86-1517

Confronting War

*An Examination of
Humanity's Most Pressing Problem*

Ronald J. Glossop

Jefferson & London : McFarland

Frontispiece: A view of the statue "Let Us Beat Our Swords into Ploughshares," a gift of the Soviet Union to the United Nations, installed in 1959. (Photo courtesy United Nations.)

second printing, with corrections and minor revisions

Library of Congress Cataloguing-in-Publication Data

Glossop, Ronald J., 1933–
  Confronting war.

  Bibliography: p.
  Includes index.
  1. War. 2. International relations. 3. Conflict
management. I. Title.
U21.2.G54 1983   303.6′6   82-23950

ISBN 0-89950-073-0

Manufactured in the United States of America

McFarland & Company, Inc., Publishers
  Box 611, Jefferson, North Carolina 28640

For Kent and the other
young people of planet Earth

Preface

There was a time when slavery was considered to be a natural and necessary part of human affairs. Then some sensitive and thoughtful persons began thinking of slavery as a social problem. Eventually outright slavery was virtually eliminated from human society.

The same type of evolution is taking place with regard to the problem of war. For most of human history the only perceived problem related to war was how to win. It is only within the past hundred years that more than a few philosophers and statesmen have regarded war as a social disease, a problem to be solved. As the weapons of war have become more devastating and as the proportion of people affected has increased, it has become clear that war is more than just one of many social problems. The war problem has become the most urgent problem facing the human race. Either the war problem gets solved or humanity becomes extinct.

Various efforts have been made to alert humanity to the problem of war and to indicate how the problem might be solved. But just as some people argued that slavery should not and could not be eliminated because it was a necessary part of human society grounded in human nature, so it has also been argued that war should not and cannot be eliminated because it is a necessary part of human society grounded in human nature. On the other hand, just as some persons put forth arguments about why slavery must be ended, so some persons have put forth arguments about why war must be ended. They have also made proposals concerning how to do it.

The purpose of this book is to familiarize the reader with some of the facts, ideas, and arguments related to the war problem and its solution. It is my hope that it will also prove useful to high school and college students and that it will stimulate their teachers to offer formal courses on the subject of war and peace.

This book has in fact grown out of my own experience in teaching a course called "The Problem of War and Peace" at Southern Illinois University at Edwardsville. During the past ten years I have learned much from team-teaching this course with many different colleagues: William Feeney and Tetsuya Kataoka of the Department of Government and Public Affairs; Robert Erickson, J. Gerald Gallaher, Samuel Grant, Richard Millett, and James Weingartner of the Department of History; Robert Engbretson of the Department of Psychology; Jerome Hollenhorst of the Department of Economics; R. Paul Churchill and Edward Hudlin of the Department of Philosophical Studies; and John Davis, former legal counsel for the University. I have also benefited from hearing a number of guest lecturers for this course: Sugata Dasgupta, Gene Hsiao, Gene

LaRocque, Anatol Rapoport, Dudley Weeks, Murray Wiedenbaum, and Jules Zanger. Ideas have also been gathered during the team-teaching of another course, "Global Problems and Human Survival," with Rasool Hashimi of the Department of Economics, Ernest Schusky of the Department of Anthropology, and Richard Parker and Marion Kumler of the Department of Biological Sciences.

Still another source of ideas and stimulation has been conversations with John Broyer, John Danley, Sang-Ki Kim, Tom Paxson, and Gerald Runkle of the SIUE Department of Philosophical Studies, Herbert Spiegelberg of the Philosophy Department of Washington University, and Jean Robert Leguey-Feilleux of the Political Science Department of St. Louis University. I am also grateful to Theodore Lentz and William Eckhardt of the Peace Research Laboratory in St. Louis who have shared their insights with me in conversations over the years. My thinking on this subject of war has also been influenced by fellow members of the World Federalists Association including Lawrence Abbott, Harold Chestnut, Eric Cox, Norman Cousins, Walter Hoffman, John Logue, Robert Myers, Sandford Persons, Everett Reflor, and Bill Wickersham and by St. Louis area peace activists including Stephen Best, Chuck Guenther, James Laue, James McGinnis, Louise Robison, and Bill Stuckenberg. Stan Norris of the Center for Defense Information assisted by providing answers to my questions about quantities of nuclear weapons available for use by the United States.

I wish to express my appreciation to the staff at Lovejoy Library at Southern Illinois University at Edwardsvile for their assistance; to the administration of Southern Illinois University at Edwardsville for support of this project through the Department of Philosophical Studies and the School of Humanities; to the Office of Graduate Studies and Research at Southern Illinois University at Edwardsville for a Summer Research Fellowship and other support; and to typists Mary Diedam, Karen West, and Ann Morgan.

Ronald J. Glossop
December 1982

Table of Contents

TABLE OF CONTENTS

The biggest lesson of all to be learned
about contemporary civilization is that
nothing anyone is doing today makes any
sense unless it is connected to the making
of genuine peace. — *Norman Cousins*

Part One

Introduction to the War Problem

I. The Nature of the War Problem

In humanity's earliest days the most urgent problems involved the struggle to survive against the forces of nature — against wild animals and exposure to freezing temperatures, against floods and droughts, against insects and disease. These problems with threats from nature are not completely solved but the progress of humankind in overcoming them provides a basis for optimism about our capacity to deal with similar kinds of problems in the future. The situation is quite otherwise with regard to the danger of death and destruction from other members of our own species.

The Importance of the War Problem

Of the great problems facing humanity in the last quarter of the twentieth century, which one is most important? Certainly the great increase in the numbers of people on the earth, largely as the result of the benefits of modern sanitation techniques, new pesticides, and scientifically-based medicine, constitutes a problem of the first magnitude. How can all these people be fed? Can there possibly be enough water for them to use, not only for drinking and bathing but also for cleaning things, for irrigating crops, and for carrying away agricultural and industrial wastes? How can the debris of so many people living at ever higher levels of consumption be absorbed by nature? How can there possibly be enough nonrenewable resources such as petroleum and metals to meet the demands of these larger and larger numbers of persons each of whom uses more and more? In fact, even if there were no growth in population at all, the continuous increase in consumption and waste production of each individual would constitute a great burden for humanity, especially in view of the limited resources still remaining in nature in a readily exploitable form and the already high pollution levels in many areas.

But there is an even more urgent problem for humanity than any of those mentioned above. Perhaps the point can best be made with a story. Suppose that a pair of astronauts have just been launched on their way to the moon in a space vehicle. At first there are some minor difficulties in getting the spaceship on exactly the right course, but with the aid of ground control the proper manuevering is accomplished. After a while as the burden of taking care of the various tasks abates, the two astronauts on the spaceship fall into discussing religion and politics. There are differences of opinion between the two astronauts, and as the discussion

2

continues it becomes more and more heated. These astronauts become more and more absorbed in their dispute. A red warning light begins to glow in the spaceship, but because of their involvement in the religious–political debate the astronauts pay no heed. Another light comes on, and then another. There is trouble with the oxygen supply system. There is trouble with the water supply system. There is trouble with some of the waste-removal systems. But the astronauts are so involved in their dispute that they pay no attention to these difficulties. Ground control calls to them in desperation: "Please stop arguing with each other and give full attention to the problems which threaten your survival." But there is no cessation of the arguing. In fact each of the astronauts is now plotting how he might be able to preserve himself while putting an end to the other.

We who are observing this scene from our secure places on the earth would undoubtedly be appalled. We could all see clearly that the priorities of these astronauts have been distorted by their emotional involvement in their dispute. It would also be obvious to us that even if one were to do away with the other while managing to preserve himself, it would not prove that the survivor's ideas were superior. Although these astronauts were having various problems with regard to their spaceship, it would be evident to us who are witnessing this event that their main problem is their over-involvement in their quarrel. To be sure there are some problems requiring attention such as oxygen supply and water supply and waste removal, but these problems could readily be solved by co-operative action. Their most urgent need is to control their disputations so they can tend to these other problems. They don't necessarily need to come to an agreement on the religious and political issues they are debating. All that is required is that they control their conflict so that it does not interfere with their taking care of their mutual problem of survival.

In a similar manner, an outside visitor to the earth would be appalled by the stupidity of the people on this planet. They are pouring scarce resources and problem-solving talent into a struggle to do away with each other while problems crucial to their mutual survival receive only the most marginal attention. Lester Brown has summarized the present human situation on planet Earth in one sentence: "It is one of the great paradoxes of the late twentieth century that the really serious threats to man's future existence are receiving so little attention while leading powers fritter away their financial resources, scientific talent, and the time of their leaders on ideological conflicts."[1]* Even ecological leader Barry Commoner tells us that "peace among men must precede the peace with nature."[2]

The Four Aspects of the War Problem

There are several aspects to the war problem. So far we have mentioned only the first, the huge expenditure of available public funds and research talent getting ready for war. That expenditure is a great impediment to our quest for survival even if actual war never comes. It has been estimated that world military expenditures now amount to over $600 billion a year,[3] that is, $1.6 billion each day! These military expenditures exceed the total income of the poorest 40 percent of the world's population.[4] Furthermore, they have been increasing at a rate of 2 percent a year in addition to increases due to inflation.[5] Forty percent of the world's highly qualified scientists and engineers are devoting themselves to research and development for "defense."[6] And this pattern is not confined to the developed countries. In the developing countries where 41 percent of the people are illiterate[7] the amount spent on the military exceeds the public expenditures for education by 25 percent.[8] This completely ridiculous situation, which seems to be accepted without question or concern by most of the political leaders of the world, is not unlike that of the quarreling astronauts in our story.

The second aspect of the problem of war, the one that usually comes to mind first, is the danger of a nuclear holocaust[9] in which the superpowers unleash on each other the many thousands[10] of nuclear warheads they presently have ready to launch. We have been living with this danger so long we have become somewhat insensitive to it. We haven't really been vividly reminded of it since the Cuban missile crisis of October 1962.[11] But the continued Arab–Israeli differences in the Middle East, the Russian–Afghan conflict, the white–black confrontation in southern Africa, the possibility of big power involvement in internal struggles in Asia and Africa and Latin America, the build-up of arms by both sides in Europe, the struggle for control of oil resources around the Persian Gulf, and so on suggest that we could be abruptly reminded of the missiles at any time. After all they are ready to go. It takes only the turn of two keys to send them on their way. And they are very fast — thirty minutes from launch to target. Some of the nuclear warheads on these missiles are 1500 times more powerful than the bombs dropped on Hiroshima and Nagasaki. The radioactivity from an all-out nuclear exchange between the superpowers might well eliminate all higher life forms on this planet. We don't like to think about the possibility of nuclear war so we don't often allow the idea to enter our minds, but denial does not solve the problem or make it go away.

The third aspect of the war problem consists of the occurrence of "conventional" (nonnuclear) wars that seem to be taking place all over the world — Ethiopa versus Somalia, Israel versus her Arab neighbors, Vietnam versus Cambodia and China, Iran versus Iraq, Tanzania versus Uganda, India versus Pakistan, Britain versus Argentina, and so on. "Wars of Liberation" in which former colonies seek to win their independence also fall into the category of "conventional wars." The destruction of lives and property in these wars is very great.[12] Further-more, since the end of World War II these conventional wars fought on the soil of the poorer nations, have become the usual kind.[13] For most people in much of the world the danger of destruction from conventional war is much greater than the danger of destruction from nuclear weap-ons. The weapons used in these conventional wars are much more de-structive than those used in World War II. During the three-week Middle East War of 1973 there was an average of more than one aircraft de-stroyed every hour and more than one tank destroyed every fifteen minutes.[14] About one-third of all aircraft and one-half of all tanks avail-able for use at the beginning of the war were destroyed.[15] Finally, there is always a danger that a war occurring in developing nations will expand to countries with nuclear weapons.

Connecting the second and third aspects of the war problem dis-cussed above is the issue of the proliferation of nuclear weapons. At present nuclear weapons are known to be possessed by the United States, the Soviet Union, Britain, France, and China. But India has detonated a nuclear device, and many observers believe that Israel and the Union of South Africa have nuclear weapons in their arsenals. Also Pakistan and Iraq seem to be embarked on efforts to develop a nuclear capability for the Arab countries. Nations such as Canada, Japan, West Germany, Sweden, Italy, South Korea, the Chinese on Taiwan, and Brazil un-doubtedly have the capability of making nuclear weapons should they choose to do so. Beyond the know-how to build nuclear weapons a nation which wants to construct such weapons must have either enriched uranium or plutonium. The supply of these two crucial materials has so far been fairly readily controlled by the present nuclear powers and Canada and West Germany. The control is not perfect, however, as the cases of Israel, India, and Pakistan show, and the continuing introduction of more nuclear power plants throughout the world will make control in the future even more difficult. Furthermore, the new breeder reactors, likely to be the preferred type as uranium becomes more and more ex-pensive, actually produce more fissionable material than was put into them. A small terrorist group could get its hands on some of this nuclear material and make a bomb.

The danger of terrorist use of nuclear weapons brings us to the fourth aspect of the war problem, wars between groups who are citizens of the same country. These intranational or civil wars are still wars and cannot be dismissed. Many of the wars fought since the end of World War II in 1945 have been essentially intranational even though other nations may have become involved. Examples are the Vietnamese War, the Cuban revolution, the secession of Bangladesh from Pakistan, the Biafran separatist movement in Nigeria, the attempt of Katanga Province to secede from the nation then called the Congo and now called Zaïre, the ongoing battle between Greeks and Turks on Cyprus, the struggle in Northern Ireland, the overthrow of the Shah in Iran, the revolution in Nicaragua, and the struggle for control in El Salvador. These wars are really wars. A complete discussion of the problem of war cannot be limited to that between nations; it must also take account of those wars within national boundaries.

Solutions to the war problem must encompass all four aspects of it. Any solution that does not, for example, cut expenditures for arms is not a complete one. A solution must likewise encompass conventional wars and civil wars as well as nuclear exchanges.

II. The Conceptual Framework

What exactly is meant by the terms "war" and "peace"? It should be helpful to the reader to learn how these words are used in this book, and also to consider the meaning of "justice," another term which is crucial to the war problem. Finally, some observations about the relations between peace and justice will be made.

The Meaning of the Term "War"

How shall we use the term "war"? We need a definition broad enough to include both civil wars and international wars but narrow enough to exclude feuds (such as between the Hatfields and the McCoys), riots (such as destroyed the Watts area of Los Angeles in 1965), and intense political action (such as the effort of some persons in Quebec to separate that province from the rest of Canada) which we would not ordinarily call "wars." The definition to be used in this book is as follows: *War is violent conflict between organized groups that are or that aim to establish governments.*

The first point to be noted is that not all conflict is war but only *violent* conflict. Of course we sometimes do speak figuratively of war between the sexes or of the cold war, but when pushed we are inclined to say that these are not really wars but only *like* wars because the conflict is so intense. Consider how strange it would sound to speak of a "hot war." Wars are necessarily "hot." They necessarily involve violence. A cold war, on the other hand, involves only a readiness to use violence though none actually occurs; there may be crises when it seems that the conflict will break into real war, but there are no acts in which people get killed and property is destroyed.

In trying to apply our definition of war to actual situations there will be a problem of indicating exactly when a conflict has become violent enough to call it a war. What if property is destroyed but no lives are lost? What if only a few people are killed? Must there be some minimum number of deaths before we say a war is occurring? There are certainly borderline cases in which it is difficult to decide whether there is enough violence to call them wars. Social scientists interested in comparing the amount of warfare in different historical periods or in different geographical regions will be forced to decide somewhat arbitrarily that a violent conflict is to count as a war only if a certain minimal number of deaths have occurred or a certain number of soldiers have been committed to battle.[1] Fortunately, our general discussion of the war problem

7

does not require this level of precision. There are some situations so violent we can unhesitatingly describe them as war. We can focus our attention on these situations and view ourselves as having made considerable headway in solving the war problem if we can successfully deal with these unquestionable cases.

The second crucial idea in our definition of war is that the participants must be members of organized groups. Even the most violent conflict between one person and another is not a war. We might be inclined to make an exception in the case where these two persons are functioning as official representatives of their respective groups and where their one-on-one battle will determine which group is victorious, as was the case in the Biblical meeting of David and Goliath; but even then we would want to say that this one-on-one confrontation between selected warriors is a substitute for a battle in which two opposing armies fought. Moreover, if two groups just happen to fall into fighting with each other (as might possibly happen if two groups of different races or nationalities were in the same locale) we would not be inclined to call it a war unless the groups were organized with leaders who give orders and followers who carry them out. War involves the notion of coordinated group action and thus cannot take place without some organization within the groups which confront each other.

The third crucial idea in our definition of war is the notion that it involves government. A government is a system for group control in which a certain individual or group of individuals is recognized by other governments as well as by those who are ruled by it as having the authority to make decisions which are binding on that whole group. It is only when the governance of some society is at stake that we call a violent conflict a "war."

Our definition of war as conflict between groups that are or that aim to establish governments implies there are two main kinds of wars. The first occurs when one governed society fights another governed society. Today this is expressed as *inter*national war (literally, war *between* nations). The second occurs when there is a struggle for control of the government within a governed society. This is *intra*national war (literally, war *within* a nation). Further distinctions can be made within these two basic types. For example, international wars may be between nations technologically and militarily nearly equal or they may occur between a technologically advanced nation and a not-so-advanced one. In the latter case the war would be called an *imperialistic* or *colonial* war when the more advanced nation is seeking to establish control and a *war of national liberation* when the less advanced nation is seeking to reestablish its independence. Within the class of intranational wars we can distinguish between a *territorial civil war* in which each of the opposing groups occupies a fairly well-defined geographical area of the country and a *revolutionary war* in which an organized group seeks to overthrow the present government throughout the whole nation.

It should be noted that a particular war may exemplify more than one type. For example, there may be a struggle for control of the government between two groups within a nation–state where one or both of these groups gets assistance from other nation–states. In that case the war is both intranational and international. The wars in Vietnam and Bangladesh were both of this type. In fact, this kind of war which is both intranational and internation is in the 1980's rapidly becoming the most common.

If we define "war" as "violent conflict between organized groups that are or that aim to establish governments," it should be obvious that the goal of warfare is the acquisition of political power. The groups engaged in a war each want to play the role of decision-maker for some society. This suggests that the alternative to war must consist of a *nonviolent* resolution of conflicts over decision-making power in a society. Broadly speaking, it would seem that the alternative to war is politics.

The Meaning of the Term "Peace"

The term "peace" may be taken to mean simply "the absence of war." Some writers on this topic have distinguished between what they call "negative peace" (the mere absence of war) and what they call "positive peace" (a peace in which there is no exploitation of some individuals or groups by others). This distinction is parallel to that which might be made between "negative healthiness" (the mere absence of sickness) and "positive healthiness" (not only the absence of sickness but also physical fitness, good muscle tone, and so on). For those who make this distinction, positive peace is necessarily a good thing while negative peace is not. Consequently, they frequently suggest that the term "peace" be used only for positive peace.[2]

The motivation for using the term "peace" to mean positive peace is admirable. The aim is to ensure that the discussion of how to solve the problem of war is not divorced from the issue of justice. Still, the effort to define "peace" this way seems not to be faithful to our normal use of the term. Also, if the term "peace" is to be reserved for positive peace, what term are we to use to describe negative peace? Furthermore, restricting the term "peace" to positive peace actually interferes with our thinking clearly about the issues of peace and justice and their interrelations. Peace and justice are both desirable things to have in a society, but they are not on that account the same thing. If we were to use the word "peace" to mean only a just peace, we would be forced to overlook certain distinctions which must be made if we are to understand the problems involved in creating an ideal society. This point should become clearer after the discussion of "justice" that lies before us.

Suppose then that we use the word "peace" to mean simply the absence of war, that is, the absence of violent conflict between organized groups that are or that aim to establish governments. Is peace in this sense necessarily a good thing? At first glance it seems to be better than war.

In a peaceful situation there may or may not be injustice, but in a war there is bound to be injustice. People are killed or maimed and their property is destroyed simply because they are on the other side or sometimes, simply because they are in the way. Bombs and machine-gun fire do not always hit the objects at which they were aimed and they almost always hit other things besides. And even the "enemy soldiers" at which they are aimed may have had little or no choice in becoming "enemy soldiers." Furthermore, peace tends to make people more humane and sympathetic toward those in other groups while war tends to make them more suspicious and spiteful toward all persons even remotely related to the enemy group.

Still it is possible for peace to be a very bad thing. A society in which a ruthless dictator rules with an iron hand in an arbitrary and oppressive way may be a peaceful society. There may be an abundance of resentment and hatred, but there still is peace because no one even dares to begin resisting the commands of the dictator. Thus it is quite possible to conceive of a peaceful situation in which there is so much injustice that even war would be better if it meant a chance of getting rid of the dictator. This situation is precisely what advocates of the "just war" theory[3] have in mind when they claim that under some conditions injustice becomes so gross that even violence and war seem to be justified.

But the benefits of peace are such and the horrors of war are such that it does not make sense to start a war over every injustice. An important part of the "just war" theory is the notion that the means must be proportional to the ends which can be expected. If a little violence, not too destructive, can get rid of a great deal of injustice, then war may be justified. But if, like modern war, it is likely to create more evil than it will remove, then violence is not justified. In view of the destructiveness of modern war, "just war" theorists are tending toward the idea that war is virtually never justifiable.

Once it is agreed that even an unjust peace is still peace, the role of government in maintaining peace within the society becomes evident. Government serves many purposes, such as defending the society against other societies and organizing collective action to provide transportation facilities, education for the young, clean water, regulation of trade, and so on, but one of its main purposes is the preservation of public order, that is, the preservation of peace. In order to do this, the government must have some device for keeping conflict among its own members under control. Thus governments have police forces and jails in order to physically subdue those who try to disturb the peace. Usually there are laws so that people will know in advance what types of behavior will be punished by the government. In a republic these laws are made by representatives elected by the people, but in other governments they may be made by a king or dictator or by some other group with absolute authority, and may not be "laws" at all. Especially in a republic, but to some extent in most other governments as well, the art of politics develops. This art consists of adjudicating the conflicting interests of different groups when making laws so that peace is preserved within the society. It is especially imperative that injustices severe enough to cause general rebellion be avoided.

Even though governments function as peace-makers within their own domain, they function as potential war-makers in relation to each other. Each government pursues its own interests and, theoretically at least, the welfare of its own people. Thus there is competition between governments for the goods of the earth. Strong governments (in the military sense) will tend to take land and resources from weak governments. As a result, weak governments tend to build up their military might so that they can take from others rather than having things taken from them. In situations where it is not obvious which government is stronger or where the weak government will not merely yield to the stronger, war frequently takes place. Thus governments tend to be war-makers vis-à-vis other governments and peace-makers within their own boundaries.

It should be noted that there could conceivably be peace in a society even though no government exists to adjudicate conflicts between individuals and groups. Conflicting individuals and groups are often able to work out their differences among themselves. In the same way national governments are often able to work out differences among themselves and thus to be at peace with each other. But the fact is that over a period of time there are almost always some intense conflicts which cannot be resolved by the parties involved. Within a government these conflicts are resolved in the political process and by the courts, with the enforcement assistance, if necessary, of the police. When there is no government with law-making and enforcement powers by which conflicts can be resolved, which is the present case among nations (there is no world government, in other words), then violence or threats of violence may be used to try to resolve the conflict. Since this possibility is a very real one, most nations maintain a powerful military force so that they do not need to give in when a conflict reaches the stage where it will be resolved by a contest of force.

Even within nations there may be violent conflict and civil war. The purpose of government is to maintain peace, but it doesn't always succeed. Still it seems to be the case that within a governed society violence and readiness for violence occasionally break out while peace is the usual situation, but in the absence of government violence and readiness for violence are common.

The Meaning of the Term "Justice"

We have noted that one possible justification for the use of violence, even within a governed society, is the removal of gross injustice. Thus is raised the question of what is meant by "justice." The appeal of war as a means to end injustice also ultimately shows the incorrectness of assuming that justice consists merely of doing whatever the law requires.

The view that justice consists of obeying the law, whatever the law says, is not completely without insight, however. We have noticed in our discussion of "peace" that one function of government is to adjudicate in a nonviolent way the conflicts of its members as they individually and collectively pursue their interests. When the government serves as a truly neutral arbitrator in these disputes, each party to the conflict has the obligation to restrain itself in accord with the judgments of the government in order to preserve the peace. If the government really is impartial, each party to the dispute is faced with a choice between living in a society where conflicts are peacefully resolved or living in a society where conflicts are resolved by resort to force. Thomas Hobbes, a prominent seventeenth-century English political philosopher, called this latter situation where there is no government to resolve disputes a state of war of every individual against every other. Where all conflicts are resolved by the use of force, there is no security of person or possessions for anyone. As Hobbes noted, in such a situation life would be "poor, nasty, brutish, and short."[4] There would be neither peace nor justice. The institution of a truly neutral arbitrator, on the other hand, with the force to subdue those who will not voluntarily obey the laws and judgments of the government would bring both peace and justice. In this ideal situation where the government is completely unbiased, justice might well be defined as doing what the law requires.

The trouble is that in actual situations the government is usually not a neutral arbitrator either when making laws or when enforcing them. For example, in a Western-style democracy groups and individuals with large amounts of money are usually able to influence the law-making process much more than people with small amounts of money. Thus the laws are more likely to protect and promote the interests of the very rich than of the very poor or even the middle class. On the other hand, after a Communist revolution has occurred, a government may be instituted with the explicit purpose of making laws which favor the poorer "working class" at the expense of the more affluent members of the society, whose property in fact may simply be confiscated by the government. The same kind of bias exists also in the enforcement of the law. In most courtrooms in the West the well-dressed and well-educated are often dealt with less harshly than the poorly-dressed and poorly-educated. The richer person will probably have a better lawyer representing him. On the other hand, under a new Communist government a person from a wealthy family can expect harsher treatment than a poor person. So where is justice? Governments are often biased toward some and prejudiced against others.

Whenever we speak of the decisions of a government as unjust, it is implied that we have some independent standard of justice by which we are able to judge. What is this standard of justice? Plato quoted the poet Simonides as offering the suggestion that justice is done when everyone gets what is due him.[5] It seems that there is little with which one can quarrel in this definition, but it still leaves open the question of how we should go about determining what people deserve.

This issue of how we should determine what people deserve is one of the most controversial issues in social philosophy, so it should not be supposed that a short discussion can do justice to it. Still, some basic points can be made. There are two central but opposite principles that must somehow be reconciled or balanced when this question of justice is being considered. On the one hand there is the principle that *those who contribute more to the general welfare should reap greater individual rewards*. The basic belief here is that people need to be encouraged by personal gain to exert themselves for the welfare of others. Such a belief does not imply that there is no altruism in human nature, but it does assume that people will work harder over a longer period of time for personal gain than they will when the only motive is the welfare of the whole society. This principle of merit or competence is supported by the actions of consumers who generally display a readiness to pay more for better quality.

On the other hand there is also another principle of justice, the principle that *everyone should be equal*. The basic belief here is that all people are shaped to be as they are by factors over which they ultimately have no control. No one chooses where he will be born, what traits he will inherit, or what kind of environment he will have as a child. No person chooses to be handicapped or to be slow in learning or to be lazy or to be born in a poor undeveloped country rather than a rich developed one. As he grows older, he will make choices, but even then the choices he makes will have been determined to a great extent, if not completely, by these other earlier factors over which he had no control. This principle of equality displays itself in the claim that workers should be paid on the basis of how many hours are worked rather than on the basis of the quantity or quality of the work completed.

Arguments can be given to support both of these principles. Defenders of the *principle of merit* argue that if talent and hard work are not rewarded then the society as a whole will soon have a lower standard of living. People who have accumulated property must be allowed to keep it. Talented people won't use their talents and no one will exert himself much if he will be just as well off when he loafs. There will be little or no concern for excellence. On the other hand, defenders of the *principle of equality* argue that those who are well off in society are not necessarily more talented or harder working than those who have less. The social system, including the government, has usually been designed to make sure that those persons and groups who have wealth and privileged positions maintain them for themselves and their children. Those who contribute more to society are able to do so only because society or some part of it has first contributed more to them.

It might seem that the ideal way of reconciling these two principles of merit and equality is to emphasize *equality of opportunity* for everyone while having actual personal rewards based on the use made of one's opportunities. If people were completely isolated individuals, such an approach might have some chance of working; but in fact people live in families and have children. If a husband and wife own things in common, how is it possible to reward one and not the other? And the situation gets even more intricate when we consider children, since one of the things parents most want is a good future for their own children. They want their children to have *better* educational opportunities and *better* social opportunities than other children. They want their children to be *more* affluent and *more* influential than other people's children. They are more concerned that *their* children not be threatened by starvation and sickness than that other people's children be preserved from these dangers. It is not that they don't care about other children, it's that they care more about their own.

Furthermore, people want this concern about their own children reflected in the policies of their government. For example, think of the outcry from Americans if it were suggested that the United States government make contributions on the order of $50 billion a year to UNICEF or some other agency concerned with the welfare of children in poorer countries in order to modify just slightly the difference in opportunity between American children and the children who live in these other countries. Or consider the outcry which would occur even if the quality of educational opportunities had to be equalized throughout all the schools, public and private, in the United States. Or consider the likely opposition to a law that would prohibit the inheritance of more than $10,000 by any individual on the grounds that such gifts destroy equality of opportunity for everyone. People in positions of privilege do not want equality of opportunity for all children; they feel that one of the important things they have earned by virtue of their talents and hard work is the privilege of sending their children to better-than-average schools and giving them advantages which other children don't have. Yet where is the justice when some children have so much greater opportunities than others? So goes the struggle between the principle of merit and the principle of equality.

It does not take much imagination to see that persons who are well off, either within a society or in relation to the human race as a whole, will see great wisdom in the principle of merit. They will believe that their privileged position is due to their superior intelligence, their greater industriousness, their generally superior genetic make-up, or their social structure. They have much more than others, but they believe this situation is fair because they deserve to have more. On the other hand, persons who are not so well off, either within a society or in relation to the human race as a whole, will see great wisdom in the principle of equality. They will believe that their inferior position is due to the poverty of their parents, to poor health which is debilitating no matter how hard they would like to work, and to historical developments completely outside their control which have put them in a disadvantaged position. They have much less than others, but they do not believe that it is because they are in any way inferior. In fact it seems to them that they work even harder than the more privileged persons but end up with less.

These differing viewpoints about what principle of justice should be emphasized produce a new basis for the perception of social situations and consequently for social conflict. We will return to these ideas when we consider the ideological aspects of the contemporary world scene. For the moment we can say that different opinions about what is just arise from the fact that people and nations, whether rich or poor, find it difficult to maintain a disinterested point of view. Their own interests always seem much more important than other people's. Furthermore, they do not see how much their own viewpoint is conditioned by their present position. The poor believe that if they were rich, they would be much more generous in helping the poor than the present rich are. The rich believe that if they were poor, they would be much less resentful than the present poor are. It is doubtful if either of these beliefs is generally true, either within national societies or within the global society of nations.

Meanwhile, what can be said about justice? It seems that justice involves some kind of delicate balance between the principle of merit and the principle of equality. The fact that people in positions of privilege usually make and enforce the laws would suggest that most governments have overemphasized the principle of merit and underemphasized that of equality. They have been more concerned about "law and order" and preserving the present situation than about equality of opportunity for everyone. On the other hand, those who are protesting against the injustice of governments may be inclined to overlook the value of merit entirely and to view justice as nothing but equality. They tend to be more interested in getting equality, even by violent means, than in preserving a peace which they perceive as designed to maintain an unjust society.

Surely it is not easy to establish just governments, that is, governments which properly balance these two principles of merit and equality, even for national societies. The ultimate challenge of the future, as will become more evident as we proceed, is to establish a governance system on a global basis that will provide a just peace for the whole world. That project will be even more difficult.

Peace and Justice

As we have just noted, the question of justice concerns the proper distribution of the goods and benefits of a society among its members. We have also noted that the general tendency of governments is to be conservative, to preserve the present social order, with its greater opportunities for the children of privilege, rather than to institute changes which would create more equal opportunities for the less privileged children. Three additional observations on the relations between peace and justice are in order.

In light of what has been said above, it might be assumed that once government is established there will be less justice with regard to the distribution of goods and benefits than if there were no government because the government will probably be controlled by the powerful to maintain their positions of privilege. But what is the situation without a government to keep peace? We have already noted that no one would have much security; but it should also be noted that ruthlessness and violence would be rewarded by gains in possessions and power and that consequently there would be a tendency of the powerful to use their power in an unrestrained way to become even more powerful. Once a government is established, the powerful may use it as an instrument to maintain their power, but in the absence of government the powerful will have other instruments (paid body-guards and warriors, specially designed weapons, and so on) to maintain their power. The point might be put this way. Government does not necessarily produce justice, but the lack of government probably will allow, and even reward, a great deal of injustice. Whether the injustice with government will be greater or less than the injustice without government is a matter of the particular situation and the particular kind of government to be instituted.

If a world government were instituted over the national governments, would the distribution of the goods of the earth among the various nations be more or less just than it is at present? It can be supposed that such a government would be dominated by the more powerful nations, at least at first.[6] Otherwise, those nations would not even allow it to be formed. Once a government was established, the more powerful nations would undoubtedly try to use it to maintain their positions of privilege. Would the less powerful, poorer nations be better off with such a government or without it? Without it, they are virtually at the mercy of the more powerful nations, which can use superior economic and military power to impose whatever terms they desire. With it, they are still in a situation dominated by the more powerful nations. Which situation would be more just would depend on specific things such as the spread of nuclear weapons and long-range delivery systems to the poorer nations (which would make them less at the mercy of the more powerful nations) and the precise voting arrangements and structure that would exist in the world government (which might be arranged so that the poorer nations were less at the mercy of the richer ones). Only after examining details would it be possible to say whether a fairer distribution of goods among the nations would be more likely with such a government or without it.

The second point to be considered with regard to the relation between peace and justice concerns the desirability of conducting war to eliminate what are considered to be unjust inequalities in wealth. To understand this point we must begin by noting that there are two different viewpoints that can be taken with regard to the measurement of wealth. People may evaluate their wealth *relatively* in terms of what they have compared to others, or they may evaluate their wealth in *absolute* terms, that is, in terms of what goods and services and burdens they actually have regardless of what others have. In a peaceful situation there may be a great discrepancy between what the rich have and what the poor have, but the poor may still be better off in absolute terms than they would be if they were to conduct a war against the rich. That is, the poor within a society may unite in a war against the rich in order to end what is perceived as an unjust situation with the result that everyone in the society ends up worse off than before. War can destroy the wealth of the rich, but it cannot by itself make the poor as a whole richer because war does not produce goods but only destroys them. To be sure some of the leaders of the poor may confiscate some of the leftover goods of the rich for themselves, but then all that has happened is that one group of rich persons has been replaced by another group of slightly poorer persons. And that is the situation if the poor *win* the war! If they try to rebel but *lose*, it can be expected that they will be even more oppressed than before.

It could be argued that a violent revolution by the poor against the rich might change an oppressive system and thus would be worthwhile in the long run even if a failure from the short-term point of view. Conceivably such a change for the better is possible. The crucial issue is whether the new leaders will prove to be different from the ones they replaced and whether the new system will put more restraints on the power of the leaders than the old system did. The first one or two generations of leaders after the revolution might well be vividly aware of what they fought to change and might be particularly on guard against special privileges for leaders and their families and friends, but at least by the third generation the leaders are much less likely to be concerned about such issues. Also it is very unlikely that the new leaders will be more restricted in their powers than the old leaders had been because the new rulers will claim that they must be unrestrained in order to make all the changes they feel are so necessary.

Suppose the poorer nations of the world eventually acquired enough nuclear weapons to be able to cause considerable damage to the richer nations. Suppose they then threatened the richer nations saying that wealth must be shared more equitably or they will use the weapons. The richer nations would probably not yield to such a threat and might even issue a counter-threat. The poor nations could argue, "You have more to lose than we do" (which is true), but the richer nations could argue, "You will be even worse off after a war with us than you are now" (which is also true). It is conceivable that the poor nations might launch a surprise nuclear attack destroying a great deal of the wealth of the richer nations and eventually developing a new international system to modify the distribution of goods among nations. Even if things worked out as the poor nations had planned, from an absolute point of view all nations would be worse off than before the war. It is also not certain over the long run that the new system would be more just than the old one. Furthermore, it is really much more probable that in a war the rich nations would prevail over the poor ones. They also might well be provoked by such a war to be even more oppressive toward the poorer nations than they had been before.

The third point to be considered with regard to the relation between peace and justice is that justice in a society produces both peace and prosperity. In a society where there is a general consensus that opportunities are approximately equal, that the goods and burdens of the society are fairly distributed, and that the laws of the society are equitable and impartially enforced there is little likelihood of group violence. Even if a few individuals have some personal gripes, they will be unable to get any substantial following if they try to organize violence against other groups or against the government. Also, when the poorer people who are in greater need of more goods have the money to buy them, the industries of the society are stimulated. Unemployment is reduced, and consequently crime is reduced. As more people work, production is increased and the demand for goods is further increased. Prosperity is promoted by having some wealth in the hands of poorer people.

Let us consider how this principle would work at the international level. Suppose that all tariffs and restraints on international trade now erected by the richer countries were eliminated so that these markets would be opened to the poorer countries. Suppose also that some system were in place to guarantee that a small portion of the income of the richer nations were transferred to the poorer ones. The present resentment felt by the governments of the poorer nations toward the richer nations would be greatly reduced. Although there might be some concern in some of the richer nations as patterns of employment shifted to accord with the new situation, the long-term reaction would be one of satisfaction as the price for many consumer goods is reduced and the market for exports expands. Unemployment in the less developed countries would decline, and the demand for goods from the developed countries would increase. Threats of violence against the investments of those living in richer nations would be virtually eliminated. The gap between poor and rich nations would be reduced, every nation would be better off in absolute terms, and the likelihood of any kind of violence would be greatly reduced. This hypothetical program of peace and prosperity through greater justice can be contrasted with the present world system in which the more powerful nations maintain their positions of superiority through military might and control of the rules of international trade. This present system focuses on preserving the relative superiority of the richer nations, but all nations are poorer in absolute terms than they could be under an international system with greater equality of opportunity. Even if the present system preserves the peace between richer nations and poorer nations, it is a coercive peace, not a just one.

On the basis of this observation that a just social system produces peace and prosperity, it has been argued by many writers that the best way to produce peace is to promote justice.[7] But there are problems here, too. One person's view of what is just is not the same as another's. Also, for some persons the use of violence can be justified if it promotes justice.[8] Care must be exercised by those who adopt such a view since the quest for justice may itself be the cause of war. On the other hand, leaders concerned about peace but insensitive to issues of justice are not blameless when their maintenance of a grossly unjust social system results in war.

III. The Historical Framework

In a sense, war is as ancient as the existence of territorial human communities. Anthropological evidence indicates that many, though not all, primitive communities engage in violent struggles with their neighbors.[1] The striving for power by the rulers of the most ancient city-states of Mesopotamia is basically not unlike the struggles for power among the leaders of modern nations. Nevertheless there is change, a never-ending evolution of the weapons used in fighting these struggles. The continuing occurrence of war in human society, even while the ways in which wars are fought are changing, leads naturally to the question, "Are there any long-range trends with regard to the nature of war?" and then to the question, "Is a solution to the war problem any more urgent now than it was in past ages?"

The Ongoing System of Sovereign States

Since our definition of war refers to government, it is evident that there could not be any war until governments came into existence, and it is difficult to know with any precision when that happened. The observation of primate groups suggests that the older males may constitute an informal "government" even among monkeys and apes.[2] Nomadic groups of people may have an informal, or even formal, structure for making decisions for the society as a whole. But it seems that government in the sense of conscious and deliberate control by a small group over the life of the community as a whole probably arose about the same time as the creation of permanent "urban" settlements and the art of writing 5,000 to 10,000 years ago.

Among the earliest known city-states are those which flourished about 5000 B.C. in the Tigris-Euphrates Valley. The rulers of city-states such as Eridu, Nippur, Ur, Uruk, Assur, Umma, Sumer, Lagash, and Kish engaged in the same kind of struggles for wealth and power that we find among modern nations. Evidence of this exists in the form of peace treaties inscribed in clay about 3000 B.C.[3] Thus the pattern of struggles for power among sovereign states is at least 5,000 years old. At times the struggle is interrupted when one sovereign state establishes an empire by conquering all the others close enough to contend for land and other advantages, but the peace is always temporary. When the leader who has created the empire dies, it may disintegrate as a struggle for power takes place among his previous subjects. Or the newly-created empire may come into conflict with other empires built of previously competing states.

19

One of the earliest recorded empires was brought into being in the Tigris-Euphrates Valley about 2500 B.C. by Lugal-zaggasi of Uruk. This Sumerian empire was then conquered and incorporated into the much larger empire of Sargon of Akkad, which continued until the twentieth century B.C. In the eighteenth century B.C. Hammurabi established a unified Babylonian empire over most of Mesopotamia which lasted two hundred years. In the fifteenth century B.C. a group of people called the Mitanni established an empire which reached from the Mediterranean to western Iran. The Assyrians freed themselves from Mitanni control in the fourteenth century B.C. and then established an empire of their own.

Starting as a separate, unrelated political entity first unified about 3000 B.C., the Egyptian state eventually spread its influence northward into Syria where it came into conflict with the Hittites from Asia Minor and the Mitanni living along the eastern shores of the Mediterranean. About 1400 B.C. these three nations entered into a nonaggression pact, and about a century later the Hittites and Egyptians formed an alliance against the expanding Assyrian empire. Nevertheless the Assyrians established control over Palestine in the eighth century B.C. and took control of Egypt in 675 B.C. But the Egyptians and Babylonians revolted and with the help of the Medes from the east destroyed the Assyrian capital of Nineveh in 612 B.C.

The rise and fall of one power after another continued as the Persians from the north conquered Lydia in western Asia Minor and then Babylon (538 B.C.). Under Darius I the Persian empire in the fifth century B.C. reached from the Danube River to the Indus River and from what is now southern Russia to southern Egypt. The city-states of Greece had managed to fight off the Persians even while fighting sporadically among themselves but fell in 338 B.C. to the Macedonians under Philip. Under Alexander the Great the Greeks then extended their domain to include Egypt and the rest of the territory previously held by the Persians (331 B.C.).

To the west the Romans began their expansion in the third century B.C. by defeating the Carthaginians. Then they conquered Macedonia, Greece, and their Numidian rivals in northern Africa. Despite class struggles in Rome which eventually led to the replacement of the Roman Republic by the Roman Empire, Roman power had spread to western Europe, Asia Minor, Egypt, and the east coast of the Mediterranean before the beginning of the Christian era. Although confronted by the Germanic "barbarians" on the north, the Roman government succeeded in maintaining the rightly famous *Pax Romana* in the Mediterranean for five hundred years. Nevertheless, as a result of invasions by the Visigoths, Huns, Vandals, and others the western part of the Roman Empire ceased to exist as a political unit after 476. In the seventh century the eastern part of the Empire came under attack as the Muslim Saracens conquered Palestine, Egypt, the rest of north Africa, and Spain. The Muslim advance into Western Europe was stopped at Tours in 732 by the Franks under Charles Martel. In 800 Martel's grandson, Charlemagne, was crowned Emperor of the new western Roman Empire by the Pope. In the tenth century the Vikings, Varangians, and Norsemen from the north, the Magyars and Bulgarians from the east, and the Turks from the southeast made new incursions into what had been the Roman Empire. The result was a Christian Europe composed of many separate political entities plus the remains of the Byzantine Empire in southeastern Europe.

The largest land empire ever known was then carved out of Asia and eastern Europe by the Mongols under Genghis Khan (1162–1127). But as often happens, the victors were conquered by the culture of the vanquished both in China and in Muslim western Asia. The aggressive Ottoman Turks put an end to the eastern Roman Empire, conquering Constaninople in 1453. The separate Christian kingdoms of Europe banded together to stop the Turkish expansion and won a naval victory at Lepanto in 1571, but when the threat was gone they again went their separate ways.

In Western Europe the period 1350–1650 was marked by violence and more violence as peasants fought feudal nobles, townspeople fought feudal nobles, kings fought Emperor and Pope, Protestants fought Catholics, and one nationality fought another. The fighting came to a climax in the Thirty Years War (1618–1648). The Treaty of Westphalia at the end of that war is usually taken to mark the beginning of the European state system which still exists on that continent. National boundaries were established for Spain, France, England, the Netherlands, Denmark, Sweden, Switzerland, Poland, Austria, Hungary, and Russia while the areas which now make up Germany and Italy consisted of many smaller states. At the same time competition among these nations was escalating with regard to control of territory in the Americas, Asia, and the coasts of Africa. From this point on, the history of these areas, which has not been discussed although it generally reveals the same kind of struggles for power found in Western history,[4] becomes woven into the history of the competition and warfare of the European state system.

The late seventeenth and early eighteenth centuries saw the British successfully checking the expansion of Spanish and French power. The Seven Years' War (called the French and Indian War in America) was ended by two treaties. The Treaty of Paris (1763) gave the British control of all of Canada, all of what is now the U.S. east of the Mississippi, and the east coast of India; the Treaty of Hubertusberg (1763) recognized Prussia as a European power.

The last quarter of the eighteenth century saw two very important revolutions. The United States of America came into existence as British colonists in North America successfully revolted against British rule with help from the French, the Dutch, and the Spanish. The second revolution took place in France in 1789 when the middle classes rebelled against the king and the landed aristocracy.

The victorious French revolutionaries became the enemy of the nobility in all the rest of Europe. Napoleon Bonaparte extended French rule over much of the European continent, but eventually the combined forces of Russia, Sweden, Prussia, Austria, and England, aided by nationalistic uprisings against the French in Spain and Austria, put an end to the Napoleonic effort. The Congress of Vienna (1814–1815) redrew the map of Europe with territorial gains for the victors. In America, the Louisiana Purchase (1803) greatly expanded the size of the U.S. while simultaneously many Latin American countries were winning independence from European control. In Europe nationalism became an important factor in the unification of Italy and Germany.

The late nineteenth and early twentieth centuries found the European powers, led by Britain and France, extending their control over Africa and Asia. Only Japan, which had adopted Western industrialism as the result of American prodding, was immune from conquest. In fact Japan embarked on expanding its own sphere of influence and ousted Russia from Manchuria and the Liaotung Peninsula in the Russo-Japanese War (1904–1905). For the most part, however, the Big Powers negotiated their conflicts with each other while using military power to subdue non-industrialized societies. While the European powers focused their efforts on Africa and Asia, the United States expanded its territory at the expense of the native American Indians, Mexicans and other Latin Americans, and a declining Spain.

Antagonisms developed in the early twentieth century as the race for colonies and for military superiority became more intense. The Italians, irked by France's takeover of Tunis, joined Germany and Austria-Hungary in the Triple Alliance. The French, still smarting from defeat in the Franco-Prussian War (1870–71), formed an alliance with Russia. The British, concerned about the growing power of Germany, entered into alliances with Japan and then with France and Russia. Competition for influence in the Balkans between Austria-Hungary and Russia provided the fuel for war, and the assassination of the heir to the throne in Austria-Hungary by Serbian terrorists provided the spark that started World War I in 1914. Austria-Hungary attacked Serbia in an effort to end support for Serbian nationalists in Austria-Hungary. The Germans were committed by their alliance to assist Austria-Hungary. Their Schlieffen plan called for fighting a two-front war by focusing their main effort at first against France on the supposition that it would take the Russians some time to mobilize their forces. When the Russians began to mobilize to help the Serbs against Austria-Hungary, the Germans demanded that they stop, but the Russians refused. The Germans then declared war on Russia and its ally France. When the Germans attacked France through neutral Belgium (another part of the Schlieffen plan), Britain joined the battle against the Germans. As the war continued Turkey and Bulgaria joined Germany and Austria-Hungary while Italy (despite its previous alliance), Romania, the United States, Japan, and some smaller nations joined France and Britain. The Russians withdrew from the war in December of 1917 after the Bolshevik revolution, yielding a great deal of territory to the Germans and allowing the Germans to throw all of their forces into the fight on the western front. Nevertheless the battle lines across France changed little as large numbers of troops from both sides lost their lives in futile attacks on the entrenched opposing forces. Finally, fresh American soldiers were able to drive the Germans back and bring an end to the war.

The Treaty of Versailles (1919) provided that Germany should lose all of its overseas possessions, some of its territory in Europe, and most of its military power. Germany was forced to pay reparations to the victors, particularly to France, on whose soil most of the fighting had taken place. The territory which the Russians had yielded to the Germans became the independent nations of Estonia, Latvia, Lithuania, Poland, and Czechoslovakia. Several smaller Balkan nations were combined to form Yugoslavia. At U.S. President Woodrow Wilson's insistence the Treaty of Versailles also provided for the establishment of the League of Nations to preserve the peace, but Wilson was unable to persuade the U.S. Senate to ratify the treaty. Consequently the U.S. never became a member of the organization he had fathered.

Unfortunately, the peace was not preserved, for power politics went on as usual. In 1931, Japan took Manchuria by force from China, and in 1935–1936 Italy conquered Ethiopia, which had been one of the few independent nations in Africa. The worldwide depression of the early 1930's led to the rise of Hitler and the Nazis in Germany. The failure of France and Britain to act decisively against Japan, Italy, or the first militaristic and expansionist efforts of Germany only resulted in further aggressive moves by the fascist nations. In the Spanish Civil War (1936–1939) the fascist Franco, with help from Mussolini in Italy and Hitler in Germany, won control of Spain from the newly-elected combined democratic-socialist-Communist forces, who got only token support from France and the Soviet Union. The democratic capitalists in Britain and France and the Communists in Russia each tried to direct Hitler's growing military might against the other. At Munich in 1938 the British and French gave their permission for Hitler to move eastward into part of Czechoslovakia, but he responded by taking the whole country. The Soviets made their move in the summer of 1939, signing a nonaggression pact with Hitler and agreeing to divide Poland between themselves and the Germans.

The German invasion of Poland in September of 1939, usually regarded as the actual beginning of World War II even though the Japanese invasion of China began in 1937, finally triggered a response from France and Britain. Nevertheless, the fast-moving German forces quickly took Denmark, Norway, Luxembourg, Belgium, the Netherlands, and France while the Russians took not only their part of Poland but also Estonia, Latvia, Lithuania, part of Finland, and part of Romania. The Japanese captured French Indo-China. The Germans continued their expansion into Yugoslavia, Greece, and North Africa. In June of 1941 Hitler attacked the Soviet Union (which apparently was planning to attack him the next year) while in December of that same year the Japanese attacked the U.S. at Pearl Harbor. At first the Soviets in Europe and the Americans in Asia suffered large losses, but gradually the Allies changed the tide of battle. Soviet forces began pushing the Germans back on the eastern front while American and British forces crossed the English Channel into France in 1944. Germany surrendered in May of 1945, and Japan surrendered in August of that same year after the Americans had dropped newly-developed atomic bombs on Hiroshima and Nagasaki.

President Franklin Roosevelt, aware of the U.S. Senate's rejection of Wilson's League of Nations after World War I, led the effort to bring the United Nations into existence even while World War II was being fought. The nations which had fought together to defeat the fascists were to unite to preserve the peace. Within three years after the war's end, however, the cold war broke out between the Soviet Union and the Western powers. The U.S. had launched a giant relief program, the Marshall Plan, to help Europe recover from the war and prevent the people there from turning to Communism. The U.S.S.R. had kept its military forces in eastern Europe in order to keep the people there from turning to capitalism. Quarrels developed over the terms of peace, especially in eastern Europe. Stalin did not permit the free elections to which Americans thought he had agreed. In 1948 the Communists staged a coup d'état in Czechoslovakia and then tried to keep the western powers from moving into or out of West Berlin. The Western powers responded by forming a new military alliance, the North Atlantic Treaty Organization. The Communists countered by forming an alliance of the Communist-controlled eastern European countries called the Warsaw Pact.

In China the Nationalists and the Communists continued their civil war which had begun even before the Japanese attack of 1937. The Communist forces under Mao Tse-tung drove the Nationalist forces from mainland China to the island of Taiwan in 1949. Communist forces in the northern part of divided Korea attacked the non-Communists in the southern part in 1950. South Koreans resisted this attack with the help of American troops and eventually that of many other nations after the United Nations declared the North Koreans guilty of aggression and in violation of the U.N. Charter. As the predominantly South Korean and American U.N. forces pushed northward toward the border of China, Chinese "volunteers" entered the war and drove them back. A truce finally set the border between North and South Korea close to where it had been when the war first broke out.

A prime feature of the period after World War II was the gaining of independence by many former colonies of Western European nations. In many cases independence came only after a military struggle against the old colonial power. In Algeria, Indonesia, and Angola the former French, Dutch, and Portuguese rulers were driven out after long battles. The Communist-led Vietnamese drove the French out in 1954 and then the American supporters of non-Communist Vietnamese in 1973. In other cases colonies became independent nations with little or no military action against the former colonial power. In 1946 the U.S. granted the Philippines the independence they had been promised 45 years earlier during the Spanish-American War. In India-Pakistan the British were nudged into leaving both by sabotage and the nonviolent resistance effort led by Gandhi, but enmity between Hindus and Muslims led to fighting that continued even after Muslim Pakistan was separated from Hindu India. Many former British colonies were granted independence but remained loosely tied together as independent republics in the British Commonwealth.

In the Middle East, British and French withdrawal led to fighting between the Jews, who were intent on creating a new Israeli state in Palestine, and the Arabs, who were already living in Palestine and who were unwilling to be incorporated into a nation officially dedicated to following the Jewish religion. In 1947 the United Nations recommended the partition of Palestine into a Jewish state and an Arab state, but the Arabs rejected this plan. When the British forces withdrew the Arabs attacked, intending to put an end to the Jewish state but the Israeli forces successfully resisted. In 1948 a U.N.-policed truce was put into force. In 1956 the Israelis combined with the French and the British to attack Egypt when Nasser, who was getting arms from the Soviet Union, nationalized the Suez Canal. The U.S. worked with the Russians in the U.N. to condemn the attack on Egypt and end the fighting. In 1967 and again in 1973 the Arab-Israeli conflict broke into open warfare with the Israelis demonstrating their military superiority each time.

Attempting to end this series of conflicts, in 1978 Carter of the U.S., Sadat of Egypt, and Begin of Israel signed a "Framework for an Agreement on the Middle East." This agreement provided that Israel would return all of the Sinai to Egypt, that Egypt would recognize the right of Israel to exist, and that the U.S. would provide a great deal of financial aid to both nations. The Palestinian Arabs living in areas under Israeli control were to be given some type of nominal control of their own affairs. The Palestine Liberation Organization (PLO) was unhappy about Sadat's willingness to recognize the existence of the state of Israel, but the recent dispersion of PLO military forces from Lebanon by Israeli forces has led the leaders of several Arab countries to hint that recognition of Israel may be the price which must be paid in order to get general support for the idea of establishing a separate state for the Palestinians.

One of the most significant recent developments in international politics is the split between Russian Communist leaders and Chinese Communist leaders which began in 1959. The Russian Communists had offered only minimal support to Mao Tse-tung in his battles with the Chinese Nationalists and even after Mao's victory, when they did begin to provide more assistance, the Soviets tended to treat the Chinese as inferiors. Mao criticized the Russian leaders for losing their revolutionary fervor and for maintaining an elitist society within the Soviet Union. He suggested that the Russians should return lands taken from China by the imperialistic czars before the Communist revolution of 1917, and noted that if all Communists were brothers then the Soviets should share their nuclear weapons with the Chinese.

The Soviets, on the other hand, apparently believed that Mao was a bit too reckless to be entrusted with nuclear weapons and a bit too demanding about what the Russians should do, especially at a time when they were already engaged in a substantial effort to help the Chinese build up their productive capabilities. In 1959–1960 the Russians pulled out of China and refused to render any more assistance. After the Chinese developed their own nuclear weapons, the Russians apparently were prepared to launch a pre-emptive nuclear attack on the Chinese nuclear research and production facilities in 1969, but were dissuaded by a message from U.S. President Nixon warning that such a Soviet attack "might bring the Russians into confrontation with the U.S."[5] China responded to this unanticipated assistance by developing more friendly relations with the U.S. Since Mao's death China seems to be turning to new domestic policies which emphasize economic development while maintaining an anti-Russian foreign policy. Chinese-American relations have cooled to some extend recently, but the Chinese seem less than eager to renew close ties with the Russians.

The scene of struggles for power has thus evolved from city-states contending for control of a river valley to nation-states contending for a control of a continent to superpowers armed with nuclear weapons contending for control of the world. The scene of action has been enlarged, but the basic principles of interaction seem to remain the same. Military power has been the key ingredient because conflicts of interest between sovereign states are ultimately resolved by force.

The Changing Nature of War

As we have noted, war is as old as civilization. Yet wars fought in the twentieth century are very different from wars fought four or five thousand years ago. For example, the scope of the world wars of the twentieth century is much wider than that of the purely regional wars of earlier periods. Even more evident is the difference in the weapons with which wars are fought. The story of the evolution of war is essentially the story of the evolution of weapons.[6]

During the period from 5000 B.C. through the fourteenth century A.D. there were only minor changes in the manner in which wars were fought. The chief weapons were swords, spears, and bows and arrows. The chief defensive strategy was to build a high wall around the city to be defended, while the chief offensive strategy was to prevent those inside the city walls from getting food or other supplies. Those attacking the walled city might also try various devices such as battering rams or catapulted stones for damaging the gates or the walls, while those inside would use devices such as arrows and boiling water to keep the attackers away from the walls. Over a period of time methods developed for protecting the fields outside the walls in order to preserve the food supply; each city equipped an army with shields, swords, and spears to try to maintain control of the land surrounding the city.

All the fighting was done on foot at first, but after about 1000 B.C. horses gradually came into use. Armor was worn both by the foot soldiers and those mounted on horseback. Various special skills were developed — javelin throwing, throwing stones with a sling, shooting a bow while mounted on horseback, and operating a catapult to throw large stones. Field fortifications (walls and trenches) were built. Ships transported troops and supplies. Eventually other ships were designed to ram the transport ships, either sinking or disabling them and leaving them at the mercy of the attackers. In the ninth and tenth centuries the Vikings capitalized on using ships as vehicles for surprise raids on settlements along rivers and sea coasts. Inventions before the fourteenth century such as stirrups for those on horseback, the crossbow, and the long bow expanded the size of the battlefield but did little to change the overall conduct of war.

Major changes in the way war was fought took place over a 400 year period starting about 1350 when gunpowder was introduced to Europe from China. As a result catapults were replaced by cannons while bows and arrows were replaced by guns and bullets. The first guns were not nearly as effective as bows, but the cannons soon proved to be superior to catapults as devices for bombardment. A crucial victory for gunpowder occurred in 1453 when the Turks used cannons to break openings in the walls of Constantinople, proving to all that a stone wall no longer provided a secure defense against attack. Smaller firearms using gunpowder were gradually being improved and became more widely used during the sixteenth and early seventeenth centuries. Nevertheless the musketeers were still accompanied by pikemen armed with spears who could protect them in close combat. Not until bayonets were mounted on muskets in the late seventeenth century did the pikemen become obsolete.

From the late seventeenth century to the last part of the eighteenth century, war almost took on the character of a game between opposing commanders. The soldiers were trained professionals who were too valuable to lose in battles where rows of men armed with muskets fired volleys at each other from a distance of 50 paces. The spirit of the Enlightenment also suggested that the conduct of war should be rational. Consequently armies tried to maneuver for advantageous positions, and the outmaneuvered commander of a unit might simply surrender before much fighting took place. The majority of the population had little to gain or lose as the result of war games being played between the armies of one king and those of another.

A new age in warfare was ushered in by the American Revolutionary War (1775–1781), the French Revolution (1789–1802), and the Napoleonic Wars (1803–1815). The change came partly as the result of the invention of the rifle and partly as the result of the rebirth of the old Greek idea of a state controlled by the citizens rather than a king. The rifle, first used to shoot game, had a longer range than a musket and was much more accurate. It was aimed at a very specific target, not simply pointed in the general direction of the enemy. The participants in these revolutionary wars were different too. Less ready to risk becoming a target because some king commanded it, the soldiers were also motivated by a new loyalty to the national community and government rather than to the king.

In the American Revolution colonial legislatures called on citizens to join in the battle for independence from Britain and King George III. In the French Revolution nonprofessionals took up arms against the professional soldiers paid by the king. In the Napoleonic Wars citizen-soldiers fought for the glory of France, and the rest of the citizenry identified with the successes and defeats of that national army.

Since 1815 the changing conduct of war has been largely a case of more of the same; that is, on the one hand new and more destructive weapons are made available by new technology, and on the other participation in war expands both actually and psychologically to greater proportions of the population. The evolution of weaponry includes not only improvements in rifles and artillery but also the development of land mines, wire entanglements, grenades, torpedoes, machine guns, tanks, submarines, and bombs dropped from airplanes. Inventions originally intended for civilian uses — telegraph, railroads, steam-powered ships, trucks, radio, airplanes, helicopters — have been adapted to military uses. Military needs dictated other inventions — tanks and other armored vehicles, poison gas, antiaircraft guns, aircraft carriers, radar, jet-propelled missiles, rocket-powered missiles, nuclear bombs, thermonuclear (hydrogen) bombs, nuclear-powered submarines, artificial satellites for information gathering and navigational assistance, and so on.

War and preparation for war have come to occupy more and more people in more ways, including the building of weapons, the production of food and clothing and medical supplies, the invention of new weapons, and the development of new technologies that may have military uses. The education of young people so they will be able to invent new weapons and otherwise contribute to the war effort is also a part of the national defense program, not only during war but also during peacetime. The distinction between military personnel who are essential to the war effort and civilian personnel who have nothing to do with war, a distinction that was so obvious in the middle of the eighteenth century, no longer seems applicable. The judgment that military-dominated planning is desirable during war but not during peace is no longer generally accepted.

When wars occur, each nation involved commits a great deal of its resources to the fight; even during peacetime the top priority of most national governments is to provide national security. War, which began as localized struggles using primitive weapons and strategies and involving only a small proportion of the population, has now become a matter of worldwide conflict using sophisticated weapons and strategies and potentially involving the whole population.

Overall Trends in Warfare

As one reviews the history of war and the changes which have taken place in the way war is waged, certain questions naturally come to mind. Are wars occurring more frequently or less frequently? Are wars becoming more destructive than they once were? Do more people get killed in wars? Are there any long-term trends of any kind related to the scope, intensity, and general nature of war?

Reliable answers to such questions require a great deal of historical research. Before one can check for trends, details must be known about wars of the past. Ideally one should be able to make a list of all wars ever fought, the nations that were involved, how long each war lasted, how many military personnel were committed to battle, how many casualties were suffered by each side, and so on. To determine the proportion of people involved in a war and the proportion killed, one would need to know the total population both of the nations involved in that war and that of the whole world at that time. There are problems of selection, too. Should civil wars, or only interstate wars, be included? How should one determine whether to include a conflict as a war? On the basis of the number of people committed to battle? On the basis of the number of casualties? On the basis of the size of the states involved? On the basis of whether the participants perceived themselves as engaged in a war? Since different investigators answer these questions in different ways, it is difficult to directly compare one study with another.

Several attempts have been made to list various wars and to estimate the number of persons engaged in battles, the number killed, and so on.[7] These studies provide the raw data from which generalizations must be drawn if they are to have any kind of a factual basis, but a review reveals that much of the data consists more of "guesstimates" than estimates.[8] Furthermore, the most careful of these studies, that done by J. David Singer and Melvin Small,[9] covers a period of only 150 years. Can we trust generalizations about trends based on such a short period of time? That period is so short that it may suggest trends that do not exist over a longer period of time, or it may fail to reveal trends that do exist over a longer period.

In his monumental work *A Study of War*, Quincy Wright compiled data about wars fought from 1480 to 1940. On the basis of this study he concluded that a number of trends can be observed with regard to war.[10]

> It is clear that during the modern period there has been a trend toward an increase in the absolute and relative size of armies whether one considers the peace[time] army, the number mobilized for war, the number of combatants engaged in battle, or the number of military and civil populations devoting themselves to war work.
>
> ...Another general trend has been toward a decrease in the length of wars and in the proportion of war years to peace years.[11]
>
> ...A third trend has been toward an increase in the length of battles, in the number of battles in a war year, and also in the total number of

battles during a century.... The number of battles in a war has also tended
to increase.[12]

...A fourth trend has been toward an increase in the number of belligerents in a war, in the rapidity with which a war spreads, and in the
area covered by a war.[13]

...A fifth trend has been toward an increased human and economic cost
of war, both absolutely and relative to the population.... [But] the proportion of persons engaged in a battle who are killed has probably tended
to decline [from 30–50 percent in the Middle Ages to only 2 percent in the
twentieth century]....

The proportion of the population engaged in the armies, however, has
tended to become larger, and the number of battles has tended to increase. As a result, the proportion of the population dying as a direct
consequence of battle has tended to increase.[14]

Many of these trends cited by Wright are what one would expect as a
result of technological advances, especially those made from the fifteenth
century on. Changes in communication and transportation made larger
armies feasible. These same factors, along with more effective weapons of
destruction, suggest that war would break out less frequently, that it
would be over more quickly once begun, and that the pace of fighting
would speed up. Similarly, a given war would cover a wider area and include more nations, and the cost of war would become greater. The decline in the proportion of combatants who die is readily attributable to
advancements in medicine plus the fact that more and more of the armed
forces (considered "combatants" by Wright) are not actually engaged in
front-line fighting.

Conclusions which are a bit more surprising are drawn by Singer and
Small in their very careful study of international war from 1816 to 1965.

Is war on the increase, as many scholars as well as laymen of our
generation have been inclined to believe? The answer would seem to be a
very unambiguous negative. Whether we look at the number of wars,
their severity [number of battle deaths for combatants], or their magnitude [number of nations involved multiplied by the number of months
each was at war], there is no significant trend upward or downward over
the past 150 years [*as long as we make allowance for the increasing population and the increasing number of nations that might get involved in
war*]. ...[T]he number of interstate wars per decade has risen no faster
than the number of nations in the interstate system....[15]

It is important to note that these conclusions of Singer and Small are in
relative, not absolute, terms. Wars in the central international state
system are becoming more bloody, but the number of battle deaths is not
increasing much faster than the total population of the nations in the
international system.[16] The number of battle deaths for combatants went
from 9,000,000 in World War I to 15,000,000 in World War II, but the
total population of the nations in World War II was much greater.[17] The
magnitude of wars is increasing, but no faster than the number of nations
in the international state system. It should also be noted that in certain

statistical treatments of the raw data Singer and Small themselves find a downward trend in the number of wars in a given period of time (both absolutely and relatively) and an upward trend in the magnitude and severity of wars (both absolutely and relatively).[18] These conclusions agree with those of Wright cited earlier. Also it should be noted that Singer and Small conjecture that violence resulting from civil war, which was not included in their study, is on the rise.[19]

Making use of the data gathered by Singer and Small as well as that of others, Francis Beer arrives at a conclusion which also agrees with the trends noted by Wright.

> ...[I]f there has been an overall historical trend, it has probably been toward the concentration and aggravation of war. Such a trend implies a decline in the incidence of wars, but an increase in casualities—both in absolute terms and relative to population.[20]

Thus according to Beer's analysis of the data, which agrees with the judgments of others, in more recent times there have been fewer wars with longer intervals of peace between them than in earlier times. When war does occur, however, it is bloodier both with regard to the actual number of persons killed and the percentage of the population suffering death from war. If these trends continue in the future, "long interwar periods may be way stations for subsequent wars which may inflict even greater casualties than the ones which preceded them."[21]

The Present Urgency of the War Problem

Is a solution to the war problem any more urgent today than in the past? Or has the availability of weapons of mass destruction created a stalemate in which no nation will dare to attack another? Are wars with conventional weapons any more dangerous now than in the past? Is preparation for war any more expensive than in the past?

In dealing with the urgency of solving the war problem, we need to recall the various aspects of the war problem outlined in the first chapter. The first aspect is the huge outlay of money and effort which presently goes into getting ready for war. As we have noted previously, the worldwide expenditure for military purposes is now over one and one half billion dollars a day and increasing at an average rate of 2 percent a year in constant dollars.[22] The cost of developing ever more sophisticated weapons will continue to push it higher. The need to keep ahead of the potential enemy technologically as well as in actual weapons on hand grows ever more urgent whether the race is between superpower and superpower, between one less developed country and another, or between national governments and revolutionary groups aiming to overthrow them. Even if war never breaks out, the rapidly rising cost of military preparation makes a solution to the war problem especially urgent.

It is also disturbing to realize that with further economic development of both the richer and poorer countries military expenditures will probably increase as total production increases. There seems to be a long-range and general tendency for developed nations to devote between 2 and 10 percent of their production to military purposes during peace-time.[23] Thus not only the increasing cost of weapons but also the tendency to spend more for the military when there is more money available suggests that military spending is likely to continue increasing even if the proportion of the world's gross product devoted to military spending does not.

The second aspect of the war problem is the danger of war between the superpowers. The destructiveness of the available weapons makes it obvious that such a war would be vastly more devastating than anything humankind has previously experienced. One U.S. nuclear-powered submarine carries more destructive power than was unleashed by both sides during all of World War II.[24] There are now in the world 50,000 nuclear warheads bigger than the bombs dropped on Hiroshima and Nagasaki, and there is no chance of stopping the missiles which carry most of these warheads from reaching their targets once they are launched. With each detonated warhead spreading large amounts of deadly radiation in addition to the damage done by blast and heat, it is unreasonable to believe that there would be much left of the nations involved. Even the nations not directly attacked would be adversely affected by the radiation and atmospheric dust from nuclear explosions. In the past the trend toward more destructive weapons was basically a gradual one. The introduction of nuclear weapons and intercontinental ballistic missiles represents a shift in destructiveness and the range at which it can be employed unlike anything in earlier history. It is a vastly greater break from the past than that which occurred when gunpowder was introduced or when airplanes were put to military uses. We are faced with "a qualitatively new situation in relation to war — the possibility and probability of annihilating the human race and all other forms of life on the planet earth."[25]

The notion that the superpowers might get involved in a war but not use their nuclear weapons overlooks the logic of a war situation. The aim of war is to use military power to win, to impose one's will on the other side. In such a situation if either side is facing defeat, it will use nuclear weapons rather than surrender. At the same time the side which is winning the war would want to use its nuclear weapons before sustaining such an attack from a desperate opponent. The side facing defeat would know that the prevailing side would feel that way, so it would be led to use its nuclear weapons before the other side expects it. But the same logic would lead the prevailing side to want to use its nuclear weapons before the losing side tries to launch an unexpected attack. Following this logic through to its end, each side would want to use its nuclear weapons as soon as the situation has deteriorated to one in which the conflict is to be resolved by force. Those who argue for nuclear surgical strikes in a limited nuclear war assume a detachment on the part of the leaders of both sides which, if it existed, would not allow a war to develop in the first place. It seems that the only alternative to a nuclear holocaust is to prevent *any* war between the superpowers from breaking out in the first place.

We cannot overlook the possibility that a nuclear war between the superpowers might be triggered by accident. Charles Osgood[26] reports an incident in October 1960 when the newly-installed Ballistic Early Warning System flashed signals indicating that a multimissile attack was coming from the direction of the Soviet Union. The Canadian officer in charge at NORAD headquarters in Colorado refrained from giving the signal for release of a retaliatory attack because there was no substantial evidence of ground firing of the missiles. When he tried to contact the radar installation in Greenland, from which the warning of attack had come, the line was dead (due, it was discovered later, to the cable being broken by an iceberg). Still the Canadian officer delayed acting for over half an hour (a delay which would have been disastrous in the event of an actual attack) because he knew that Khrushchev was in New York at the U.N. and thought that the Soviets were unlikely to attack the U.S. at such a time. Eventually it became evident that the warning resulted from radar signals bouncing off the rim of the rising moon. But, as Osgood asks, what would have happened if Khrushchev had not been in New York or if the same incident had occurred at a time when tensions were high? Consider too the fact that over a recent 18-month period, the U.S. warning system produced 147 false warnings of Soviet missile attacks![27] As more nuclear weapons are employed by more nations and as the need for a quick response to any threat becomes ever greater, the chance of a nuclear holocaust occurring even though there is no intent to start a war by the government of either side also becomes greater. Murphy's Law, the notion that if something can go wrong it will, could receive a disastrous confirmation given the present international situation and the attitudes of some military leaders on both sides.[28]

The third aspect of the war problem is the possibility of conventional wars between nonnuclear powers. There is a real danger that the nuclear powers would get dragged into such a war just as the Big Powers got dragged into World War I as the result of disputes between smaller nations. Also the weapons being used in conventional wars are themselves becoming much more destructive. During the Six-Day War in the Middle East in 1967 there were about 21,000 battle-related deaths[29] in just six days—about 3,500 per day. The rate of death in that war involving only four nations is more than half of the 6,897 per day killed all over the world by 28 nations during World War II[30] and is nearly twice as much as the 1,770 deaths per day in the Korean War.[31] It should be obvious that these "little" conventional wars are small only by comparison with what might be expected in a war using nuclear weapons.

The fourth aspect of the war problem is the occurrence and the threat of the occurrence of civil wars. We have already noted that these wars seem to be occurring more frequently now than in the past. The ready availability of weapons with substantial firepower plus the development of techniques of guerrilla warfare plus the existence of devices for duplicating printed materials at low cost have given those dissatisfied with a government and its policies a much greater opportunity to promote revolt. Another important factor of civil war is the widespread belief that the government has the responsibility to promote the general welfare of the society. If important problems go unsolved, the government is blamed. Also, the privileged classes no longer have a monopoly on knowing how to use weapons or how to read, write, and think about social issues.

Since the poor now have more awareness of what will promote their interests and since those interests are usually not the same as the interests of those with political power, civil war between these groups with opposing interests is much more likely than in the past.

There is still another way in which the war problem is more urgent today than in the past, at least from the perspective of the ordinary citizen. There was a time, as late as the eighteenth century, when anyone who didn't want to participate in a war could simply ignore it. Armies employed by kings fought against each other and did little to disturb ordinary citizens, who for the most part were indifferent concerning whether they were subject to King A or King B. But, as we have noted, that is no longer the case. Now every citizen is expected to assist if the society is engaged in war. Even civilian jobs have military significance, and any citizen is likely to be the subject of enemy attack. World War II meant a gigantic upheaval in the lives of millions of people, but there were some places (parts of Latin America and Africa) where the war made little difference, at least directly, to the lives of the people. If there is a World War III, however, no one will escape. Even people in nations which want nothing to do with war, which are completely neutral, would be affected by radioactive fallout, by large amounts of dust in the atmosphere, and by the alteration of the ozone layer which presently protects the earth from a great deal of ultraviolet radiation from the sun.

Smaller wars now have a wider impact, too. Americans learned in 1973 that war in the Middle East made a great deal of difference in the price they paid for oil. The same was true of the civil war in Iran and the resulting shortage of gasoline. Civil wars in Central America may have an impact on the prices Americans pay for fresh fruits and vegetables, especially in winter and early spring. On the other hand, such wars may eventually open up new opportunities for people in some less developed countries — education, medical care, and better housing.

The problem of war is more urgent now than in the past also because of the higher cost of war preparations which must be borne by the general public. For example, in the United States, current military expenditures run about $71 per month per person.[32] This cost of preparing for war even in peacetime means less goods for everyone both directly and in terms of less productivity in the long run. In less developed countries as well as more advanced ones military spending means less government money for schools, medical care, and other social services.

Today no person anywhere on earth can truthfully say that solving the war problem makes no difference to his own life.

Part Two

Causes of War

IV. The Cause of War: Some General Considerations

It is not uncommon to think of war as a disease of society. This analogy has led to the expectation that war could be prevented if we learned more about what causes it. As a result of this pattern of thinking, a great deal has been written and said about the cause of war. In dealing with this issue it is worth pausing to consider exactly what is involved in saying that one thing is a cause of another. Then we need to look at the phenomenon of individual human aggressiveness and to consider what relationship it has, if any, to those violent conflicts we know as war.

Investigating the Cause of War

There are at least four senses in which the word cause can be used: a necessary condition, a sufficient condition, a necessary and sufficient condition, and a contributory factor.

A "cause" in the sense of a *necessary condition* means that the effect cannot occur if the "cause" is not present. If one knows the necessary condition of something, he will know how to prevent that thing from happening. For example, the presence of oxygen is a necessary condition for the burning of materials such as wood and paper. It follows that one can put out a fire by using a gas such as carbon dioxide to prevent oxygen from getting to the fire.

A "cause" in the sense of a *sufficient condition* means that the effect must occur whenever the "cause" is present. If one knows the sufficient condition of something, he will know how to make that thing occur. For example, the flow of electricity through a wire made of a metal such as aluminum or copper is a sufficient condition to produce heat. It follows that one can make heat (for a toaster or an electric blanket, for example) by having electricity flow through a metal wire.

A "cause" in the sense of a *necessary and sufficient* condition means that the effect cannot occur if the "cause" is not present *and* that whenever the "cause" is present the effect must occur. If one knows the necessary and sufficient condition of something, he will know both how to prevent it and how to produce it. For example, the flow of electricity through the filament of an incandescent light bulb is the necessary and sufficient condition of the bulb giving off light. One can stop the bulb from glowing by cutting off the supply of electricity, and one can make it glow by letting electricity flow through the filament.

36

A "cause" in the sense of a *contributory factor* means that the effect is more likely to occur when the "cause" is present, but the relationship is not a necessary one. The cause may be present and the effect not occur, or the cause may be absent and the effect occur anyway. If one knows a contributory factor of something, he will be able to make it more probable or less probable but will not be able to guarantee any results. For example, smoking cigarettes seems to be a contributory factor to lung cancer. Some people smoke cigarettes and don't get lung cancer, and others don't smoke but nevertheless get lung cancer. Nevertheless, someone who smokes cigarettes is much more likely to get lung cancer than someone who doesn't.

How do these four different senses of "cause" apply to the problem of the cause of war? It seems that if our goal is to prevent all warfare, we will want to know the *necessary condition* of war. We could then eliminate war by eliminating this necessary condition. The problem is to discover some necessary condition that we could and would want to eliminate. Consider, for example, that the existence of war as we have defined it requires the existence of groups of people. If we eliminated all people or somehow made it impossible for people to form groups, we would eliminate war. But the proposed cure is worse than the disease.

What about the notion that group conflict is a necessary condition of war? It does seem to be the case that if we eliminated all conflicts between groups, we would then have eliminated war, that is, violent conflicts between groups. The difficulty with this proposal is that eliminating all conflict between groups is more difficult than simply eliminating the *violent* conflicts which constitute war. Those who think that the only way of eliminating war is to eliminate all conflicts of interest between groups set before themselves an even more difficult problem than the one with which they began.

What can be said about the notion that since individual human aggressiveness is a necessary condition of war, the way to eliminate war is to eliminate all individual human aggressiveness? Once again, it seems that eliminating all human aggressiveness is a more difficult task than eliminating war. We need not achieve that difficult and in some ways undesirable goal in order to rid the world of war.

When we turn to "cause" in the sense of *sufficient condition*, it seems that what we want to know is not the cause of *war* but the cause of *peace*. Is there anything which when present always produces peace? Theodore Lentz suggests that just as medical researchers sometimes focus their attention on unusually healthy groups of people to learn what produces such good health, so peace researchers should focus their attention on peaceful societies to learn what produces them.[1] Efforts in this direction, however, have not yet come up with any promising hypotheses.[2] The search has just begun, however, and there are some nations such as Switzerland and Sweden which seem to have very good records in avoiding wars with other countries. Investigators may also turn their attention to the cause of peace *within* countries. There are many nations which have been relatively free from internal strife for long periods of time, and it seems it would be worthwhile to examine these societies and their institutions to try to discover the cause of peace within governed communities.

Since the concept of "cause" as necessary and sufficient condition does not involve any issues not already discussed in connection with the separate concepts of necessary condition and sufficient condition, only the concept of *contributory factor* remains to be considered in connection with the issue of the cause of war. This sense of "cause" is most likely to be relevant when very complex phenomena are being investigated, and there can be little doubt that war is a very complex phenomenon. Consequently, when people say that nationalism is a cause of war or that individuals who make profits from selling arms are a cause of war, they are most likely using the word "cause" in this sense of contributory factor rather than in the stronger sense of necessary condition. They can be viewed as claiming merely that if nationalism were reduced, or if the profits from selling arms were reduced, the likelihood of war would be reduced.

One must remember, however, that the mere correlation of one thing with another does not prove that one is the cause of the other, even in the sense of being a contributory factor. Suppose, for example, that one finds a positive correlation between military spending and the number of casualties suffered in war for many different nations over some period of time. Does this prove that high military spending *causes* a nation to get involved in war and suffer many casualties as a result?[3] Saying that a nation with high military spending is *more likely* to engage in war and suffer casualties is different from saying than high military spending *causes* (is a contributory factor to) involvement in war and casualties. There may be tension between two nations which leads them to increase their military spending. A war accompanied by high casualty counts may follow. But this war may have occurred even sooner and been even bloodier if one of the nations had refused to increase its military spending in the face of tension. The correlation between military spending and war may be the reflection of some common cause for both (increased tension) rather than a causal connection between military spending on the one hand and war on the other.

There is still another point related to the issue of causation which needs to be considered by those seeking to discover the cause of war. We have previously noted the analogy which can be drawn between war and disease. Suppose that a physician were to address himself to the cause of disease. He would probably begin by noting that there is no cause of disease in general but only particular causes of particular diseases. He would probably note that these particular diseases can be put into classes on the basis of their causes — diseases caused by bacteria, diseases caused by viruses, diseases caused by genetic factors, diseases caused by toxic chemicals in the environment, and so on — and that any attempt to make statements about *the cause* of all these various kinds of diseases is bound to fail.

Couldn't a similar point be made with regard to the subject of the cause of war? Perhaps it is inappropriate to try to make judgments about *the cause* of war in general. Perhaps one should begin by examining the particular causes of particular wars and then make an effort to classify these cases on the basis of different kinds of causes. World War I and World War II may be superficially similar in that they are the only two world wars in history, but in terms of their causes they may in fact be very different. Trying to discover some cause of war which is operative in both World War I and World War II (as well as all other wars) may be an exercise in futility.

Once wars had been classified on the basis of their causes, the next step would be to identify symptoms that appear before the war actually breaks out. Only then would there be any chance of using one's knowledge about the various kinds of causes of war to try to prevent wars. Ideally one could learn what type of "medicine" to use when certain symptoms appear so that the threatened war could be avoided. Even if such knowledge became available, however, it is questionable whether a knowledgeable "physician" of society would be consulted by political leaders or that anyone would pay much attention to taking the "medicine" prescribed.

In any case, it is evident that we are far from being able to deal with the problem of war in this manner. The previous efforts to classify wars usually focus on their size rather than their cause, a situation comparable to classifying diseases in accord with the number of persons who suffer from them. Even studies which start with the examination of the causes of particular wars often end by trying to make generalizations which apply to all wars[4] rather than trying to distinguish different types of wars on the basis of their causes.

Consequently, our situation is that we have little choice but to follow tradition and discuss the cause of war in general. Still, what has been said in this section is relevant to the examination of various theories concerning the cause of war to be undertaken in Chapters V and VI. These theories must be viewed as being about *contributory factors* which are purported to be operative in some wars but not necessarily in all wars. To return to the medical analogy, it might be asserted even on a very general level that bacteria are *a cause* of disease. This statement would not be taken to mean that every single disease is caused by bacteria but only that bacteria are a contributory factor in some diseases. It is regrettable that our discussion of the cause of war should be carried on at such a level of generality, but the present state of our knowledge permits no other approach.[5]

Individual Human Aggression

Aggression can be defined as "behavior whose goal is the injury of some person or object."[6] It is equivalent to violence and therefore seems to be relevant to war, which we have defined as "violent conflict between organized groups that are or that aim to establish governments." It is important, however, to make a distinction between the aggressive behavior of *individuals as individuals* and the aggressive behavior of *individuals as representatives of groups* which are at war with each other. The explanation of the former type of behavior may have very little to do with understanding the latter type of behavior. Giving causes for the aggressive behavior of individuals as individuals is not the same as giving causes for war.[7]

Even though there is some question of the extent to which understanding individual human aggression is helpful for understanding the war problem, it is appropriate to discuss the topic simply because many of those who have dealt with individual human aggression have thought that it is particularly relevant to warfare.[8] Furthermore, even if the relationship between individual aggression and warfare is not as direct as some writers have assumed, whatever relationship does exist can be better understood once the basis of individual aggression is understood.

Three main groups of theories have been advanced to account for individual aggressive behavior. The first group sees aggression as rooted in man's biological nature. The second group sees aggressive behavior as flowing from feelings of hostility which are the result of frustration. The third group of theories sees aggression as the result of man's social conditioning. Let us consider these three types of theories at greater length.[9]

According to the biological-instinctual theories, humans, like other animals, are born with a propensity or drive to be aggressive. This aggressive behavior may be triggered by specific kinds of situations, such as defense of one's territory, but it may also, according to Konrad Lorenz and others, just "explode"[10] with no external stimulation. Sigmund Freud wrote of an instinct of destruction.[11] Robert Ardrey links aggressive behavior with what he calls "the territorial imperative"[12] and writes of the "weapons instinct"[13] which he believes developed in the killer apes from which man is descended. Another defender of this ethological approach is Desmond Morris.[14] A more recent quite different version of the same general approach has been put forth by Peter Corning. He emphasizes the evolutionary adaptiveness of the various inborn aggressive responses to specific kinds of situations.[15]

Biological-instinctual theorists rely on studies of animals where aggressive behavior is exhibited in three situations. First, there is aggressive behavior, primarily but not exclusively among males, for status in the "pecking order" within the group. Second, there is aggressive behavior among males of territorial species for individual territory within the group's territory. Third, there is collective aggressive behavior by males to defend the group and its territory from other groups. Defense of the young, primarily by females, may be mentioned as a fourth specific situation where aggressive behavior occurs, but among the theorists mentioned above only Corning seems much interested in this particular manifestation of aggression.

One problem for the biological-instinctual theorists is to indicate in what sense the aggressive instinct is to be regarded as a "cause" of aggressive behavior. Do these theorists want to maintain that the aggressive instinct is a *sufficient condition* for aggressive behavior? In that case they will have a problem accounting for the lack of aggressive behavior in groups of people such as the Tasaday of the Philippines,[16] the Arapesh of New Guinea, the pygmies of Zaïre,[17] the Pueblo Indians of the American Southwest, and the Lepchas of Sikkim.[18] The notion that there is an inborn instinct which is sufficient by itself to produce aggressive behavior is what arouses the antagonism of other theorists, and even the spokesmen for the instinctual theory admit that the aggressive instinct can be controlled by civilization.[19]

On the other hand, what is the situation if these biological-instinctual theorists want to maintain merely that the aggressive instinct is a *necessary condition* of aggressive behavior? In this case, why use a term such as "instinct"? It seems more appropriate under these circumstances to speak of a *capacity* for aggressive behavior which must exist as a basis for such behavior, but then it would follow that under some circumstances such a capacity might not be developed. In that case, these biological-instinctual theorists would not be espousing anything different from what is being maintained by social-learning theorists.

A third possibility is that the biological-instinctual theorists want to maintain that the aggressive instinct is only a *contributory factor* to aggressive behavior. Again we must ask: If that is the thesis, then why use the term "instinct," which seems to indicate that there is some inborn drive sufficient by itself to produce aggressive behavior regardless of environmental constraints? If that which is inborn only serves as a contributory factor, it might be more appropriate to speak of a tendency or disposition for people to engage in aggressive behavior under certain circumstances. The point of the biological-instinctual theory could then be stated in terms of some people having inherited a greater tendency to engage in certain types of aggressive behavior than others. The evidence suggests that there are significant differences in this regard between males and females in humans as well as other animals, but some of these studies also indicate that the tendency to be aggressive can be overcome by training.[20]

A second problem for the biological-instinctual theorists is related to the fact that two of the three aggression-arousing situations on which they focus deal with defense of territory. With territorial animals like some fish and birds, there are many examples of territorial fighting; but when it comes to humans, and even other primates, there is some doubt that they are territorial animals either individually or collectively. David Pilbeam maintains that "territoriality ... is not a 'natural' feature of human group living; nor is it among most other primates."[21] It might be argued that humans sometimes seem to be very dedicated to defending their homeland or their neighborhood against external invaders, but on other occasions people simply migrate to other lands and other neighborhoods with no desire whatever to defend the territory they are leaving. It is also generally believed that at one time all human life was nomadic. These observations seem to cast doubt on the claim that in humans there is an instinctive drive to defend territory. Furthermore, the fact that American and British soldiers fighting on the mainland of Europe in World Wars I and II did not behave less heroically than French troops fighting for their own homeland suggests that the notion of group territoriality, even if such exists in humans, is not relevant to the problem of modern war.

Some biological-instinctual theorists, recognizing the problems just noted, fall back to postulating a nonterritorial herd instinct that leads people to empathize with members of their own group (the in-group) while being antagonistic to other groups (out-groups). That there is a tendency to such empathy and antagonism is obvious to any observer of human behavior, but that it is instinctive is again questionable. It seems, for example, that one must be taught how far one's in-group extends. It is certainly not instinctual for Americans to feel that residents of Detroit, Michigan are part of our in-group while residents of Windsor, Ontario are not. Furthermore, it seems that people must be taught which out-groups to hate, especially since the situation changes rapidly. Consider, for example, American attitudes toward Germany, Japan, and China over the last 50 years. This matter of in-groups and out-groups will be taken up again in the next chapter when we discuss nationalism.

A second group of theories about the cause of individual human aggression are those which view aggressive behavior as the result of hostility brought about by frustration. According to this approach, human beings are viewed as goal-oriented organisms. As long as they are making adequate headway in achieving their ends they do not become frustrated and aggressive, but when they are blocked from reaching a goal they are likely to become more hostile. John Dollard and his colleagues at Yale at one time claimed that frustration was both a *necessary condition* and a *sufficient condition* for aggressive behavior.[22] Later advocates of the theory such as Leonard Berkowitz have made the weaker claim that frustration is merely a contributory factor to aggression.[23]

If the frustration theorists are correct, aggressive behavior will be more readily controlled than if either of the other approaches is correct. To produce aggressive behavior, it is much easier to frustrate the person in some way than to alter his genetic make-up or to change habits of responding that have been built up over a lifetime. Alternatively, to control someone's aggression, one would need only to discover what goal is being blocked and then give the person some assistance in making headway toward this goal. If no help can be given with regard to that goal, one might still hope to reduce the aggressive behavior by providing some other substitute satisfactions.

The main doubt to be raised about the frustration-aggression approach concerns the extent to which frustration affects the amount of aggressive behavior displayed. The biological-instinctual theorists emphasize that certain situations will produce aggressive responses of a particular kind whether or not there appears to be any frustration. Those who adopt the social-learning approach note that people learn to accept different levels of frustration in different situations before displaying aggressive behavior. Also there is evidence to indicate that aggressive behavior is displayed in the absence of any frustration or hostility by persons who are merely obeying orders to be aggressive[24] and that the intensity of aggression displayed by various individuals does not seem to depend on how frustrated they are.[25] In fact, the amount of aggression seems to depend much more on the strength of the attack which triggers the aggressive response and on the anticipated response to aggressive behavior expected by the aggressor from others who witness his behavior.[26] Thus it seems that the frustration-aggression view is challenged by a good deal of evidence. It may be that frustration produces hostility which produces aggressive behavior, but this approach seems to neglect the fact that aggressive behavior may be brought about by factors other than hostility. People can behave aggressively without being angry.[27]

The third group of theories about individual human aggression emphasizes the role of social conditioning in aggressive behavior. According to this approach it is a mistake to assume that humankind has some fixed human nature that makes people either aggressive or nonaggressive.[28] Human beings have the capability of learning to behave in many different ways depending on what kind of behavior is observed and consequently imitated, as well as on what kind of behavior is rewarded. Although this view is particularly associated with behaviorist psychologists such as John B. Watson and B.F. Skinner, many psychologists of other schools of psychology also favor the social-learning theory. Anthropologists such as Margaret Mead and Geoffrey Gorer also tend to be supporters of the social-learning approach to explaining human aggressive behavior.

The evidence for the social-learning view of the origin of aggression comes mainly from two sources: psychological studies which show how people's behavior and attitudes can be modified by conditioning and education, and anthropological studies which find very different behavior patterns in different cultures. Anthropologists can point to some societies, such as the Eskimos, where individuals are pugnacious but there is no group warfare; among others such as the Pueblo Indians, individuals are not pugnacious but there is group warfare.[29] This situation would suggest that both individual aggressiveness and group aggressiveness must be learned — separately. The social-learning theory is supported also by the fact that adopted individuals reared from infancy in a culture different from that of their natural parents will display the attitudes and behavior patterns of the culture in which they are reared rather than that of their biological parents.

When the social learning theorists say that the environment causes the presence or absence of aggressive behavior, they seem to mean that the environment is a *sufficient condition* of the behavior. Their claim is that, except in extreme cases of genetic abnormality or the like, the aggressiveness of an individual will be the result of the social conditioning to which the person is exposed. The evidence about sex differences in aggressive tendencies mentioned in connection with the biological-instinctual theory cannot be ignored, but the social-learning theorists claim that these inborn tendencies can be completely overcome by the proper training, as is demonstrated by the existence of the nonaggressive societies mentioned previously.

The casual observer might question the social-learning approach on grounds that certain individuals, even offspring of the same parents, are very different in their aggressiveness though reared in the same environment. The social-learning theorist responds that no two people, even children in the same family, have exactly the same environment. For example, there is a great difference between being a boy with a younger brother and being one with an older brother even when the boys are in the same family. It seems that, even though there may be some slight differences in the inborn tendency to aggressive behavior among individuals and even though people may be more likely to behave aggressively when frustrated, the overwhelmingly predominant factor determining the degree and kind of aggressive behavior displayed by individuals is their social conditioning.

Individual Aggression and War

Having discussed various views about the cause of individual human aggression, let us turn our attention to the issue of how such individual aggression may be related to that violent group conflict we call war. Three rather different situations need to be considered. The first deals with the aggressiveness of group leaders who have a great deal of influence on the behavior of the groups they lead. The second deals with the ways in which hostility, built up in members of a group as a result of frustration, may be directed against other groups. The third deals with the way in which soldiers are prepared to actually engage in acts of violence.

There is a remarkable incident involving rhesus monkeys that gives support to the notion that a particularly aggressive individual leader can be a cause of war. Robert Ardrey relates[30] how ethologist C.R. Carpenter had transported several groups of rhesus monkeys from India to Santiago Island off Puerto Rico to observe their behavior in a natural environment. One matter which he wanted to study was the dominance relationships of the males in the various groups of monkeys. The usual pattern of dominance among these monkeys is such that the top monkey prevails in disputes about four or five times as often as the bottom male monkey. While making his observations Carpenter was surprised to find that one group of monkeys began conquering territory from five neighboring groups. In such struggles between groups the usual pattern was much threatening, little actual fighting, and no exchange of territory, but this situation was different. Furthermore, there seemed at first to be no explanation for the expansionist activity since an adequate food supply was distributed to all the groups each day and the size of all the groups was roughly the same.

But Carpenter soon found an explanation. The conquering group was led by an extremely strong, courageous, and domineering male. His factor of dominance over the second male in the group was the 5:1 ratio usually found between the top male and the bottom male. This commanding leader had a dominance factor of about 50:1 over the bottom male in his group. It was he that led his group on the warpath against the neighboring groups. When Carpenter removed the master monkey from the group, it went back to its own territory and stopped attacking its neighbors. When he returned the master monkey to the group, it again began imposing on the territory of its neighbors. One could not ask for a more striking case of the effect of an aggressive leader on the behavior of a group. In this case the master monkey was both the necessary and the sufficient condition for aggressive behavior on the part of the group as a whole.

This incident suggests that the individual aggressiveness of leaders may be a very relevant factor in the causation of war. When we look at human history, we are struck by the names of individual leaders who led their peoples along the path of conquest—Alexander the Great, Genghis Khan, Napoleon Bonaparte, Adolf Hitler, and so on. It may be too simplistic to believe that aggressive leaders are either a necessary or a sufficient condition for war, but it is hard not to believe that they are an important contributory factor.[31] This seems to be one situation where individual aggression is a factor rather directly related to war.

A second way in which individual aggression may be related to the problem of war involves the psychological phenomenon called "displaced aggression."[32] A person who is frustrated may not be able to direct his hostility toward the real source of his frustration and may, consequently, take it out on others. The typical example of displaced aggression is the man who is frustrated in his job by his superiors. He may become angry, but he cannot direct his hostility toward his superior without losing his job or damaging his chances for promotion, so when he gets home he acts aggressively toward his wife and children.

The phenomenon of displaced aggression can be related to war in the following way. If there is widespread frustration among the members of a society, possibly because economic conditions are bad, a leader may be able to direct the resulting hostility toward some particular group, possibly toward some minority within the country or toward some foreign nation.[33] When economic conditions were very bad in Germany in the early 1930's, Hitler's attacks on the Jews gained a considerable following while just a few years earlier, during prosperity, very few persons paid any attention to him. Today we can expect that when the anticipation of rapid economic advancement in less developed countries is disappointed the hostility toward richer nations will be great, but since the people of these poorer nations are unable successfully to attack these rich countries their hostility is likely to be directed toward their own leaders or toward their poor neighbors.[34] In fact, the leaders of these frustrated nations may deliberately direct their people's hostility toward neighboring countries in order to keep it from being directed toward themselves. It is an old device of political leaders to protect themselves from troubles at home by starting a crisis abroad, but the recent experience of Argentinian leaders with regard to the Falkland Islands–Malvinas indicates why political leaders adopting such a strategy ought to make sure they take on a weak enemy rather than a strong one.

All of the above suggests that prosperity is likely to make peace more probable while economic adversity is likely to produce hostility and war, even though the hostility and war may not be directed against the real source of frustration. It should be noted, however, that this phenomenon of displaced aggression seems to be more closely related to the issue of how leaders get their followers ready to participate in a war than to the issue of how the wars get started. Still, persons who call for aggressive action are more likely to make their way into leadership positions when the population as a whole is frustrated, and leaders are much more likely to embark on a course of action which will lead to war when they feel their followers are ready and eager for the effort.

A third way individual aggressiveness is related to war is in the preparation of soldiers to do the actual fighting of a war. This matter has nothing to do with how wars get started, but only with how individuals are induced to engage in violent behavior once the leaders have decided to go to war. Both the frustration theory of aggression and the social learning theory of aggression are relevant. Much of military training, especially basic training, is based on the principle that a frustrated soldier is more likely to be a hostile person and therefore an aggressive person. The task then becomes one of directing this aggression against the enemy rather than the military leaders in charge of the training or the political leaders who have been responsible for pulling the young person away from his personal pursuits to fight for the glory of his country. A frequently-used device is to describe atrocities committed by the enemy. There is also an effort to get the soldiers to view the enemy soldiers as less than human and thus not deserving of the respect usually accorded to humans. A concerted effort is made to get these soldiers to follow orders without questioning them. Of course this military training is supported by a long period of social conditioning leading the young soldier to identify with his country and to place a positive value on the idea of losing one's life for his country. This identification with the national group, nationalism, is one of our subjects in the next chapter.

V. Group Competition and Group Identification

We have defined war as "violent conflict between organized groups that are or that aim to establish governments." This definition implies that whatever serves as a focus of competition between groups may become a cause of war. Still these conflicts of interest between groups could not become wars if the individuals in the groups did not identify their own welfare with the welfare of the group. Special attention needs to be given to that identification with the group which is called "nationalism," since it has been a particularly significant factor in the wars of the last 200 years.

Arenas of Group Competition

The main things for which groups compete are the same things for which individuals compete: acquisition of goods, propagation of their ideas, and status. Consequently, our discussion will focus on economic competition between groups, ideological competition between groups, and the struggle for status between groups. At the same time we will need to consider the competition between groups for formalized political power since only such power provides a group's recognized authority to maintain control over goods and people. As we noted in the second chapter, wars are fought ultimately for political power.

Economic competition among groups is focused mainly on the goods provided by nature, including land, good soil and a favorable climate for growing food, access to water, and supplies of raw materials such as wood, metals, and petroleum. The wants of human beings seem virtually limitless, but the goods provided by nature are quite limited. Over thousands of years humans have learned how to get more of what they want from nature than nature would have provided without human management. The introduction of agriculture and the domestication of animals are two of the earlier developments in this process while the introduction of fertilizer for crops and the production of energy from uranium and plutonium are more recent developments. Regardless of the great progress that has been made, people continue to want more than they have.

After governments are established in human societies, the leaders of these governments are better able to pursue their aim of increasing the number and kind of goods available to themselves. Three approaches can be used by these leaders. One approach is to tax the people of their own society in order to get goods for themselves. Second, they can promote the development of technology within their society so that more goods are produced, either for their own use or for trading to other societies for other goods. Third, they can organize an army composed of members of their society in order to take goods from other societies by force. The first approach is limited by the fact that if the people are very poor the leaders will not get much by taxing them. There is also the danger of rebellion if the discrepancy between the goods available to the leaders and those available to others in the society is too great. The second approach of using technology is much more attractive today than when human knowedge and technology were more limited, but even today, especially in less developed countries, technology may not be able to produce what is needed more cheaply than it can be obtained by force. Thus the third approach, war, has been widely used as a way of getting more goods even though the cost is high when the other society fights to keep its goods for itself.

Originally the goods acquired by war belonged to the leaders and the soldiers who took part in the fighting, but with the development of more democratic societies the government was expected to look out for the welfare of the general citizenry. Competition between ruling groups in the different societies was transformed into competition between nation and nation with the government of each seeking to enhance the standard of living of its whole society. Even authoritarian governments now usually take as their goal getting more goods for everyone in the society, not just more for the leaders.

A great deal of ancient war seems to have been motivated by the desire for the goods of another society, but war for economic gain is by no means confined to the ancient world. From the sixteenth through the early part of the twentieth centuries there were continuing imperialistic wars in which the more technologically advanced European nations were able to gain control over the territory of less advanced peoples in the Americas, Africa, and Asia. These wars usually did not last very long because the military forces of the European nations were equipped with guns and other modern weapons unknown to the inhabitants of these less developed countries. Victory for the more advanced nations gave them access to goods of nature beyond those available in Europe. The advanced nations were also usually able to restrict the flow of technological know-how into the less developed countries, consequently preserving the arrangements by which natural resources continued to flow to Europe rather than being converted into manufactured goods within the less developed countries.

Since taking control of the natural resources of less developed countries was a very profitable operation, a new kind of economic competition developed among the imperialistic nations themselves. Each advanced nation wanted to control as much territory as possible in order to have access to the natural goods that might be found there. Sometimes nations made deals with each other, such as when Spain and Portugal agreed to divide Latin America between them, but at other times the competition led to war. Thus competition for the goods of the Earth led to wars not only between technologically advanced countries on the one hand and less advanced countries on the other but also among the advanced countries themselves as each tried to expand at the expense of the others.

As some of the people in the less advanced countries gradually acquired some of the weapons produced by the more advanced countries and as the advanced countries became embroiled in wars among themselves (especially the two World Wars), a third kind of war caused by economic competition became a reality. People in the less developed countries now engage in "wars of liberation" to gain control over their own natural resources. These wars usually start as guerrilla wars, and the liberation fighters who seek national economic and political independence are usually motivated by nationalistic loyalty.

At present economic competition continues among the nations of the world. Rich nations compete against other rich nations, but the rich nations as a group also compete against the poor nations as a group. And the poor nations compete among themselves. The more advanced nations for the most part no longer have political control over the less advanced nations, but they have the capital, the technological knowledge, and the equipment needed by the less developed countries and consequently usually are able to work out arrangements favorable to themselves. The outstanding exception to control by the advanced countries is OPEC, the Organization of Petroleum Exporting Countries. By forming a producers' cartel, these less developed nations were able to dramatically increase the price of crude oil, to the great disadvantage of the more advanced nations. Is it possible that one or more of the advanced countries might be led by economic considerations to use its superior military might to control once again the oil fields in these less developed countries? The existing state of conflict between the capitalist and Communist nations, the changed norms of international relations, and the possible cost politically as well as militarily of such a move together have thus far prevented such an attack, but it is not inconceivable that economic competition could eventually lead to war in this type of situation.

We also should not neglect economic competition as a contributing factor to war within nations. We earlier mentioned the possibility that a ruling elite which has a great deal more wealth than the rest of the people in the society needs to be concerned about rebellion. The ruling elite are usually able to hire a superior police force armed with superior weapons to maintain control over the rest of the society in much the same way that a technologically advanced nation is able to control its colonies. But a split may occur among the ruling elite which would present opportunities for others in the society to gain power by agreeing to support one or the other faction. Or some other nation may provide military assistance to the poorer people so they have a chance to rebel against the military and economic domination practiced by the elite in that society. In either case it is possible that a civil war will occur resulting at least in part from the economic competition between groups within that nation.

A second kind of competition that may lead to war is the effort by groups to spread their own ideology. A group may have a set of beliefs about the nature of the world, how individuals should behave, and what sort of institutions a society should have, and believe these ideas should also be adopted by other groups. This "truth" usually involves beliefs or views about how wealth and political power should be distributed in the society. The real issue in this type of conflict is control of information generally and control of the formal educational system in particular. People's beliefs and values depend on the information available to them. Children tend to believe whatever ideas they are taught first. Any conflicting ideas which they hear later will usually be viewed as false and wrong. For most adults, any ideas which conflict with what seems to be believed by the majority of people around them will be viewed as false and wrong. Thus control of information and education is crucial for promoting an ideology. Competition between groups for control of information and formal education may lead to war.

If the aim of the leaders of a society were simply that people should come to believe whatever is true and approve of whatever is objectively good, the appropriate means of accomplishing this aim would be the exposure of both children and adults to the whole range of views that might be held on any topic. There would be a constant effort to challenge prevailing beliefs and values so that mistaken views would be corrected through investigation and debate.[1] Unfortunately, most people, including the leaders of the society, do not want other people to explore ideas and reach their own conclusions. They want their children and other members of their society, and even members of other societies, to believe what they themselves believe and to value what they themselves value. Consequently in most societies there is an effort to control education and information so that people will come to the "right" conclusions about what is true and what is good. Those who question the accepted beliefs and practices are discouraged, ignored, silenced, or even actively persecuted.

The goal of promoting the views approved by the decision-makers in the society and discouraging those which they disapprove often is not limited to their own society. If two different nations have opposing ideologies, each will probably make efforts to promote its views within the other society. Each will also probably try to get its ideology accepted in other countries. Each may even try to make its ideology the prevailing ideology in the whole world. Such an ideological conflict may ultimately lead to war.

Intense ideological differences may also lead to war within a society. People of different religious persuasions may come to believe that they just cannot continue to live together in the same society. Sometimes a single issue such as the abolition of slavery may become a focal point for intense feelings that contribute to the outbreak of war. A group which advocates a sharing of political power or economic wealth may find itself persecuted by the leaders of the society who would be losers if those views were widely accepted. If this group uses force to defend itself, a civil war may develop. These instances show that war as the result of ideological conflict is not confined to the international arena.

It might be supposed that people would fight more vehemently for physical goods than for abstract doctrines and ideals, but in fact ideologically-motivated wars seem to be especially bloody and unrestrained. Each side tends to believe that it has a holy mission to bring the other side to the "Truth", no matter what the cost or sacrifice. It is firmly believed by people on both sides that it is better to die than to be forced to live in a society in which the ideology of the opposing side prevails. This viewpoint has been succinctly expressed in the U.S. by the slogan "Better dead than Red." Examples of wars motivated largely by ideological conflict are those which occurred between Christians and Muslims in the twelfth and thirteenth centuries and those between Protestants and Catholics in the sixteenth and seventeenth centuries. It has been argued that the destructiveness of modern war makes it likely that if there is a World War III the primary cause will be ideological conflict rather than hope of material gain.[2] It seems that many wars which take place within nations will also involve some kind of ideological conflict.

To anyone who thinks carefully and impartially about the matter, war to resolve ideological differences is ridiculous. Ideas which are true and values which are good will prevail if given a chance. The notion that the ideas of the winner of a war are closer to the truth and that their values are superior to those of the loser cannot be accepted by anyone who knows how often in human history the speakers of truth have been silenced and the toilers for good imprisoned or killed by those with greater physical force at their command. Violence may be a temporarily effective way of extending one's control over others, but it is not an appropriate method for advancing truth and goodness.[3] The search for truth and goodness requires open discussion of alternative views rather than coercion designed to promote the views of those who happen to be physically in charge at the moment.

A third arena of competition between groups is for status. Status is an abstract concept, but it is also a very real thing. It is the result of a combination of fear and admiration. It depends on things such as military power, economic power, and scientific or cultural achievements. As in the case of individuals, the group which has status will be deferred to and imitated. Having status means having power even though it may not be formally recognized or authorized in political institutions.

Let us consider an example of how status functions in international affairs. Suppose that two nations are negotiating a trade agreement. The richer nation intends to export manufactured goods to the poorer nation while the poorer nation intends to export raw material to the richer nation. As the negotiations proceed the richer nation makes the proposal that all goods going either direction would be transported in its vessels. The poorer nation does not want to accept such arrangements, but the rich nation takes the position that if the goods are not shipped in its vessels it will simply stop negotiating with this poor nation and work out something with another more cooperative nation. At this point the poorer nation is trapped because this rich nation is one of the few which can afford to buy large quantities of its raw materials and the only one which can supply some of the manufactured goods it needs. Thus the poorer nation is coerced into accepting a trade agreement where all the goods involved will be shipped in the vessels of the richer nation. There has been a struggle concerning which nation will get its way, and the rich nation has prevailed because the poorer nation needs what the rich nation has more than the rich nation needs what the poorer nation has. But this particular trade agreement also means that a situation of dominance has been established. Having yielded to the demands of the rich country on this occasion, the poorer country can expect to be coerced into accepting similar demands in the future.

The example just cited focuses on economic coercion in a struggle for dominance, but one nation might also establish its dominance over another on the basis of military superiority. A militarily weaker nation might be coerced into accepting trade agreements or other policies which it really does not want as a result of a threat of invasion if it does not go along with the demands of the militarily stronger country. Coercion on the basis of the military superiority is as common as economic coercion. Military superiority is also more curcial in a head-to-head confrontation. Since the ultimate test of a nation's strength lies in its capability of defending itself in a war, military superiority is the most crucial aspect of national status.

A good example of competition for status outside the economic and military spheres is the race between the U.S. and the Soviet Union with regard to accomplishments in space. Many aspects of the space race have military implications; for example, the size of satellites which can be kept in orbit and the length of time a person can stay in space before returning to earth. But one event of the space race had very little to do with military needs: the landing of men on the moon. The U.S. was able to do this after making an open challenge to the Soviets to enter the race. What was gained? Perhaps some discoveries useful to the military were made, but the main gain for the U.S. was status. United States scientists were able to do something which the Soviet scientists could not do, or were unwilling to attempt.

So far we have noted that economic or physical coercion may be used by one nation or group to establish dominance over another. But what happens if the state or group which has been submissive decides not to be submissive any longer? In that case the struggle for dominance may take the form of a violent physical confrontation. Such violent physical conflicts occur among animals to determine which one will be "top dog" of the pack. Similar violent conflicts for dominance may take place between nations or between groups within a nation. They are called wars.

Ultimately, however, the dominant nation or group within a nation wants not only status but also formal recognition of that status by means of a treaty or other formal political document. It also wants others to accept its right to determine what policies will be followed in a particular territory and over a particular population. It wants political power.

It should be noted that political power is essentially a means to some other end rather than an end in itself. A group which has power is able to accomplish whatever it is that it wants to accomplish, but having power still leaves open the question of what to do with it, of what ends will be sought. In this respect the quest for political power resembles the quest for money. If a person accumulates a great deal of money, he will be able to buy whatever he wants or give away as much as he wants to whomever he wishes, but having the money simply provides means to some ends. He still must decide how to use his money.

There is also another similarity between the quest for money and the quest for political power. A person whose aim is to acquire more and more money may at the beginning of his quest have some idea of what he wants to use the money for, but after a while the aim of acquiring more money may itself become a goal. While trying to acquire more and more money, the person may have no idea of what to do with it once it is in his hands. Similarly, the leaders of nations or of groups within nations aim to acquire more and more political power; at the beginning they usually have some idea of what they want the power for, but in time the aim of acquiring more power may itself become a goal. These leaders may want even more power but have no idea of what to do with it once they have it.

The fact that leaders may not know what to do with their political power once they have it does not stop them from trying to get more power and a position of recognized dominance relative to other countries or other groups. The desire for political power for its own sake may be a cause of war.[4] At the same time it should be remembered that power can be used to get other things. The struggle for power is usually associated with the other three types of competition previously discussed in this chapter. The nation or group which has political power will be able to use that power to get a larger share of the available goods for its own people, to promote the acceptance of its ideology, and to enhance its own status. Thus the struggle for political power among and within nations may be instrumental to these other ends or it may become an end in itself. In either case, the desire for political power may serve as a contributory factor to the outbreak of war.

Group Identification

Groups could not come into sustained conflict with each other if individuals did not think of themselves as members of these groups. It is also necessary that they identify with these groups. A person is said to identify with a group when he feels that whatever is good for the group is good for him, and that whatever harms the group harms him. To put it another way, if the group experiences some type of success it will make him feel better because the group's welfare is perceived as his own.

The phenomenon of identification is a common part of human life. For example, students tend to identify with their school and its athletic teams. If the team wins, they feel good. If the team loses, they feel bad. People identify with the religious or ideological group to which they belong, with the racial or ethnic group to which they belong, with their labor unions or professional organizations, with the company which employs them, with their age group, with the sex group to which they belong, with the local community where they live, with their state, with their nation, and so on. Whenever people think in terms of "we" (for example, "We won" or "We got recognized"), they are identifying with some group.

Group identification seems to be increased by competitive situations, especially when the group or its representatives are experiencing success or confronting a particularly crucial struggle. Winning athletic teams are thought to increase school loyalty. When a representative of a racial group wins a prize, other members of that group experience a greater pride in their racial identity. When a religious or ethnic group faces persecution, other members of that group feel a special awareness of being members of that group. Group identification usually continues, however, even in losing situations and noncritical confrontations.

Since members of a group identify with the success or failure of the group, leaders of the group are under a great deal of pressure to advance the interests of the group. They have a role to play: to do what is best for the group. If they do not succeed or if they seem not to be aggressive enough in pursuing the interests of the group, they are likely to be replaced by other leaders who promise to do better. All groups want to be gainers, winners, the best of their kind. Such a situation necessarily fosters group conflict.

One of the more obvious ways of lessening conflict between two groups is to persuade them both to see themselves as members of the same larger group which is united against some other group. Thus, Catholics and Protestants may experience less tension if they perceive themselves as Christians struggling against Muslims. In turn Christians and Muslims may have less conflict with each other if they view themselves as believers in God struggling against atheistic Communists. Perhaps believers and Communists could in turn see themselves as humans struggling together against the forces of nature, including the demonic forces within themselves which threaten their continued existence.

Nationalism as a Cause of War

Of all the various types of identification, the one most relevant to the war problem in recent times is nationalism. Nationalism is not a necessary condition of war since prior to the last quarter of the eighteenth century wars were fought to a great extent by mercenaries, that is, men who hired themselves out as soldiers. They fought for the king who paid them and felt no nationalistic sentiment. In many wars people were motivated by identification with a religious group rather than a nation. Neither is nationalism a sufficient condition of war since it is possible for people to have strong nationalistic feelings and yet not engage in warfare; the Swedes and Swiss are both good examples. Yet nationalism seems to be an important contributory factor to war, especially in the last 200 years.

To clarify the issue of nationalism as it relates to war, however, we must distinguish three different ways in which this term is used. The first two meanings both involve the psychological phenomenon of identification we have just discussed. The third meaning of nationalism refers to a doctrine about how the scope of governmental control should be determined.

In order to distinguish the first two types of nationalism we must note the difference between a *nation* and a *nation-state*, a difference which requires special attention because of a tendency of people to use the term "nation" when they in fact mean "nation-state."[5] A *nation* (or *people*) refers to a group of people who are of the same racial stock, use the same language, share the same religious beliefs and cultural traditions, and perceive themselves as a homogeneous group. In this racial-ethnic sense of nation there is no reference to any political unit or nation-state; some nations lack nation-states of their own. Thus we speak of American Indian groups such as the Mohawk nation or the Dakota nation. Another good example is the Jewish nation after the destruction of ancient Israel and before the creation of the modern state of Israel.

A *nation-state*, on the other hand, refers to a government which rules all the people living in a certain territory. This meaning of "nation" differs from the first meaning, for in some nation-states the people are not a homogeneous group. Switzerland is a particularly good example of a nation-state. It is a political unit, even though it is composed of several different cultural groups with different languages and traditions. The Soviet Union and the United States are also examples of nation-states whose populations are composed of several different cultural groups.

Nationalism in the first sense, *racial-ethnic nationalism*, refers to a person's identification with a homogeneous nation or people. This type of nationalism develops naturally when one is reared in a homogeneous group. We tend automatically to identify with other people who look like us, act like us, use the same language we do, and have the same religious and cultural heritage we have. Within a homogeneous ethnic group an intense feeling of group solidarity develops. There is a strong tendency to view people who look different, act differently, use a different language, or who have a different religious and cultural heritage as "strange," "odd," or maybe even "uncivilized."

Nationalism in the second sense, *loyalty to the nation-state*, refers to a person's identification with a nation-state and the people who live within it. This type of nationalism does not develop naturally but comes about as the result of a deliberate effort to inculcate loyalty to the nation-state and its institutions. Symbols such as a flag, a national anthem, and a pledge of allegiance are used as a focus of loyalty. Education of the children emphasizes the history of the nation-state and the value of sticking together against outsiders. National holidays are celebrated. A national military force maintains allegiance to the national government, and persons in this force as well as those who hold office in the national government are accorded honor. By such devices the "we" perspective of the people is extended beyond their own cultural group to the heterogeneous nation-state as a whole.

The third meaning of the term *nationalism* is quite different, but it depends on understanding the previously discussed difference between "nation" and "nation-state." In this third sense, *nationalism* refers to the doctrine that each racial-ethnic national group should have its own independent political nation-state and that all members of the same racial-ethnic national group should be in a single political nation-state. This situation does in fact exist in countries such as Norway, Sweden, Portugal, and Japan. *Doctrinal nationalism* is usually associated with nineteenth-century Italian political writer and activist Guiseppe Mazzini who used it in arguing for the desirability of unifying the various Italian city-states into a single political unit. It has also served as a theoretical support for separatist movements among minority racial-ethnic groups within nation-states and for independence movements in territories ruled by foreign colonialists.

This doctrinal nationalism has been behind various movements, especially in Europe, which have been intimately connected with war. In a general way, doctrinal nationalism will almost certainly produce dissatisfaction where there are various racial-ethnic groups intermingled in several geographical areas. Suppose that there are some Italians living within the boundaries of France and some Frenchmen living within the boundaries of Italy. How is this situation to be resolved according to doctrinal nationalism? Should there be a small area of land within France that becomes part of the political nation-state of Italy and a small area of land within Italy that becomes part of the political nation-state of France? What should happen to those areas that are about 50 percent French and 50 percent Italian? If these Italians surrounded by Frenchmen want to be under the political control of Italy, why shouldn't they move into territory that is already part of Italy? And a similar question could be addressed to the Frenchmen living in Italy.

Even more basically, we can ask why it is essential that all persons of the same racial-ethnic nation live in a single nation-state. Why is it unacceptable for them to live in three or four separate nation-states? The answer to this question must be that in unity there is strength against other racial-ethnic nations. But in that case perhaps a better approach would be to try to eliminate the struggle for power with the other nation-states in favor of some overall political structure that protects everyone's security.

This approach, however, runs afoul of another part of doctrinal nationalism: All political nation-states should be racially and ethnically "pure," that is, homogeneous rather than heterogeneous. Why is it undesirable to have heterogeneous nation-states? The answer seems to be that in a heterogeneous nation-state one racial-ethnic group will be in control and can be expected to use its political power to discriminate against other racial-ethnic groups which are less powerful. There is no doubt that such situations do occur, but perhaps other devices could be used to prevent this from happening. This is preferable to assuming that each racial-ethnic group must have political autonomy.

Nationalism is related to war in several ways. There are three different situations in which doctrinal nationalism, with its heavy emphasis on racial-ethnic nationalism as the proper basis for political structures, may produce tensions and eventually war. Nevertheless the aspect of nationalism that has probably been most significant in modern international war is loyalty to the nation-state. Let us consider the various ways in which nationalism may serve as a cause of war.

First, doctrinal nationalism may spawn *separatist movements* within a politically unified nation-state. One example of this possibility is the effort of some French-speaking Canadians to lead Quebec to secede from Canada and form a separate nation-state if the Quebec provincial government is not allowed greater autonomy. The French-speaking Canadians resent the pro-English bent of the national government and most business operations. They fear gradual elimination of French culture and language. The Canadian national government has responded with efforts to protect French culture and the use of the French language, but there is constant tension because it is very cumbersome to try to do everything in two languages. According to doctrinal nationalism, the French-Canadians should have their own nation-state.

Separatist movements have actually led to war in many situations. One example is the effort made by the Ibos in Nigeria to establish a separate nation-state of Biafra, an effort overcome by the Nigerian central government. Another example is the Bengalis of what was once East Pakistan but who now, as the result of a successful separatist war in which they received help from India, have their own independent nation of Bangladesh. Many other examples could be cited.[6]

The second kind of movement generated by doctrinal nationalism that might lead to war is *irredentism*. This term comes from the nineteenth century. After the nation of Italy was politically unified, the new Italian national government claimed that there were other areas containing cultural Italians which were *not yet redeemed* (irredenta), that is, which were not yet incorporated into the new Italian nation-state. These areas were within the boundaries of other nation-states. The Italian government did not invite the cultural Italians in these areas to come and live within the political boundaries of Italy but instead claimed that these areas should become part of Italy. The other political nation-states in which the cultural Italians lived did not look kindly on this effort to take some of their territory. It is easy to see how this kind of conflict can lead to a violent confrontation. Some examples of irredentism leading to war are the moves by Germany to control Austria and parts of Czechoslovakia and Poland, which led eventually to World War II, and the claim of Morocco to the Tindouf area of Algeria. In some cases one country claims that culturally and historically the whole of another country belongs to it. Examples are the claim of China to Tibet (which was taken by force by China in 1951 and put more directly under its control in 1959), of Ghana to all of Togo, and of Morocco to Mauritania.

An interesting case of how doctrinal nationalism can lead to separatist and irredentist movements at the same time involves the Somalis of East Africa. The Somalis share a common language and culture, but when the European conquerors drew national boundaries the Somalis were placed in five different political jurisdictions: Italian Somaliland, British Somaliland, Djibouti (under French control), the northeast part of Kenya, and the southeast part of Ethiopia. After gaining their independence, the first two nations united to form Somalia. Uniting the rest of the Somalis has proven more difficult. The Somalis constitute only a small proportion of the population of Ethiopia and Kenya and just over half of the population of Djibouti. The Somalis in Ethiopia are engaged in a separatist effort while Somalia is engaged in an irredentist effort to expand its boundaries to include all Somalis. The other countries claim that Somalia is merely trying to take from them land which has valuable resources. Furthermore, these other countries resisting the Somali effort have the support of the Organization of African Unity, an organization composed of the present ruling governments in Africa who have decided that all national boundaries should remain as drawn by Europeans because any effort to redraw them could only lead to chaos. This situation apparently leaves the Somali nationalists with a single option for fulfilling their dreams: war.[7] On the other hand, the governments of the newly independent nations of Africa seek to promote nationalism in the sense of loyalty to the political nation-state in order to try to overcome the racial-ethnic nationalism that threatens to tear their nations apart.

The third kind of movement generated by doctrinal nationalism that might also lead to war is that in which an ethnic group within an independent nation-state seeks to have that whole nation absorbed into another nation-state which it culturally resembles. This type of effort is a *reintegrationist* movement. It is similar in a way to irredentism, but here it is the people in the "unredeemed" territory who are actively seeking to be reattached to what they regard as their homeland, rather than the homeland actively seeking to annex the area in which they live. The resistance in this case comes from other ethnic groups in the independent nation-state who do not want to be absorbed into the larger political unit. Cyprus is a good example of this type of situation. Cyprus is presently an independent nation-state, having won its independence from Britain in 1960. Many of its 80 percent ethnically Greek population would like to see it become part of the nation-state of Greece. On the other hand, the 20 percent of the population which is ethnically Turkish is adamantly opposed to such a move. With the nation of Greece ready to defend the interests of the Greek Cypriots and the nation of Turkey ready to defend the interests of the Turkish Cypriots, the potential for violent conflict is obvious. The United Nations peacekeeping force on Cyprus has been able to keep the situation under control most of the time, but there have been many violent outbreaks including an invasion by Turkish troops in 1974 which resulted from Turkish fears that the island was about to be annexed by Greece. The desire of Catholics in Northern Ireland to reunite that state with Ireland may be viewed as another example of a reintegrationist movement which has led to violence.

We can now turn our attention to the way in which nationalism as loyalty to the nation-state is related to war. It is this kind of nationalism that comes into play in most international conflicts.[8] During conflict situations the people of the countries involved are urged not only to love their own country but to hate some actual or potential enemy. During World War II, for example, propaganda in the U.S. urged Americans not only to love their own country but also to hate the Germans and Japanese. After that war was over and the cold war had begun, Americans were told that the Germans and Japanese are not really such bad people after all but that the Russians and Chinese, our allies in World War II, are the people we should hate. Recently the Chinese have become "good guys" again.

This nationalistic group hatred gets people ready to kill if there is a war. It also distorts people's perceptions of events so that war becomes more likely. Nationalism is nourished by focusing on the good things done by one's own nation and the bad things done by "the enemy," simultaneously ignoring the bad things done by one's own nation and the good things done by "the enemy." It tends to accentuate the differences between "us" and "them" and to dismiss the similarities. In this way the members of the opposing nations are led to be proud of their own nation and to be indignant about all of the horrible things done by "the wicked enemy."

A particularly good example of nationalistic hatred is the antagonism that developed between the French and the Germans as the result of being opponents in one war after another from the time of Napoleon through World War II. It became difficult for either group to see any virtue in the other. They accentuated their differences in food, drink, language, and so on. Under such circumstances it was relatively easy for the German and French governments to mobilize their people for war against each other.

But in this relationship between Germany and France there may be a lesson concerning the connection between nationalism and war. It may be that nationalism in the sense of hatred of another group is more an effect of war and preparation for war than a cause of it, though it may certainly be both. Because the cold war has created a political situation requiring the Germans and French to cooperate against a possible invasion from the Russians, the nationalistic hatred between these two nations has diminished considerably. The shift in American attitudes since World War II toward Germans and Japanese also supports the notion that nationalistic hatred is more the result of wars and indoctrination dictated by political interests than it is a cause of wars. It appears that nationalistic hatred is produced deliberately by leaders and propagandists as the result of opposition to another nation's political policies, and is not the result of some inherent hatred of the people of one nation for the people of another.

Still, we should not overlook the way in which nationalism provides the basis for support of national policies which lead to war. People want their own nation-state to have a high status; they feel good when their nation has the highest gross national product or the highest per capita gross national product or the largest number of nuclear warheads. People feel bad when their nation falls behind others in these and other categories. They feel good when their nation expands its territorial holdings and bad when the extent of territory controlled by their nation is reduced. Especially people feel good when their nation wins military battles or is successful in getting another nation to back down in a head-to-head confrontation, and they feel bad when their nation loses a military battle or retreats in a head-to-head confrontation.

These nationalistic feelings support national leaders who aggressively defend the nation-state's economic interests and lead the nation to military strength and dominance over other nations. The difficulty is that status is a relative thing. It is impossible for all nation-states to be first, or even near the top, with regard to wealth or military power. Struggles for superiority and "honor" (not backing down) thus take place between nation and nation. It is nationalism which generates public support for those national leaders who behave aggressively in these struggles. This support for aggressiveness certainly does not decrease the likelihood of international war.

Nationalism in the sense of loyalty to the nation-state may also be an important factor contributing to war in a situation where the people of one nation have been subjugated or controlled by those of another. The conquered people develop an intense hatred for the people who have kept them in subjection. They also will tend to regard members of their own nation who cooperate with the conquerors as traitors. When the time is right, the nationalistic feeling of the oppressed people will support a *war of liberation* to throw off the control of the other nation. This set of events has occurred time after time in nations which were once colonies, such as India, Algeria, Vietnam, Angola, and Mozambique. The same type of resentful nationalism may also be manifested in situations where foreign political control is subtle (as in Eastern Europe) or where the foreign domination is more economic than political (as in Central America). In these cases nationalistic feeling may support a revolutionary movement directed against those native leaders who are viewed as being too cooperative with the foreign oppressors. In Cuba and Nicaragua such wars of liberation have succeeded while both the 1965 uprising in the Dominican Republic and the 1968 uprising in Czechoslovakia failed.

Thus we see that nationalism contributes to war in several ways. Doctrinal nationalism supports separatist movements, irredentist movements, and reintegrationist movements, all of which may lead to war. Loyalty to the nation-state supports aggressive leaders in their struggles for power and their efforts to liberate nation-states from subjection to other nation-states. It would be difficult to point to any war in the nineteenth and twentieth centuries in which nationalism in one or another sense has not been a significant factor.

VI. Other Views About Causes of War

We have discussed the hypotheses that war is the result of individual human aggression; that it is caused by groups competing for goods, for control of information, for status, and for political power; and that it is due to group identification, especially identification with the nation. Now we will consider some other views.

Arms Races as a Cause of War

If the ultimate test of a nation's strength is its capacity to defend itself in a war, then any nation which anticipates war seems to have little choice but to build up its military forces to be superior to those of the anticipated enemy. It could even be argued that, in the face of a possible attack from another nation, failure of a nation to increase its military forces might in fact encourage attack because the other nation could be confident of a quick and easy victory. On the other hand, if two nations confront each other and each aims to make its military forces superior, a steady increase of arms on both sides will result. This escalation of arms construction and deployment will be further intensified if military planning on each side includes a little extra build-up just in case the potential enemy's forces are stronger than estimated.

This situation in which two potential enemy nations (or groups of nations) each try over a period of time to gain armed superiority over the other is called an arms race. Such a race seems to contribute to the likelihood of war between the nations involved. The temptation to start a war seems to be especially great when one nation possesses a newly developed, significant weapon which its potential opponent does not yet have but will probably acquire in the near future. Why not start a war when the prospect of victory is greatest? Why wait, when waiting might eventually result in the enemy gaining military superiority?

To get a better understanding of what it is like to be a leader of a nation involved in an arms race, the reader is invited to play a simple game.[1] Ideally there should be three participants, but with the proper arrangements and understandings, two can play. When there are three persons, one acts as supervisor, referee, timekeeper, and scorekeeper while the other two represent the heads of nations involved in an arms race. Each player needs a small piece of paper or cardboard which can be concealed under his hand on a flat surface. This piece of paper should have a plus-sign on one side and a minus-sign on the other, so the player can indicate whether he has chosen to increase or decrease the military spending of his nation.

To begin the game, the timekeeper tells the players that they have 30 seconds before they will be required to render their first arms decisions (which can be considered the first annual budget). The players are permitted to communicate with each other and to make "treaties," but as in actual international situations no one enforces any agreements that might be made. As the 30-second deadline approaches, each player places his piece of paper on the table with either the plus-sign or the minus-sign face up, but conceals it until the timekeeper says, "Now." Players then uncover the papers allowing the others to see the decisions. The timekeeper calculates, records, and announces the score and then informs the players that the next decision is due in 30 seconds. The entire sequence is then repeated. The game can be as long or short as players desire, but 20 decisions is about the proper duration of one's first game.

The scoring of the game is crucial, and the players must understand it before beginning play. Each player receives 10,000 points at the start of the game. This figure represents the average standard of living, or per capita gross national product, of the people in each player's country. The object of the game is to score as high as possible, that is, to improve the average standard of living of one's nation as much as possible. Each time a decision is made, scoring depends on the combination of the decisions of the two players. If both players put the minus-sign up, indicating a cut-back in military spending, each is awarded 100 points. If both put the plus-sign up, indicating an increase in spending, each loses 100 points. If one puts the plus-sign up and the other the minus, they receive different scores: the player with the plus-sign gains 500 while the one with the minus-sign loses 500. This scoring represents a situation in which the military superiority of one nation allows it to make coercive arrangements with other nations to the disadvantage of its opponent.

This game illustrates the logic of arms races and the difficulty of controlling them even when both parties realize objectively that it would be best for both to disarm. The rules can be varied to make the game more sophisticated. For example, one might allow the players to choose a third option of keeping military spending at the present level. The scoring might be changed so that disarming while one's opponent arms is even more costly, perhaps involving a loss of 1,000 points rather than 500. Perhaps the scoring could be revised so that the loss to both sides of continuing to increase arms expenditures would be greater. Other modifications might also be made.

What strategy should a player use in this game? One might adopt a tit-for-tat strategy, opting each time to do what the opposing player had done on the previous turn. One could adopt a hawkish strategy and increase arms spending every turn, regardless of what the opponent does, on grounds that this would maximize gains and minimize losses whatever decision the opponent made. A player might adopt a dove-like strategy and consistently decrease arms expenditures regardless of what the opponent does on grounds that this seems to be the only way of ending the arms race. (Empirical evidence suggests that this strategy does not work in many situations and in fact often encourages the opponent to be aggressive.[2])

One could also adopt different strategies with regard to communication with the opponent. For example, a player might decide to announce what strategy he intends to use and then use it, or he might decide to *say* that he will use one strategy and then actually use another. One must decide whether or not to abide by agreements entered into with the other player. Games like this one have been played and observed with a view to determining which strategies different kinds of people do actually use and which strategies are most likely to succeed in bringing an arms race under control.[3]

In what sense, if any, are arms races a cause of war? It seems that arms races themselves are always an *effect* of some other "cause of war" such as a struggle for power. Nations do not simply fall into arms races against some nations and not against others; there is always some other cause such as economic or ideological conflict which leads to the arms race. For example, before World War I there was an arms race between Britain and Germany but not between Britain and the United States. Why? The difference can be explained at least in part by the conflict of ideology between Britain and Germany while Britain and the U.S. were ideological allies.

Nevertheless, once an arms race begins it may serve as an additional contributory factor to the outbreak of war. It has been argued by Lewis Richardson that the behavior of nations involved in an arms race can be described by a mathematical model.[4] This model indicates that under certain circumstances arms races could conceivably tend toward a stable situation rather than growing out of control and resulting in war, but these circumstances are unlikely to exist in the twentieth century.[5] Of the wars that occurred between 1820 and 1929, arms races were considered a significant factor in the outbreak of war in about one-ninth of the cases.[6] Still that means that arms races are sometimes considered to be a contributory factor to the beginning of war even though they are also the effect of other causes.

Particular Villains as a Cause of War

If we look at the problem of crime within a society, it seems reasonable to believe that a good portion of it is caused by a few antisocial people. It seems that the best way to eliminate, or at least greatly reduce, crime is to lock these criminals away so they can no longer harass the rest of society. Some see an analogy between crime and war and believe that the basic cause of war is the existence of a few villains who are ready to use force and violence to exploit the rest of society in order to get wealth and power for themselves. Wars are caused by these war-mongers, it is claimed, and the way to reduce the likelihood of war is to get rid of these troublemakers.

Different versions of this approach point to different types of villains. One view focuses on power-hungry individuals who work their way into leadership positions in nations or other groups which are ready to use violence. A second view sees the troublemakers as groups such as military leaders and weapons manufacturers who stand to realize substantial personal gains as the result of violent conflict. A third view sees the culprits as the elite of a society who are ready and willing to use violence to try to stop inevitable social changes which will eventually eliminate their positions of privilege.

The importance of the aggressiveness of the group leader was discussed earlier in connection with the relation of individual aggressiveness to the outbreak of war. As was noted then, it would be difficult in the human context to defend the view that these aggressive leaders are a necessary or a sufficient condition for war, but the more limited contention that power-hungry leaders are a contributory factor is plausible.[7]

A related thesis claims that particularly aggressive individuals are more likely to gain leadership positions in an authoritarian political system while democratic political systems are less likely to allow such individuals to get to the top.[8] This implies that if all governments were democratic rather than autocratic the danger of war would be considerably reduced. Woodrow Wilson's slogans during the first world war, that it was "the war to end all wars" and "the war to make the world safe for democracy," seem to be based on the acceptance of this thesis. The difficulty for this view is that democratic nations have had their share of aggressive leaders and oppressive foreign policies. The British and Americans have been just as imperialistic as the Spanish and Russians. One can hardly review the policies and practices of the U.S. government toward American Indians, Filipinos during the Spanish-American War, and Latin Americans since that war and conclude that democratic governments are not aggressive toward other societies. Also it should not be forgotten that Hitler came to power in Germany in accord with democratic procedures. It is doubtful that democracies have any special advantages in keeping aggressive individuals from gaining positions of leadership.

A second view about particular villains is that war is caused by munitions makers, high-ranking military officers, and others who profit from war. The expression *military-industrial complex*[9] has been used to refer to a relatively small group of people who benefit from war and preparation for war, a group that includes not only the professional military and the arms manufacturers but also others such as bankers who finance the arms industry, leaders of labor unions engaged in arms production, scientists and engineers engaged in weapons research, politicians eager to promote federal spending in their political districts, and veterans' organizations.

The thesis that arms manufacturers and their allies in the military, the government, and the newspaper-publishing business might deliberately promote war scares to stimulate military spending seems to have been first seriously argued by Richard Cobden in Britain in 1861.[10] He noted the repeated occurrence of a series of events beginning with expressions of concern by high-ranking naval officers (widely publicized by the newspapers) that France was preparing to invade Britain. An increase in appropriations to the navy soon followed, and then the threat disappeared. One event which provides a particularly good piece of evidence to support the view that arms manufacturers have deliberately stimulated arms races occurred a few years before World War I. H.H. Mulliner, the managing director of a British shipbuilding firm, told his friends in the military that he had secret information that the Germans had suddenly speeded up their building of battleships.[11] The story was leaked to the press who cooperatively published it. The British public demanded that more battleships be built to meet the German challenge. The Germans denied having increased their efforts, but once the British speeded up theirs the Germans felt they had to do the same. After this naval arms race was in motion, Mulliner wrote a series of letters which were published in the London *Times* indicating how he had started the whole thing, but the arms race did not stop and Mulliner himself was fired. Another incident worthy of mention occurred in 1927 when American steel companies sent William Shearer to the Geneva Disarmament Conference for the express purpose of disrupting it.[12]

In the United States the notion that the U.S. munitions manufacturers had been responsible for involving the U.S. in World War I became popular in the 1930's as a result of public investigations by a Senate committee chaired by Senator Gerald Nye, although the committee failed to prove the allegations.[13] The idea that the military-industrial complex is a possible source of danger to U.S. policy-making was brought to public attention again by President Eisenhower in his 1961 farewell address.[14] During the Vietnamese War some opponents of the war claimed that the military-industrial complex was responsible for U.S. involvement. The notion that the present arms race between the U.S. and U.S.S.R. is largely due to the activities of the American military-industrial complex is widespread.[15]

Some observers claim that there is also a military-industrial complex which promotes war and preparation for war in the Soviet Union.[16] Even though there are no owners of arms industries in the U.S.S.R., there are managers of such industries whose influence is greatly affected by the importance ascribed to their work. The military and the hawkish members of the political leadership have the same interests as their counterparts in the U.S. It has even been suggested that the military-industrial complexes of the Soviet Union and the U.S. keep the arms race going as an informal cooperative enterprise which is very profitable to both of them.[17]

What about these claims? Do certain people who profit from war actually cause wars to occur? Even Senator Nye claimed only that American munitions makers had caused the U.S. to be dragged into World War I, not that they had caused the war in the first place. And even if one took seriously the idea that there is an informal cooperative effort between the American and Soviet military-industrial complexes in support of a gigantic arms race, it does not follow that these groups actually want to cause a war or that they could do so if they wanted.

We need to use the distinctions about the various senses of "cause" we have previously discussed. Are the advocates of the military-industrial complex theory claiming that these conspirators are a sufficient condition for war or merely a contributory factor? The former claim would suggest that this complex of individuals has so much influence that it can force political leaders to go to war. But even though the military-industrial complex in many countries is now more influential than before World War II, it seems far-fetched to believe that this group has greater influence on government policies than the huge nonmilitary sector of the economy and the nonmilitary population.

The claim that the military complex is a contributory factor to war is much more credible. Before the age of the long-range bomber and the intercontinental ballistic missile, high-ranking military officers and owners of arms-producing facilities could be relatively sure that they would not personally be hurt by war and that they stood to gain a great deal by it. In the current military situation, one can readily see that even in an age of intercontinental missiles certain kinds of war can be very profitable for military-industrial complexes in the richer countries. Furthermore, these are just the kinds of wars that have been occurring. The fact that these situations are profitable for the military-industrial complex does not prove that they bring them about, but it does raise suspicions. One such profitable situation is for the country in which a military-industrial complex operates to engage in a limited war with an enemy which has no chance of hurting the wealthier country. This is exemplified by U.S. engagements in Korea and Vietnam and Soviet involvements in Hungary, Czechoslovakia, and Afghanistan. A second type of profitable situation for the military and arms producers is a war involving smaller allies of their own country in which the wealthier country supplies military know-how and weapons which need to be replaced again and again as they are destroyed in the fighting. Wars such as those in the Middle East have provided an excellent opportunity for the U.S. and U.S.S.R. to test some of their military equipment under actual battlefield conditions. Add to these wars the arms races occurring in various parts of the world and it is evident that the post-World War II era has been a very profitable one for the military-industrial complexes in the U.S., Britain, France, and the Soviet Union.

Nevertheless, it is more plausible to suppose that national governments struggling for power with each other create the military-industrial complexes than to believe that the military-industrial complexes control the governments. The decision to spend large amounts of government money for military purposes so that arms-making is profitable is a political decision. Governments could make it equally profitable for industry to make typewriters and tractors to donate to less developed countries. Then a products-for-development complex would come into being which would be as self-perpetuating as the military-industrial complex. Why isn't there an influential products-for-development complex? It is because governments are willing to spend large amounts for weapons to use in the struggle for power against other national governments while they are unwilling to spend large amounts to assist less developed countries.

As long as crucial international conflicts are to be resolved by force and threats of force, governments of nations likely to be challenged by others seem to have little choice but to try to make their military forces "second to none." Once a military-industrial complex is created to produce this military superiority, it tends to be self-sustaining and to encourage attitudes and policies which will work to its own advantage. This probably contributes to the existence of arms races and to the outbreak of limited wars, but like the arms race it seems to be an effect of other, more fundamental causes rather than an ultimate cause of war.[18]

A third view about villains who are responsible for war is asociated with the names Karl Marx, Frederick Engels, and V.I. Lenin. According to this view the villains are the elite of a society who try by force to maintain their positions of privilege in the face of economic and social changes which eliminate the underpinning which gave rise to their status.

Understanding this view will require a brief discussion of some of the basic ideas of Marx, Engels, and Lenin.[19] According to them the most important thing about a society is how its goods and services are provided. A society in which people hunt, fish, and forage for food will be much different from a society in which agriculture and domesticated animals provide the food supply. In fact, they believe that the whole social structure and cultural outlook will depend on the mode of production. In a feudal society where agriculture and domesticated animals are the basic sources of goods, those who own land will be the elite and the culture will develop around their outlook and interests. On the other hand, in a bourgeois society where small-scale manufacturing is the basic means of producing goods, those who own the shops will be the elite and the culture will reflect their concerns.

According to this theory, if the mode of production continues to be the same, the society will be stable and violent conflict at a minimum. But if the basic mode of production changes, then the situation is different. Consider, for example, what happened at the beginning of the industrial revolution when simple machines were introduced which enabled one person to produce a great deal more than previously could be produced by several persons in the same period of time. The introduction of these machines changed the mode of production from one in which each family milled its own grain and wove its own cloth by hand to one in which machines did this work. Before the introduction of these machines wealth would depend basically on how much land you owned; afterward it would depend basically on how many of these machines you owned. In the old feudal society the big landowners, the nobility, were the elite. A whole social structure and cultural outlook had been built around their interests. The newly-rich bourgeoisie did not fit into this structure and outlook. Consequently, a struggle for power resulted. The old landed aristocracy tried to preserve the social structure which supported their positions of privilege while the owners of machinery strove for recognition in accord with their new wealth and power in the society.

If the old elite would have modified their social structure to make room for the owners of machinery, a peaceful transition could have taken place, but the old elite didn't make such a move. Why not? First, they did not intend to surrender their positions of privilege simply because some other people wanted them. Second, the old social structure with which they were familiar was "natural," the only social structure they could imagine. On the other hand, the bourgeoisie had power represented by the productive capacity of their machines. If the old nobility wouldn't step aside peacefully, there was no choice but to throw them out of power violently. The French Revolution in 1789 is a good example of the violent overthrow of the old aristocracy by the new middle class.

One might be inclined to say that it was the new middle class rather than the old nobility who caused this violent upheaval. It was, after all, the bourgeoisie and their followers who were the active agents of the revolution. But according to Marx and Engels such a view of the situation overlooks the force used by the old order to try to prevent change. It is true that the repressive violence used by the police was authorized by the laws of the existing government, but that fact merely shows that the government was just one more part of the social structure controlled by the old nobility. The blame for the violence, according to the Marxists, should be placed not on the revolutionaries seeking to establish a social order based on the objective reality of the new dominant mode of production, but rather on the old elite who use force to preserve a social order which is no longer in tune with the objective situation.

What has been said so far may lead the reader to believe that Marx and Engels were supporters of bourgeois capitalism. In one sense they were. They thought capitalism was a great advance over feudalism and that it was desirable for the bourgeoisie to use force to overthrow the social structures of the landed aristocracy. But in another sense Marx and Engels were opponents of bourgeois capitalism. They opposed the capitalist society in which they lived because they believed that still another qualitative shift had taken place in the mode of production, a shift from small-scale individualistic manufacturing to the social production of goods by cooperative effort in huge factories. The social structures (such as private ownership of factories) and cultural outlook (such as rugged individualism) of the capitalists were built on the foundations of small-scale manufacturing, but Marx and Engels felt that the shift to mass production made these social structures and this cultural outlook obsolete. Thus the capitalists were now to be opposed by the new revolutionary socialists, just as the landed aristocracy had previously been opposed by the revolutionary capitalists. Now it was the capitalists who were using government-sanctioned force to obstruct needed social change. It may seem that the socialist revolutionaries are the instigators of war, but according to Marx and Engels the blame belongs to the capitalists who refuse to permit the social changes required by the shift to the collective production of goods. In the nineteenth and twentieth centuries, according to the Marxists, the capitalists who resist the needed change to socialism are the villains responsible for war.

In order to evaluate this view, let us return to our distinctions about the various senses of the word *cause*. Are the present capitalist leaders supposed to be a sufficient cause of war? That is, do they by themselves bring about war? The answer seems to be "No." They might, according to Marxists, bring about oppression, but war occurs only when there is also violent resistance to this oppression. Consequently, it does not seem that Marxists maintain that the capitalists are a sufficient condition for war.

Are the capitalist leaders a necessary condition for war at the present time? (Obviously at an earlier time the question would need to be raised concerning the landed aristocracy rather than the capitalists.) It would seem that Marxists answer this question in the affirmative, believing that if all capitalists were out of the way then war would be eliminated. At any stage in history, the Marxists seem to be saying, if the old elite would just step aside when their privileged positions are no longer objectively supported by the mode of production, then there would be no wars.

Such an extreme claim seems difficult to defend. A survey of history reveals many wars in which one feudal society fought against another feudal society and one capitalist society against another. We can even find instances in recent history of one socialist society fighting against another socialist society. If the only basis for war is the unwillingness of the old elite to give way to the new order, why do these nonrevolutionary wars occur? It seems that Marxist thought focuses for the most part on wars *within* societies rather than wars *between* societies, and even *within* societies it is questionable whether the Marxist view adequately accounts for wars such as those resulting from nationalistically-motivated separatist movements.

Recognizing that Marxist theory did not seem particularly relevant to the wars taking place between countries in the late nineteenth and early twentieth centuries, Lenin extended Marx's analysis of social conflict to the international sphere.[20] The capitalist countries were engaged in two kinds of wars, he said: colonial wars against less developed countries and wars between themselves. The first type of war could readily be explained by an extension of Marxist principles. The capitalists were countering a possible revolution in their own societies by subjugating distant peoples, exploiting them, and giving some of the benefits to the workers in the home country. This arrangement allowed large profits to continue to flow into the pockets of the capitalists without objection from the working classes at home.

The second type of war, that due to economic competition between capitalist nations for control in colonial regions, introduces a cause for war not present in the original Marxist position. This position still ascribes blame to the capitalists for all wars but no longer defines all wars as conflicts between an old elite class and a new revolutionary class. And once Marxist-Leninists allow that economic competition between one capitalist nation and another may be a cause of war, then it would seem that they must also allow that wars may be the result of economic competition between one *noncapitalist* nation and another. Then they must also allow that wars within countries can be caused by economic competition between groups which represent the same economic class.

Furthermore, Lenin's revision seems unable to account for recent wars between one socialist country and another. Were any capitalists involved in the border dispute which developed between China and the Soviet Union? Were any capitalists involved in the Communist Vietnamese invasion of Communist Kampuchea? Once it is admitted that other factors such as nationalism may be involved in these disputes, the question is raised whether nationalism might not be the crucial factor in other wars.

The Marxist-Leninist thesis that the capitalist class is the cause of all war depends on accepting a debatable theory of history which views the ruling class as the cause of all violence. Recent history seems to refute the notion that the capitalists are a necessary condition of war. The most that can plausibly be claimed is that capitalists are a contributory cause of war, a claim that seems to be strongest in the case of colonial wars and efforts to squash liberation movements in less developed countries.

War as an Effort to Suppress Internal Dissension

The famous German philosopher Hegel observed that "peoples involved in civil strife also acquire peace at home through making wars abroad."[21] There seems to be little doubt that when a group or society is engaged in a violent conflict with a common enemy, differences of interest within that group or society are temporarily ignored. For example, in revolutions to overthrow a government such as have recently occurred in Iran and Nicaragua, the revolutionary forces are able to unite in the fight to overthrow the old regime even though they may have very different views about what sort of new government is to be established. In the same way quarreling groups within a nation tend to forget their grievances against each other when that nation is engaged in a war against another nation. Labor and management perceive that they must work together. Rich and poor see that they must join together in defense or go down to defeat together. Different racial or cultural groups will unite in the common effort even though they might be quite antagonistic toward each other in peacetime.

Under these circumstances it is easy to see that a leader who is being criticized by various factions within a movement or by various groups within a society might be tempted to begin using violence against a common enemy in order to quell the dissent. If internal strife is threatening, a war could be started to keep the internal disturbances under control. The leader must be subtle about accomplishing this outbreak of warfare, however, so that the other side can be blamed for it.

Has this sort of thing ever really happened? Has there ever been a war which was begun with the motive of overcoming internal dissension? One example frequently cited is that of Otto von Bismarck, President of Prussia and then Chancellor of the German Empire during much of the last half of the nineteenth century. At one time he observed that his various wars had undercut the influence of the left-wing revolutionaries in Prussia, but he never said that he started the wars to accomplish this aim. The wars he started in the middle and late 1860's aimed to bring the previously separate German states under Prussian control. One might be tempted to say that he started wars with external enemies to unify the German nation and that he succeeded in accomplishing this goal after peaceful efforts to unite the German states had failed.[22] But it can be asked whether this case is truly an example of wars begun to alleviate internal dissension. It seems rather to be a case of a leader being particularly clever at gaining new territory without arousing any resentment among the people who have been conquered.

The recent effort by the government of Argentina to take over the Falkland Islands–Malvinas from Britain is viewed by many as an example of a government starting an external skirmish in order to counteract domestic unrest. If that was the aim, the project proved to be a gigantic failure. On the other hand, it may have been triggered primarily by the desire of the Argentine government to have control over those islands when a treaty about ownership of ocean resources comes into effect. Regardless of the motives in this particular case, efforts to discover any general correlation between internal discord and the fighting of external wars have been inconclusive.[23]

War as an Effort to Eliminate Injustice

We have previously discussed the issue of the relation between peace and justice. It was noted that peace may refer to the persistence of a situation in which some group or some nation is being treated unjustly. If this injustice is flagrant, the resentment may become so intense that people are ready to use violence to change the situation, especially if nonviolent efforts have proved to be unsuccessful.

It is interesting that both Thomas Jefferson and Karl Marx argued that violence is justified in such situations and that both the American and Russian revolutions are examples of wars fought to remove what were perceived to be injustices not removable in any other way. Jefferson even suggested that the use of violence to protect liberty would need to be repeated with some regularity. He wrote in a letter to Colonel Smith in 1787:

> What country can preserve its liberties, if its rulers are not warned from time to time, that this people preserve the spirit of resistance? Let them take arms.... What signify a few lives lost in a century or two? The tree of liberty must be refreshed from time to time with the blood of patriots and tyrants. It is its natural manure....[24]

Of course, the notion that violence should be used if necessary to combat injustice is not confined to Americans and Russians. In fact, almost all efforts to justify the use of violence, other than the rationale of self-defense, point to the need to remove some perceived injustice. For example, much civil strife has resulted from issues such as opposing claims concerning which person is the rightful ruler of a nation, and even Hitler's earliest aggressive actions were "justified" on grounds that the Treaty of Versailles ending World War I had been unfair to Germany.

A good contemporary example of war being waged in order to remove a perceived injustice is the battle of the Palestinian Arabs against the new nation of Israel. This nation was established by Jews with the aid of Britain and the United States on land inhabited largely by the Palestinian Arabs. When the British relinquished their control of the Middle East after World War II, these Palestinians wanted to establish a new independent nation. They had no objections to Jews already living there joining with them in a secular state, but did object to the creation of a Jewish state which would be administered in accord with Jewish religious views and which would as a matter of policy try to attract more Jewish people to the area. Why, they asked, should Palestinians be required either to accept second-class citizenship in such a state or to move out of homes their families had occupied for generations? They used violence to try to prevent the establishment of a Jewish state, and continue to use violence to try to bring an end to it. The Palestinians feel that it was very unjust for such a state to be created, without their consent, on territory which they regard as their own. A comparable situation for Americans would be to have American Indians reestablish their "nation" where we now live, with the requirement that we abide by the Indian laws or get out. Of course, the Jews and the Indians might feel that they were finally getting back what had unjustly been taken from them at an earlier time. Such are the intricacies of questions of justice. One great problem related to using violence to remove perceived injustices is that different parties have different perceptions of what is just.

Questions of justice are even more likely to be the cause of war within nations. We have previously discussed the Marxist view that one cause of war is the unwillingness of the elite to give up positions of privilege when changed conditions indicate they should. We also noted earlier that governments tend to be more sensitive to the problems of people with wealth and power than to the poor and powerless. It is not surprising that sometimes people feel so oppressed that they believe the only viable action is to resort to violence. The 1979 revolution in Nicaragua is an example.

Using violence to fight injustice constitutes a problematic situation: The use of violence will probably result in much injustice itself. There is usually a question of whether some nonviolent approach might be effective in alleviating the injustice. There is also a danger that the use of force will fail and make the oppressors even more oppressive. Finally, there is the problem of whether or not one's own perceptions of what is just or unjust are merely biased views reflecting self-interest. Regardless of these considerations, the desire to remove some perceived injustice has been a contributory factor in many wars, especially those taking place within countries.

The Absence of Peaceful Alternatives as a Cause of War

War comes about as a result of conflicts between groups, but such conflict situations need not be resolved by resort to violence. Bargaining, arbitration, and the institutions of government represent some other avenues for resolving conflict. There are some conflict situations, however, where none of these alternatives seems to be a viable option. Bargaining depends ultimately on threats of force and stubbornness. Arbitration depends on the availability of an arbitrator perceived as fair by both parties and also as so strong and independent that he will not be intimidated by either. The institutions of government exist only in the most rudimentary forms with regard to handling conflicts between nations. Even within a nation a fair resolution depends on the government being really neutral between the parties to the conflict, a situation which often does not exist. Consequently, it frequently happens that the parties to a dispute decide on trial by force simply because there seems to be no other way.

Within a country, the belief that the conflict cannot be resolved by any approach short of violence produces new sources of antagonism on both sides. Groups intent on overthrowing the government or on establishing an autonomous state for some national minority cease to rely merely on propaganda and peaceful protests to promote their point of view. They inaugurate the use of violence against the police and sabotage against the government generally. On the other side, the government begins arresting and torturing anyone who might in any way be suspected of aiding the revolutionary or separatist forces. Tensions mount. Each incident involving violence calls for more violence by the other side. The perception that violence is the only way to settle the issue thus becomes itself a contributing factor to the outbreak and escalation of violence.

In international conflicts the same situation exists. Once it is believed that the use of violence is the only way to resolve the dispute it follows that if either side momentarily gains a substantial advantage, it should strike at that moment. When it is believed that there will be a war anyway, why not fight it when one has the best chance of winning it? It is apparent that this type of thinking, viewing war as inevitable, can itself be a cause of war.[25] If it had prevailed, the U.S. might well have attacked the Soviet Union in the early 1950's when Americans had a marked superiority in atomic weapons and the means of delivering them against the enemy. This type of reasoning seems to have been the basis for the Soviet Union's plans to attack China in 1969 and for earlier American thoughts about attacking China during the Korean War. There is some hope for humanity in light of the fact that this thinking did not result in action on these occasions. Still there is no assurance that restraint and the possibility of third-party intervention will continue to inhibit action among either the superpowers or other nations.

We must conclude that the absence of trustworthy nonviolent ways of resolving conflicts of interest at both the national and international levels constitutes a contributory factor to the outbreak of war. The absence of fair and nonviolent instruments for resolving conflict is in fact a particularly important cause of war, because the presence of such instruments would diminish the likelihood of war even in the face of the existence of the other causes of war previously discussed.

VII. The Value of War

The general assumption of our inquiry about war is that human society is now faced with the problem of how to eliminate it. But is war really all bad? Hasn't war, at least in certain respects, been a good thing for human society? Although it would be a mistake to argue that wars occur *because* they serve good purposes such as controlling population and stimulating technological progress,[1] still it might be claimed that we should not seek to prevent them because they do have some favorable results. Let us examine some of the alleged positive values of war.

The Biological Value of War

At the end of the eighteenth century Thomas Malthus first published his thesis that there is a natural tendency for the population of humans to increase in a geometrical progression (2, 4, 8, 16, 32, etc.), while food production tends to grow only in an arithmetic progression (2, 4, 6, 8, 10, etc.). Consequently, population will tend to outgrow food supply, and there must be some devices by which the population growth is checked. According to Malthus, disease, famine, and war are three such devices. Thus war, it is claimed, has a positive value: People are killed off so they and the children they would have produced need not face death from disease or starvation.

Has war been an important factor in controlling human population? The facts seem to suggest not. Fifty-one million people were killed in World War II,[2] or about 2 percent of the world's population.[3] The people killed in that war were replaced in a single year. In South Vietnam the population actually grew at a rate of 3 percent a year during three years (1964–67) while a war was being fought on its soil.[4] Statistics from earlier wars, all of which were considerably less lethal than World War II, indicate that "during the Christian Era, warfare has not been a major force controlling the size of human population."[5] It is disease, rather than war, which has been the major factor in controlling human population growth, and the recent surge in population growth can be attributed to the use of DDT, public sanitation projects, and modern medical knowledge rather than any decrease in deaths due to war.

A second view about the biological value of warfare claims that war improves the genetic quality of humans because it provides a means by which the less skilled and less cooperative members of human society are killed or disgraced, while the better warriors win mates and produce offspring. But since such a small proportion of the population is killed

76

even in a war as tragic as World War II, there could be no significant selection of the fittest even if one grants the very debatable premise that war results in the less fit becoming less likely to produce offspring.[6] Anthropologist Frederick Thieme has observed that "racial discrimination, selective immigration policies, imperialistic exploitation of peoples, and a host of other forms of behavior have had a much more significant effect on demography or genetics of many populations than has warfare."[7] It seems then that during the last 5,000 years or so war has not been an important factor in either population control or genetic selection.[8]

What about the future? There has been a steady trend toward more casualties in each war, and the development of modern weaponry, both nuclear and nonnuclear, would not seem to promise any reversal of that trend. An all-out nuclear war between the superpowers could in a few hours produce many times the fatalities that occurred during all of World War II, and subsequent deaths from radiation and burns and other causes would swell the death count even further. Conventional weapons are being greatly improved in accuracy and destructiveness so that a much higher number of deaths can be expected even in nonnuclear wars. Future wars may consequently have a much greater impact on the population of the earth than recent wars have had. At the same time, the possibility of genetic damage from radiation means that any war fought with nuclear weapons will surely be detrimental from a biological point of view.

The Technological Value of War

Another alleged positive value of war is that it stimulates social change. Societies tend to get into ruts and continue doing things in the same old way until some crisis, such as a war, forces them to adopt a more efficient social system, to do without some resources to which they are accustomed, or to be creative in the development of new weapons. Progress requires challenge, and war serves as the most intense kind of challenge to the society as a whole. Those who advocate this point of view may note the rapid development of aviation, electronics, medical technology, weather forecasting, synthetic materials, and so on during the past world wars. They may point to the large-scale government planning that was nonexistent before World War I and to the changed roles of women, a result of World War II. They may call attention to the great changes in the distribution of goods brought about by the Communist revolutions in Russia and China and point to the changed situations of the former colonies of the Western European nations which have now become independent countries. Their claim is that all of this progress would not have occurred without the stimulus of war.

But it is impossible to say what would have occurred without the world wars. Before World War I the world had been moving toward a global community with a minimum of trade barriers and nationalistic feelings. Within a few decades inventions such as the telegraph, the telephone, the light bulb, the phonograph, the radio, the motion-picture camera and projector, the automobile, the airplane, and the agricultural tractor were brought forth with no stimulus from war. The technique of assembly line production was developed. The Suez and Panama Canals were built and put into operation. Remarkable advances were made in controlling malaria, yellow fever, and typhoid. Freud was publishing his theories about the psychological origins of various forms of mental illness, and X-rays were discovered. Einstein published his paper on the theory of relativity in 1905. What would have happened if there had been no World War I? Didn't World War I, with its demand for battleships, submarines, artillery pieces, tanks, and military aircraft, act as a detriment to scientific progress? On the other hand, it was the necessities of war that led the Germans to pioneer the large-scale production of synthetic rubber and use of the Haber process to make the nitrates needed for explosives.

What was the situation between the world wars? New plastics were developed, along with synthetic materials such as rayon and nylon. The effectiveness of penicillin against bacteria was discovered. The basic principles of television, nuclear energy, and rocket propulsion were known before World War II broke out in 1939.[9] During that war, as during most wars, the scientific knowledge already available prior to the war was devoted to technological advancements for the military: nylon parachute cords, radar, V-2 rockets, atomic bombs, and the like. World War II caused a delay of at least five years in the development of nylon clothing, television, and the use of nuclear energy to generate electricity. On the other hand, the war probably hastened the development of antibiotics, DDT, jet engines, helicopters, rockets, and substitutes for petroleum.

The thesis that war and preparation for war yield "spin-offs" that improve human life needs to be countered by the observation that similar investments of money and effort made with the direct aim of improving human life would undoubtedly yield even greater benefits. If it is the case that scientific and technological progress increases during war, it seems due primarily to the willingness of governments to spend large amounts of money on the development of weapons and related research. Suppose that governments were willing to spend similar amounts on medical research, better transportation and communication systems, and eliminating crime. Suppose that governments were willing to undertake massive expenditures to improve the educational levels of their citizens and to research better ways of teaching and learning. It seems safe to predict that the resulting social progress would be several times greater than that which occurs as "spin-offs" from military programs. It is not war and preparation for war that produce technological change. Instead, massive public expenditures for research and development achieve this result. Most governments are willing to pay these costs when stirred up by the threat of external attack but are less willing to do so simply to improve the lives of their citizens.

It is true that social changes would probably come more slowly without war. Change would tend to be evolutionary rather than revolutionary, but this seems to be desirable because revolutionary change usually involves violence and also tends to elicit more violence later. There is also the issue of whether change is always desirable, a question that especially needs to be considered with regard to the kinds of changes war brings. For example, during war there tends to be a greater concentration of power in the hands of a few leaders, a situation which may continue after the war ends. Is that desirable? During war there tends to be less questioning of public policies and the decisions of those in command, which may also continue after the war is over. Is that desirable? Wars may accelerate social changes, but the changes may be undesirable.

Another aspect of this issue of technological and social progress as a result of war concerns the costs involved. Even if it were granted that more technological and social change takes place during war and that this change is desirable, one must still ask whether the cost of war exceeds the benefits. What might have been accomplished by those killed in a war? What additional things might have been accomplished even by those who survived the war uninjured but who devoted several years of their early lives to fighting in it? Even in the simplest economic terms the public debt incurred during a war continues long after the war ends, contributing to inflation and taking funds that might be used instead for improving the quality of life. As the destructiveness and costs of war continue to escalate, it becomes more doubtful that war can be justified on the basis of any technological and social progress it might generate.

The Psychological Value of War

Another claim made for the value of war is that it provides a feeling of significance for the individuals who participate, challenging the citizen to sacrifice for the welfare of the society as a whole rather than pursuing his own personal welfare. What else besides war can lead the individual to give up the pursuit of his own petty aims and devote his efforts to an endeavor which is crucial for human destiny? It is only during war, some claim, that the existence of the society and its values are really threatened. It is only then that citizens can reasonably be called upon not only to forego certain amenities but perhaps to lose their lives for the sake of a larger good. People are forced to think in terms of the overall course of history and the relative insignificance of their own personal goals and activities. As the German philosopher Hegel put it:

> War is the state of affairs which deals in earnest with the vanity of temporal goods and concerns — a vanity at other times a common theme of edifying sermonizing.... War has the higher significance that by its agency, as I have remarked elsewhere, 'the ethical health of the peoples is preserved....'
>
> In peace civil life continually expands; all its departments wall themselves in, and in the long run men stagnate.[10]

Similar sentiments are expressed by World War II Italian fascist leader
Benito Mussolini.

> War alone brings up to its highest tension all human energy and puts
> the stamp of nobility upon the people who have the courage to meet it.
> All other trials are substitutes, which never really put men into the
> position where they have to make the great decision—the alternative of
> life or death.[11]

That there is some truth in the general point being made by Hegel
and Mussolini can be confirmed by talking with persons who have been
involved in a war in which they truly believed. Among Americans such
persons are more likely to be veterans of World War II than of the Korean
or Vietnamese Wars. These people are likely to have fond memories of the
war period, when the humdrum existence of everyday life was broken by
a new feeling of the significance of every act which contributed to the war
effort and thus to the victory of "our" values over "their" values. When
discussing war, they are likely to tell of a feeling of being a part of something bigger and to confirm the insight that war not only requires self-
discipline and self-sacrifice but also provides a psychological lift, a sense
that one's life will make some difference in the course of the world.

What can be said in response to this claim concerning the psychological value of war? The American philosopher and psychologist William
James recognized the need for self-discipline and self-sacrifice for a larger
cause which is met by participation in war, but he also realized that war
was becoming too destructive to be a satisfactory way of meeting this
need. Consequently, he recommended an alternative. In his essay "The
Moral Equivalent of War"[12] James advocated having the government
direct a "war" against the injustices of fate and nature, a war for which
the young people of the nation would be drafted, trained, and then supported as they attempted to right the wrongs of the world.

James's list of tasks to be performed suggests that he was thinking
mainly of requiring the men of the upper classes to get their hands dirty
doing the kind of work ordinarily done by people of the lower classes, but
his basic idea could be modified by having youth go to work in less developed countries or parts of their own country too poor to pay for their
services. These young people would constitute an "army against injustice," something like the Peace Corps or Vista, but James's proposal
called for compulsory service for all young people rather than voluntary
service for a few. These young people would thus be forced to dedicate
themselves to problems beyond their own personal advancement and
would find some significance in their lives as a result of being part of a
general war on injustice. James realized that the task of establishing this
battle against injustice as the moral equivalent of war would be difficult,
but he thought it could be done. "It is but a question of time, of skillful
propagandism, and of opinion-making men seizing historic opportunities."[13]

The psychological lift which comes from participating in war might
also be duplicated by educating people to take a certain attitude toward

their own lives. Even in peacetime people should be made constantly aware of how much difference their actions can make to the furtherance or hindrance of values they hold dear. There presently exist people who view their whole lives as dedicated to promoting the welfare of humanity even at personal cost to themselves. Such persons can be found in religious orders, and in service organizations dedicated to advancing one or another good cause. They work in various public service jobs, perpetually underpaid, as teachers, firemen, and policemen.

While it is the awareness of being completely caught up in a good cause which transcends one's personal fate that makes participation in war such a significant experience, it seems that people should be able to become similarly involved in other efforts to advance the welfare of the human community. The problem of developing a human society which is both peaceful and just on the local, state, national, and global levels is a big enough problem to absorb the energies of any who care to join. There may not be danger of losing one's life in the sense of being killed, but there is a challenge to lose one's life in the sense of making continuous personal sacrifices of time and money in order to promote the general welfare. During wartime the challenge may be more readily recognized and more difficult to escape, but it is there even in peacetime for those who have the eyes to see it. Perhaps we should follow William James's suggestion and require all our young people to participate in such an endeavor for a couple of years, but it may be that an even better approach is to try to open the eyes of all, young and old, to the challenge of serving humanity. Let them respond as they will. In either case, one hopes that the psychological lift generated by participation in war can be replaced by a similar satisfaction from sharing in the never-ending battle to eliminate injustice, violence, and ignorance.

The Social Value of War

Two theses about the social value of war need to be considered. The first maintains that war is an instrument of struggle among various societies which, like the struggle for survival among individual organisms, results in the survival of the fittest societies. War is thus an instrument of social evolution. The second thesis maintains that warfare functions as a safety valve allowing the hostility among members of a society to be directed toward an external enemy.[14] War thus promotes social cohesion.

The thesis that war is a useful device by which more advanced societies eliminate less fit societies was popular with Europeans from the fifteenth through the first part of the twentieth centuries, for it provided a rationale for subjugating native populations in the Americas, Asia, and Africa. The question which must be raised here is whether technological superiority in weaponry proves social or cultural superiority. Were those societies which first used iron weapons socially and culturally superior to those which fought simultaneously with weapons of bronze? Is the

Spartan society to be judged culturally superior to that of Athens simply because it was victorious in the Peloponnesian War? Making weapons and winning wars is but part of the business of a society; an inferiority in this activity does not imply an inferiority in other respects. It seems as inappropriate to evaluate societies on the basis of their capacity to win violent conflicts as to evaluate individuals on this basis.

What about the thesis that war has the positive value of promoting social cohesion by allowing hostility to be displaced to an external enemy? Other crises such as earthquakes or tornados also stimulate group cohesion but do not provide the outlet for hostility that war does. Thus the challenge is to find some other activities which promote group cohesion while at the same time providing a legitimate outlet for aggressive feelings. One obvious substitute for war in this regard is participation in athletic contests. For example, an American basketball team composed of individuals from different racial groups competing against teams from other nations does wonders for reducing domestic tensions between these racial groups. At the same time, however, these contests, like war itself, may stir up antagonisms between nations. In 1969 a three-game series to determine who would represent Central America in the World Cup soccer championship touched off a short war between El Salvador and Honduras![15] Athletic contests should be a substitute for war, not a stimulus to it. Another possible alternative to war is competition among societies in scientific activities such as the exploration of space or the conquest of disease. Among less developed countries there could be contests to increase the literacy rate, reduce the infant mortality rate, or raise agricultural production.

The possibility of implementing alternative forms of competition is not the only way to respond to the thesis that war is desirable because it creates internal cohesion. It can be noted that even if war was once valuable as a means to this end, that is no longer the case. The destructiveness of modern warfare is so great that the cost now exceeds any benefits to be expected in terms of group cohesion. Another response is that group cohesion is not always a good thing. It seems that internal dissension is somewhat better than the conformity and uniformity of expressed opinion which is typical of a society at war with an external enemy. The belief that war is desirable because of the internal cohesion it maintains within a group cannot be justified.

The Moral Value of War

We earlier noted that a possible cause of war is the desire to eliminate injustice. We have also observed that there is a tendency for people with power to establish institutions by which their privileged positions can be maintained and that this situation exists both within national governments and among national governments at the global level. Frequently political institutions will be used not only to protect power but to extend it. Thus government itself becomes an instrument of exploitation. In such a situation ordinary citizens cannot effectively appeal to the government for protection because the government itself is controlled by the exploiters. History is full of instances where people have used violence to overthrow an oppressive government. One of the positive values of war, it is claimed, is its use to gain freedom from tyrannical government. The threat of such a possibility is also useful in checking governments that otherwise might be more oppressive. This same principle seems to apply in the international sphere: If weaker nations possessed no possibility at all of resisting the more powerful nations by some use of force, they would probably be exploited even more than they are.

The use of violence and threats of violence has probably had some influence at times in reducing or eliminating tyranny and the exploitation of weaker nations by stronger ones. An evaluation of the thesis that war and the threat of war is therefore desirable, however, requires taking account of the whole picture. The possibility of violence against the government may serve to keep the government from becoming tyrannical, but a tyrannical government may react to threats of violence by becoming even more oppressive. It may establish secret police to ferret out even the beginnings of protest, and try to control every facet of life so that no revolution can even get started. The possibility of violence against the government thus becomes an excuse for even more tyranny. The same situation exists on the international level. One nation may try to dominate another one entirely on the grounds that even a little freedom could be used later to move to total independence and result in less power for the previously dominant nation.

Suppose that a different approach were adopted both by the rulers and the ruled. Suppose that a tradition were established that there would be no armed revolt against the government, and that the government would be restrained in pursuing the interests of the privileged people of the society. In this situation the government probably would not be very tyrannical since it would not be fearful of overthrow. A new and delicate balance would be brought into existence in which distortions of justice and exploitation of the poor are kept under control while those not in power would be permitted to publicize their views and even to try to change the social structure as long as it is done within the rules set up by the government. If these rules seemed unfair, then the danger of revolution would, of course, again be increased. On the international level, a less powerful nation which appears to be somewhat cooperative toward a more powerful nation would probably be allowed more internal freedom than a smaller nation which seems constantly ready to reject all cooperation. The balance here again requires the more powerful nation to control its desire to exploit and the small nation to forego strident demands for rights.

It is distressing to realize that in these situations power is only partly restrained by considerations of justice and that the claims of the less powerful for justice must be tempered by a recognition of the realities of power. This type of compromise, widely practiced, is not the morally perfect situation. Yet these situations seem immensely preferable to an unrestrained, violent struggle for power between the privileged and the underprivileged. In the latter situation, the success of a violent revolution may produce a new group of leaders who will themselves become a new privileged group even more oppressive than those they replaced. Cognizant of how it was able to come to power, this group will seek to prevent others from overthrowing its rule. On the other hand, if there is absolutely no possibility of violent resistance by the have-nots regardless of the level of exploitation and oppression, a real danger of tyranny exists.

The best situation seems to be a system of governance with built-in checks against tyranny. Nevertheless, it must be admitted that despite such efforts the injustice perpetrated by those in power may become so gross and the exploitation of the weak so outrageous that resort to violence seems to be the only reasonable course of action. Peace is desirable, but so is justice. Ideally governments should be vehicles of both peace and justice, but experience shows that they are often merely new instruments by which the privileged extend their power. This analysis suggests that the only way to eliminate resort to violence as a legitimate means of securing justice is to establish governments which are impartial and which allow for peaceful change. To the extent that this goal is realized, resort to violence as a means of eliminating injustice becomes unnecessary.

Part Three

The Contemporary Situation

VIII. Ideological Aspects of
the Contemporary Situation

An *ideology* is like a religion whose main concern is the proper structuring of society rather than the salvation of the individual. It consists of a set of beliefs about the human situation and the way society ought to be organized to which a substantial number of persons have committed themselves. Our present goal is a better understanding of the ideologies most relevant to the social conflicts of the contemporary world. After reviewing some basic distinctions in the first section, we will devote our attention to the predominant ideology in the United States, Western Europe, and Japan: capitalistic democracy. Then we will deal with the basic tenets of Marxism-Leninism or Communism. In the fourth section we will make a direct comparison of capitalistic democracy and Communism. The last section deals with the ideologies of democratic socialism, Maoism, and fascism.

Some Basic Distinctions

In our earlier discussions of justice we noted that there are two opposing principles which must somehow be reconciled or balanced in order to have a just society. These two principles are *the principle of merit*, that some people deserve to have more than others because they contribute more or are more qualified in some way, and *the principle of equality*, that everyone should have the same amount of goods because ultimately how much of a contribution one makes or how qualified one is depends on factors outside one's own control. These two principles are so basic in social philosophy that adherence to one or the other is used to determine the seating arrangements in most of the legislative bodies of the world. Legislators who tend to emphasize the principle of merit are usually seated on the right while those who tend to emphasize the principle of equality are seated on the left. Consequently, to call someone a *rightist* indicates that he emphasizes the principle of merit with regard to the distribution of goods and political power within the society, while to call someone a *leftist* means that he is a champion of the principle of equality.

It is evident that there can be degrees of emphasis on one or the other of these principles. A person who is so committed to the principle of merit that he wants to use violence, if necessary, to subdue those who favor the principle of equality is an *extremist of the right* while a person who is similarly committed to the principle of equality is an *extremist of the left*. *Moderates*, on the other hand, of both the right and the left believe in the use of persuasion and the right of the opposition to be heard. Thus extremists of both right and left favor authoritarian forms of government while moderates favor Western-style parliamentary democracies where freedom of expression by the opposition is an important part of the political process.

We have noted that social structures, including governments, are usually controlled by the elite in the society and are consequently usually designed to maintain privileges which these people and their families enjoy. We have also noted that people in these top positions tend to believe that they hold these positions because they deserve to have them. Thus in most societies those at the top are defenders of the principle of merit and will want to preserve the *status quo*, that is, they will want to conserve the present values and structures of society. When such rightists take a moderate stance, they are called *conservatives*. On the other hand, moderate leftists who want to reduce impediments to social change and create more equality of opportunity are called *progressives*. (These moderate leftists are sometimes called "liberals," but this term is also used to refer to persons who favor individualism rather than collectivism, so "progressive" is a less ambiguous term for someone who favors more equality of opportunity.) Extreme rightists who strive for even more privileges for the ruling class are called *reactionaries* while extreme leftists who want to completely uproot the present institutions and arrangements of the society, thus eliminating all influence of the privileged class, are usually called *radicals*.

These terms are widely used to refer to politicians and others with regard to their views on the nature of the ideal society, but another distinction has usually been neglected. This is the distinction between a person's *economic ideology* (his views on how the goods of society should be distributed) and his *political ideology* (his views on how the political power of society should be distributed). This distinction seems useful because a given individual could be a rightist with regard to his economic ideology (that is, he may believe that goods should be distributed primarily on the basis of merit) and a leftist with regard to his political ideology (that is, he may believe that political power should be distributed primarily on the basis of equality). It is also possible for a person to be a leftist with regard to economic ideology (that is, he may believe that goods should be distributed primarily on the basis of equality) and a rightist with regard to political ideology (that is, he may believe that political power should be distributed primarily on the basis of merit). The significance of this distinction becomes more evident when we note that the first combination is precisely what we find in the capitalistic democratic ideology prevalent in the U.S., while the second is characteristic of the Marxist-Leninist view, the official ideology of the Soviet Union.

This distinction between economic ideology and political ideology raises another very important issue in social philosophy: the influence of a nation's economic and political systems on each other. One possible view is that the economic system is basic and that the political system is merely a reflection of it. According to this view economic power necessarily creates political power. Another possible view is that the political system is basic and that the economic system is ultimately dependent on it. According to this view political power assisted by the military power of the state may be used to control and redirect economic power. We will refer again to this issue of the priority of the economic or the political system in our discussion of the relationship between capitalistic democracy and Communism.

Capitalistic Democracy

The prevalent ideology in the United States, Western Europe, Japan, and many other parts of the world is capitalistic democracy. Capitalism refers to an economic system in which the instruments of production are owned by private persons rather than the government while democracy refers to a political system in which political power is ultimately in the hands of the people as a whole.

The term *capitalism* is derived from the term *capital*, which in this context refers to things such as machines which can be used to produce more wealth. A person who possesses such wealth on a large scale is a capitalist, and the income derived from this capital is called *profit*. To earn profit one must save some of his wealth and use it for capital investment rather than spending it on present needs and wants. Thus, profit ideally represents a reward for saving rather than spending. Of course, saving will not automatically produce a profit; the money must be invested in something which is productive, such as machinery. Suppose a machine enables a man to produce five times as many goods as he could produce without it. These goods can be sold, and some of the money received can pay the worker's wages and some can provide profit to the investor whose money made it possible to buy the machine in the first place.

A capitalistic system depends on the existence of some kind of capital such as machinery that will increase productivity and on there being some people who are willing to invest their money in this productive capital rather than spending it on themselves. It also depends on the manufacturer's ability to sell the goods which are produced and on having people who know how to operate the machines. To be able to sell the goods produced, the capitalist must make things of the type and quality which will appeal to potential buyers. To get workers he must pay them enough that they will work for him rather than someone else. Consequently, in theory a system of competition develops among capitalists (or groups of capitalists who have merged their savings in a single enterprise such as joint-stock company or a corporation). Each capitalist tries to give potential buyers a better bargain than they can get from others.

Each capitalist competes for the best workers, and because income depends on the goods sold, the capitalist will pay a higher wage to the more efficient workers. Capitalists will also be willing to pay more for more efficient machines, which in turn motivates inventors and other capitalists to produce such machines.

This *market economy* rewards inventiveness, good business management, and skill. Saving one's money rather than spending it will be rewarded with profit. Inefficient businesses will go bankrupt while efficient ones will prosper and earn more money with which to make further investments and expand their operations. While each person, capitalist and worker alike, aims only to better his own personal situation, the system as a whole works naturally to increase productivity, efficiency, and the variety of goods available to the consumer while at the same time prices, wages, and profits reflect the supply and demand for goods, labor, and savings.[1]

This capitalistic system seems ideal in principle. There is no need for people to be altruistic or even concerned about the welfare of others. They are assured that their long-term selfishness will do more to help others than any charitable acts. The one imperative to be followed by each individual is to save rather than spend, since saving alone will provide more goods in the long run.

In actual practice, however, some difficulties occur in the capitalistic system. Sometimes one capitalist or a small group of capitalists manage to gain a monopoly in the production of goods of a particular kind; then the competition, which had previously kept prices down, disappears. Another difficulty is that even without monopolies competition is imperfect, for those with very large assets generally have an inherent advantage because they can take greater risks, buy more expensive machinery, and wait longer to realize profits from their investment. This situation means that there is a built-in incentive to seek to develop those very monopolies which destroy the competitive system.

There are also several other difficulties. In setting wage levels, the greater assets of the capitalist puts him in a much better bargaining position than that of the poor laborer looking for a job, since the laborer needs work immediately to get money for food while the capitalist can wait until someone is found to work at the wages he is willing to pay. Unscrupulous capitalists may produce unsafe products whose defects are not visible to the buyer. Also, since products can be sold only to those who have money to pay for them, there is a tendency to produce luxury items which appeal to the whims of the wealthy rather than to make things which meet the basic needs of those who have little or no money. Furthermore, the intrinsic advantage for the richer in bargaining situations, as well as their ability to save and invest, produces a strong tendency throughout the system for the rich to get richer while the poor get poorer.

Most distressing of all for the capitalists themselves is the tendency for the whole system to undergo a continuing cycle of boom followed by bust. When business is going well, the capitalists invest more in production, hire more workers, and pay each more as the competition for labor increases. Since the workers have more money, they buy more. This produces a demand for the production of more goods. The capitalists respond by building more factories to produce still more. Since each capitalist is thinking only in terms of more profits, each expands as much as possible. Soon more goods are being produced than can possibly be sold, and the bust begins. The capitalists start laying off workers. These workers no longer have any money with which to buy goods. Others who are still working keep their expenditures down as much as possible, fearing that they also may soon lose their jobs. This cutback further decreases sales, leading eventually to more layoffs. Capitalists then try to sell their machines because they are sitting idle, but no other capitalists want to buy them. Production comes to a virtual halt. Workers are unemployed, and capitalists are not making any profits. Eventually the oversupply of goods is consumed and the boom part of the cycle slowly begins again.

To control these various problems a system of *government-regulated capitalism* has been developed. Under this system it is the task of government to break up or regulate monopolies. The government establishes laws to protect smaller firms against unfair competition from larger ones and enacts laws to protect the right of laborers to join unions and bargain collectively with the employer. Agencies are established to protect the public from unsafe products. The government institutes progressive rates of taxation on income and adopts other measures to try to mitigate somewhat the natural tendency in a capitalistic system for the rich to get richer. Welfare programs are adopted so the unemployed, the disabled, the very old, and others will have at least some money to provide for their basic needs. The government also tries to moderate the boom and bust cycles by controlling the money supply, tax rates, and government spending. Thus government-regulated capitalism aims to preserve the positive values of capitalism — productivity, efficiency, variety of products, and personal freedom — while controlling its less desirable features.[2]

Let us now turn to the democratic part of the capitalistic democratic ideology. *Democracy* refers to a political system in which political power rests ultimately in the hands of the people as a whole. Political leaders need not come from any particular family, class, or political party. They are elected by a majority vote of the citizens. In the words of Abraham Lincoln, democracy is "government of the people, by the people, and for the people." The ideology of Western-style democracy includes not only the notion of majority rule but also the principle of minority rights. Voting means nothing if there is no chance to be informed of the issues or to hear the arguments offered by persons defending various points of view. Opposition candidates as well as those representing the group in power must be on the ballot, and the voting must be secret so that it is impossible to determine how any person voted. People must be free to give their opinions, ask questions, hear the opinions of others, form voluntary associations to promote one or another point of view, travel about, and so on. These rights or freedoms are rooted in the notion that in a democracy public policy should be the outcome of rational discussion and deliberation rather than the dogmatic pronouncements of some group.

A fundamental asset of the democratic political system is that it allows for peaceful change. People who don't like a public policy are free to speak against it. They are free to enlist the help of others and even to run for political office themselves. Consequently, there is no point in trying to start a violent revolution. It could succeed only if one had the support of many people; with such support one should be able to win an election. At the same time those in power need not use force except in the case of an attempt to use violence against the government.

Sometimes the question is raised whether in a democracy persons ought to be permitted to openly advocate the overthrow of the government. It is clear that democratic theory requires that such a viewpoint be allowed to be openly expressed. If those who espouse this view can gain enough followers to win elections or to pose a real threat to the government, then the government itself has failed to persuade many people of its value. On the other hand, to try to silence those who advocate overthrow of a democratic government is to resort to an undemocratic approach, which is inconsistent with the rational defense of democracy. Such a course of action would leave this dissatisfied group with no option but to turn to violence to promote their views, the very sort of thing which democracy is designed to make unnecessary.

Capitalistic democracy is sometimes attacked on grounds that, although there are formal freedoms such as expressing a point of view and running for public office, there are in reality only a few wealthy or otherwise influential persons who can take advantage of these freedoms. It is noted that participation in politics requires time both for keeping oneself informed and for the actual political activities and that such time is not available to all persons in the society. Such participation also requires at least minimal amounts of money. There is undoubtedly a great deal of truth in these criticisms. It is obvious that some people are able to exert a great deal more influence on the political process than others. Nevertheless the freedom to participate does exist and many people do participate in various ways that go beyond voting. Furthermore, most people find plenty of time and money for recreational activities and time to watch a great deal of television. It seems that the biggest factor lacking in most cases of nonparticipation is not so much the opportunity but the inclination. People may complain about the influence of special-interest groups on government policy, but their own nonparticipation permits these groups to exert such influence. In a democracy, people get what they deserve.

Marxism-Leninism (Communism)

The official ideology of the Soviet Union and its satellite countries is Marxism-Leninism, often called Communism. The basic ideas of this philosophy were formulated by Karl Marx and Frederick Engels in the nineteenth century. The central thesis of socialism is that capital goods, the machines and other means of production, should be owned jointly by the whole society rather than by individuals or private corporations. Marx and Engels called their view *scientific socialism* to distinguish it from earlier socialist views which they regarded as utopian. The *utopian socialists* believed that socialism could be brought into existence merely by convincing people how desirable such a system would be, while Marx and Engels claimed that social change could come about only as the result of the operation of historical forces.

What are these historical forces? The answer to this question is given by the *materialistic interpretation of history* developed by Marx and Engels.[3] The basic factor in historical change is not divine intervention as Christians believed or philosophical thought as Hegel had taught but rather the manner in which the goods of a society are produced, that is, the material or economic factor. This historical materialism maintains that the predominant mode of production determines all the other aspects of a society. Most importantly, it determines what class of people will be in positions of power and what class will be exploited by them. If the goods of society are produced by slave labor, then the slave-owners will be the privileged class and the slaves will be the exploited class. If the primary mode of production is small-scale agriculture as in a feudal society, then the landowners will be the ruling class and the serfs who do the physical labor of farming will be the exploited class. If the primary mode of production consists of using machinery, then those who own machines will be the class in control while the workers who run the machines will be the exploited class. The mode of production and resulting social relations will also influence religious views, the nature of art, legal concepts, and government structure. It is especially important for understanding the history of conflict to note that the ruling or dominant class will always establish political and judicial institutions which protect its own interests.

Violent social conflict arises when the predominant mode of production changes and the old ruling class refuses to graciously step aside. Consider, for example, the transition from feudalism to capitalism that took place in Europe in the sixteenth, seventeenth, and eighteenth centuries. The feudal kingdoms, complete with archdukes, dukes, marquesses, earls, viscounts, and others had established a system of government to serve their purposes and solve their particular problems. The productive and commercial activities of the up-and-coming bourgeoisie (or burghers, so called because they lived in the towns) did not fit with the land-centered thinking of the feudal lords. In cases of conflict between landowners and merchants, the laws and government structures always favored the landed aristocracy. The bourgeoisie wanted more power and more government concern about the kinds of problems they faced, but the old dominant class would not willingly surrender control. Although the bourgeoisie may in some cases have been able to gain political power peacefully, the usual course of events was a violent revolution which ended the feudal government.

Marx and Engels argued that by the nineteenth century a new transition was taking place. Once again a shift in the predominant mode of production had taken place and the old ruling class was refusing to graciously step aside. This time it was the bourgeoisie that had created laws and government structures to protect their interests; the emphasis was on private ownership and individual enterprise. But the mode of production had now shifted from privately-owned machines in workshops employing a few people to corporately-owned machines in large factories employing hundreds and managed by people other than the owners. According to Marx and Engels, the production of goods had become a social enterprise, not a private one, and production no longer depended mainly on the owner of the machines, but on the workers who used the machines.

These workers, the proletariat, were the new up-and-coming class[4] whose interests were neglected and thwarted by the laws and government of the bourgeoisie. Although the proletariat might be able in some cases to gain political power peacefully, the usual course of events would be a violent revolution to eliminate the capitalist-dominated governments. Marxists do more than predict that this will happen, however. Their aim is to make it happen. The Marxists' readiness to push history along by promoting violent revolutions against bourgeois governments makes them unpopular in capitalist countries.

Marx and Engels argue that the system of private ownership which was suitable for the small-scale enterprises of the bourgeoisie is not appropriate for the large-scale enterprises of mass production. When a large number of people work together to produce an object such as an automobile, then that product should belong to them, not to the small group which happens to have enough money to buy stock in the company. Capitalists may object that those who bought stock made it possible to purchase the machines which in turn provided employment for the workers, but according to Marxists these capitalists were able to accumulate this extra money for purchasing stock only by some previous exploitation. How do these capitalists get their money? They do not need to work, but only make money from the money their families accumulated from earlier exploitation. Suppose a person inherits $500,000 from capitalist parents. Without any special talent for investing wisely, the heir should be able to get a 12 percent return on the money. That income of $60,000 per year is much more than factory workers can hope to earn, no matter how hard they work. As the Marxist sees it, the laws of the capitalist society protect this continued exploitation of the workers by the capitalists. At the same time, for the most part capitalist-controlled governments do not show an enthusiastic concern for the problems of the proletariat such as unemployment, the availability of affordable health care, and an assured minimum supply of the basic necessities of life regardless of one's financial situation.

The Marxists also claim that the capitalistic free enterprise system, even when regulated by government, is unable to take full advantage of the productive capabilities of mass production. Although each individual enterprise plans its operations with a view to making as much profit as possible over the next few years, there is no effort to coordinate the productive capabilities of the whole nation or the whole world. During the bust part of the capitalist business cycle, factories sit idle and workers are unemployed even though there are plenty of unmet needs in the society. Even when the system is working rather smoothly, production is geared to what people with money will buy, not to the needs of the general population. So factories still operate well below their maximum capabilities.

The writings of Marx and Engels are devoted primarily to a criticism of capitalism. Workers are encouraged to overthrow capitalist governments, but they are not provided with much guidance about what to do after they gain control. They are told that a transition period will be needed before they can move to the higher phase of communist society when the slogan "from each according to his ability; to each according to his need" can be implemented.[5] During this transition period private ownership of the means of production would be eliminated but differential pay on the basis of one's contribution to society would continue. Soviet spokesmen maintain that the Soviet Union is now in this socialist transition period and will not be able to shift to the higher phase of communism until all capitalist societies are overthrown.

Marx's views are not free from difficulties. He accepted the labor theory of value from earlier writers, a theory which maintains that the value of any product depends completely on the amount of labor required to get it out of nature and into usable form. Even when patched up with questionable notions such as the idea that machines represent stored labor, the labor theory of value presents difficulties. Labor undoubtedly is a big factor in the value of most things, but supply and demand also make a great difference. Scarce but useful raw materials such as petroleum will be very valuable even if relatively little labor is required to take them from nature. Sometimes people are willing to pay a great deal for an art object which did not take long to make, while they won't pay much at all for another which required more labor.

Marx also made several predictions which have turned out to be incorrect. For example, he predicted that as capitalism progressed the middle class would become smaller and smaller. In fact, it has become larger and larger. For another example, he expected that proletarian revolutions would occur in the most industrially-advanced nations such as France and Germany while in fact the first successful revolutions have occurred in Russia, at that time probably the least advanced country of Europe, and China, a predominantly agrarian and feudal nation. Furthermore, the revolutions which have occurred seem to be more the result of the influence of Marx's philosophy than of any objective historical forces. For a third example, he predicted that the capitalists would amass such an abundance of capital that they would be searching around for places to invest. In fact, just the opposite has occurred. Everywhere there is a shortage of capital for investment. From a scientific point of view so many wrong predictions must raise doubts about the correctness of the theory.

Since Marx and Engels had not provided much guidance on the issue of what the proletariat should do once they gained power, Lenin had to work out his own program after the Bolshevik Revolution in Russia in 1917. He decided to base the government on the *soviets*, organizations of workers, soldiers, and peasants who had been elected by their fellows to serve as representatives. These soviets had been the prime movers in the overthrow of the czar. Nevertheless, it was claimed by Lenin that the soviets needed the leadership of the Communist Party for guidance, so the Party was organized in such a way that it could be controlled by the intelligentsia who had led the revolution.[6]

The procedural arrangement which governs the operation of the Communist Party is called *democratic centralism*, a system which is basic to politics in the Soviet Union. The basic features of democratic centralism are that representatives are elected at the local level; that these lower level representatives then elect higher level ones who elect higher level ones, and so on; that decisions are made by majority rule; that after a decision has been made no further dissent or questioning of that matter is permitted; and that decisions of higher level organs are binding on all lower level organs.[7] It is the last two features which give the central decision-making bodies so much power in the Soviet system. It is also these two features, plus the fact that the Communist Party is the only party allowed to exist in the country, which distinguishes the political party structure in the Soviet Union from that found in Western-style democracies. The monopoly maintained by the Communist Party in the Soviet Union means that the real political power belongs to the party even though there are elections for many government positions.

Capitalistic Democracy Versus Communism

We have examined briefly the two ideological positions which vie for supremacy in the world today. As noted earlier, tension exists between rightist and leftist tendencies in both systems. The capitalistic economic system emphasizes merit (some people deserve to have more goods than others) while the Western-style democratic political system emphasizes equality (each person has one vote). On the other hand, in Communism the economic system emphasizes equality (all income is from labor and income differentials should be relatively small) while the Party-controlled political system emphasizes merit (only those who have proved their competence and loyalty should be involved in political decision-making). Furthermore, in both systems the emphasis on equality takes place in that area which is regarded as the most fundamental in the society. Defenders of capitalistic democracy tend to believe that the political system basically controls the economic system; if the people should decide they want socialism, then they will have it. On the other hand, defenders of Communism tend to believe that the economic system basically controls the political system; consequently their primary concern is to prevent any large accumulation of wealth in the hands of individuals or families. They are much less concerned about the accumulation of political power by a few individuals or families.[8]

In their appeals to Third World countries, both the U.S. and the U.S.S.R. emphasize the egalitarian aspect of their ideologies. The U.S. puts itself forth as the proponent of democracy and political rights while the U.S.S.R. champions socialism and economic rights. When they propagandize against each other, each emphasizes the nonegalitarian aspect of the other's ideology. Thus the U.S. criticizes the Russians for trying to silence political dissenters and for their authoritarian political system, and the U.S.S.R. criticizes Americans for neglecting the poor and for a political system that they maintain is really only a façade behind which capitalists do whatever they want in order to increase their profits.

The fact that both nations emphasize the egalitarian aspects of their own ideology raises the issue of whether these two different systems are totally incompatible or whether they might even gradually converge. Some relatively minor modifications could produce significant changes. For example, in the Soviet Union the "progressive" and "conservative" wings of the Communist Party might be permitted to nominate alternative candidates in some elections. Provisions already exist to assist these candidates in making their views known. Public dialogue and debate would be opened. On the U.S. side, stricter controls might be imposed on the manner in which economic power can be converted to political power. Recent efforts to control private financial contributions to political campaigns and to provide public funding for Presidential elections already mark a step in this direction, as do efforts to more strictly control lobbyists. If these efforts are continued and expanded, the U.S. political system will become much better insulated against control by wealthy individuals, corporations, labor unions, and other special-interest groups.

Convergence between the two opposing ideologies can already be observed in some areas. In the Soviet Union there have been efforts to decentralize planning, to adjust production to consumer demand, and to reward individual effort. These changes seem to be making the Soviet system more similar in some respects to a market economy. At the same time, in the United States there have been proposals for a guaranteed annual income for all, for a universal health insurance program, and for tax reform to eliminate or greatly reduce those tax deductions which benefit only the very wealthy. Such changes would make the U.S. system slightly more socialistic. There has also been a long-term trend in the U.S. political system to expand egalitarianism, as the right to vote has been extended to more members of minority groups, to women, and to 18-year-olds. There is a similar trend in the judicial system as efforts are made to appoint judges on the basis of merit and to provide legal assistance for those who cannot afford to pay for their own.

Regardless of the possibility of future convergence, however, the fact remains that at the present time there are important differences between capitalistic democracy and Communism. What is not so obvious is why we should have a nuclear war between West and East over these ideological differences. After all, there was a time, not so long ago, when Catholics and Protestants believed that they could not possibly live together in peace. If the question which needs to be considered is what type of social system best promotes the welfare of its citizens, it seems that a war is a poor way to go about finding the answer. Furthermore, neither of these competing ideologies maintains that its system is best because of its effectiveness in military conflict, though both recognize the legitimacy of using force to remove what they consider to be injustices. It must be remembered that nonideological factors such as the desire for status, nationalism, and competition for the goods of the Earth also play an important role in the present conflict between the U.S. and the U.S.S.R.

Although our discussion of the ideological conflict between capitalistic democracy and Communism has focused on the international situation as it relates to the big powers, this same ideological conflict is a significant factor *within* many nations. Whenever the capitalistic economies of the developed countries begin to falter, the support for Communism grows. In the less developed countries, there are fierce contests between those who espouse the capitalist road to development (as exemplified by Japan, South Korea, and Taiwan) and those who espouse the socialist way (as exemplified by the Soviet Union, China, and Cuba). These battles may be fought at the ballot box in those few countries that have elections but are more likely to be fought between guerrilla forces on the one hand and the secret police and security forces of the government on the other. Even the seeming advocates of democracy frequently claim that the situation is too unsettled and the people too ignorant to have elections and consequently find themselves supporting capitalistic totalitarianism. In such a situation there is a tendency for force to become the arbiter between a totalitarianism favoring the elite and a totalitarianism favoring the poor. Ideological conflict becomes mixed with personal ambition and intense feelings of hate and revenge to produce bloody and drawn-out struggles for control in many of the newly-independent countries. Frequently, Americans and Russians or their surrogates are involved too, providing weapons, supplies, training, and intelligence information. Thus ideological conflict becomes relevant to the problem of war not only on the international level but also on the intranational level.

Other Contemporary Ideologies

So far our attention has been focused on the ideological conflict between capitalistic democracy and Soviet-style Communism. We will now discuss briefly two other varieties of Marxism and the ideology of fascism which played such an important role in World War II.

It should not be assumed that all Marxists are pleased with what has happened and is happening in the Soviet Union. Many Marxists in other parts of the world, especially in Western Europe, believe that capitalism should be replaced by socialism, but that political control should remain in the hands of the general population, not in a bureaucracy controlled by professional revolutionaries who are supposed to direct the thinking and action of the proletariat. Marx himself indicated at one time that the proletariat might be able to come to power in Britain and the U.S. by means of the ballot box.[9] Those Marxists who favored a democratic, peaceful overthrow of capitalism struggled against the revolution-oriented Marxists for control of the socialist movement in Europe during the early 1900's. After the Lenin-led Russian revolution of 1917, a division took place between the *orthodox Communists* who supported an author-itarian Russian leadership and the *revisionist Socialists* who opposed it.

The *Democratic Socialists* or *Social Democrats* thus emerged as advocates of both Western-style democracy and government ownership of the means of production. They attempted to get voters to put them in power via the ballot box. When they were successful in getting elected, instead of doing away with private ownership of the means of production as their ideology seemed to require, they became satisfied to nationalize only certain large and crucial industries and to take the lead in national economic planning. After World War II, the Socialist Parties of Western Europe for the most part were content to maintain the level of govern-ment ownership that already existed and to focus attention instead on economic planning and support for welfare programs which benefit not only the working class but also the unemployed, the retired, and others with little or no income.

As a result of the gradual movement of the socialists away from full-fledged socialism, the earlier position of the revisionists (government ownership of all the means of production combined with parliamentary democracy) became available to a new group, the so-called Euro-Communists. These Euro-Communists, such as Berlinguer in Italy, Marchais in France, and Carillo in Spain, are leaders of the Communist Parties in Western Europe. They have been increasingly critical of the Communist leaders in the Soviet Union both for their efforts to silence dissenters within their borders and for their attempts to use the Russian military to impose their will on other nations, as occurred in Eastern Europe and Afghanistan. In order to attract votes, the Euro-Communists have made public statements that, if elected, they will abide by tradi-tional Western standards of democracy, including free speech for the opposition. They will stay in power, they say, only so long as the voters keep reelecting them. They will even keep their countries in NATO. The critical issue for voters in Italy, France, Spain, and Portugal is whether they can trust these Communists to keep their word if they do come to power.

Another significant variation in Marxist ideology took place under the leadership of China's Mao Tse-tung. While Marx and Engels had focused attention on the conflict between workers and capitalists, Mao emphasized the conflict between the poor rural peasants and the more affluent elite of the cities. Mao exhibited great faith in the ordinary, unsophisticated powerless people of the society and was always on guard against any elitist tendency even within the Communist Party of China. He made special efforts to place university students and professors in the fields working beside the poorest peasants, and at the same time he championed the idea that hard-working peasants should be given priority in access to education. One of his main concerns was that an elitist group, out of contact with the hard life of the peasants in the rural areas, would again gain control of China and overturn the revolution of the dispossessed which he had led.

Mao's focus on the rural poor versus the urban rich bears on his analysis of international affairs. He saw the world as divided between the rich, developed "urban" countries and poor, undeveloped "rural" countries. He thought that Communism on the international level meant getting the poor rural areas to revolt and throw off the control exercised over them by the rich urban areas, just as his revolution in China had begun with the rural areas throwing off the control of the cities. Mao took issue with Lenin's view that all imperialism was due to capitalism. He claimed that the two superpowers, the capitalistic imperialistic U.S. and the socialistic imperialistic U.S.S.R., were vying with each other for hegemony over the whole world. These two nations constituted what he called the First World. The other developed countries he called the Second World, while the undeveloped countries constitute the Third World. Mao believed that the best hope for the Third World countries was to unite with each other and perhaps some of the Second World countries against the influence of the superpowers. Since Mao's death in 1976, the new Chinese leaders have shifted away from his obsession with equality at the expense of specialization within Chinese society, but with regard to foreign policy they seem to be following his view that at present China's most dangerous enemy is the Soviet Union.

Fascism has not been in the spotlight since the end of World War II, but there are incidents from time to time which indicate that fascism is by no means dead. Fascism, or *National Socialism* as it was called in Germany, emphasizes the organic unity of the nation. The people of the nation are bound together by a common language, a common cultural heritage, and a common leader. The whole nation is to be organized in a military fashion in order to be able to prevail in contests with other nations. Loyalty to the nation and the national leader ("Il Duce" or "Der Führer") is supreme and absolute.

Fascism represents a reaction against both the Marxist emphasis on economic class consciousness and the Western liberal emphasis on the basic equality of all persons. Fascism's emphasis on power and will rather than on law and reason is fundamentally opposed to the democratic ideals of free speech, parliamentary debate, deliberation, and voting. The fascist glorifies aggression, violence, and war and shows a corresponding disdain for restraint, reasonableness, and peace. Peace is regarded by the fascist as both boring and contrary to nature. The fascist usually links nationalism with a belief in the absolute superiority of his own race, language, and culture, thus justifying the ridicule and even persecution of people of other races and cultures. Fascism consequently also opposes efforts to promote international tolerance.

The most obvious examples of fascism in recent history are the Axis Powers (Germany, Italy, and Japan) which were defeated in World War II, but fascist movements also held control or exerted considerable influence at one time in Spain, Portugal, Argentina, and other countries. Some Marxists claim that Israel and the Union of South Africa are fascist countries because of their fervent nationalism and their religious and racial policies, but neither of these countries has both the authoritarian political structure and the glorification of violent strife which is typical of fascism. The fact is that nationalism is a powerful force throughout the world which might readily be converted by a dynamic leader to support for a fascist outlook in almost any nation.

IX. Economic Aspects of the Contemporary Situation

The distribution of wealth and the ways in which public funds are spent have an impact on the problem of war in various ways. The manner in which the goods of the earth are distributed among the various nations raises a question of justice at the international level. The maldistribution of wealth within nations has implications for the possibility of war within countries. The cost of war preparations is another economic aspect of the contemporary situation which must be examined. Both at the international level and within countries, the rich use violence to keep the poor from changing the social order and the poor use violence to try to take power from the rich.

The Rich and the Poor among the Nations

A widely-used distinction in international economics is that between the economically developed countries and those that are less developed. To say that a country is developed means that it has a large number of labor-saving machines for the production of goods and services. Labor-saving devices have the effect of increasing the productivity of the workers in the society. The more the machine does, the more can be accomplished by one worker using this machine. Consequently, less developed countries with few machines will have a much lower level of production per person, resulting in a much lower average income compared to that of the developed countries. Experience indicates that less developed countries also have lower literacy rates, higher birth rates, less readily available clean water, and a much larger proportion of the population engaged in agricultural production than the developed countries. In general the developed countries consist of the European nations plus the U.S., Canada, Japan, Australia, New Zealand, and Israel while the countries of Africa, Asia, and Latin America are less developed countries. Lists of the developed countries usually include 25 to 30 countries[1] while the other 130 or so countries of the world are considered to be less developed countries.

One of the most significant facts about the world today is the extremely wide gap between the material conditions of life in the developed countries compared to those in the less developed countries. From time to time we hear of thousands of people starving to death in some Asian or African country. These people starve not because of a shortage of food in the world but because they have no money with which to pay for food.

No one with money starves to death. The basic problem is the distribution of wealth in the world. The 1979 per capita GNP[2] was $15,623 in Switzerland, $12,157 in Sweden, and $10,554 in the United States while it was only $131 in Ethiopia, $109 in Bangladesh and $99 in Laos.[3] These figures indicate that the average income level in the three developed countries mentioned is over 100 times greater than that in the three less developed countries cited. In the developed countries as a whole the 1979 per capita GNP was $7,698 while for the less developed countries as a group it was $730,[4] a ratio of greater than 10 to 1.

How does it happen that some countries are developed and others are not? The answer requires a review of the events of history. In the fourteenth century there was little difference in the standard of living among the various nations of Europe, Asia, and northern Africa, but by the middle of the nineteenth century there were vast differences. The change came as a result of the industrial revolution, the making of machines to help people do their work. The industrial revolution itself was the result of increasing scientific knowledge about how nature works, coupled with a desire to use this knowledge of nature to serve the goals of people; it started in Great Britain. To explain precisely why it started in Britain would involve dealing with a complicated combination of factors including the distribution of easily extracted raw materials, the existence of certain kinds of political structures, the history of religious and philosophical thought in the various parts of the world, and so on. From Britain the practice of using machines for production spread to northern continental Europe and North America, then to the rest of Europe, Oceania, and Japan. It is now in the process of spreading throughout the whole world.

To better understand the present gap between the rich countries and the poor countries, one must focus attention on what happened from the beginning of the eighteenth century through the middle of the twentieth century. During this period the newly-industrialized countries of Europe, especially Britain and France, were able to use their superior machines of war to bring areas in America, Africa, and Asia under their control. The colonies of the European countries shipped agricultural products and raw materials for industry back to Europe. After the raw materials were converted into manufactured goods, these goods were sold by the colonizing nations to their own people and to other countries. Such sales provided the money for new investment in more machines to make more goods. The activities of gathering raw materials, making goods, selling the goods, and reinvesting in more machinery was all under the control of the leaders of the industrialized nations, and they profited immensely from such an arrangement.

In Africa and Asia this process usually included political control by the European nations coupled with special training and privileges for the native people who assisted them, but in Latin America a slightly different kind of development took place. The United States, having originally been a colony itself, was opposed to the practice of outright political control over other nations. As a result of its readiness to guarantee the safety of any foreign investments in Latin America, the U.S. was able to keep European nations from exercising political control over any land in the Americas except for Canada and a few small colonies. As a result of its policy of protection, however, the U.S. was forced to establish a new kind of nonpolitical control over Latin America. Latin Americans were thus allowed to control their own countries politically as long as they permitted the foreign investors to operate without interference. The foreign investors established corporations to mine raw materials or to grow agricultural products for sale in the United States or Europe. The aim was to make as much profit as possible, and there was little concern about the impact that the money-making might have on the local population. Latin American political leaders who did not cooperate were replaced by others who did. Apart from the absence of actual foreign political control, this American system of *neoimperialism* was not very different from the more traditional *imperialism* exercised by the European countries over their colonies.

It might be asked why the big businesses operating out of the developed countries didn't build factories in the new colonial areas. One reason is that making manufactured items requires skilled persons to run the machines, and these skills were not possessed by the people in the colonial areas. The native peoples could have been taught these skills, however, if the desire to do so had been present, but it wasn't. The colonizing countries wanted to protect their own industries and the jobs of their own people. Consequently they established tariffs against finished products made in other countries but not against the importation of raw materials from overseas. Entrepreneurs who invested overseas could make money as long as they sent raw materials to the homeland, but if they tried to send finished goods they would find that the tariffs would make those finished goods too expensive to be marketable in the homeland. Thus the tariff arrangements discouraged the industrialization of the colonies while furthering the industrialization of the colonizing powers. The developed countries became more developed while the undeveloped nations remained undeveloped. The situation began to change somewhat only after World War II, when most of the former colonies won their political independence.

Approaches to Economic Development

What can the less developed countries do to move toward becoming developed countries? Three alternative models for development are available: the capitalistic or conventional approach, the socialistic or radical approach, and the cooperative approach. Regardless of the model to be followed, there are two basic problems: how to get the machines that will increase productivity, and how to develop the know-how to use and repair the machines, market the products, and so on.

The *capitalistic approach* to economic development assumes that the capital for buying needed machinery will be in the hands of private persons or corporations, mostly in the rich countries. The problem for the leaders of a less developed country following this approach becomes one of getting those with money to invest in their country rather than in some other country. The solution is to give investors what they want, including healthy profits, security of investment, and freedom to operate as they desire. When investors are assured that a country will provide these things, they will build the factories needed for development. They will bring the machinery and the highly skilled people needed to manage the factories and market the products, and they will teach the local population how to run and repair the machines. People will be employed and will be paid wages much higher than they could have earned otherwise. The government can tax some of these wages for public improvements, and what is spent in the marketplace will provide jobs for others in the society. Economic development will be on its way.

There are, of course, some difficulties for this capitalistic approach. The healthy profits that the investors make are for the most part taken out of the country. Any inclination to impose a substantial tax on these profits conflicts with the fact that investors dislike much of their profits taken away in the form of taxes. If the less developed country requires that a certain proportion of the profits be reinvested in that country, the danger becomes that the foreign investors may soon control a good deal of that nation's economy. Providing security for the private investors may require strict government controls on those within the society who might advocate the take-over of all foreign investments by the national government. Giving these firms freedom to operate as they desire also means refraining from passing laws about safe working conditions or pollution controls or the rights of workers to organize unions. These companies may also require the government to provide services such as transportation facilities, water supply, waste removal, and educated workers. In agriculture, foreign investors may buy land and use it to grow crops for export to richer countries while many of that poor country's population starve. Furthermore, the foreign investors may concentrate on capital-intensive rather than labor-intensive production, thus providing a minimum number of jobs for people in the less developed country.

The Japanese developed a unique version of the capitalist model which eliminated the need to attract investment from outside the country. The key move was the government's persuading those who held large areas of land to trade that land to the government in exchange for governmental administrative positions or for bonds which would mature many years later. This land was then given to those who worked it, who in return paid taxes to the government. The government then used this money to build factories devoted to those kinds of industry which could not attract private capital. As these government-sponsored industries became profitable, they were sold, often to the former landowners in exchange for the bonds. Thus many of the old aristocracy became members of the new capitalist class. In most less developed countries those who own large amounts of land are so wealthy that they are reluctant to see any social changes take place, but the Japanese approach succeeded in moving the elite into positions of leadership in an industrialized society with little risk to them during the transition. The Japanese model, with local modifications, has also had some success in Taiwan and South Korea.

Another possible source of capital for countries following the capitalistic approach is borrowing from other countries, from foreign banks, and from international development banks such as the International Bank for Reconstruction and Development (the World Bank) and its related organizations, the International Finance Corporation which loans to private enterprise projects and the International Development Association which provides interest-free loans to the poorest of the poor countries. To get these loans, however, the countries and individuals involved must abide by strict regulations. In some situations less developed countries are so deeply in debt that the foreign lending organizations come to control the economic policy for the whole country. The country may complain that it has lost some of its sovereignty, but the lending organizations refuse to give any further financial assistance until specified conditions are met.

The *socialistic approach* to economic development assumes that the needed capital for industrialization will come from within the country and that the investment in new machinery will be made by the government itself. Foreign investment and loans from outside the country are viewed as invitations to foreign meddling and foreign control. The problem for the leaders of a less developed country following the socialistic approach becomes one of finding money in a society where most people are very poor. One device is to confiscate land and other available wealth, especially things owned by foreigners or the very rich within the country. Another is to control the whole economy with the aim of producing a minimum amount of consumer goods so that a good share of the available wealth can be used to build factories and produce machines. The need to cut back on the production of consumer goods is summarized in the expression that "one generation must be sacrificed" for the sake of economic development. Production is to be guided by what is most needed for the long-term welfare of the society as a whole rather than the short-term needs of individuals. The socialistic approach also requires putting a substantial proportion of the society's wealth into education so that people will learn how to read and to build, use, and repair various kinds of machines.

There are, of course, also some difficulties for this socialistic approach. Those people from whom things have been confiscated will certainly be upset. If they live in other countries, the governments of those countries will exert pressure for payment for the confiscated property. If they are natives, they will feel a continuing resentment toward the government. In fact, governments embarking on the socialist path have little choice but to chase out, kill, or imprison substantial numbers of their own well-to-do citizens from whom they have confiscated property. Furthermore, they will probably need to adopt harsh policies toward the whole population for some time because there will likely be a great many who dislike being part of a "sacrificed" generation. Another difficulty for nations which choose the socialistic path is acquiring those things which they can't produce for themselves. This problem will be much more severe for small countries than for large countries such as the Soviet Union and China. If a country has confiscated property from citizens of many other nations, difficulties may arise when it tries to trade with these other nations. It can perhaps trade with other socialist countries, but if it becomes very dependent on them it risks falling under their domination.

A third approach to economic development is the *cooperative approach*. The basic assumption of this approach is that the less developed countries must work together to change the international pattern of economic relationships which have been carried over from the colonial era. It is claimed that the poorer countries of the world must bargain collectively with the richer countries just as workers bargain collectively to get the best terms they can from an employer. The problem for the less developed countries is how to get the developed countries to pay attention to their demands. One forum used in this way is the General Assembly of the United Nations. In 1974 at a Special Session of the General Assembly, a Declaration of the Establishment of a New International Economic Order was adopted. Since then other meetings have been held, but little progress has been made in restructuring the international economy.

What the less developed countries want is nondiscriminatory and possibly even preferential treatment with regard to tariffs and restrictions on the manufactured goods they export to the developed countries, a reserve system to stabilize the prices of the raw materials they sell to the developed countries, renegotiation of the terms of their huge debts, regular multilateral foreign assistance from the developed countries amounting to .7 percent of their GNP, a greater voice in making the rules for the world's monetary system, and some internationally-approved restrictions on the practices of transnational corporations.[5]

One success story for the cooperative approach is the action of the Organization of Petroleum Exporting Countries (OPEC), which at the end of 1973 succeeded in quadrupling the price of crude oil in the world market. By working together some of the less developed countries were able to greatly increase the amount they received from the developed countries for the petroleum they export. Efforts by the less developed countries to raise the price on other raw materials in the same manner by formation of producer cartels have so far not been very successful, and recently OPEC itself has suffered from disagreements among the members.

The main difficulty for the cooperative approach is that the developed countries can and do act together to thwart the efforts of the less developed countries to gain more influence in the international marketplace. Although OPEC gave the less developed countries a temporary psychological lift, the developed countries are now in a much stronger position in negotiations because they have succeeded in stockpiling huge amounts of petroleum, dampening future threats from OPEC. The poor countries need what the rich countries have more than the rich countries need what the poor countries have. Even the suggestion that the poorer countries trade more with each other is not very promising, since the developed countries have the technologically advanced goods which the poorer countries can't provide for themselves. The main hope for the co-operative approach is that more rich countries will respond, as the Scandanavian countries have, on the basis of humanitarian concerns.

There is one other hope for a less developed country: that oil should be discovered in its territory. The oil-rich countries have that crucial ingredient for development, money to buy machinery and educate their citizenry. For example, the government share of the revenue from oil in Saudi Arabia at one time amounted to a million dollars every 15 minutes.[6] Recently the price of oil has dropped, and the amount of oil available to other oil-exporting countries is not nearly so great, but still oil provides the money that allows some of these less developed countries to look to the future with some optimism.

The Bleak Outlook for the Poorer Countries

Most of the poor countries of the world have no oil, however, so their futures do not look very promising. To see more clearly the situation facing most of the less developed countries, consider some mathematical calculations comparing a developed country (DC) which now has a per capita GNP of $5,000 with a less developed country (LDC) which now has a per capita GNP of $500.[7]

Suppose that in a given year the DC and the LDC each manage to increase their per capita GNP by 5 percent, a figure which represents a good increase for the DC and a very good one for the LDC, especially in view of the fact that the population growth rate would probably be somewhat greater in the LDC. A 5 percent increase for the DC means that on the average each person in the DC has had a standard of living increase of $250 (5 percent of $5,000) while a 5 percent increase for the LDC means that the average income increased from $500 to $525, an increase of only $25 (5 percent of $500). Thus the *absolute gain* in terms of more income would be ten times greater in the DC even though the *percentage gain* is the same in both countries. In order to increase the income of its citizens by $250 the LDC would need to experience an unheard-of 50 percent increase in per capita GNP. Because the per capita GNP is already so low in the LDC even high percentage gains in productivity mean little gain in terms of actual additional income.

The second calculation is based on the supposition that the DC makes absolutely no gain whatever in per capita GNP year after year while the LDC gains at the healthy rate of 5 percent a year. Even making these totally unrealistic suppositions, how long would it take the LDC to achieve a per capita GNP equal to that of the DC? The first year the LDC's per capita GNP would go from $500 to $525. The second year it would go from $525 to $551.25. At the end of ten years it would be $814.46. At the end of 25 years it would be $1,693.18. Finally, after 47.5 years the LDC would have a per capita GNP equal to the DC's present $5,000 per year!

The third calculation is based on suppositions that are a bit more realistic but still very implausible. It reflects what might happen *if* the developed countries accepted the full implementation of the program of the New International Economic Order. Let us suppose that the DC's per capita GNP increases at only 2.5 percent a year while the LDC's goes up 5 percent a year. Under these conditions, how long would it take for the LDC's per capita GNP to match that of the DC? During the 47.5 years that it took the LDC to go from $500 per year to $5,000 per year, the DC's per capita GNP would have increased from $5,000 per year to over $16,000 per year. Altogether it would be 96 years before the LDC would catch up to the DC at a per capita GNP of over $53,000 per year!

As indicated, the last two calculations are based on very unrealistic suppositions. The *absolute gap* between the average income in the developed countries and that in the less developed countries will almost surely continue to widen. There is even a good chance that the *percentage increase* each year will be greater for the developed countries than for the less developed ones (except for those with oil to export) because the richer countries will not need to contend with the large population increases facing most of the poorer countries. In addition, they will probably continue to control the terms of international trade in accord with their own interests and continue to be very niggardly with regard to assisting the less developed countries. Since 1960 the gap in per capita GNP between the developed countries and the less developed countries has continued to widen,[8] and unless something quite unexpected and different occurs, this gap will continue to grow.[9]

It is a grim picture for the poorer nations. Even if they get the New International Economic Order for which they are working, it will be at least 50 years before they can expect to approximate the standard of living which now exists in the developed world and at least another 50 before they would near equality with the ever-increasing standard of living of the developed countries. Actually the time period would be longer for many countries. In our calculations we have used an LDC with a $500 per capita GNP in 1979 as an example, but there are several LDC's with per capita GNP's under $200. Also, it is very unlikely that much of the New International Economic Order will be implemented.

Furthermore, there are two other significant issues. First, we have been discussing *income* levels rather than *wealth*. In developed countries there are many things such as roads and bridges and public buildings which were built in the past and go on adding to the quality of life even though they are not reflected in data about present levels of income. Second, if the LDC's increased their per capita GNP even halfway to the current level of the DC's, from where would come the raw materials and resources to provide for higher levels of consumption? Depletion of both the renewable and nonrenewable resources of the planet now seems to be an urgent problem even if no one's material standard of living is increased.[10] This very fact may make the developed countries even less willing to assist in any very positive way with the development problems of the less developed countries. The outlook for poorer nations is indeed bleak.[11]

The Distribution of Wealth within the Nations

The very uneven distribution of income among the various nations of the world vividly raises the question of justice. No one chooses where he will be born; yet the very fact of being born one place rather than another makes a tremendous difference in whether one will face a lifetime of starvation or live in abundance. A similar uneven distribution of income and wealth occurs within nations and similarly raises the question of justice since no one chooses the family into which he will be born. There may be individual Horatio Alger cases where a person from a poor family becomes wealthy because of special talents or special breaks (just as a less developed country may suddenly learn it has rich deposits of petroleum), but there is no doubt that in general persons born into wealthy families can expect a much different kind of life from those born into poor families even within the same nation.

There are two common ways of measuring the amount of inequality of income or wealth within a group. One is to compare the proportion of the total income or wealth of the society belonging to the richest fifth of the population with the proportion of the total income or wealth of the poorest fifth. A ratio can be determined by taking the percentage of the total belonging to the top fifth divided by the percentage of the total belonging to the bottom fifth. The smaller this ratio, the more equally distributed is the income or wealth of that group. As a specific example, in the United States in 1970 the richest fifth of the population received 38.8 percent of the income while the poorest fifth received 6.7 percent of the income.[12] By dividing 38.8 by 6.7 we get a ratio of 5.79 to 1 as the ratio between what the richest fifth get and what the poorest fifth get. That is, the richest fifth get 5.79 times as much as the poorest fifth. For another example, in Ecuador in 1970 the richest fifth of the population received 73.5 percent of the income while the poorest fifth received only 2.5 percent of the income.[13] By dividing 73.5 by 2.5 we get a ratio of 29.4 to 1. Comparing the figures of 5.79 to 1 and 29.4 to 1 reveals that the distribution of income in the United States is much more nearly equal than it is in Ecuador. Here are the ratios for the income of the top fifth to the income of the bottom fifth in some other countries based on various studies done between 1963 and 1970[14]:

	Share of income to richest fifth	Share of income to poorest fifth	Ratio of top fifth to bottom fifth
Kenya	68.0	3.8	17.90 to 1
Mexico	64.0	4.0	16.00 to 1
Egypt	47.0	4.2	11.19 to 1
India	52.0	5.0	10.40 to 1
Japan	43.8	4.6	9.52 to 1
Sweden	42.5	5.4	7.87 to 1
West Germany	45.6	5.9	7.73 to 1
South Korea	45.0	7.0	6.43 to 1
Hungary	33.5	8.5	3.94 to 1
East Germany	30.7	10.4	2.95 to 1

It may be noted that Communistic societies which aim for a greater equalization of income apparently achieve that goal.

Another way of indicating the degree of inequality in the distribution of income or wealth in a group is a graph called the Lorenz curve.[15] Such a graph looks like this:

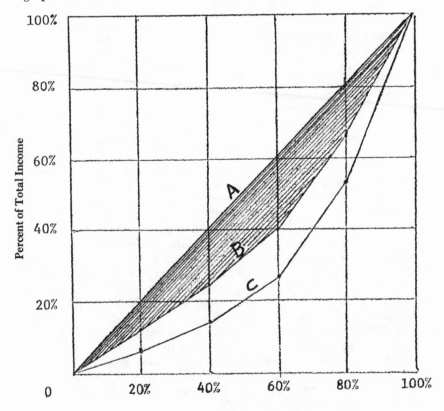

Percent of Total Population

Diagonal line A indicates how the income would be divided if there were absolute equality. That is, the poorest 20 percent of the people would have 20 percent of the income, the poorest 40 percent of the people would have 40 percent of the income, the poorest 60 percent of the people would have 60 percent of the income, and so on. Curve B represents a society in which there is a moderate amount of inequality. The shaded area between line A and line B indicates the amount of inequality in that society. Curve C represents a society in which there is a great deal of inequality. As can readily be seen, the area between line A and line C is much greater than the area between line A and line B, reflecting a greater amount of inequality in the society represented by line C.

Using data which have been collected and processed in accord with the two approaches described above, what generalizations can be made about the distribution of income and the distribution of wealth within nations and among the nations of the world? First, the distribution of *income* tends to be more equal than the distribution of *wealth*.[16] Wealth is accumulated over the years while income refers to only one year. Even if less developed countries can bring their per capita GNP (which represents *income*) up to the level of the developed countries, the developed countries will have an accumulation of goods from the past that will still not be matched. The same thing is true of a newly-rich family as compared to a family that has had a high income over a period of time. The second family's high income year after year has been used to accumulate wealth which cannot be readily matched by a family that has only recently begun to receive a large income.

A second generalization is that the distribution of income tends to be more unequal in less developed countries than in developed ones. As we have noted, in developed countries the ratio between the income of the top fifth and the bottom fifth tends to range between 3 to 1 and 10 to 1, while in the less developed countries it tends to range between 10 to 1 and 30 to 1. Lorenz curves also show that the inequality in income in Sri Lanka and India is greater than the inequality in the U.S., Great Britain, and Sweden.[17] It must be remembered, of course, that a tendency is not an absolute rule. There are individual differences among both developed and less developed countries, and certain less developed ones may have more equal distribution of income than some more developed ones.[18]

A third observation is that the distribution of income among the nations of the world is even more unequal than the most unequal distribution of income among families in any country. When nations are ranked with regard to per capita GNP, in 1980 the richest fifth of the world's population had a per capita GNP of $7,690 while the poorest fifth had only $170.[19] That means that the ratio of the richest fifth to the poorest fifth of the world's population is *45 to 1*. Furthermore, the poorest *half* of the world's population gets only 8 percent of the world's income.[20] Construction of a Lorenz curve also demonstrates clearly that the inequality of distribution of income for the world as a whole is much greater than that in less developed countries such as India.[21]

It is certainly not to be assumed that absolute equality of income and wealth would necessarily be a good thing. The point is merely that there are vast inequalities in wealth and income both within nations and among nations and that such inequalities undoubtedly mean inequalities of opportunity for children of different families as well as for children of different nations. If it is believed that these inequalities are due merely to the accidents of history and that they can't be rectified under the existing social order, then there will be resentment and a readiness to use violence to try to change that social order. This desire to change the status quo will be present whether the social order which is perceived to be unjust exists within a nation or among the nations of the world. As more and more poor people within nations and in the world as a whole become capable of reading and learn about their own situations, we can expect this desire for change to become a more and more significant force in social affairs.

Military Expenditures, Social Needs, and Foreign Aid

Another economic aspect of the contemporary situation concerns the amount of public funds being spent for military purposes compared with the amount being used to alleviate poverty and meet the needs of the poor. This matter was mentioned briefly in the first chapter.

Since the poorer countries have massive problems of illiteracy and poor health and a great need to invest for economic development, and since they have no hope of competing militarily with the developed countries, one might expect to find undeveloped countries putting most of their scarce public funds into nonmilitary endeavors. Some less developed countries that are not involved in confrontations with their neighbors are following such a policy. Less developed countries which year after year are devoting .5 percent or less of their GNP to military expenditures are Barbados, Botswana, Costa Rica, Fiji, Gambia, Lesotho, Mauritius, Surinam, and Trinidad and Tobago.[22] The usual amount of military expenditures for countries not having conflicts with their neighbors is 1 to 2 percent of GNP. Less developed countries engaged in confrontations with their neighbors, however, have much higher military expenditures. In the Middle East, Syria, Iraq, and Iran are spending up to 16 percent of their GNP for the military while Israel's military expenditure is 20 to 38 percent of its GNP. Oil-rich countries are especially fortunate in terms of having money for economic development, but many are putting large amounts of their new wealth into the military. For example, Saudi Arabia is devoting over 16 percent of its GNP to military expenditures while the figure for Oman is 36 percent. The less developed countries as a group in 1979 spent $112.4 billion representing 4.6 percent of their gross product on the military while their collective public expenditures for education amounted to only $89.2 billion and for health to only $37.3 billion.[23] Thus in these countries as a group the military got 26 percent more money than did education and over three times as much as health. This is not a happy situation when the need for public education and public health is so great.

But one can hardly blame the less developed countries for wanting strong military forces. They are merely following in the steps of the developed nations, who in 1979 as a group spent $365.6 billion representing 4.52 percent of their combined GNP's on the military.[24] At the same time these developed countries gave only $24.3 billion or three-tenths of one percent of their combined GNP's for assistance to the less developed countries,[25] a figure which could have tripled had only a little over 13 percent of military spending been diverted to foreign aid. Developed countries are reluctant to give money to the LDC's on grounds that these funds could be invested in their own economies for further growth, but the same could be said of the money spent on the military. On the other hand, the point about shifting funds from the military to development also applies to the LDC's. If these poorer countries use their limited resources for military purposes, then why should the DC's cut military spending to increase foreign aid to the LDC's?

In discussing the matter of foreign aid from DC's to LDC's, we should also note that the Soviet Union and its satellites have consistently refused to extend much foreign assistance to the less developed countries[26] on grounds that the present plight of these countries is due to exploitation by the capitalistic nations, a situation in which the Communist nations supposedly played no part. In response it could be argued that the assistance from many nations, such as Sweden and Norway, can hardly be considered reparations and that the aim of aid is to help the LDC's for the future rather than to repay them for damages in the past. It could also be noted that East Germany would seem to be just as obliged to pay reparations as West Germany. If the East Germans complain that it was not they but rather a different government of Germany that exploited these less developed nations, then the West Germans and others could make the same plea. Also the Chinese have claimed time and again that imperialist Czarist Russia took lands from them that the Soviets have refused to give back. The less developed countries are beginning to make more of an effort to get the Communists to join with the other developed countries in giving some help to the poorer nations of the world.

A good test of the values of both nations and individuals is how they spend their money. The patterns of expenditure by national governments suggest that most national leaders are more interested in military power than in improving the condition of life for large numbers of people. In the poorer countries especially the resentment continues to build when this occurs. It is hard for mothers and fathers to see their children starving, dying from lack of medical care, or growing up without learning to read. They become angry when they learn that their children wouldn't need to suffer if only a small portion of what is being spent for military purposes was instead used to meet the human needs of the poorer people of the world. This situation should also arouse the indignation of those whose own children are not suffering to the same extent (though their own children may also be short-changed in part because of military spending). Even those without children may be moved to question the priorities presently being pursued by most government leaders.[27]

Economic Conditions and the War Problem

How are the economic conditions we have been discussing related to the war problem? How might the conflict of interests between those in control and those who feel oppressed break out into open violence? One possibility is that the wealthy may use open violence against the poor if the poor seem to be making too many gains by nonviolent means. A second possibility is that the poor will conduct guerrilla warfare, terrorism, or some other type of nonconventional war against those in power. Let us consider these possibilities as they relate to the international scene and to the situation within countries.

The possibility of war by the rich against the poor on the international scene almost became a reality in 1974. The previously-noted success of OPEC in quadrupling the price of crude oil at the end of 1973 was doubtless a blow to Western Europe, Japan, and the U.S. The U.S. in particular considered a military attack to take over the oil fields in countries such as Saudi Arabia and the United Arab Emirates. These countries had virtually no military forces to resist such an attack. The overt use of violence was a real possibility.

Why didn't the rich countries use their superior military forces to take over the oil fields? Cynics might say that it was because the Western-based oil companies also stood to profit immensely from the price hike, but this suggestion overlooks the fact that many other influential Western-based businesses suffered greatly from the higher prices. This reply also ignores the more significant fact that a complete military takeover would have been even more profitable for the Western oil companies. It could be argued that there was fear that the Soviet Union would intervene to halt a takeover, but the Russians were not in a position to stop such action. They would have been risking an all-out war over a struggle which, from their point of view, was merely a battle between one group of capitalists and another. It might be argued that the Arabs would have blown up the equipment and pipelines, but it would not take long to repair the damage and start the oil flowing again. From an economic point of view, a quick military takeover would have been cheaper for the U.S. than all the extra payments made for oil since the price hike.

So why was there no attack? The lack of a military response seems in large part due to public opinion in the developed countries. It should not be forgotten that the U.S. had just experienced large-scale protests concerning its involvement in Vietnam. Some experts in international relations may not like to admit it, but it seems that in this situation moral considerations influenced public policy. The governments of the Western countries were constrained by the fact that many of their own people would view a military takeover of the oil-rich countries as wrong, as a violation of the principle that the possessions of other nations should not be taken by brute force. Such open international thievery would have made a mockery of the basic notion in Western democratic political theory that force should be restrained by law. Cynics may say that morals don't influence politics and that the policies of democratic national governments are no more moral than those of totalitarian governments, but this striking example from recent history suggests otherwise. This development should also provide some hope to the less developed countries that public opinion in the Western democracies may to some extent restrain these powerful governments in their dealings with weaker, poorer nations.

Nevertheless, there is no guarantee that public opinion will always act as much of a restraint on international policy. Public opinion shifts rapidly, and a short war with a quick victory is not likely to meet with much opposition. Consequently, it is always possible that the poorer nations will find themselves being attacked militarily if they adopt policies which are too damaging to the rich countries.

The use of violence by those in control can also occur within nations when the poor are making too many gains by nonviolent means. A classic case of this occurred in Chile. Salvador Allende was elected in 1970 and began instituting a socialist program. In 1973 he was overthrown by a military coup which aimed to protect the interests of the rich, including foreigners with investments in Chile. This incident is not unique, but in most situations the poor do not get so far before being repressed. The elite are able to exercise control by using government powers to arrest, imprison, or otherwise silence anyone who might in the future threaten them. This small-scale "authorized" violence is carried out against individuals and small groups before their followers become numerous enough to constitute one side in a war. Nevertheless this use of force to prevent peaceful change often serves as a stimulus to the use of violence to overthrow the existing government.

The use of violence by those not in power is the second way that the current economic situation is relevant to the war problem. Since those who control the reins of government usually have sophisticated weapons and well-paid professional military forces, those out of power are not likely to be able to challenge them successfully in a traditional military confrontation. They need to resort to nonconventional efforts. An unlikely possibility might be hidden nuclear weapons or secret biological weapons which can be used to blackmail the richer countries into giving more economic assistance to the poorer ones; a more likely approach is the use of guerrilla warfare. Guerrilla warfare is fought by ideologically-motivated citizen-soldiers who use violence in unanticipated settings with the ultimate aim of overthrowing the existing social order.[28] Guerrillas seek not the control of territory but rather the commitment of more persons to the support of their antigovernment activities. They may assassinate or terrorize those in power, but they also engage in acts of sabotage which are likely to produce more government repression and in turn motivate more people to join their struggle. Guerrillas hope eventually to generate enough support to create a regular army capable of defeating the forces of the government.

On the international level guerrilla warfare frequently takes the form of a "war of liberation" to force a colonial power to allow a former colony to become an independent nation. Such wars have been fought in Algeria, Vietnam, Indonesia, and Angola, to name but a few instances of the many which have taken place since the end of World War II. In these situations the guerrilla fighters appeal not only to concerns for economic justice but also to feelings of national pride. The people can readily understand that the guerrillas are helping them to get rid of foreign rulers. Efforts by the colonial power to repress the guerrillas often help the guerrillas by giving them what they most need: more recruits to their movement. Such efforts are also likely to end up providing the guerrillas with more arms, since their major source of military equipment is usually what they can steal or capture from their opponents. Of course, the guerrillas are often also able to acquire arms in the international market or from other national governments which would like to see their revolutions succeed.

When we turn to the situation where the aim of the guerrilla movement is the overthrow not of a foreign colonial power but a native national government, there is no longer a nationalistic component in the struggle. The ideological aspect of the conflict becomes central. As we have noted, in less developed countries there is usually a wide gap between what the rich have and what the poor have, and the government typically strives to preserve this situation. Thus the guerrillas can usually count on support from much of the population, especially in rural areas. The leaders of the government, however, are in a position to use both coercion and enticement to try to get the people to help them against the guerrillas. Consequently the guerrilla fighters must be able to persuade the people that the chances of overthrowing the present government are good and that life will be much better if the guerrillas are successful.

It should be evident that the distribution of wealth within a society is directly related to the phenomenon of guerrilla warfare. The guerrilla fighter sees himself as a social reformer in a situation where peaceful change seems impossible. Public support for guerrillas is based on sympathy with that outlook. As more and more people become educated about the society in which they live, as they come to know more about the great differences in wealth which exist and the role of government in maintaining them, we can expect that there will be more and more guerrilla warfare unless governments become much more sensitive to the needs of the poor.

X. Military Aspects of the Contemporary Situation

When nations confront each other in war, military power determines the outcome. Economic power, technological capability, size of population, and morale of the people are relevant only in so far as they can be converted into military power. Military power depends on military leadership, the quality and quantity of the personnel in the armed forces, and, most importantly, on the weaponry available. Our discussion of military power will focus on this last ingredient.

The Post-World War II Struggle for Power

The end of World War II in 1945 left two major powers with strong military forces: the United States and the Soviet Union. The Americans were in a much stronger position than the Russians, having come through the war without any destruction to their homeland and also having developed the first atomic bombs. The Russians, on the other hand, had lost 9 percent of their population during the war, and the most densely populated part of their country had served as a battlefield for a couple of years. The U.S. was eager to forget war and bring its troops back home, but the Soviet Union under Stalin's leadership maintained some military forces to ensure that the newly-established governments of Eastern Europe would be friendly to Communist Russia. Although it may seem that the possession of nuclear weapons by the U.S. could have allowed American President Truman to be particularly tough in dealing with the Russians, it should be remembered that the Soviets and Americans had worked together against the Nazis, so Americans tended to think of the Russians as friends. Furthermore, in 1945 the U.S. had built only three atomic bombs, one by one, and the last two had been dropped on Hiroshima and Nagasaki.[1] Thus no atomic bombs were available to use against the Russians had war broken out. It is unlikely, however, that the Russians or anyone else except the highest American officials knew this.

Russian efforts to create a buffer of friendly governments in Eastern Europe and American efforts to spread Western-style democracy throughout the world soon came into conflict in Poland, Czechoslovakia, Hungary, Greece, Turkey, and conquered Germany. A Communist coup d'état in Czechoslovakia plus a Russian move to cut off Western access to Berlin led to the creation of the North Atlantic Treaty Organization by the Western nations to prevent any further Communist expansion.

The Soviets responded by organizing the Communist-controlled nations of Eastern Europe into the Warsaw Pact, and the existence of a cold war between West and East become obvious. In 1949 the unexpected detonation of an atomic device by the Russians and the takeover of China by Mao's Communist forces added to American fears of further expansion by the Communists. The U.S. detonated a thermonuclear device (a hydrogen bomb) in November of 1952, and the Russians followed with theirs in August of 1953. In 1957 the Russians successfully tested an intercontinental ballistic missile and launched an artificial satellite called "sputnik." These events greatly shocked Americans who for the most part had assumed that American technology was vastly superior to that of the Russians. Three months later Americans launched a much smaller satellite, which Krushchev ridiculed as a "grapefruit." It had now become evident that these two opposing powers would soon be capable of attacking each other with nuclear weapons carried by long-range missiles.

Deterrence Theory

This situation where each side could directly attack the homeland of the other presented a new military situation. Imagine that you are responsible for the military defense of your nation. Previously, you could always protect your nation from attack by defensive military efforts. A protective buffer of other allied countries could be maintained, through which the enemy must proceed before striking, or there might be bodies of water which the enemy must cross before being able to inflict any damage on your homeland. You could count on having some time to launch a defensive effort against attacking enemy forces. Even if the enemy used airplanes, it was at least possible to try to shoot them down before they were able to drop bombs on your cities. With long-range missiles, however, everything was different. How could you hope to stop missiles which are guided to their targets by gravitational and inertial forces and which travel so fast that they can go a sixth of the way around the earth in half an hour? Furthermore, these missiles carry nuclear warheads. One hit could destroy a whole city! If the enemy fired 100 missiles and you could somehow destroy 90 percent of them, ten of your cities would still be demolished.

Although the notion of some kind of anti-missile missile enjoyed popularity for a time, the prevailing view came to be that there simply was no dependable defense against a missile attack. The only conceivable military strategy seemed to be to try to prevent such an attack in the first place. The aim became one of deterring the potential enemy from launching a missile attack by threatening a retaliatory attack of equal or greater magnitude. It was necessary to persuade the enemy that you had the capability to launch a retaliatory attack, even if he launched a surprise attack first, and also that you had the "guts" to do it after your strategy of deterring an attack had failed. Emphasizing a quick retaliatory attack meant that you needed radar units and spy-in-the-sky satellites to detect a missile attack by the enemy, not because anything could be done to stop the incoming missiles, but so that you would know when to launch your own missiles in return.

But the military must consider all the possibilities. What if the enemy were able somehow to knock out or neutralize your radar units and spy satellites? How could you protect your own missiles from destruction by a surprise attack? One solution would be to build hardened silos for your land-based missiles so they would not be destroyed except by a direct hit. Another solution would be to put at least some of your missiles aboard submarines so that the enemy would not know where they are. You might also keep some bombers carrying nuclear bombs in the air at all times so that they could respond to an attack which even wiped out your military airfields. With your own nuclear weapons thus protected, you would have what is called *second-strike capability*. That is, you could absorb a first strike by the enemy and still retaliate. You would desperately want to prevent a situation where an enemy could destroy all your own retaliatory capability. Thus, you want to be sure that the enemy does not acquire a *first-strike capability*. If the enemy were to develop systems which could defend against your bombers and detect the whereabouts of all your submarines while at the same time making his own missiles so accurate that they could score direct hits on your missile-launching silos, radar sites, and spy satellites, you would be in deep trouble. Still it would be difficult for the enemy to launch an attack so swiftly and with such a fine degree of accuracy and timing that you would have no chance to launch at least some missiles. Thus what would pose a particularly great threat to your capacity to retaliate would be the development by the enemy of a truly effective anti-missile weapon because then, even if you were able to launch several missiles in retaliation, he could knock them out before they did any damage.

The doctrine of deterrence through the threat of massive retaliation required that your own missiles be targeted on the enemy's population centers. The enemy theoretically would be deterred from making an attack for fear of suffering a tremendous number of casualties in return. But, asked the military, what if there were some type of limited military engagement and you wanted only one or two of your nuclear weapons to knock out a few of the enemy's military installations? Then you would want your missiles targeted on his missile sites and military bases rather than on his population centers. Such targeting represents what is called *counter-force* targeting as compared to *counter-population* targeting. The notion of limited nuclear war presumes that you could announce to the enemy that you are not launching a full-scale nuclear attack but are merely going to knock out one or two military bases. According to this way of thinking, you warn him that if he retaliates to your limited attack, an all-out attack will be staged in response. It is hard to see why the enemy would do anything but launch an all-out attack under these conditions,[2] but many military planners think otherwise and are considering various possible moves in a limited nuclear war. Consequently both Russians and Americans now have some of their missiles aimed at military targets while others remain targeted on population centers. The knowledge that some missiles are aimed at military targets which one might want to destroy in a so-called *surgical strike* increases the tension in the cold war because it suggests that such missiles might be used as part of a general first strike, while missiles aimed only at population centers are known to be destined for a retaliatory role.

At the present time there is still no reliable defense against ballistic missiles. Consequently, the U.S. and the U.S.S.R. each remain vulnerable to attack by the other. The use of hardened silos and submarine-based missiles means that both sides have a second strike capability against the other and that neither has a first-strike capability. Such a situation has a certain stability in it, but more than ten years ago it was realized that the development of an extensive, reliable anti-missile defense by either side would upset this stable situation. Consequently the U.S.S.R. and the U.S. agreed to limit their development and deployment of anti-missile missiles. This agreement was based in part on the fact that at that time such weapons didn't seem very promising anyway, but it was also motivated in part by a desire to maintain a situation in which each side is vulnerable to a retaliatory attack by the other. This arrangement is called *mutual assured destruction* or MAD. It must be agreed that there is a bit of madness in this type of international stability, for it is a balance of terror. Still the situation would become much more dangerous if either side should succeed in developing some type of effective anti-missile defense.

Coercive Diplomacy

Nuclear-tipped missiles sit in their silos or in their tubes in nuclear-powered submarines. The turn of two keys will send any of them on its way. One half hour later nuclear explosions will vaporize whole cities and leave radioactive clouds to be dissipated over the surface of the earth. Is it really believable that these nuclear weapons will ever be used?

Every once in a while the world is reminded that the missiles are there and might really be used. One particular occasion was the Cuban missile crisis of October 1962. Fidel Castro had established a Communist government in Cuba in 1959. An invasion attempt by non-Communist Cubans who had been chased off the island by Castro's forces had been launched from the U.S. in 1961 but had failed miserably. Apparently to discourage future U.S.-based invasion attempts, Castro and the Russians decided to install some Russian missiles in Cuba. U.S. reconnaissance flights spotted the building of the missile sites. The U.S. claimed that this presence of a non-American nation's military forces in the Americas was a violation of the long-established Monroe Doctrine, which stated that non-American nations should stay out of American affairs. The U.S. also succeeded in getting the Organization of American States to endorse this viewpoint. The Russians could have responded to American complaints by noting that the Monroe Doctrine is simply a U.S. pronouncement which is not international law, even if it had been endorsed by the U.S.-dominated Organization of American States. The Russians might have argued that Cuba was a sovereign state which could legitimately invite the Russians to put missiles on its soil if it wished to do so. Instead, when confronted with the American accusation, the Russians denied that they were installing missile bases in Cuba. At a dramatic meeting of the United Nations General Assembly, U.S. Ambassador Adlai Stevenson displayed aerial photos proving to the whole world that the Russians were liars. President Kennedy sent American ships to intercept the Russian ships bringing parts needed to complete the missile sites. The world held its breath as the Russian freighters neared the U.S. Navy ships. It seemed that a nuclear war might begin at any moment. But Khrushchev directed the Russian ships to turn back, and a nuclear holocaust was averted.

Why did Khrushchev direct the Russian ships to turn back? It may have been because the two nations had reached an understanding that the U.S. would not assist any further efforts to overthrow the Castro regime. There may also have been other factors, but an important consideration undoubtedly was the fact that at that time the U.S. had about a 5 to 1 superiority in the number of atomic weapons which could be delivered by long-range missiles and bombers. The Soviet Union had been coerced into ceasing its missile-building efforts in Cuba even though the Russians had some missiles capable of delivering atomic warheads onto U.S. cities. It was the overwhelming superiority of the U.S. in the quantity of available nuclear warheads and delivery systems which had been decisive.

As a result of this incident, the Russians were convinced that it was not sufficient to have some missiles with nuclear warheads which could strike the U.S. They began a massive missile-building effort and increased their defensive capabilities against U.S. bombers. It was the stimulus of the Cuban missile crisis and its outcome that led the Russians to conclude that military power was necessary not just for defense of the homeland but also for success in international bargaining. In an anarchic world a nation which is obviously second in military power will be coerced into accepting terms dictated by the nation which is first in military power. Since most American leaders also recognize the validity of this principle, unless something is done there will be a virtually unlimited arms race to develop ever more destructive weapons and a technological race to try to create some kind of defense against a missile attack.

Modern Nuclear Weaponry

Humankind's first weapons, the club, the spear, and the bow and arrow, could kill one person at a time. The invention of the exploding grenade in the fifteenth century meant that a single weapon might kill four or five persons at once. By the beginning of World War I in 1914, artillery shells and torpedoes made it possible for one weapon to kill 10 or 20 people at once, and by the end of that war a single shell from the Germans' "Big Bertha" cannon might kill 40. During World War II, the large bombs dropped by the Allies might kill 60 or 70 persons. But the atomic bomb dropped on Hiroshima at the end of World War II in 1945 killed at least 75,000 persons! The first thermonuclear bombs were 20 times as powerful as the Hiroshima bomb, and now some nuclear warheads are available which have more than 1,500 times the explosive power of that first nuclear bomb.[3] Since some of the explosive power will necessarily be wasted because of the physical principles involved in large explosions, it doesn't follow that these newer thermonuclear weapons would kill 1,500 times as many people, or even do 1,500 times as much damage, but there is little doubt that one of these superbombs could kill millions of people in a big city. In fact, atomic weapons generally are so powerful that the primary military problem has been how to make them smaller so that they won't be more destructive than desired.

There is no doubt that the quantity of nuclear warheads has grown steadily over the years even though secrecy makes it difficult to get exact numbers. It was not until the 1950's that nuclear warheads of many different sizes and kinds came rolling off the assembly lines. By 1960, the U.S. had 7,000 nuclear weapons in Europe.[4] In 1975 it was estimated that the U.S. had 8,000 nuclear warheads on its strategic (long-range) weapons and at least 22,000 on its tactical weapons.[5] During the period 1971–1976 the U.S. was building 100 new nuclear warheads a month for strategic weapons.[6] The Soviet Union was estimated to have 5,000 nuclear warheads on its strategic weapons alone at the end of 1978.[7] Since the U.S. has approximately three nuclear warheads on tactical weapons for each one it has on strategic weapons, it is not unreasonable to assume that the Soviets have at least twice as many nuclear warheads on their tactical weapons as on their strategic weapons. Thus it can be estimated that at the end of 1978 the U.S. and the U.S.S.R. together had 45,000–50,000 nuclear warheads in their arsenals.[8] For the world total, one would need to add the nuclear warheads possessed by the British, French, and Chinese. There may also be a few in the hands of the Israelis and the South Africans. It seems almost certain that there are now at least 50,000 nuclear warheads in existence and that the number is growing.

Nuclear warheads are not particularly useful for military purposes, however, unless a nation has some means of delivering them to the target. It is the long-range bomber and the ballistic missiles as much as nuclear warheads which make today's military situation different from that of World War II. The first delivery system for nuclear warheads was the airplane. By 1948 the U.S. had bombers with intercontinental range. Then in 1957 came the Russian development of the intercontinental ballistic missile (ICBM). A ballistic missile is started on its way by a rocket engine which does not need oxygen from the atmosphere. The missile goes high above the atmosphere and then free falls onto its target; it is in effect a space shot which does not quite go into orbit. Since it goes so high, its launching is readily detectable by radar, but its speed is so great that the distance between the U.S.S.R. and the U.S. can be traversed in half an hour. The first intercontinental ballistic missiles were liquid-fueled, making it difficult to keep them ready for launching on a continuous basis, but before long they were equipped with solid propellants. Solid propellants also made it possible to develop submarine-launched ballistic missiles (SLBM's) which could be launched even while the submarine was submerged. Nuclear warheads have also been placed on artillery shells and bazooka rockets and developed for use as aerial bombs, depth charges, and demolition munitions.[9]

Eventually strategic missiles were armed with more than a single nuclear warhead. At first these separate warheads, launched by a single missile, simply separated a bit from each other while descending so that the target area would be sprayed with several warheads rather than a single one. Then a system was developed for guiding the separate warheads from a single missile onto different targets; that is, multiple independently-targetable reentry vehicles (MIRV's) were developed. The next step was to make the reentry vehicles maneuverable (MARV's) so they could evade anti-missile devices. The most recent developments relative to long-range ballistic missiles are the use of a mobile rather than a stationary launching pad for land-based missiles and the development of substantially increased accuracy.[10]

In the past few years we have also seen the development of cruise missiles. They differ considerably from ballistic missiles in that they depend on continuous power after launching until they strike their target. They are in fact pilotless jet aircraft with very small wings. Cruise missiles do not travel nearly as fast as ballistic missiles, but they can fly very close to the surface of the earth, a feature which makes them difficult to detect with radar. Thus they may give an enemy less time to respond than the much speedier ballistic missiles. Cruise missiles are also very maneuverable and can even be called back after they are part way to their target. In addition, they are smaller and much less expensive to build than ballistic missiles. Cruise missiles also pose a special problem for arms limitation agreements because they are much more easily concealed than ballistic missiles and because it is difficult (though perhaps not impossible) to distinguish between short-range and long-range versions of the weapon.[11]

Research and development on new weapons is proceeding in many areas. The range of submarine-launched ballistic missiles is steadily being extended. Both land-based and submarine-launched ballistic missiles are becoming much more accurate because of new guidance systems based on the use of more satellites, and the average number of warheads on each long-range missile is steadily increasing. Air-launched cruise missiles are being joined by sea-launched and ground-launched cruise missiles while ground-launched and submarine-launched ballistic missiles are being joined by ballistic missiles launched from airplanes. Neutron bombs which produce a great deal of deadly but short-lasting radiation have been developed for possible use against military forces, especially those inside armored vehicles such as tanks. Long-range bombers are being developed which because of their design and construction are very difficult to detect by radar. Efforts are underway to develop military uses for lasers and charged-particle beams, especially in the area of missile defense.[12] Modern military technology is truly awesome.

Changes in weaponry require changes in strategy too. For example, before long-range missiles were so accurate, it was feasible to harden ICBM launch-sites and expect that a substantial proportion of them could survive a nuclear attack by the enemy because they could be destroyed only by direct hits. This situation permitted a nation to wait until after an enemy's nuclear weapons actually exploded before launching a retaliatory attack. Now the situation has changed. If a nation waits that long, it may have very few land-based ICBM's left. Consequently, a new strategy is needed, namely, to launch missiles when a warning is received that the enemy has launched his. Since it takes only a half hour at most for the enemy missiles to strike a nation's launching sites, the response will need to be quick. But this situation substantially increases the likelihood of a nuclear war beginning by accident. What if the warning of an enemy attack turns out to be mistaken? Once ballistic missiles have been fired, it is impossible to call them back. But this possibility leads to another idea: Why not develop a system where your ballistic missiles boost the nuclear warheads into orbit so that they stay aloft until they are commanded to come down? Then a nation could launch missiles on warning without danger of starting a nuclear war by accident. If there is a mistake about an enemy attack, a space shuttle vehicle can retrieve the warheads from space.[13] Of course, such a system carries with it the imperative that the enemy not be able to interfere with commands to the orbiting warheads. Thus new strategies also require new technology.

Arms Control Agreements

The notion that arms races and the huge expenditures required to continue them might be controlled by an agreement between the adversaries is not new. The 1817 Rush-Bagot Agreement between the U.S. and Great Britain permitted each side only one lightly armed vessel on Lake Champlain, one on Lake Ontario, and two others on all the other Great Lakes together.[14] In 1902, Chile and Argentina entered in an agreement not to add any more battleships to their fleets and also to disarm and put in dock the three battleships which the two countries between them already possessed.[15] In 1905, Norway and Sweden agreed to establish a permanent demilitarized neutral zone along their border.[16] The Five Power Naval Limitation Treaty resulting from the Washington Conference of 1921–22 sets limits on the tonnage of capital ships and aircraft carriers establishing a ratio of 5 for Great Britain and the U.S., 3 for

Japan, and 1.67 for France and Italy. At the London Naval Conference of 1930 the same five nations agreed to observe a five-year moratorium on any further construction of battleships, and the first three nations signed an agreement setting limits on the strengths of each nation with regard to cruisers, destroyers, and submarines at the ratio of 10 for Great Britain and the U.S. to 7 for Japan. These naval agreements were observed until they expired in 1936.[17] The Geneva Protocol of 1925, which is still in effect, prohibits the use of poisonous gases and bacteriological warfare.

The success of these various arms agreements may be the reflection of other factors rather than an indication of what arms agreements can accomplish. Still, the evidence seems to indicate that if nations can work out arrangements which all involved view as advantageous to themselves, they will tend to observe their agreements. Furthermore, if nations find an agreement becoming disadvantageous, they will publicly announce their withdrawal from it rather than trying secretly to take advantage of other parties to the agreement, a course of action which would lead to special difficulties if they later wanted to enter into other international agreements. In other words, nations generally do not enter into arms control agreements (or most other kinds of agreements) unless they intend to abide by them. This fact is confirmed by the hard bargaining which goes on when nations strive to reach arms agreements. If there were no intention to abide by the agreement, why struggle so intensely over the terms?

Before reviewing the various arms control treaties adopted since the end of World War II, let us consider briefly how such treaties may be classified. First, some treaties are bilateral (between two countries) while others are multilateral (among more than two countries). Second, we can classify the treaties according to the type of weapons they seek to control: nuclear weapons and the accompanying delivery systems, biological weapons, chemical weapons, and conventional weapons. Third, we can classify the treaties on the basis of whether they completely prohibit something, such as the deployment of weapons of a particular kind, or merely limit the number permitted. Fourth, we can classify the treaties as zonal (applying only to certain geographical areas) or general (not limited to particular regions). Finally, we can distinguish among those treaties which focus on the development and testing of weapons, those which focus on the deployment of weapons, and those which focus on the transfer of weapons from one nation to another. We shall briefly review existing multilateral arms control agreements and then the bilateral agreements which have been made by the U.S. and the U.S.S.R.

A good example of a multilateral zonal arms prohibition agreement is the *Antarctic Treaty*, which was signed in 1959 and which got enough signatories to go into effect in 1961. This treaty covers nuclear and other kinds of weapons and prohibits both their development and their deployment in the Antarctic. At the end of 1980, it had been acceded to by 21 countries including the U.S., the U.S.S.R., the United Kingdom, Japan, and France.[18]

The *Partial or Limited Test Ban Treaty* (1963) prohibits the testing of nuclear weapons in the atmosphere, in outer space, under water, or anywhere else where the radioactive debris may enter the territory of a nation other than the one which exploded the device. In effect this agreement prohibits testing of nuclear devices except when done underground. It is a multilateral treaty which applies only to the testing of nuclear weapons, a step which is crucial for their development. One aim of this treaty is to hinder the development of nuclear weapons capability by countries which do not already have it. Although this treaty has been acceded to by 112 countries, including the U.S., the U.S.S.R., and the United Kingdom, it has not been signed by certain key nations such as China and France.

The *Outer Space Treaty* (1967) prohibits placing nuclear weapons or other weapons of mass destruction in outer space, including celestial bodies such as the moon. It also forbids the establishment of any military bases, the testing of any kinds of weapons, and the conducting of any kind of military maneuvers on celestial bodies. It is a multilateral treaty which has been signed by 82 countries, including the U.S., the U.S.S.R., the United Kingdom, and France.

Another multilateral zonal treaty is the *Treaty of Tlatelolco* (1967) which prohibits the testing, manufacture, production, acquisition, receipt, storage, installation, deployment, or possession of nuclear weapons in Latin America. The second protocol to this treaty allows non-Latin American countries which have nuclear weapons to pledge themselves not to contribute to acts involving a violation of the treaty and not to use or threaten to use nuclear weapons against Latin American nations which have signed the treaty. This treaty has been ratified by 22 Latin American countries, and the Protocol indicating cooperation on the part of nations possessing nuclear weapons has been signed by all five nuclear-weapon states.

The *Non-Proliferation Treaty* is a multilateral treaty which was signed in 1968 and went into force in 1970. Its aim is to prevent the spread of nuclear weapons to countries which do not already possess them. The nuclear powers also pledge themselves to pursue negotiations to stop the nuclear arms race and to work for a treaty on general and complete disarmament. Provision is made for a review of the operation of the treaty at five-year intervals at the request of a majority of the signatories. This provision allows the nonnuclear countries to exert some pressure on the nuclear powers to stop their own nuclear build-up, though so far it has not proved to be very effective. The Non-Proliferation Treaty has been acceded to by 115 countries including the U.S., the U.S.S.R., and the United Kingdom, but not including the key countries of China, France, Brazil, India, Israel, and South Africa.

The *Sea-Bed Treaty*, signed in 1971 and in force in 1972, prohibits the placement or storage of nuclear weapons or other weapons of mass destruction on the floor of the ocean beyond the 12-mile territorial waters of coastal states. It is a multilateral treaty designed to prevent nuclear powers from using the sea-bed as another place from which nuclear weapons might be fired. This treaty has been acceded to by 70 countries including the U.S., the U.S.S.R. and the United Kingdom, but not including China or France.

The *Biological Weapons Convention*, signed in 1972 and in force in 1975, prohibits the development, production, and possession of biological agents or toxins as well as devices for delivering such agents or toxins for hostile purposes. Any such materials on hand must be destroyed within nine months from when the convention enters into force or from when a nation accedes to the treaty. This multilateral convention is the only disarmament agreement since World War II which has led to the actual destruction of any already existing weapons or war materials. It has been acceded to by 91 countries, including the U.S., the U.S.S.R., and the United Kingdom, but not including China or France.

The *Environmental Modification Convention*, signed in 1977 and in force in 1978, prohibits military or other hostile use of environmental modification techniques to manipulate natural processes in a way which would be harmful to other countries. This multilateral treaty has been acceded to by 31 countries including the U.S., the U.S.S.R., and the United Kingdom, but not including China or France.

Though there were earlier agreements between the U.S. and the U.S.S.R. regarding a "hot line" between the two countries and measures to reduce the likelihood of a nuclear war beginning by accident, the first bilateral arms control agreement was the SALT I agreement of 1972.[19] "SALT" stands for "Strategic Arms Limitation Talks" and the SALT I agreement was actually composed of two separate treaties. The first was the *Anti-Ballistic Missile* (ABM) *Treaty* which limited each country to two sites at which ABM's could be deployed and limited the number of ABM's at each site to 100 missiles. It also limited the number and characteristics of radar installations related to the ABM systems or surface-to-air missiles (SAM's) that might be used against ballistic missiles. Each side pledged not to develop, test, or deploy ABM systems or components which are sea-based, air-based, space-based, or mobile land-based. (This pledge seems to have been forgotten by both sides, though it could be argued that the new types of missile-defense systems now being developed are technically not ABM's as defined in SALT I.[20]) The ABM Treaty is of unlimited duration but it is to be jointly reviewed every five years and either side can withdraw from the treaty upon giving six months' notice. In 1974 a protocol to the ABM Treaty was signed reducing the number of ABM sites allowed for each country to one. After building an ABM site in North Dakota, the U.S. decided not to spend the funds needed to keep it in operation.[21] The Russians apparently are still maintaining their ABM system near Moscow.

The second part of the SALT I agreement was the *Interim Agreement on the Limitation of Strategic Offensive Arms*. This interim agreement was originally scheduled to expire in July 1977, but was extended beyond that by both parties in anticipation of the signing and ratification of a new treaty, SALT II. The aim of the Interim Agreement was to set limits on the number of long-range missiles and missile-firing submarines each side could have. It should be noted that this agreement did not cover tactical (shorter range) missiles but only those with intercontinental range, namely, those that could go farther than "the shortest distance between the northeastern border of the continental U.S. and the northwestern border of the continental U.S.S.R."[22] According to SALT I, the Soviets were to be allowed 1,408[23] land-based intercontinental ballistic missile launchers (ICBM's) while the U.S. was to be allowed 1,000.[24] With regard to submarines capable of launching intercontinental missiles, the Russians were to be allowed 62 submarines with a total of 950 launching tubes while the U.S. was to be permitted 44 submarines with a total of 710 launching tubes.[25]

One may wonder why the Russians should be allowed more missiles than the Americans. The answer is that many factors outside the treaty gave the Americans real advantages. First, the agreement did not cover long-range bombers, of which the U.S. had 466 compared to Russia's 140.[26] Second, the agreement made no mention of the number of nuclear warheads each missile might carry, and at that time the U.S. was installing MIRV's on its missiles while the Soviet Union did not yet have that capability. It has been estimated that at the time of the agreement the U.S.S.R. had 2,478 nuclear warheads for strategic weapons while the U.S. had 5,792.[27] Third, the U.S. has two allies, the United Kingdom and France, who have nuclear weapons which are not covered by this agreement. Thus the stated terms of the treaty favored the Soviets while the actual situation was that the U.S. maintained a substantial advantage in numbers of warheads that could be delivered on enemy territory.

The *Threshold Test Ban Treaty*, formally called the Treaty on the Limitation of Underground Nuclear Weapon Tests, is a bilateral agreement between the U.S. and the U.S.S.R. to limit the size of underground nuclear explosions for the purpose of testing nuclear weapons.[28] No such explosion is to be over 150 kilotons (more than ten times as large as the bomb dropped on Hiroshima!). A protocol to the treaty indicates that each side will provide the other with certain information that will assist in verifying compliance with the treaty. This treaty was signed in 1974, and both sides seem to be observing it, though the U.S. Senate has not ratified it. The fact that this treaty was signed shows that the major military problem for the superpowers at present is how to make smaller nuclear warheads for tactical weapons rather than new kinds of larger ones for strategic weapons.

The *Treaty on Underground Nuclear Explosions for Peaceful Purposes* was signed by the U.S. and the U.S.S.R. in 1976 in order to extend the 150-kiloton limit to nuclear tests for peaceful purposes.[29] This treaty provides for on-site inspections to ensure that explosions are for peaceful purposes. Like the Threshold Ban Treaty, this treaty is being observed by both sides even though the U.S. Senate has not yet ratified it. Meanwhile, Russia's Brezhnev proposed that both countries stop all nuclear explosions of any size for any purpose.[30]

The most comprehensive arms control treaty ever negotiated is *SALT II*, signed by presidents Carter and Brezhnev in June of 1979. Again, both sides are continuing to abide by the terms of this agreement even though the U.S. Senate has not ratified it. The SALT II agreement goes far beyond SALT I in that it seeks to limit the number of all kinds of presently-developed long-range delivery systems each side can have as well as indirectly setting a limit on the number of nuclear warheads permitted on strategic weapons. Unlike SALT I, the numerical limits to be put into effect are the same for both sides. Provisions for not interfering with the other side's verification of compliance are more detailed than in SALT I. The SALT II Treaty is to remain in effect until 1985.[31]

The treaty itself focuses on setting limits on the number of all types of presently operational intercontinental-range delivery systems each side can have. Such systems include intercontinental ballistic missiles (ICBM's), submarine-launched ballistic missiles (SLBM's), heavy bombers, and air-to-surface ballistic missiles (ASBM's). (With regard to all these ballistic missiles, it is the number of launching tubes that is counted rather than the number of missiles, but the launching of a second missile from the same tube would be impossible in the case of submarines and aircraft, and in the case of land-based missiles, it would require the development of new technology which is forbidden by SALT II. Each side is permitted a total of 2,400 delivery systems until the end of 1980 and a total of 2,250 after that. Within this aggregate limit there are limits for particular types of weapons. The maximum for land-based ICBM's is 820 and for MIRVed missiles (whether land-based ICBM's, SLBM's, or ASBM's), 1,200. The maximum for MIRVed missiles *plus* heavy bombers is 1,320, with each heavy bomber being restricted to carrying a maximum of 20 long-range (more than 600 kilometers) air-launched cruise missiles (ALCM's). In counting these systems, if any launcher has been tested with a MIRVed missile, then all launchers of this type will be counted as being equipped with MIRVed missiles whether they are or not. Both parties agree not to start construction of any new nonmobile ICBM's, not to relocate present nonmobile ICBM's; not to make major modifications in the size of the missiles to be fired from a given launcher; not to put extra ICBM's in the vicinity of launching tubes for quick second launches from the same tube; not to develop, test, or deploy systems for rapid reloading of launching tubes; not to develop or test or deploy any ICBM's heavier than what that nation now has; and not to flight-test or deploy any larger number of warheads on any given type of missile than is already available on that type of missile. Each side is permitted to test and deploy one new light ICBM system (which for the U.S. is the ICBM system called the MX). Both sides agree to notify the other of any planned ICBM launches where the trajectory extends beyond the launcher's own national territory, and both sides agree not to impede verification of compliance by the other side. The treaty also indicates that both sides will work toward another agreement further limiting strategic offensive arms (SALT III).

If we compare the various arms control agreements made since 1959 with those few agreements which had been made prior to World War II, we are forced to conclude that a new era has begun. These agreements have been made possible by the development first of high-flying reconnaissance aircraft and then of satellites capable of taking incredibly detailed photographs from high altitudes. These devices allow the Big Powers to keep track of each other's activities. If either side violates an agreement it has signed, the other side can immediately make this information public with detailed photographs supporting its point.

As we examine the arms control treaties which have been signed so far, a number of observations can be made. First, it seems that the U.S. and the U.S.S.R. are willing to engage in a cooperative effort to preserve their present positions as superpowers with a long lead over other nations with regard to nuclear weapons and delivery systems. The Partial or Limited Test Ban Treaty and the Non-Proliferation Treaty both aim at preventing other nations from acquiring or developing nuclear capability. Although the U.S., the U.S.S.R, and the United Kingdom have signed both these treaties, it is noteworthy that the nuclear or near-nuclear nations of France, China, India, Israel, Brazil, and South Africa have each refrained from signing all of them. Second, the U.S. and the U.S.S.R seem willing to restrict the area of competition between themselves with regard to nuclear weapons (and even conventional weapons). Note that both have accepted the Antarctic Treaty, the Outer Space Treaty, the Protocol for non-Latin American nuclear powers to the Treaty of Tlatelolco, the Sea-Bed Treaty, the Biological Weapons Convention, the two parts of the SALT I Agreement, the Threshold Test Ban Treaty, the Treaty on Peaceful Nuclear Explosions, and SALT II (though the U.S. Senate has not yet ratified the last three). In each case both countries were willing not to expand the area of their military competition with each other. It remains to be seen whether new developments in ballistic missile defense will be kept within the bounds set by the Outer Space Treaty and the Anti-Ballistic Missile part of SALT I. Third, despite the rhetoric in the U.S. about how the Soviets have violated arms control agreements in the past[32] and about how arms control agreements are really advantageous to the Soviet Union, even the Reagan administration has agreed to abide by SALT II so long as the Soviets do. Apparently some limits on the arms race are better than none, even to the most hawkish. Fourth, arms control agreements thus far have aimed at stopping the increase of certain weapons rather than eliminating those already deployed. In other words, the aim has been arms *control*, not disarmament. The effect has been to channel the technological efforts of both sides into developing weapons not strictly excluded by the arms agreements.

Détente

The term *détente* refers to a relaxation of tension. In our contemporary world it is used to refer to the lessening of tension in the cold war between the U.S. and the U.S.S.R. which began after the Cuban missile crisis. It was somewhat strained for a while by U.S. involvement in Vietnam, but was revived by the signing of SALT I in 1972 and the Helsinki Accord in 1975. Détente is now strained again as a result of Soviet intervention in Afghanistan and the crackdown on Solidarity in Poland. The basic assumption is that the conflict between Soviet Communism and Western democratic capitalism can continue without there being a direct military confrontation between the opposing sides. The ideological contest continues, but efforts are made to reduce the likelihood of war. The U.S. and the U.S.S.R. enter into arms control agreements and even trade agreements with each other, but at the same time each attempts to spread its ideology and demonstrate the superiority of its own system. The Soviets do not give up their right to assist revolutionary Communist movements in all the countries of the world, and the U.S. does not give up its right to try to promote democratic capitalism in all the countries of the world.

Although efforts to influence events in other nations are thus condoned, there is an expectation that involvement will be indirect and covert rather than direct and overt. Soviet intervention in Afghanistan put a great strain on détente because it violated this expectation.

The central point of détente is that neither of the superpowers will launch or even threaten to launch a military attack against the other. (It should not be forgotten that both the U.S. and the U.S.S.R. were victims of surprise attacks in World War II, and each compares the other to the fascists of that time. That is, the Russians see the Americans as militaristic capitalists like the Germans were, while the Americans see the Russians as supporting an authoritarian political structure similar to the kind the Germans and Japanese had. Neither of these perceptions is completely true, but they nevertheless guide the thinking of the two sides.)

The real battleground of détente becomes the rest of the world. The outcome of the conflict is to be determined by the economic and social progress each side can display in its zone of influence and by internal conflicts in various other countries on a one-by-one basis. These other countries are to choose between Communism and democratic capitalism, but it will probably not be on the democratic basis of casting votes. The outcome will depend rather on a contest of force and of the willingness of people to fight for one or the other ideology. Civil wars and coups d'état and guerrilla warfare will be the means by which Communism and democratic capitalism vie for control in many of the nations of the world.

The battles of the future will be like those we have seen recently in Vietnam, Nicaragua, Afghanistan, and El Salvador. The crucial disputes will be fought within nations, rather than between nations. Thus, détente is not a formula for the end of all war and physical violence in world affairs. It is simply a program for avoiding nuclear war between the superpowers.

Modern Conventional Weaponry

The term *conventional weapons* is used to describe all weapons that are not nuclear, biological, or chemical. But modern conventional weapons are anything but conventional if that term refers to the weapons used in World War II. The wars of the late 1960's and early 1970's in the Middle East and Vietnam revealed that nonnuclear weapons had undergone rapid development even at that time, and modern technology promises even more deadly weapons in the future.

In Vietnam, the U.S. introduced many new weapons designed mainly to kill or seriously wound individual persons.[33] One well-known example is napalm, a jellied oily mixture which burns while sticking to things like human flesh. Other examples are fire bombs that use magnesium and white phosphorus to burn through the skin and muscle to the bone. Fragmentation bombs were used to wound people by burying fragments in their flesh, and some of the fragments were made of plastic so that they would not show up on X-rays. Asphixiation bombs, also used by the U.S. in Vietnam, release a cloud vapor which ignites, quickly consuming all the oxygen in the area. Such new antipersonnel weapons, plus others being developed, promise that the number of injured people and the severity of their wounds will be much greater in future wars than has been the case in the past.

The biggest difference in new weapons is the improved accuracy of projectiles which has been made possible by radar, television, heat-seeking devices, infra-red devices, laser beams, radio control, and tiny computers. In previous times soldiers practiced for hours to learn to drop bombs near the intended target or to hit what they aimed at with rifles, anti-aircraft guns, or artillery. A huge proportion of the firepower delivered in battle did not hit the target at which it was aimed. But that situation is rapidly changing. The new precision-guided munitions called *smart weapons* are much more likely to hit the target than to miss it. The aircraft, ships, tanks, artillery sites, control centers, or other targets at which these devices are aimed are very unlikely to escape destruction. For example, in Vietnam two bridges which had escaped destruction during many regular bombing attacks were knocked out in the first effort using smart bombs.[34] The great accuracy of these new smart weapons means, among other things, that during future battles it will not be safe to be in an airplane, a tank, a ship, or anything else that is easy to locate. The military answer to this situation is pilotless aircraft and perhaps eventually crewless tanks. If an airplane is equipped with television cameras and the proper control systems, it can be flown by a "pilot" on the ground as readily as by a pilot in the aircraft. In that case the airplane would no longer need to be equipped with a life-support system or ejection device for the pilot. It could take greater risks than might be considered reasonable with a pilot aboard. It could even be used for kamikazi missions.

It will not only be unsafe to be in an airplane, tank, or ship during a battle. It will not be safe to walk or talk in the vicinity of a battlefield,

because extremely sensitive listening devices can be placed almost anywhere. These devices will let the enemy know the whereabouts of people
in the area who can then be destroyed by a missile or other device directed
from miles away. The only issue to be considered by the enemy is whether
such death is worth the cost of the missile sent to do the job.

The automated battlefield is the prospect of the future.[35] Soldiers
located far from the battlefield will launch missiles which are precision-
guided to targets like unmanned airplanes and tanks. The outcome of
battle will depend on the technological capabilities of the weapons, which
will necessarily have been designed and produced well before the war
begins. The battle will be as different from the battles of yesterday as
television table tennis is from the game played with an actual table,
paddles, and ball.

It is not difficult to see that the development of the automated battlefield will be expensive for nations which want to participate in preparing
for such battles. On the other hand, any nation which does not get involved in such research will be as helpless against this military technology
as primitive peoples with bows and arrows have been against European
armies equipped with machine guns and airplanes. The cost of developing
and producing these new weapons will obviously be high, and the contest
for superiority will be unending. The military has never been particularly
enthusiastic about nuclear weapons, since they are too powerful to produce much need for complex strategy, but the new electronic, unmanned
weapons of war are a different story. With this equipment, the game of
war becomes very challenging, and the leaders no longer need to worry
about losing large numbers of soldiers in battle. The military-industrial
complex will also gain new significance because the outcome of battles is
likely to depend as much on the weapons available as on the ingenuity of
the military leaders.

XI. Institutional Aspects of the Contemporary Situation

There are many kinds of international institutions in the world today, but the one most obviously relevant to the problem of war is the United Nations. It will be our first topic, and we will discuss it in four sections: its structure, its peacekeeping activities, the influences on it, and its accomplishments. Other international institutions also require some attention even though their relation to the war problem may be less direct. For example, there are many government-sponsored *global administrative or functional agencies* which are important to our study because of their roles throughout the world in solving social problems. We also need to examine *regional functional and political organizations* formed by national governments. Finally, we need to discuss international *nongovernmental organizations*, that is, international organizations formed by individuals and private organizations rather than by representatives of national governments.

The Structure of the United Nations

The first effort to create a global political institution was the formation of the League of Nations after World War I. Forty-two nations were original members of the League, and 20 others became members at one time or another, including all the major powers except the U.S. The main structures of the League were the Assembly (one representative from each nation), the Council (permanent representation for the Great Powers and elected representation from other nations), and a Secretariat (civil servants employed by the League). There were also a number of specialized functional agencies to handle particular international problems, all of which in one form or another have now become specialized agencies of the United Nations. One of the basic principles of the League was that no nation surrendered any of its sovereignty over its own affairs when it became a member. Measures other than those dealing with procedural issues required unanimous support in both the Assembly and the Council.

World War II seems to have come about partly as the result of the League's failure to act decisively when powerful nations such as Japan or Italy began to engage in expansionist military activities. Great Britain and France in particular seemed to be guided more by balance-of-power thinking than by the provisions of the Covenant of the League, which they tended to regard as good for public relations with their own citizenry but too idealistic for use in the real world.[1] In 1933 the Assembly of the League adopted a resolution condemning Japan for its invasion of Manchuria, but Japan responded by quitting the League. In 1936, when the League did nothing to protect Ethiopia from being taken over by Italy, several countries withdrew. The Soviet Union was expelled in 1939 for attacking Finland. After the German conquests of 1939–40, Great Britain was the only great power remaining and very few nations continued as members. For all practical purposes the League ended in June of 1940 when Secretary-General Avenol resigned, though a final "funeral session" was held in 1946 after the United Nations had been formed.

The formation of the League's successor, the United Nations, began even while World War II was still being fought. President Franklin Roosevelt, aware of the fate of Wilson's plan for U.S. participation in the League of Nations, decided not to wait until the war was over to involve the U.S. in an organization to preserve the peace. In January of 1942 representatives from 26 nations met in Washington D.C. and adopted a "Declaration by the United Nations" to fight together against Germany, Italy, and Japan and to accept the democratic and anti-imperialist principles enunciated in the Atlantic Charter, which had been signed by Roosevelt and Britain's Prime Minister Winston Churchill in August of 1941. A resolution calling for the creation of a general international peacekeeping organization was adopted by the U.S., the U.S.S.R., the United Kingdom, and China at the Moscow Conference in October of 1943. At Washington in August of 1944 and at Yalta in February of 1945 representatives of the big powers agreed on the general structure of the U.N. The actual final wording of the Charter of the United Nations was worked out by delegates from 50 nations[2] in San Francisco in April, May, and June of 1945. (Germany surrendered, ending the war in Europe on May 8, 1945). The Charter was signed on June 26, 1945 and acquired sufficient ratifications to go into effect on October 24, 1945, the date generally recognized as the beginning of the United Nations. (Japan surrendered ending World War II on August 15, 1945). The first session of the U.N. General Assembly was held in London in January, 1946. Among other things, it decided to establish permanent headquarters in or near New York City. Most of the subsequent meetings of the U.N. were held in temporary facilities in and around New York until 1952 when the organization moved into its present building along the East River in Manhattan.

The structure and principles of operation of the United Nations are similar to those of the League of Nations.[3] Each nation retains its national sovereignty; that is, each nation decides for itself what it will or won't do and can withdraw from the organization whenever it so desires. Disputes between nations are to be resolved by negotiation rather than war. Aggression by one nation against another is to be stopped by collective action of all the other nations using economic measures primarily but including military action if necessary. In both the League and the U.N. the primary bodies have been the all-inclusive Assembly and the smaller

Council in which the big powers have more influence. The greatest difference is that the U.N. has more machinery devoted to promoting economic and social progress in the poorer nations of the world.

The main body of the United Nations is the General Assembly, in which each member nation may have five representatives but only one vote. The General Assembly has the power to make decisions concerning the operation of the U.N., such as determining the budget of the organization and electing representatives to various U.N. bodies including the Security Council, but with regard to other matters it can only make recommendations to the member governments. Actions are taken on the basis of majority rule (2/3 majority on certain important issues) rather than requiring unanimity as was the case in the League of Nations. The General Assembly cannot pass laws for the world as a legislature could, but neither is the Assembly merely a "debating society" as it has sometimes been called, for it does govern the operation of the U.N. organization itself. The number of nations in the United Nations has increased from the original 51 members to 157 at the end of 1981.

The primary function of the Security Council is the maintenance of peace. The five major powers who fought together to win World War II were expected to work together to preserve the peace. Thus the U.S., the U.S.S.R., the United Kingdom, France, and China are permanent members of the Security Council. Any one of them can prevent Security Council action by casting a veto. Originally the Security Council had six other nations elected to the Council by the General Assembly, but the Charter was amended to increase that number to ten in 1965. A measure can be enacted by the Security Council only if it receives an affirmative vote of nine of the fifteen members and no permanent member is against it. All members of the U.N., upon joining the organization, commit themselves to accepting and carrying out the decisions of the Security Council. In principle, then, decisions of the Security Council are binding in a way that resolutions passed by the General Assembly are not.

A third major organ of the United Nations is the Economic and Social Council. The main function of this body is to coordinate efforts to promote economic and social welfare throughout the world. It does this by working with the many specialized agencies of the U.N. and by establishing its own committees and commissions. For example, ECOSOC has commissions on the status of women, on statistics, on population, on social development, on narcotics, and on human rights. Originally the Economic and Social Council consisted of 18 representatives selected by the General Assembly, but the number was increased to 27 by an amendment which became effective in 1965 and then to 54 by another amendment which went into effect in 1973.

The fourth main organ of the United Nations, the Trusteeship Council, has nearly completed its task of supervising the transition of 11 Trust Territories from being dependent colonies to being independent nations. The only territory which has not yet been granted independence is a group of Pacific islands (the Marianas, Marshalls, and Carolines) under the administration of the U.S. In 1975 the inhabitants of the Marianas voted to become a political territory of the U.S., so the remaining Trust Territory now consists of only the Marshall and Caroline Islands.

The fifth main organ of the United Nations is the International Court of Justice. It is simply the revised version of the Permanent Court of International Justice which had been created in 1921–22 by the League of Nations. Like the earlier Court, the International Court of Justice meets in the Hague, Netherlands, and has 15 judges. Every three years five new judges are selected for three-year terms, and no country may be represented by more than one judge. The aim of the Court is to render legal decisions in cases involving international law, the interpretation of treaties, and the like. Although the Court can give advisory opinions when asked to do so by the General Assembly or the Security Council, only nations can be parties in any actual case to be decided by the Court. Furthermore, all nations which may be directly affected by a decision of the Court must agree in advance to abide by the decision before the Court will consider it.[4] Since a nation which believes that another nation is violating international law must persuade the alleged violator to agree in advance to abide by the decision, it is not difficult to see why the International Court of Justice has not had many cases to consider.

The sixth main part of the United Nations is the Secretariat, the employees of the U.N. under the directorship of the Secretary-General. The Secretary-General not only is in charge of all the personnel employed by the U.N. but also has special responsibilities such as making an annual report to the General Assembly and bringing to the attention of the Security Council any matter which he believes threatens world peace. The Secretary-General is elected by the General Assembly after being recommended by the Security Council. Although no term of office is stipulated in the Charter, the first General Assembly decided that a Secretary-General should serve for five years and could be reappointed.[5] The Secretary-Generals of the U.N. have been Trygve Lie of Norway (1946–52), Dag Hammarskjöld of Sweden (1953–61), U Thant of Burma (1961–71), Kurt Waldheim of Austria (1972–81) and Javier Pérez de Cuéllar of Peru (1982–   ).

Peacekeeping by the United Nations

During the first few years of the U.N., the U.S. and Britain tried to use it to stop Communist expansion into Eastern Europe, but these efforts failed because of Soviet use of the veto. When Communist troops from North Korea invaded anti-Communist South Korea in 1950, however, the U.N. Security Council declared North Korea to be an aggressor and called on U.N. members to help the South Koreans and their U.S. allies. This action was possible because the Russians were boycotting the Security Council at the time to protest China's being represented at the U.N. by Chiang Kai-shek's appointees, even though Communist revolutionary forces led by Mao Tse-tung had conquered all of China except the island of Taiwan. Sixteen nations sent troops in response to the call of the Security Council, but the brunt of the fighting was borne by South Korean and U.S. forces. Nevertheless this action by the U.N. marked the first time in history that an international organization had organized a collective military force to resist armed aggression.

At first the forces defending South Korea were driven back, but eventually a counter-attack was launched. The U.N. forces pushed northward past the 38th parallel, which had been the boundary between North and South Korea. As they pushed farther north, the Chinese Communists warned that they would enter the war if the northerly advance was not halted. The warning was not heeded. Using large numbers of troops, the Chinese forces pushed the U.N. forces back toward the 38th parallel. After two more years of indecisive fighting, in 1953 a truce was worked out, and the boundary between North and South Korea was set not far from where it had been before the war.

An important development took place at the U.N. during this Korean conflict. After the Security Council had declared North Korea to be an aggressor, the Soviet Union returned to its seat in the Security Council in order to veto any further U.N. action. The U.N. General Assembly responded by passing the "Uniting for Peace Resolution." This resolution declared that the General Assembly can make recommendations to the member nations (including recommending the use of armed forces) whenever the Security Council fails to act in cases where peace is threatened or aggression has occurred. This tactic of taking action in the General Assembly when the Security Council fails to act has been utilized two other times. It was used in 1956 with American and Russian approval to establish a U.N. peacekeeping force in the Middle East after an attack by Britain, Israel, and France against Egypt; and it was used again in 1960 to authorize the continued use of U.N. troops in the Congo, although the formation of this U.N. force had originally been authorized by the Security Council.

Although U.N.-sponsored forces have engaged in actual military activity on only two occasions (Korea and the Congo), U.N.-sponsored soldiers and observers have participated in many peacekeeping operations, that is, in operations which consist of policing a truce between the warring parties.[6] The Middle East has been the scene of several such operations.[7] In 1947 the General Assembly of the U.N. passed a resolution calling for the partition of Palestine into a Jewish state and an Arab state with international status for Jerusalem. This arrangement was to go into effect after British forces left the area, but even before that withdrawal the Arabs and Jews were engaged in war with each other as the Arabs tried to prevent the establishment of a separate Jewish state in an area where much land was privately owned by Arabs. The Security Council established a Truce Commission to try to prevent violence. On May 14, 1948 the Israelis proclaimed the independence of the state of Israel and fighting resumed. The Security Council called for a cease-fire, but it lasted only four weeks. Then the Security Council called for another cease-fire and made an effort to enforce it with its own Truce Supervision Organization. Eventually a truce was made in 1949 which left the Israelis in control of slightly more territory than they would have had according to the 1947 U.N. resolution calling for partition.

In 1956 Egypt nationalized the Suez Canal which had been operated by the Suez Canal Company, chief shares in which were owned by the British government and French private companies. The British and French governments tried to work out a plan for internationalization of the Canal, but the Egyptians rejected this proposal. Then Israel, Britain, and France attacked Egypt. Putting principle above alliances, President Eisenhower condemned the attack against Egypt, and the U.S. and the U.S.S.R. worked together in the U.N. to stop further aggression against Egypt. After Britain and France vetoed the idea in the Security Council, the General Assembly authorized the U.N. Emergency Force (UNEF) to supervise the cease-fire under the provisions of the "Uniting for Peace Resolution" previously discussed. Israel refused to allow the UNEF troops on the territory it controlled, so they were stationed only on the Egyptian side of the border.

In 1967 Egypt's Nasser asked Secretary-General U Thant to remove the U.N. troops from Egyptian territory. Then, having already excluded Israeli ships from the Suez Canal, Nasser inaugurated a blockade of the Gulf of Aqaba, Israel's only access to the Red Sea. Unable to get much help from its allies in overcoming the blockade, the Israelis launched a lightning attack on Egypt, Syria, and Jordan. In six days the Israelis gained control of the whole Sinai peninsula, the Gaza Strip, the West Bank, all of Jerusalem, and the Golan Heights. The Security Council called for a cease-fire, and the call was soon accepted. This time, however, the Israelis maintained control over most of the territory they had taken. In November of 1967 the Security Council passed the now-famous Resolution 242, setting down principles for the solution of the Middle East conflict. It called for withdrawal of Israeli forces from territory taken in the recent war, an end to war in the area, free navigation for all ships through international waterways such as the Suez Canal, resolution of the problem of what to do with the Palestinian Arab refugees, and maintenance of the territorial integrity and political independence of all countries in the area.

In October 1973 war broke out again, initiated this time by Arabs who had become impatient with the lack of progress in getting land back from the Israelis. The Israelis were pushed back at first but soon regained all the territory they had lost, and more. Once again the Security Council called for an end of military activities and sent in a U.N. force to supervise the truce. The U.N. Emergency Force (UNEF II) was stationed between Israeli and Egyptian forces while the U.N. Disengagement Observer Force (UNDOF) was stationed between Israeli and Syrian forces. The establishment of these U.N.-sponsored peacekeeping forces was significant, because for the first time the Soviet Union actively supported a

U.N. peacekeeping effort and troops from some Communist countries were a part of the peacekeeping force.

Near the end of 1976 Syrian forces took over much of Lebanon in an effort to stop fighting between Muslims and Christians. The Israelis did not want hostile forces along their northern border, however, and gave strong military support to the Christian, anti-Muslim forces in the southern part of Lebanon. In 1978, after over a year of civil war in Lebanon, the Security Council voted to send in a United Nations Interim Force in Lebanon (UNIFIL) to try to maintain some public order in the southern part of that country. This peacekeeping operation in the midst of civil strife without well-defined borders between the belligerents was a new role for U.N. forces, and did not work out well. The Israelis complained that terrorist attacks were still being launched by Palestinians in Lebanon, and in 1982 they invaded Lebanon in an effort to eliminate all military activities of the Palestine Liberation Organization in that country.

This record of four wars and continuing violence in the Middle East over a 35-year period does not seem to say much for the U.N.'s peacekeeping capabilities. On the other hand, it should be noted that the 1967 war broke out only after U.N. forces had been removed, that none of the wars lasted more than a year, and that the armed forces of the superpowers have not become involved despite their sometimes-opposing interests. Furthermore, it should be noted that most, if not all, of this violence could have been avoided if the U.N. had acted more forcefully to support its own 1947 resolution on partitioning the area into a Jewish state and an Arab state. The Israelis have had to rely on their own military capability to preserve their existence; and since military force has proved to be more efficacious than the U.N.'s negotiations and resolutions, other nations and oppressed peoples seem to be learning a lesson exactly opposite of what the U.N. should be promoting. The big question now is the extent to which the U.N. can help the Palestinian Arabs so that this determined group will also not learn the wrong lesson, namely, to trust their own military might rather than the world community. There is a reluctance in the U.N. to impose solutions on warring third parties, but this reluctance to intervene has the consequence of encouraging the conflicting parties to rely on military forces and the use of violence.

The Middle East is by no means the only part of the world in which U.N. peacekeeping efforts have been active. From 1947 to 1954 a U.N.-sponsored observer and mediation team was stationed in Greece in response to a complaint by Greece that its northern borders were being violated by Albanian, Bulgarian, and Yugoslav forces seeking to assist Communist guerrillas in Greece. In 1947–48 fighting broke out in Indonesia between Dutch forces seeking to reestablish colonial control and Indonesian forces fighting for independence, and a U.N. Commission assisted by military observers was sent into the country to supervise an agreement under which Indonesia would become independent. Armed conflict in Kashmir between Pakistan and India led in 1948 to the establishment of a U.N. commission to mediate the dispute and supervise the subsequent cease-fire.

In 1958 the Security Council sent a U.N. observer group to Lebanon to investigate charges that the United Arab Republic was attempting to overthrow the Lebanese government. In 1960, U.N.-sponsored forces were sent to help the newly-independent nation of the Congo suppress a rebellion in the mineral-rich province of Katanga. This rebellion was not merely an internal affair, however, since many of those fighting for Katanga were European mercenaries flown into the area by foreign planes. The first thrust of the U.N.'s efforts was to have all foreign mercenaries removed from the area, and in 1964 the leaders of the rebellion were persuaded to accept control by the central Congolese government.

When a dispute arose in 1961 between the Netherlands and Indonesia concerning whether the western part of New Guinea (West Irian) was to be considered a part of newly-independent Indonesia, a U.N. team was put in charge of administering the area from 1963 until 1969 when representative councils in West Irian decided they wanted to be part of Indonesia. A U.N. observer mission was sent to Yemen in 1963 during a civil war between forces supported on the one hand by Saudi Arabia and on the other by the United Arab Republic; its recommendations were not accepted and it withdrew in 1964. Near the end of 1963 fighting broke out between the Greek and the Turkish residents of the newly-independent nation of Cyprus, and U.N. authorized forces were sent to maintain order in 1964. They have remained, though they were unable to do much except maintain control of the Nicosia Airport during the 1974 conflict when forces from Turkey invaded the island. In 1965 war again broke out between India and Pakistan, this time not only in Kashmir but all along the border. U.N. Security Council action led to U.N. supervision of the cease-fire agreement along the whole border for six months. After that, the U.N. observers were withdrawn except from Kashmir itself. At present, then, U.N. peacekeeping forces or observers are still on patrol in the Middle East, Cyprus, and Kashmir.

Bringing in U.N.-authorized troops to supervise cease-fires is certainly not the role laid out for the U.N. in its Charter. The provision in the Charter that a Military Staff Committee consisting "of the Chiefs of Staff of the permanent members of the Security Council or their representatives"[8] be established to advise and assist the Security Council has been carried out only as a ceremonial operation and is not likely to produce any action. On the other hand, the Charter says nothing about supervising truces which have been worked out by the warring parties. Still, this peacekeeping activity has proved to be very useful. One problem with this mode of operation, however, is that the U.N. usually acts merely as a preserver of the status quo rather than a negotiator of basic political concerns and issues of justice.

A big problem is how to pay for the U.N.'s peacekeeping efforts. In some cases the funds have come from regular assessments on the member nations of the U.N.; but in others where this approach might arouse antagonism there have been appeals for voluntary contributions. The response to such appeals has not been overwhelming. The U.N. operation in the Congo was terminated in 1964 largely because of inadequate financial support, and there is still a large unpaid debt for that operation and the first UNEF effort in the Middle East.[9]

Dominant Influences in the United Nations

One of the most important actions ever taken by the General Assembly of the U.N. occurred on October 25, 1971. By a vote of 76 to 35 (more than the two-thirds margin required), the Assembly determined that China should be represented in the U.N. by representatives selected by the Communist government of the People's Republic of China rather than by those of the Nationalist Chinese who controlled only the island of Taiwan. This vote is important because it marks the end of the United States's domination of the U.N. Compliance with U.S. interests was secured earlier not only by American economic and military power but also by the fact that the nations of Western Europe, Latin America, and the British Commonwealth, all of which could be expected to vote as the U.S. wished, accounted for almost two-thirds of the original 51 countries in the U.N. Furthermore, the U.S. could usually also count on support from China, Iran, Iraq, Lebanon, Liberia, the Philippines, Saudi Arabia, and Turkey. The Russians, on the other hand, could count on only six votes, two of them belonging to the Byelorussian Soviet Socialist Republic and the Ukrainian Soviet Socialist Republic, which are actually part of the Soviet Union but had been given separate votes in the General Assembly as a compromise for Russia's participation.

Between 1945 and 1955, nine countries were admitted to the U.N., but in 1955 16 new countries became members. In 1960 membership reached 100 countries with the admission of 17 new members, all but one being former African colonies. Most of these newly-independent nations were bound together by an antipathy to colonialism which was reflected in a resolution passed in the General Assembly in December, 1960, supporting the idea that all territories have a right to self-determination which overrides any claims of colonial powers.[10] This resolution can be characterized as one which the U.S. would not have introduced itself but also as one to which it was not intensely opposed.

The vote on Chinese representation in 1971, however, was different. The U.S. had failed to get the Chinese Nationalists to go along with a "two Chinas" policy so that a system could be worked out to give both Chinese governments representation in the U.N. Consequently, the U.S., in an effort to keep its Nationalist Chinese ally from losing its representation, vehemently opposed the 1971 resolution to seat the Communists as the representatives of China, just as it had opposed similar previous resolutions. On those earlier occasions, the U.S. had always managed to prevail, but in 1971 the results were different. For the first time the nonaligned, anticolonialist countries made their influence felt even against strong U.S. opposition, and a new era began at the U.N. From that time on, the General Assembly has belonged to the less developed countries, while the big powers still have their vetoes in the Security Council. This development means that no matter how much the structure of the U.N. resembles that of the League of Nations, a political influence has come into being which did not exist, and could not have existed, at the time of the League.

There was a big problem for this new power group, however: They were poor. Contributions to the U.N. were assessed by the General Assembly on the basis of ability to pay, and none of these former colonies made very large contributions to the support of the U.N. In fact, over a third of the U.N. budget came from the U.S. on grounds that the U.S. had over a third of the world's gross income. This situation allowed the U.S. to score a point against the less developed countries in response to the 1971 vote on China. In 1972 the U.S. successfully requested the General Assembly to set 25 percent of the U.N. budget as the maximum any single nation could be assessed. The U.S. did nothing to contradict rumors that if this proposal to reduce its own contribution was not passed it might just quit the U.N. altogether. The message from the U.S. was clear: Don't push your voting advantage too far, or you may lose a substantial portion of the money coming into the U.N. On the other hand, the less developed countries realized that neither the U.S. nor the U.S.S.R. was likely to withdraw from the U.N. because this would clear the way for the other to maintain a close working relationship with those very nations in which the ideological battle between Communism and democratic capitalism is to be fought.

The financial threat to the U.N. from the U.S. was diminished considerably at the end of 1973 when the Organization of Petroleum Exporting Countries (OPEC) quadrupled the price of oil. This event not only demonstrated the vulnerability of the developed countries to economic pressures; it also meant large amounts of money in the coffers of those oil-rich Arab nations with sparse populations on which to spend their new-found wealth. These countries could now provide some of the foreign aid which the U.S. might threaten to withhold from nations which voted against it in the U.N. They could replace U.S. contributions to the U.N. if the U.S. were to withdraw from the organization. (The total of U.S. payments to the U.N. and all its various agencies and programs was $824 million in 1979.[11]) This new situation provided the impetus for the less developed countries to become even bolder in the U.N. They passed a resolution calling for a New International Economic Order to replace the existing system of trading arrangements which favored the developing countries (1974) and another resolution declaring that Zionism is a form of racism (1975). The passage of this last resolution gives support to the view that Arab oil money has influenced U.N. voting.

Another indication of the importance of the U.N. to the less developed countries is the proportion of the U.N. budget that goes to support activities in the poorer nations. Nearly 90 percent of all funds spent by the U.N. system is expended for programs designed primarily to assist the less developed countries.[12] In addition, almost all of the loans for development made through the International Bank for Reconstruction and Development go to these poorer countries. Both politically and economically, the United Nations is an organization which serves the poor nations in their struggle to survive.

The other side of the coin, however, is the fact that the richer, more powerful nations are not enthusiastic about increasing either the influence of the U.N. or their support for it. The U.S. and the Soviet Union especially seem inclined to negotiate directly with each other on issues they feel are important. They may not want to withdraw from the U.N., but they can ignore it and try to keep it poor and weak, thus making it rather irrelevant to international affairs. The main danger for the U.N. is not ceasing to exist but rather ceasing to matter.

Accomplishments of the United Nations

The United Nations came into existence October 24, 1945. It has not been particularly successful in its announced aim "to save succeeding generations from the scourge of war." Yet the rest of that first sentence of the U.N. Charter makes reference to the two world wars, and the fact is, regardless of whether the U.N. is responsible for it or not, there has been no World War III. The League of Nations was formed in 1919 and twenty years later another world war was being fought. The U.N. has already existed for 37 years without another world war. Furthermore, a look at its record reveals that it not only has accomplished several of its aims to some degree but also has brought about other desirable developments.

One of the U.N.'s major accomplishments is simply that is has managed to maintain its existence and even to extend its membership to practically all the nations of the world. Survival is no small task for a political organization. Even a national-level political institution which maintains its existence for nearly forty years is considered a stable institution. Over half the nations which now belong to the U.N. did not have independent national governments at the time the U.N. was formed; the U.N. is older than they are! Continuing existence produces expectations and traditions. The longer the U.N. survives as an organization with almost universal membership, the more difficult it becomes for anyone to conceive of a world without it or for national leaders to conceive of their own nations as nonmembers.

With regard to the war problem, the U.N. has been the agency by which multilateral arms control agreements have come into existence as well as the vehicle for various peacekeeping operations. The U.N. has established various committees to further arms control and has called two Special Sessions of the General Assembly to discuss disarmament (1978 and 1982). With regard to peacekeeping efforts, one can only conjecture about whether any of the situations in which the U.N. intervened might have otherwise developed into a large-scale war. The U.N.'s role in Korea should not be forgotten, even if it is very unlikely that there will ever again be such an operation. At least the precedent was set for an international organization coordinating an effort to resist aggression in accord with the idea of collective security. One should also consider whether in the absence of the U.N. there could be a situation such as the one that now exists in which the U.S. and the U.S.S.R. are motivated to cooperate in Security Council peacekeeping efforts since otherwise decisions will be made in the General Assembly where the less developed countries have the controlling number of votes.

A third area of achievement for the U.N. consists of providing opportunities for formal and informal exchanges between diplomats in times of crisis and for planning cooperative efforts to resolve conflicts. The existence of the U.N. makes possible meetings in the hallway or the lunchroom which may produce important diplomatic exchanges that would never have taken place if formal arrangements for such meetings had been required in advance. Diplomats from smaller countries may be able to take part in discussions to which they otherwise would not have been invited. The Secretary-General and other U.N. personnel can participate in negotiations as representatives not of this or that nation, but of the world community. How much difference this opportunity for ready contact between diplomats has made toward preventing war cannot be determined with precision, but it is hard to believe that it hasn't helped.

Fourth, the United Nations has been developing a whole new tradition in international politics, one of conferring and debating and appealing to disinterested third parties rather than making military threats and issuing ultimatums. This new tradition involves a shift from a situation where interaction between nations is only bilateral and coercive to one where it is also multilateral and persuasive. The United Nations is thus serving as a school at which national governments and their leaders are learning how to participate in a democratic parliament. Even representatives from nations with autocratic governments are learning that different points of view must be allowed to be expressed, that the opinions of third parties are important, that appeals to reason rather than force can be influential, and so on.

Unfortunately, the United States, which prides itself on being a democratic nation, seems to have trouble at times functioning within this democratic forum. As a nation we have yet to learn the very important lesson that on the world scene we are a minority, only 5 percent of the world's population. We have yet to learn that democracy means listening as well as talking, appealing to reason rather than being coercive, and abiding by the decision of the majority even when we don't agree. We must learn that there are others in the world who care about freedom and justice just as much as we do.

A fifth area of achievement for the U.N. is its supervision of the relatively smooth transition from a world of colonizing nations and their colonies to a world of independent sovereign countries. We have already noted that the Trusteeship Council of the U.N. has practically finished its work and that over half the nations of the U.N. were colonies at the time the U.N. was formed. Even if the U.N. had accomplished nothing else, its supervision and legitimation of the decolonization of much of the world makes it one of the greatest success stories in human history.

Obviously one cannot claim that the U.N. accomplished this transition alone. There can be no down-grading of the sacrifices made by millions in wars fought for the independence of their homelands. At the same time, it can be noted that the process would undoubtedly have been much slower and much bloodier without the U.N. Many nations have won their independence without bloodshed, and the existence of the U.N. has often facilitated this development. The U.N. provides a ready means by which the independence of a nation can be registered as an objective fact. A country may declare itself to be independent, but that independence is publicly recognized by the rest of the world when it becomes a member of the United Nations, equally sovereign with every other nation.

The U.N. has not only helped these new nations to achieve recognized independence; it has also helped them to survive once they have become independent. This is its sixth area of achievement. Most of these former colonies are poor and short of the skills needed to run businesses, schools, hospitals, and governments. They need loans and other forms of development assistance. The U.N. has helped to provide these. The less developed countries have been successful in the past in using the U.N. as a vehicle to procure and secure their *political independence*. Their expectation now is that it will assist them further in their *economic development*.

A seventh area of accomplishment for the U.N. is its progress in carrying out the aim stated in the second paragraph of the Charter, namely, "to reaffirm faith in fundamental human rights." The various declarations and covenants on this subject serve as an ideal for the world's governments and peoples to pursue even though they are often far from being actualized. Their role in the development of standards may be compared to that played by the Declaration of Independence and the Bill of Rights in the formation of public opinion in the United States. The three main U.N. human rights documents (the Universal Declaration of Human Rights adopted by the General Assembly in 1948; the Covenant on Economic, Social, and Cultural Rights passed by the General Assembly in 1966; and the Covenant on Civil and Political Rights also passed by the General Assembly in 1966) were all adopted without a dissenting vote.[13] Even national governments which do not honor these rights in practice feel bound not to vote against them as public statements of the ideals toward which humankind should be moving.

The Covenant on Civil and Political Rights contains an optional Protocol which nations may also adopt when they ratify that Covenant. The Protocol indicates that the nation acceding to it recognizes the right of its citizens to file complaints about violations of their rights directly to the U.N. Human Rights Committee, a committee formed of representatives elected by those nations who have ratified the Covenant. As more and more nations accede to this very special Protocol, the pressure on the others who have not adopted it will mount. The accusations of human rights violations made against each other by potential enemies such as the U.S. and the U.S.S.R. do not carry much weight because each is known to be merely attacking an opponent, but failure to ratify the Protocol of the Covenent on Civil and Political Rights will eventually be viewed as a self-accusation before the whole world. Unfortunately, the media in most of the world have not paid much attention to these Covenants and the all-important Protocol, so the pressure of world public opinion has not yet been brought to bear on this issue.

In addition to the three basic documents on human rights, the U.N. has also adopted several treaties on specific human rights such as the prevention of genocide, protection of refugees, political rights of women, abolition of slavery, the nationality of married women, the status of stateless persons, consent to marriage, and elimination of racial discrimination. Also, in 1981 the General Assembly adopted a Declaration on the Elimination of All Forms of Intolerance and of Discrimination Based on Religion or Belief. Most of these efforts to further human rights would not have occurred without the United Nations.

An eighth accomplishment of the U.N. is directing the attention of the whole world to crucial global problems so that action can be taken toward solving these problems. The technique which has been used to focus attention on an issue is the convening of a world conference devoted to that problem. Experts from all over the world, governmental representatives and sometimes private citizens too, get together to discuss this problem and possible solutions to it. The first of these world conferences was on the environment. It was held in Stockholm in 1972 and led eventually to the creation of the U.N. Environmental Programme with headquarters in Nairobi, Kenya. In 1973 the first session of the U.N. Conference on the Law of the Sea was held in New York. Many subsequent sessions have been held in Caracas, Geneva, and New York over a period of nine years, and a treaty on the governance of the oceans was signed in 1982 by 117 nations. In 1974 the World Conference on Population was held in Bucharest and the World Food Conference met in Rome. Starting in 1975 and continuing into 1977, the Conference on International Economic Cooperation in Paris dealt with the relationship between the developed and the less developed countries. In 1976, Vancouver, Canada, and Geneva were the sites of conferences on human settlements and employment. In 1977 the World Water Conference was held at Mar del Plata, Argentina and a conference on the nuclear fuel cycle was held in Salzburg, Austria. In 1978 the Conference on Technical Cooperation among Developing Countries was held in Buenos Aires. In Vienna in 1979 a conference was held on Science and Technology for Development. In 1981 a conference was held in Nairobi on New and Renewable Sources of Energy. Vienna was host again for the 1982 Conference on the Peaceful

Uses of Outer Space. This list of U.N.-sponsored world conferences is by no means complete. The success of the earlier conferences in drawing attention to a given problem has in fact led to such a multiplication of conferences that they no longer attract as much attention as they once did. But even though the general public may not be so well informed about some of the more recent conferences, experts in the various fields involved are aware of them and appreciate their importance in focusing efforts on the solution of these problems.

A ninth area of accomplishment of the U.N. is most evident to social scientists and government officials. The U.N. secures and maintains data on societies all over the world and publishes yearbooks and statistical records containing comparative information from these societies. The information-gathering capabilities presently vary widely from country to country, so the data is not yet so standardized as desired, but the existence of the U.N. as an information-gathering and information-dispensing agency will undoubtedly lead to increasing reliability of this information as the years go by. These data about what has happened and what is happening all over the world are crucial for planning for the future whether the planning is done by private parties, by national governments, or by the United Nations itself.

The tenth contribution of the United Nations is actually a whole collection of achievements of a collection of organizations, some of which are subsidiary organs of the U.N. and some of which are fairly autonomous agencies which report to the Economic and Social Council. Among the subsidiary organs of the U.N. whose work constitutes part of the U.N.'s accomplishments are the U.N. Conference on Trade and Development (UNCTAD), the U.N. Children's Fund (UNICEF), the Office of the U.N. High Commissioner for Refugees (UNHCR), the World Food Programme (a combined effort with the Food and Agriculture Organization), the U.N. Institute for Training and Research (UNITAR), the U.N. Development Programme (UNDP), the U.N. Environmental Programme (UNEP), the U.N. University (UNU), the U.N. Special Fund, the World Food Council, and the U.N. Relief and Works Agency for Palestine Refugees in the Near East (UNRWA). The more autonomous specialized agencies, several of which existed before the U.N. and some even before the League of Nations, will be discussed in the next section.

Worldwide Functional Agencies

National governments are one of the most prominent features of social life on the earth. The boundaries of their control often mark the limits within which a certain language or a certain currency is used. But national boundaries are not inscribed on the surface of the earth, and they do not stop the flow of air and water and animals and radio waves and goods and people from place to place. As a result, problems frequently arise which cannot be handled by national governments acting separately. The League of Nations and the United Nations represent two different efforts to create a supranational organization dedicated to dealing with world problems in general. On the other hand, each of the international organizations now to be discussed aims to perform a specific function. Such organizations consequently are called *functional agencies* or *specialized agencies*. They are also sometimes called *administrative agencies* because they aim to do what needs to be done to solve a particular kind of international problem without confronting political and ideological issues.

The first permanent international functional agency was the European Commission of the Danube. It was created in 1856 to facilitate and regulate traffic on this important river of southeastern Europe. A system of tolls and licenses was developed which permitted the lower Danube to be kept navigable without all the expense being borne by Romania. It also provided for a common set of rules and regulations and a single licensing agency for all users of the river regardless of what country they might be in or go through. The Commission proved to be a success, lasting until World War II. After that war a new Danube Commission was formed. Similar international commissions have been established to supervise navigation on other waterways which flow through more than one country, but these functional agencies are regional rather than worldwide in scope and consequently are more directly related to the next section below which deals with regional functional agencies.

Another example of an early international organization, one which is global in scope, is the International Red Cross. This organization grew out of the efforts of Jean-Henri Dunant, a Swiss humanitarian who had organized emergency aid services for both French and Austrian wounded soldiers at the Battle of Solferino in 1859. The Geneva Convention of 1864 committed the nations who signed it to caring for war wounded, whether friend or enemy. National Red Cross Societies (or Red Crescent Societies in Muslim countries) have been created to provide humanitarian assistance not only in time of war but also during peacetime, especially when natural disasters occur. The international coordination is provided by the International Committee of the Red Cross, a group of 25 Swiss citizens, and by the League of Red Cross Societies which has a secretariat in Geneva.

The first of the worldwide functional agencies which eventually became incorporated into the present U.N. system was the International Telegraphic Union established in 1865. The agency was created by a multilateral convention which enunciated the general principles of the organization and set the rules to be followed by those signing the convention. The International Telecommunication Convention of 1932 brought together the International Telegraphic Union and the International Radiotelegraphic Union, which had been established by a separate convention in 1906. The new International Telecommunication Union became effective in 1934 and became a specialized agency of the U.N. in 1947. Its task is to encourage international cooperation in the use and further development of communication by telegraph, radio, cable, telephone, and television. Regulation of the use of various radio and television frequencies is one of its main functions.

One of the better known worldwide functional agencies is the Universal Postal Union. To facilitate international postal communication without each nation trying to throw the burden of postal charges for this international mail on the other, the General Postal Union was formed in 1874–75. A single scale of charges for all international mail was to be established, and transit charges through any given nation were to be based on weight and mileage. The legislative body is the Postal Congress which meets every five years. New policies are adopted by majority vote, but each nation must then separately ratify its concurrence with the change. It is so advantageous to each nation to belong to the Union that a tradition has been established of virtually automatic ratification of any changes proposed by the Congress. The Congress elects an Executive Council of representatives from 40 different countries to supervise the system between Congresses. The name of this organization was changed to the Universal Postal Union in 1878, and it became a specialized agency of the U.N. in 1948.

There are so many worldwide functional agencies that it would be tedious to try to discuss each one. We can, however, mention those that are officially a part of the U.N. system. Twelve of the specialized agencies are funded through assessments on their members: the International Telecommunications Union and the Universal Postal Union discussed above are two of these. The Food and Agriculture Organization (FAO) aims to improve the quantity and quality of the world's food supply by assisting in agricultural research programs, irrigation projects, pest control activities, development of fishing techniques, and the like. The International Maritime Organization (IMO) aims to improve ship safety and navigation procedures on the high seas, minimize environmental damage from shipping activities, and insure that damages to private property or the environment are paid for by those who do the damage. The International Atomic Energy Agency (IAEA) aims to promote the safe and peaceful use of atomic energy. The International Civil Aviation Organization (ICAO) aims to promote safe and efficient international air travel by regulating aircraft operation, safety equipment, pilot training, and language use for communications related to international flights. The International Labor Organization (ILO) aims to improve the workplace environment for laborers by setting international standards for safety and working conditions so that employers in one country cannot argue that they are disadvantaged compared to employers in another country who need not meet the same standards. The U.N. Educational, Scientific, and Cultural Organization (UNESCO) aims to increase international cooperation in the areas of education (especially literacy programs), scientific research, and the preservation and exchange of culturally and historically important buildings and objects. The World Health Organization (WHO) aims to prevent the spread of disease (especially across national boundaries), to promote health education, and to encourage medical research. The World Intellectual Property Organization (WIPO) aims to promote international cooperation in respecting copyrights, patents, and trademarks. The World Meteorological Organization (WMO) aims to coordinate the gathering and exchange of weather information from all over the world. The U.N. Industrial Development Organization (UNIDO) aims to assist the less developed countries of the world in their efforts to industrialize.[14]

Four specialized agencies dealing with financial matters are officially part of the U.N. system. The International Monetary Fund (IMF) aims to promote the stability of exchange rates between different national currencies and to promote international cooperation with regard to monetary policies. The International Bank for Reconstruction and Development (IBRD), also known as the World Bank, provides loans and other assistance for economic development. The International Development Association (IDA) is affiliated with the World Bank and focuses on helping the poorest nations by arranging loans at extremely low rates of interest. The International Finance Corporation (IFC) is also affiliated with the World Bank, but it aims at promoting private business in less developed countries. As affiliates of the World Bank, IDA and IFC can both borrow from the Bank and thus are able to loan much more than if they were limited to the funds actually given to them by national governments. The World Bank system as a whole provides a means by which richer countries can provide foreign assistance to less developed countries without confronting issues about whether the projects being proposed are in fact promising, and without getting into the position of funding worthless projects just because of the political consequences of not funding them.

In a sense, all these global functional agencies which form part of the U.N. system constitute what would be departments if a fully-developed world government existed. For example, WHO would be the Department of Health, FAO would be the Department of Agriculture, and UNESCO would be the Department of Education. These agencies are busy solving real world problems and improving the quality of life for the whole human race. For example, as the result of the work of WHO, smallpox has been eliminated from the face of the earth.[15]

Regional Functional and Political Organizations

Although our discussion of functional agencies has so far been directed mainly to those which are *global* in scope, we did mention the Danube River Commission, which is an example of a *regional* functional organization. There are many more of these international regional functional organizations than of those with a worldwide scope. Although regional functional organizations carry on many different specific kinds of tasks, the most important ones fall into one of two classes. First, there are those regional organizations whose primary function is military cooperation against a prospective opponent. Second, there are those regional organizations whose primary function is economic cooperation. In addition to these *functional* organizations there are regional *political* organizations which aim to peacefully resolve conflicts of interest among their members and to adopt a common policy toward nations outside the organization.

Regional *military* organizations may look at first glance like simple military alliances, but there is a difference. A regional military organization includes a governing council, which meets on a regular basis, and an integrated military staff, which functions at all times, not just during crises or war. In other words, an actual organization is created to implement a military agreement rather than just having a commitment to join in the fighting in case of an attack. The most obvious example of such a regional military organization is the North Atlantic Treaty Organization (NATO). Other examples are the Warsaw Treaty Organization (the Eastern European counterpart to NATO) and ANZUS (a military security organization with representatives from Australia, New Zealand, and the United States).

Regional *economic* organizations usually seek to develop a free trade area or common market among the nations which belong. Tariffs and quotas between member states are eliminated, and a common tariff policy is adopted toward nations or groups of nations outside the regional group. These regional economic organizations also seek to promote economic cooperation and development among their members. In the case of Benelux (an economic union of Belgium, the Netherlands, and Luxembourg) cooperation includes provisions for the free flow of capital and labor across national boundaries and for common tax laws, welfare policies, and postal and transport rates.

The outstanding example of regional economic integration is Western Europe. The European Coal and Steel Community was created in 1952 to integrate the coal and steel industries in France, West Germany, Italy, and the Benelux countries. The European Economic Community (the EEC or "Common Market") was created by the same countries in 1957 to establish a free trade area among them and a common economic policy toward other nations. Denmark, Ireland, and the United Kingdom joined the EEC in 1973, and Greece became a functioning member in 1981.

The success of the European Economic Community in promoting economic growth in Europe led to the formation of other international economic organizations such as the European Free Trade Association (EFTA) consisting of the capitalistic European countries not in the European Economic Community, the Council for Mutual Economic Assistance (Comecon) consisting of the Soviet Union and its socialist neighbors, the Central American Common Market (CACM), the Latin America Free Trade Association (LAFTA), the Andean Development Corporation (the Andean Group within LAFTA), and the Caribbean Free Trade Association (CFTA). There are also several regional development banks modeled on the World Bank.

Some economic international organizations are less than global in scope but also are not regional. One example is the British Commonwealth, made up of Britain and many of its former colonies. Another example is the Organization for Economic Cooperation and Development (OECD). That organization began in 1948 as the Organization for European Economic Cooperation (OEEC) whose aim was to coordinate American assistance to a devastated Europe. The U.S., Canada, and Japan joined with these Western European countries in that organization, whose name was changed in 1961 to the Organization for Economic Cooperation and Development and whose aims included the further development and economic stability of the developed capitalist countries, the coordination of aid to the less developed countries, and the promotion of world trade. Still another example of an economic international organization which is not global but which is also not regional is the Organization of Petroleum Exporting Countries (OPEC).

Continuously increasing economic cooperation within a group of countries usually will eventually lead to problems of a political nature. For example, there are frequently differences among member countries with regard to tax policies, agricultural subsidies, and benefits for the unemployed. As economic integration proceeds, it becomes necessary to decide how to reconcile these different policies. Economic cooperation reaches a point where it cannot be expanded without some type of political integration. The European community seems to have reached this point.

Consequently, it should not be surprising that when we turn our attention to international *political* regional organizations, it is Western Europe which is farthest along the path to significant political integration. The European Community now has a decision-making Council, a Commission, a Court of Justice, and a Parliament. In the spring of 1979 the people of Western Europe for the first time elected representatives to the European Parliament. The very difficult problem of how many representatives each country would have was solved by the adoption of the following formula: France, West Germany, Italy, and the United Kingdom each have 81 representatives; the Netherlands has 25; Belgium has 24; Denmark has 16 (including one from Greenland); the Irish Republic has 15; and Luxembourg has 6.[16] The powers of the European Parliament are quite limited now, but they can be expected to grow as this institution matures. Membership will also expand. In 1979 it was decided that Greece would become a member in 1981, and it is likely that Spain and Portugal will be added within a few years.

Although Europe leads the way in political integration, there are several other regional political organizations which are much weaker in nature but nevertheless dedicated to dealing with the problems of the region in a general way and not serving as merely functional or administrative organizations. The basic aim of these organizations is usually to keep nations outside that region from intervening in what are viewed as regional matters. If the nations in the region are able to settle any disputes among themselves, then action by other nations or by the United Nations will be unnecessary.

For example, the Organization of American States, which includes all the countries of the Americas except Cuba and Canada, serves to continue the Monroe Doctrine of the U.S., according to which nations in other parts of the world are to refrain from involvement in American affairs. Similarly, the newly-independent nations of Africa have created the Organization of African Unity not only to work together in moving out of their colonial status but also to settle conflicts between African nations without the involvement of either the developed capitalist states or the Communist bloc. All African nations except segregationist South Africa belong. The Arab League was established to foster Arab unity but has found little agreement except in anti-Israel sentiment, and even on the issue of how to deal with Israel there has been a great deal of disagreement. One regional international political organization which seems more interested in promoting cooperation among its members than in keeping outsiders out is the Nordic Council, composed of Denmark, Finland, Iceland, Norway, and Sweden. The aim of that Council is the promotion of more uniform legal and economic practices.

It is possible that one or another of these or other regional international political organizations will become more significant in the future, but so far only the European organization seems to have developed a higher level of integration than that found at the global level in the United Nations. Meanwhile, it is somewhat distressing to see that in the regional organizations the motive of keeping outsiders out usually seems to be much more important than that of furthering positive cooperation among the nations of the region.

International Nongovernmental Organizations

When we look at the international institutions which reflect a developing global community, we tend to concentrate so much attention on those institutions created by and for national governments that we may overlook the international institutions being created by individuals and groups than national governments. Yet these *nongovernmental* international organizations play a crucial role in promoting those attitudes and perspectives which are essential if there is ever to be peace and justice on a global scale. The United Nations has recognized the importance of these nongovernmental organizations (NGO's) by permitting many of them to have a special affiliation with the U.N. and its agencies through the Economic and Social Council as provided in the U.N. Charter.[17] At present nearly 700 nongovernmental organizations are so affiliated.[18]

Among the NGO's affiliated with the U.N., the ones most directly relevant to the problems of peace and justice are those whose efforts are focused on issues such as human rights and disarmament. Amnesty International, which won the Nobel Peace Prize for 1977, conducts independent investigations of violations of human rights and consequently has been permitted to present its findings to the U.N. Commission on Human Rights. The same privilege has been extended to the International League for Human Rights. In fact, these two NGO's have been so successful in bringing violations of human rights to the attention of the public that certain national governments such as those of the U.S.S.R., Argentina, and Chile are trying to deprive them of consultative status with the Economic and Social Council.

A historic moment occurred at the U.N. when, during the 1978 Special Session on Disarmament, representatives from some of the nongovernmental organizations interested in disarmament were allowed to address the Assembly.[19] These representatives seemed to be much more eager to move toward a disarmed world than the government representatives of many of the nations. This is why the NGO's are so important. They speak for the human interest, for peace and justice. Many of the national governments and their representatives, on the other hand, are interested primarily in protecting national interests, the interests of powerful groups in their countries, and the status quo. U.S. President Eisenhower once remarked, "I like to believe that people, in the long run, are going to do more to promote peace than are governments. Indeed, I think that people want peace so much that one of these days governments had better get out of the way and let them have it."[20] If citizen effort is ever going to succeed, it will need to be channeled through NGO's dedicated to peace, justice, and the common good.

One large group of NGO's affiliated with the U.N. consists of the international religious organizations. These affiliated religious groups include representatives from Catholic and Protestant Christianity, Judaism, Islam, Buddhism, and Hinduism as well as smaller groups such as the Bahais, the Friends, and the Unitarian-Universalists. Religious groups are important to peace because of their role in the development of attitudes. Some religious institutions have been promoters of the grossest kind of parochialism and nationalism, leading war combatants on both sides to believe that God is on their side and that opponents should be utterly destroyed because they are the incarnation of evil. Other religious institutions, however, have been instrumental in inculcating a devotion to peace and justice and the welfare of the whole human family. Which of these attitudes is promoted by religious groups makes a great deal of difference concerning what kind of world we live in and will live in.

Other international nongovernmental organizations consist of professional or vocational groups. Still others focus on special hobbies and interests. Many service organizations have an international scope. There are also athletic organizations which transcend national boundaries. Organizations such as the Club of Rome seek to promote the independent study of problems facing the global community. Only a minority of these numerous international organizations are formally related to the U.N., but they nevertheless are global institutions which accordingly tend to break down the nationalism and parochialism which have been so prominent a factor in modern warfare.

Another very important kind of nongovernmental international institution is the transnational business enterprise. These companies, frequently called "multinational corporations," tend to promote feelings of human unity. National differences in regulations, tax laws, systems of measurement, language, and the like are nuisances to these companies. Although transnational businesses are motivated by a desire for profit and may in some ways be perceived as instruments of imperialism, in other ways they facilitate the development of a global perspective and a positive attitude toward human cooperation which is free from nationalistic and other kinds of biases.

A significant problem for many nongovernmental international organizations is the absence of an international language. Governmental organizations and some transnational business enterprises operating at the international level are able to provide the equipment and personnel to make quick translations available to the participants at their meetings, but this is not true for most of the nongovernmental international organizations. For example, when the World Conference on Religion and Peace holds a world assembly, what language or languages should be used? Such organizations are usually not able to afford the equipment and personnel needed to furnish translations and copies of written material in several different languages. The leaders of the national governments, who have translations provided to them when they get together, do not seem very interested in this problem. Consequently, its solution may depend primarily on another nongovernmental international organization, the Universala Esperanto-Asocio, an organization devoted to spreading the use of the international language Esperanto. It is worth noting that when the Esperantists have a world conference they are not confronted by the same language problem as other international organizations. They all speak Esperanto.

XII. Legal Aspects of the Contemporary Situation

We are likely to suppose that laws can exist only when there is some authorized person or body to make the laws and see that they get enforced; that is, we may believe that there cannot be law without government. Since there is no government above the nations (the U.N. is not a full-fledged government even though it is a political organization), we may conclude that there cannot be anything such as international law which nations are obliged to obey. But such a conclusion would not be correct. International law exists and is recognized by national governments even though it is not always obeyed. We will begin our discussion of the legal aspects of the contemporary situation by reviewing how international law has evolved. We will then turn to the laws of war as an example of international law. After considering the sources of international law, we will discuss the issue of how effective international law can be expected to be in regulating the behavior of nations.

The Nature of International Law

International law rests on the presumption that the relations between nations are somewhat different from the relations between individual persons. Individual persons are not self-sufficient. They need other persons to bring them into existence, to care for them when young, to exchange goods and services with them (no person can take care of all his own needs), and to keep them company. They have sexual desires which lead them to mate with others and parental feelings which cause them to care for their offspring. Nations, on the other hand, are presumed to be relatively self-sufficient "organisms." They usually can survive without any interaction with other states. They do not need other states to bring them into existence or to take care of them when young. They do not need other states to help them provide for their needs or to keep them from being lonely. They do not have sexual desires which lead them to interact with other states, nor do they produce son and daughter nations which must be cared for. People must live in societies, but nations do not need to live in a society of nations; they are able to survive in relative isolation from other nations with few adverse effects.

Since people must live in societies to survive and meet their various needs, they can be expected to abide by certain restrictions on their behavior in order to remain in the society. As societies evolve, these restrictions are codified as the law of the society, and the laws are maintained by religious and political authorities. This law of the society over its own citizens is called *municipal law* as opposed to the very different type of law, *international law*, which regulates the behavior of nations with regard to each other. Because of their very different situations, individual persons are born into a society and are subject to the laws of that society, while nations are subject to no laws except those which they have explicitly accepted as binding on themselves. Another way of saying that states are subject to no externally imposed law is to say that nations are *sovereign*.

Although nations are not subject to any laws but those to which they have deliberately and explicitly subjected themselves, they may nevertheless be conquered and destroyed by other nations. Many nations that once existed no longer do. Thus a struggle for survival and power exists among the various nations presently existing. In this contest for survival and power, nations may find it advantageous to enter into agreements (treaties) with other nations. For example, consider a situation where there is an aggressive state more powerful militarily than each of two other neighboring states but not more powerful than both of them together. In this situation the two weaker nations may enter into an agreement not to attack each other and to fight together if the stronger one should attack either one.

What assurance is there that these two nations will live up to their agreement with each other? The situation is somewhat different from a contract between two citizens of the same state where the government will use its power to penalize any party which fails to fulfill its agreement. There is no government over the states to enforce the agreement if either side should try to back out. Still nations make such agreements, and most of the time they live up to them. Why? Because it is in the self-interest of each state to do so. Let us consider the situation in detail. Suppose that you are the leader of the state which finds its treaty partner being attacked. It is in your self-interest to abide by your agreement even though it means going to war. That is because if the more powerful enemy state overcomes your partner, which is likely if you refrain from fighting, then that victorious nation will probably attack you after it has solidified its conquest of your former partner. Consequently, it is better to join in the battle as soon as your partner is attacked than to wait and let the more powerful state devour your partner and you, one at a time.

There is also some motivation to join in the battle in accord with the treaty merely to establish the fact that your country can in general be counted on to live up to its agreements. If your country should get a reputation for not fulfilling its treaty obligations, then other nations will be reluctant to make other treaties with you in the future. Furthermore, since each nation enters into only those treaties that it wants to make, your country need not make any commitments which it does not intend to keep. Of course, there are cases where states have not lived up to their agreements, but in such cases the governments involved are very eager to provide some justification for not keeping their commitments, thus preserving their honor as treaty-keeping countries. States tend to abide by the treaties into which they enter because it is in their long-term self-interest to do so.

One of the most basic kinds of agreements nations make with each other is that which provides for reciprocal benefits; that is, each nation agrees to do for the other exactly what the other one agrees to do for it. For example, Nation A may agree to allow the citizens of Nation B to travel through Nation A unhindered if Nation B allows the citizens of Nation A to travel through Nation B unhindered. A good deal of international law depends on this principle of reciprocity. It is the basis, for example, of the law of diplomatic immunity, whereby each nation agrees not to harm or arrest or otherwise interfere with diplomats sent into its territory by other nations. Without such an agreement diplomats might be harassed, put in jail and held for ransom, or even killed. Under such circumstances no diplomats would go to other countries and international communication among nations would be severely handicapped. The principle of reciprocity is also the basis of the laws of war to be considered below. Such rules governing conflict are obeyed because each nation finds it beneficial to abide by them, because only then can the other side also be expected to abide by them.

Certain agreements, such as that providing for the immunity of diplomats from arrest, have become so common that nations may feel it is no longer necessary to stipulate that such an agreement exists when they begin dealing with each other. These and similar widely accepted arrangements in the dealings of countries with one another have come to be viewed as the rules of international *customary law*. To avoid possible misunderstandings about exactly what these customary rules are, however, they were codified in 1961 in the Vienna Convention on Diplomatic Relations.

The sovereignty of the nation is basic in all international law. Even though the rules of international customary law have the weight of wide acceptance and tradition behind them, any country which wished to renounce them or to join with another nation in some agreements which are not consistent with the customary law may do so. As sovereign, any nation can decide which other nations it will recognize. It can decide to take on obligations to another nation or to an international body such as the United Nations. It can unilaterally declare a previous agreement with another state to be void if in its own opinion the other party has not fulfilled its obligations under the agreement! Furthermore, no nation can be bound by the agreements of other nations. Consequently, even if all nations but one agreed to follow certain principles (for example, that all should completely disarm), that single sovereign nation could still refuse to go along. If the other countries were determined to make the agreement universal, their only option would be to physically subdue the recalcitrant country, consequently depriving it of its existence as a sovereign nation. This example also illustrates how some nations may be subject to coercion by other more powerful nations even though, in principle, all nations are sovereign. The reality is that nations are sovereign, but only so long as they can maintain their existence as independent nations.[1]

The Evolution of International Law

It should be evident that international law is not static, but is instead a changing body of obligations which may even differ from nation to nation. Although the counterpart of modern international law was developed among the Greek city-states, present international law has grown out of the dealings of European states with each other in the Middle Ages when nations were generally much smaller than those of today. At one time it was supposed that nations were at war with each other unless they had specifically entered into an agreement to be at peace. Unless there were specific agreements to the contrary, rulers could do as they pleased with any foreigners in their territory. To assure that a treaty would be kept, one party frequently provided the other with hostages who could be killed or otherwise abused if the provisions of the agreement were not fulfilled.

As the European community grew in wealth and technology, certain traditions and expectations with regard to international behavior developed. Frequently, principles of municipal law were extended by analogy to the international situation, especially when the ideologies and institutions of the nations involved were similar. Different views about the nature of international law were used to support efforts to argue for or against the adoption of certain proposed rules. Some philosophers appealed to *natural law*, that is, to the dictates of reason, as a guide to what is required of nations in their relations to each other. Others took what has come to be known as the *positivist position*, maintaining that countries had no obligations to each other except what they had specifically agreed to do in formal treaties. Still others appealed to *custom and tradition* as the basis for determining present obligations of one nation to another.[2]

Regardless of what philosophy of law might be used to provide a rationale for the principles of international law which came to be followed in the European system, the principles adopted were those which were acceptable to the more powerful nations. Thus, freedom of the seas became an accepted principle. Likewise the notion that the discoverer of a land was entitled to claim it for his own country was generally accepted. The right of conquest over "inferior" native peoples was accepted without question. As these European nations extended their control over the Americas, Africa, and Asia, they took these concepts of international law with them. Needless to say, if the peoples being subdued could have learned about this "international law" which was being used to justify their subjugation, they would not have regarded it as very desirable. It merely served as a device by which the powerful could exploit the weak, all the while maintaining that this was done by a legal process. It also functioned, however, to regulate the dealings of the European countries with each other, so that the danger of war between the colonizers would be minimized.

By the nineteenth century Europe had become a society of nations where interactions were not just between one state and another but frequently among several as a group. Treaties ending wars, for example, usually involved several countries. After World War I, President Wilson persuaded the Europeans of the desirability of an international organization to regulate international affairs. The creation of this League of Nations, which was intended to include not only European nations but also nations of other parts of the world, was conceived as being completely consistent with the notion of national sovereignty on which international law was based. Any nation which wanted to join could do so without giving up any of its sovereignty, since all decisions of the League were to be unanimous. No nation could be compelled to join the League or to remain in it once it had joined.

Although the development of the League of Nations was completely consistent with national sovereignty, it did develop a new principle in international relations, the notion of collective security in the face of an aggressive attack. Until the creation of the League, war had been regarded as a natural and legitimate way of expanding national power and any nation that was attacked was expected to defend itself. The League introduced a new idea in international law, namely, that launching a military attack against another nation was a reprehensible act and that it was the responsibility of sovereign nations to assist other sovereign nations in the enforcement of this principle, even when they were not themselves victims of the aggression.[3] It is obvious from history that nations found ways of avoiding this responsibility when it did not serve their own interests, but nevertheless the principle of the illegitimacy of military aggression and of the responsibility of all nations to act against an aggressor had been stated and at least nominally accepted by the nations which joined the League.

Another important development in international law came when the League established the Permanent Court of International Justice. For the first time an international tribunal was established to interpret international law as it applied to particular cases. If there were any dispute about what was required by international law in a particular situation, the nations now had a third party to which they could turn for an answer if all the disputants involved agreed to do so. This development also meant that there would be some pressure on every nation to accept principles of international law that had been accepted by most other nations. Strictly speaking, however, it was still true that no principle could be applied by the Permanent Court to a nation which had not accepted it.

The establishment of the United Nations after World War II also marked new developments in international law, at least in terms of what nations committed themselves to doing. The Security Council, composed of representatives from a small group of countries, was authorized to decide what kind of action should be taken with respect to threats to the peace, breaches of the peace, and acts of aggression. It was also given the right to determine what actions member nations and their military forces should take in such circumstances![4] Although any countries supplying forces must ratify arrangements made by the Security Council, there seems to be an important move away from the notion of national sovereignty in these provisions. The principle enunciated in the U.N. Charter is no longer simply that of collective defense as found in the League Covenant, but rather *internationally organized* collective defense under the direction of the Security Council and its Military Staff Committee. To be sure, no country is compelled to join the United Nations, but once it has signed the Charter it takes on a new kind of obligation not previously found in international law. The existence of such a commitment has led Switzerland to stay out of the U.N. itself, even though it belongs to most of the U.N.'s specialized agencies.

A second new development in international law ushered in by the United Nations concerns the commitment to human rights mentioned in the Charter and developed by the Universal Declaration of Human Rights and two later treaties, the International Covenant on Economic, Social, and Cultural Rights and the International Covenant on Civil and Political Rights. Especially significant for the development of international law is the Protocol to the Covenant on Civil and Political Rights.[5] Nations which adopt this Protocol give their citizens the opportunity to appeal directly to an international body, the U.N. Human Rights Committee, if they feel their human rights are being violated by their own national government. Here, for the first time, the possibility exists of a nation entering into an international agreement which restrains the sovereignty of that government over its own citizens.

A third development in international law since the end of World War II has been the much greater emphasis on violations of international law by individual persons. There has been an effort to delineate and prescribe penalties for those individuals who have broken international law. The wide and early acceptance of the principle of the freedom of the seas resulted in pirates being considered international criminals some time ago, but the problem of piracy at sea was virtually eliminated in the nineteenth century. The new problems are piracy in the air in the form of hijacking airplanes, taking of international hostages, crimes by individuals against diplomats and citizens of other countries, and terrorism by individuals. International conventions have been adopted defining these crimes and indicating what national governments may do when such crimes are committed. The effort to penalize individuals for breaking international law got a big boost from the Nuremberg trials after World War II, where Nazi leaders were tried as individuals for war crimes.[6] Although one can be cynical about whether the persons tried in these cases were really any more responsible than others not brought to trial and about whether these trials are not simply a device used by the victors to humiliate the vanquished, one can also see them as part of a trend toward singling out for punishment those individuals who break international law. In this connection it is significant that a few of the German defendants at Nuremberg were found *not guilty* of violating international law.[7]

This brief survey indicates that international law is developing gradually in the direction of world law, a law which is above the national governments and which puts some restrictions on national sovereignty. Consider the changes that have taken place: While it was once assumed that nations are at war with each other unless they had explicitly signed a truce, it is now assumed that nations are at peace unless they have declared war on each other. Furthermore, fighting a war is now viewed as acceptable behavior only if it is in response to aggression either against the nation itself or some other nation.

The old presuppositions on which international law had rested no longer hold. In a modern technological world, nations are no longer self-sufficient. Even a large and powerful nation such as the United States must import large amounts of oil and other raw materials from abroad, and it must also sell some of its goods to other nations. In the present world the behavior of every nation makes a great deal of difference to all the others, whether it consists of testing nuclear weapons, adopting new tariffs to protect domestic production, adjusting the exchange rate of its currency, raising the prices on its exports, broadcasting propaganda, or building up its armed forces. Consequently, it no longer makes sense to conceive of nations as essentially isolated "organisms" which once in a while come into contact with their immediate neighbors. A society of nations has been developing and, along with it, a code of conduct suitable for such a society.

Laws of War

One of the most interesting aspects of international law is that even when nations are engaged in open hostilities against each other they still follow rules, the laws of war, which restrain their behavior. How is this possible? It stems from the same principle as all international law, namely, mutual self-interest. For example, in war both sides will experience situations where some of their military forces are so outnumbered that they will want to surrender rather than be slaughtered. Consequently, a rule of war exists by which armed forces are permitted to surrender rather than being killed. Furthermore, it is to the advantage of each side to keep observing this rule. If one side starts slaughtering opponents who have surrendered, it can expect the same to happen to its own personnel who are trapped. Consequently, the rules of war are designed to keep war from becoming any more brutal than it already is.

A fundamental distinction made in the rules of warfare is that between military personnel (combatants) and civilians (noncombatants).

It is presumed that the contest in war is between the military forces of the nations involved and that the aim of warfare is military victory. According to this way of thinking, there is no point in killing civilians because it does not contribute to military victory to do so. Since the governments on both sides want to preserve their civilian populations from any more harm than necessary, the rules of war indicate that it is acceptable to try to kill military personnel (as well as to destroy the armaments they use or could use) but that it is improper to try to kill civilians (or to destroy the equipment they use for farming or their other civilian pursuits). Trains and ships and airplanes carrying military personnel or military supplies are fair game, but others are not. Following this same outlook, prisoners, wounded military personnel and those who care for them, pilots who have parachuted from their aircraft, survivors of sunken ships, and the like are not to be attacked since they no longer constitute a military threat.[8]

In modern warfare the distinction between military and civilian sectors of a nation's wartime efforts has become very blurred. Whole nations are mobilized for warfare. The high school student of today is the soldier of tomorrow, so why wait until he gets into uniform before trying to kill him? Some of the food which the farmer grows may go to civilians, but part also goes to the military, who would have a hard time continuing the war without it. The workers who are producing tanks, airplanes, ships, and ammunition are civilians, but the goods they produce are as crucial to the continuation of the fighting as the soldiers who use them. The wounded soldier of today is the already-trained functioning soldier of tomorrow, so why wait until he has recovered before trying to kill him?

Also, if we look at war carefully, we see that it is the governments rather than the military forces which are ultimately responsible for carrying on the war. If the civilian population is bombed and otherwise intimidated, won't they eventually pressure their own government to stop the war by surrendering? Why not make the population of the other side suffer just as the other side will cause suffering to one's own population if the area where they are living were to be conquered? Such questions came to the fore especially during World War II when aerial bombing made it possible to attack far behind the front lines. Furthermore, now that nuclear weapons with their extensive destructiveness are available, it becomes hard to see how an attack could any longer be pinpointed on military targets even if the attacker wished to do so. The present planning for the use of strategic nuclear weapons by the U.S. and the U.S.S.R. is not inhibited by any wish not to harm civilians. The traditional distinction between military targets on the one hand and civilian areas and personnel on the other is in danger of being lost completely. Yet, if this distinction is eliminated, then those international laws protecting prisoners and the wounded on grounds that they are no longer active members of the enemy's military forces would seem to lose their justification too.

If there cannot be humane war, why not try to prohibit war itself as inhumane? An effort to renounce war as an instrument of national policy was made in 1928 in the form of the Treaty for the Renunciation of War (also called "The Pact of Paris" and "The Kellogg-Briand Pact"). Unfortunately, this treaty did not stop World War II from occurring (though it did serve as a basis for some of the indictments of German leaders at the Nuremberg trials). The U.N. Charter also contains statements renouncing war, and even renouncing the *threat* of using force![9] The trouble is that international laws of war have not always been obeyed during war, and there is no basis to expect that an international law against starting a war would be observed any more faithfully. In the final analysis, nations tend to act in terms of their perception of their own national interest; and when obeying international law comes into conflict with national interest, it is national interest which prevails.

The Sources of International Law

We have already noted that international law differs from municipal law in that there is no authorized person or body which enacts or enforces it and that international law evolves as other things change. We have mentioned in passing some of the sources of international law, but will now explore this issue in more depth. Suppose that you were a member of the International Court of Justice hearing a case. Since there is no world legislature whose acts would produce world law, where can you turn to discover what the international laws are that might bear on the case at hand?

Article 38 of the Statute of the International Court of Justice spells out precisely what sources are to be used.[10] First, you could turn to "international conventions [including treaties], whether general or particular, establishing rules expressly recognized by the contesting states." Note that it does not matter what principles of international law may have been accepted by other nations. All that counts are the principles explicitly acceded to by the parties involved in the present dispute.

Second, you could refer to "international custom, as evidence of a general practice accepted as law." As we noted earlier, there are certain principles involved in the relationships between nations which have become so common that they are assumed rather than being written into treaties. We have already indicated that these rules of international customary law were codified in the 1961 Vienna Convention on Diplomatic Relations.

Third, one could use "the general principles of law recognized by civilized nations." It is understood that this source of law is to be used only when the matter cannot be resolved using the first two sources. It is only the very general principles of law which are accepted by all the major legal systems of the world which are relevant. The main point of specifying this source of international law is to preclude a situation where the Court could not decide an obvious issue because the principle involved had not come up for consideration in earlier treaties or conflicts.

Fourth, appeal could be made to "judicial decisions" previously rendered by international, and even national, courts and to "the teachings of the most highly qualified publicists of the various nations." Scholars of international law are constantly publishing arguments for one or another position, and if there were a consensus among these experts on international law from various legal traditions, then their opinion might be used to support a judgment. Still, it must be remembered that appeal to previous judicial decisions and to the opinion of experts are "subsidiary means for the determination of rules of law" and consequently become significant only when the first three sources leave the issue unresolved.

One of the more interesting sources of international law is that which grows out of treaties and covenants in a secondary way. For example, states which have joined the United Nations have signed a treaty (the U.N. Charter) upon entering the organization. The Charter establishes the whole U.N. structure, including the General Assembly. Suppose the General Assembly unanimously passes a resolution dealing with a particular aspect of international law, for example, that the oceans are "the common heritage of mankind" rather than the property of any nation. If none of the nations protested or voted against this principle when given the opportunity to do so, it can be assumed that all have accepted it, just as if they had signed a treaty containing this declaration. No nation could later claim during a judicial proceeding that it had not accepted it. On the other hand, if a given nation had voted *against* that declaration, it would not be obliged to conform to that declaration no matter how many other nations in the General Assembly had voted for it. Thus, there is no assumption that the General Assembly can make international law. The situation is rather that nations put themselves on record when they cast their vote in the U.N. and that those votes might later be taken by the International Court of Justice to indicate acceptance of a measure acted on by the General Assembly.

Enforcing International Law

Just as there is no legislature or other authority to make international law, so also there is no police force or other agency to enforce it. What is to be done if a decision has been rendered by the International Court of Justice and a nation refuses to abide by the decision? Ideally, the Security Council of the U.N. should coordinate enforcement efforts, but it is also conceivable that the U.N. General Assembly might recommend measures to the member states of the U.N. or that individual nations might act on their own. In any case, efforts to enforce the decision might include cutting off trade, severing diplomatic relations, eliminating international exchanges with regard to mail or transportation, or initiating military action.

How effective would such enforcement efforts be? It seems to depend a great deal on the power and self-sufficiency of the "outlaw" country and the level of support among the more powerful nations for enforcing the sanctions. If the country which refused to abide by the Court's decision was a weaker nation and there was enthusiastic support for enforcement among all the big powers, the actions suggested above would undoubtedly be effective; there probably would be no need to go beyond the imposition of economic sanctions. On the other hand, if the country which refused to abide by the Court's decision was a powerful country or had even a single powerful ally who would not support sanctions against it, efforts to enforce the decision would be vetoed in the Security Council or thwarted in some other way.

A further examination of this hypothetical situation shows how completely power politics dominates the international situation. Even though the International Court of Justice is supposed to be an impartial body, it would probably not render a judgment contrary to the vital interests of one of the superpowers, realizing that its judgment could not be carried out and that consequently the authority of the Court would be undermined. If the Court did nevertheless hand down a decision unfavorable to a superpower, there would be little likelihood that such a judgment could be enforced. If action were attempted in the Security Council, the superpower would simply cast a veto to stop it. If the General Assembly tried to generate support for sanctions, the superpower might threaten to leave the U.N. Without one or the other of the superpowers, the U.N. would lose much of its prestige as a world organization. Consequently, while the U.S. and the U.S.S.R. would both be reluctant to actually leave the U.N., any threats they might make to do so would probably be sufficient to deter action against them. Another aspect of trying to enforce a decision against a superpower is the fact that carrying out sanctions, such as cutting off trade, might be more disadvantageous to the other nations than to the nation supposedly being punished.

Even though we might abhor the fact that international law will be much more of a constraining factor on weak nations than on strong ones, we should not forget that unfortunately the same thing is true to some extent even within domestic legal systems. Very wealthy individuals, politically influential people, corporations, labor unions, and the like have enough power that legislatures and courts are much more protective of their interests than of the interests of poor, powerless, unorganized people. What makes the national political and judicial systems as workable as they are is that even the most powerful individuals and groups constitute only a small proportion of the nation as a whole and thus their capacity to resist the dictates of the common interest is restricted. On the other hand, on the international scene the U.S. alone accounts for about a quarter of the world's production of goods and services. Its allies in Western Europe and Japan account for another quarter. How could any world organization hope to endorse decisions to which the U.S. and its allies were intensely opposed? Perhaps the only hope for either international law or world law is to deal with individuals rather than large groups or nations. Then the problem of enforcement becomes much more manageable.

We should not suppose, however, that the only motivation which national governments have for obeying international law is the possible coercive activities of other nations. As noted previously, another important motive is long-range self-interest. International law has been built on the basis of agreements which are mutually satisfying to the nations entering into the treaties. Any loss which may come from the application of international law in one situation will probably be small compared with the gains that can be made in the long run by making use of international law. Consequently, although nations can be expected to struggle to their utmost to advance their national interests, they can also be expected to exercise some restraint instead of openly violating international law. For the smaller, less powerful nations the gains from a strengthened system of international law will be even greater than for the more powerful countries.

A third motivation which national governments have for obeying international law is furnished by the relation of such governments to their own citizens. In many democratic nations, and even in some non-democratic ones, there is a concern for the morality of law which will be marshalled against any national government which blatantly transgresses it. In the 1930's when the governments of Great Britain and France were making deals with Mussolini to try to lure him onto their side against Hitler, even though the Covenant of the League of Nations required them to resist Italy's aggression in Ethiopia, they had to keep what they were doing secret.[11] They knew that a substantial proportion of their own citizenry backed the League and its principles of collective defense against nations engaging in aggression. In 1974, when OPEC quadrupled the price of oil, there was some talk of using military force to conquer the oil fields of the Middle East, but such a blatant use of force and indifference to international law would have generated mass protests in the U.S. and other Western democracies.

National governments must also keep up at least the appearance of abiding by international law because of the dangerous example they would provide to their own citizens if they openly defied established principles of international law. Although there is a considerable difference between municipal law and international law, the subtleties of this distinction will not be apparent to most of the citizenry. Consequently, most national governments will do everything they can to avoid being perceived as violators of international law because they do not wish to provide an example of lawlessness to their own people.

Finally, it should be kept in mind that there is one way in which the enforcement of international law is not as much of a problem as the enforcement of municipal law, namely, that in international law each nation is subject only to those rules which it has explicitly accepted as binding, while in municipal law individual persons are subject to rules which they did not personally consent to obey but which were imposed on them by the government. A nation need not commit itself to any rule that it doesn't intend to follow. This situation means that nations will have fewer legal obligations but will usually abide by the ones to which they have committed themselves. An obvious exception, however, is the situation where nations have just lost a war and are coerced into signing agreements which they would not make voluntarily. Under such circumstances they may not feel obliged to fulfill the terms which have been imposed on them.

Regardless of theoretical considerations, however, one cannot be very optimistic about the enforcement of international law after what happened with regard to Iran in 1980. The Iranian government acquiesced in the seizure of American diplomatic personnel and property by some of its own citizens in direct violation of the principle of diplomatic immunity, one of the oldest principles of international law. The International Court of Justice ruled unanimously that Iran had violated the 1961 Vienna Convention on Diplomatic Relations, which Iran had signed. Nevertheless, no international sanctions were adopted against Iran, even though it was not a superpower or the close ally of a superpower and all diplomats everywhere were threatened by the weakening of this particular international law. There may have been a feeling that the Iranian government was not strong enough to take the supposedly unpopular action of freeing the American hostages from the hands of their captors. The fact that many countries were dependent on Iran for oil may have also been an important factor. Nevertheless, the failure of the international community to enforce the decision of the International Court against Iran was a disaster from the point of view of promoting future reliance on international law and the International Court of Justice.

Part Four

Proposals for Solving
the War Problem

XIII. Reforming the Attitudes of Individuals

Since the war problem is a complex problem, one cannot expect to find a single simple solution for it. Many proposals for trying to solve the war problem must be examined, and some combination of them will undoubtedly be required to rid the world of war. This chapter will focus on modifying the attitudes of individuals as a way of promoting peace. Subsequent chapters will deal with the internal social structure of nations, with the foreign policies pursued by nations, and with the basic structure of the international system.

The preamble of the constitution of the United Nations Educational, Scientific, and Cultural Organization says: "Since wars begin in the minds of men, it is in the minds of men that the defenses of peace must be constructed." In one way or another, education seems to be at least part of the solution to almost any social problem. But when we speak of education, we must beware of jumping to the conclusion that education is for young people alone or that it refers only to what happens within classrooms in schools. Education refers to all teaching of some by others in all kinds of situations. Most of our attitudes come from our parents, our close associates, and the mass media. Teachers are close associates of their students only for a brief period of time. Consequently, although it is to be hoped that teachers and the formal educational system of which they are a part can be instrumental in furthering the objectives discussed below, it would be a gigantic mistake to believe that the institutionalized educational system, by itself, can do a great deal to reform the attitudes of individuals. If the attitudes of individuals are to be reformed in a manner that will make war less likely, many persons in the society will need to take part. The efforts of the mass media will be especially important, and several kinds of attitudes will need to be addressed.

Interest in Social Issues Including International Affairs

Attitudes about the importance of certain kinds of events are affected by how much we know about them. It is true that when we think that something is important we make an effort to find out about it, but it is also true that we tend to regard as unimportant anything about which we know very little. Consequently, the development of attitudes and interests depends to some extent on the knowledge we acquire, especially when young. If this knowledge is only about our own immediate family and close friends, we may unconsciously come to believe that what is happening to others in other places is unimportant. The same holds at another level, too: If we learn only about our own nation and its history and traditions, we may unconsciously come to believe that what has happened and is happening to people in other lands is unimportant. Interest in the problems of the larger society and of the global community is not inborn. It must be developed in younger people and nurtured in older people.[1]

A good deal of injustice that exists in society is the result not of malevolence but of indifference. People are very much aware of their own personal and family problems, but a special effort is required to develop a sensitivity to the problems of others and to the problems faced by the society as a whole. The beginning of social injustice is the attitude of indifference on the part of large numbers of people. Consequently, a just society requires that its members acquire an interest in the problems of others and the problems which confront the group as a whole.

It is important for peace and justice at the global level that this interest go beyond domestic issues. People need to be informed about international affairs and about the problems being faced by other nations as well as those confronting their own country. They need to know how and why decisions are made. Understanding events requires background knowledge about governments and other institutions and about the various ideas and ideologies that motivate people. If we never learn about the competing interests and the various outlooks which guide social decision-making, we probably will never understand the significance of the individual events which are reported in the news. Also if we have never been encouraged to think of war as a problem for humanity to solve, we will probably not be aware of how particular political decisions help or hinder the solution of this problem.

We can conclude, then, that one thing that may help to solve the war problem, and also the public indifference to that problem (which is also part of the problem), is teaching people about social issues, the problems facing different nations and different groups within our own nation, social philosophy, and war as a social problem. Learning about such things is especially important for younger people, but the mass media should also provide continuing education about these matters for those no longer in a formal educational setting.

Skepticism and Tolerance

Developing awareness about social issues, the problems of different nations and different groups, social philosophy, and the war problem is not sufficient, however. It is also important that certain attitudes be developed if the war problem is to be solved. A crucial one is an attitude of skepticism toward what others tell us and toward the beliefs we have already adopted. We are credulous creatures. We tend to believe whatever we are told unless there is some good reason to doubt it, and sometimes we believe what we are told even when there is reason to doubt it. We are also creatures of habit. If there should be a conflict between one idea and another, we tend to believe that the idea we heard first is the correct one. We find it difficult to discard any belief we have once held, and the longer we have held it the harder it is to give up.

It is because of our natural credulity and our natural dislike for changing our views that we must make a special effort to develop a skeptical attitude in ourselves and others. Although what people tell us is generally a reflection of what they believe to be true, no one is infallible. Consequently, at least part of what we are told by others is false. We are not infallible, either. Consequently, it follows that at least some of our own present beliefs are mistaken. Of course, if we knew which of our ideas are false, we would discard them. The only rational procedure is to be somewhat skeptical both about our own beliefs and the beliefs conveyed to us by others.

Skepticism is especially important for solving the problem of war because wars often have an ideological basis. There is usually an effort by the leaders of each nation or social group to impose their "obviously correct" views about religious, economic, political, or other matters on the rest of their own group as well as on other societies. In each nation or group, people come to be convinced of the correctness of their own beliefs because those beliefs were the ones they heard first and most often from persons most dear to them. They just *know* that their own views about religion and about the ideal political and economic arrangements in a society are true. The views of "the enemy," on the other hand, have come to their attention only late in life, if at all. These views are unfamiliar and are often conveyed by strangers or books written by unknown authors, so it is assumed that they are obviously mistaken. Thus each side, being composed of people who are credulous creatures of habit, is sure that it is fighting for truth and justice. Most people in each nation or social group believe themselves to be the agents of good and the enemy to be the embodiment of evil. Even violence seems justified since the issue is perceived as a struggle of truth and justice against falsehood and wickedness.

One way of trying to prevent this situation is for all people everywhere to develop skeptical attitudes toward all their beliefs and toward the "information" which is being conveyed to them. The prejudices of others which differ from our own and the propagandistic nature of devices used by others to spread ideas with which we disagree are obvious to us. What is necessary is that we be alert to the fact that we also have our own prejudices (most of them learned in our earliest years), and that the ideas which we have been led to accept may also have been spread by propagandistic devices. We need to examine even our most basic beliefs to determine whether they have a sound foundation or are merely reflections of prejudices. Even after we have critically examined our beliefs, we must continue to keep in mind that we may be mistaken.

Closely related to the attitude of skepticism is the attitude of tolerance for beliefs and practices which are different from our own. If we are absolutely sure of the correctness of our own beliefs and practices, then it may seem appropriate to impose these beliefs and practices on others even if they are not willingly accepted. If we happen to be in a position where we cannot impose them on others, we still are tempted to make fun of different beliefs and practices. But we need to combat these inclinations. Just learning about the various beliefs and practices of others at an early age will help to make them seem less strange, but special efforts should also be made to develop an attitude of appreciation of the different perspectives of others. Such an attitude does not develop automatically. It is the natural inclination of people to be intolerant of beliefs and practices different from their own, and this tendency supports a readiness to engage in wars against foreigners or others who differ in some way. Consequently, the deliberate development of an attitude of tolerance for those who are different is one instrument for making wars less likely.

Reluctance to Use Violence

Another attitude which needs to be fostered to promote peace is the reluctance to resort to violence in situations of disagreement and conflict. Each of us has ideas of what is true and right and good (with what is good usually being taken as equivalent to what is good *for me*). We regularly find others disagreeing with us. When we are in a position to do so, it is tempting to coerce the other party into following our point of view. The mistreatment of children, old people, minority groups, and women testify to the readiness of people to use violence to impose their will on others. But the attitudes of skepticism and tolerance just discussed imply another way of handling conflict situations. The use of violence overlooks the possibility that our own ideas may be mistaken. It also neglects the consequence that resentment is aroused in those who are coerced into acting against their own will.

A nonviolent approach to conflict situations will involve a recognition that one's own beliefs about what is true or right may need to be corrected, as well as an effort to appreciate the point of view of the other party. The conflict situation can thus be viewed as an opportunity for learning and developing a wider range of concern. The opportunity for learning can best be exploited if each party can state not only its position but also the grounds or reasons for this position. Each party to the conflict should be free to raise objections to beliefs which it thinks are mistaken. Ideally, the parties would become aware of the weaknesses in their own positions and the strengths in those of their opponents. Eventually a compromise of some sort may be possible. Each party should also develop a sensitivity to the concerns of the other. In conflict situations it is desirable to engage in role-playing where each party argues for the opponent's position. This exercise helps develop an awareness of the interests of the other party. Undoubtedly, this nonviolent approach to conflict situations is not one which will occur automatically. If we want life to be more peaceful, we will need to make an effort to have both children and adults learn about it and want to use it.

Although peace requires that people learn to develop a reluctance to use violence in conflict situations, many young people today are being taught just the opposite. Boys are still often told that the "manly" way of resolving differences of opinion is to use their fists against those who disagree. Propagandists urge their followers to stop at nothing in promoting their cause. On television, violence is glorified as the quick and proper way of resolving conflict, and the long-term consequences of using violence in conflict situations are conveniently neglected. In discussing international relations, many government leaders and media representatives assume without even considering alternatives that the use of force and threats of force is the only proper way to handle conflicts between nations. The question of what is right or just is often not asked; the only issue is how to coerce the other party into accepting one's own terms. When many people feel that violence and the threat of violence is the proper way to resolve differences among them, there is little hope of avoiding war and eliminating arms races. On the other hand, if there were a general feeling that conflict situations should be resolved by nonviolent means, the chance for peace would be much greater.

One way of reducing the readiness to use violence in social situations would be to expand public knowledge about the philosophy and techniques of nonviolent resistance and to promote a wider awareness of some of the situations where nonviolent actions have brought about social change.[2] A wide-spread familiarity with the teachings and lives of Mohandas Gandhi and Martin Luther King, Jr., would provide a good beginning.[3] Peace on all levels will be furthered if people develop a negative attitude toward the use of violence in conflict situations.

Unselfishness

It is a commonplace that warfare would be greatly reduced if people were less greedy and selfish. It seems that no matter how much people have, they always want more. The situation is aggravated in a society where advertising creates wants in order to sell goods and services to those who have the money to buy them. People who never thought about a midwinter vacation of a week or two in Hawaii or the Caribbean may, as the result of advertising, find themselves not only wanting such a vacation but positively needing one. Furthermore, the vicissitudes of life are such that it is impossible for most people to have enough insurance and savings to take care of all the emergencies that might arise. Faced with what appear to be unlimited "needs" for our own welfare, it is difficult for most people to be much concerned about the welfare of others. The expenditure of $1,000 or more for a vacation seems sensible, while a gift of half that amount to educate illiterate people in other parts of the world might lead some to think that the giver had lost his sense of the worth of money. Our own "needs" seem pressing and urgent, while those of others seem insignificant and remote. It is certainly natural to be more concerned about ourselves than others, but a peaceful world will require people to develop more concern for others and a more realistic appraisal of their own needs than what is generally found at present among the affluent persons of the world.

It is not only individual selfishness which must be tempered but group selfishness as well. One of the interesting aspects of society is the existence of small groups, such as families, whose members display the greatest unselfishness toward each other but who are reluctant to give assistance to those outside this group. For example, parents may sacrifice a great deal so that their children can acquire a college or university education but will be reluctant to give a penny so that other children can learn the very basic skills of reading and writing. They will make sure that their own parents are cared for but at the same time display complete indifference toward other old people who may be in much more desperate need of help. In this situation, the individuals may be very unselfish, but the family group could well be described as selfish. While generosity confined to the family group is a very natural human trait, peace will be much more likely when not just individuals but also families (and other larger groups such as nations, too) become much less selfish.

Globalism and Humatriotism

We have just considered the needs for families and other groups to become less selfish not only as individuals but also as groups. Another way of examining what is essentially the same problem is to expand the "we"-group, the group with which we identify. The attitude of identifying with members of our family and with close friends seems to develop naturally. With a bit of effort, nations are able to extend the group with which the individual identifies. When there is a single language, a single cultural heritage, and a racially homogeneous group, the identification with the nation is likely to be easily established, but even in nations such as Switzerland, where a variety of languages and cultures exists, it is possible to develop a sense of "we" which extends to the whole country.

An obvious question arises. If people can be taught to identify with all the others in a heterogeneous nation, why can't the same devices be used to stimulate identification with all the people of the world? If a national flag can be used in helping to develop a sense of identification with the nation, why not use the United Nations flag to help develop a sense of identification with the whole global society? If nationalism can be furthered by a pledge of allegiance to the national government, why not use a pledge of allegiance to the whole world in order to further a commitment to globalism?[4] If nationalism can be developed by celebrating national holidays, why can't a sense of globalism be developed by celebrating world holidays?

A step in the direction of a world holiday has already been taken by the United Nations General Assembly. In December of 1971, a resolution was adopted 63-6 proclaiming U.N. Day, October 24, to be an international holiday and recommending that it be observed as a public holiday by all nations which are members of the U.N. Dorothy Schneider of San Diego, who was instrumental in persuading delegates from various nations to introduce this resolution, has now shifted her efforts to getting the United States to follow the recommendation and make U.N. Day a national holiday in the U.S.[5] A somewhat related annual event in the U.S. and some other countries which helps to develop an attitude of globalism is the annual collection for UNICEF conducted near the end of October.[6]

Of course, the fact that such devices *can* be used to develop a sense of globalism does not prove that they *will* be used. In fact, the persistence of the system of sovereign nations and the enduring possibility of war means that national governments, schools, and mass media which are directly or indirectly under their control will probably continue to try to develop *patriotism* (loyalty to the homeland) rather than *humatriotism*[7] (loyalty to the human race). National governments can't afford to have their soldiers hesitating to kill enemy soldiers just because they are also human beings. In case of war they need young people who are unquestioningly loyal to them, not to the whole human race. If a world government were instituted over the national governments, the situation would be different. Then an effort could more readily be made to develop humatriotism because national governments would no longer have a potential need for soldiers. It is worth noting, for example, that the state governments in the U.S. formally control the educational system but do not need to develop intense loyalty to their own state governments because they have no need for soldiers to fight against other states. The irony of the situation is that a world government probably will not be feasible until there are large numbers of people who have already adopted an attitude of loyalty to the world community. It seems then that the development of humatriotism cannot wait until after a world government is formed. Loyalty to the whole human race is needed now.

It is sometimes argued that creating a sense of globalism will not work in the same way as creating a sense of national loyalty because there will be no out-group or enemy to serve as a stimulus for group cohesion. It is claimed that the love for one's own group (amity) must be accompanied by the hatred of some enemy group (enmity). For example, Robert Ardrey says, "The primate amity-enmity complex cannot exist without enemies."[8] Earlier, Sigmund Freud had observed, "It is always possible to unite considerable numbers of men in love towards one another, so long as there are still some remaining as objects for aggressive manifestations."[9] Historically, nationalism seems to have been strongest when there has been a traditional enemy, such as occurred when Germany and France confronted each other in the 19th and first half of the 20th centuries. On the other hand, there are cases where national pride and patriotism are strong even in the absence of any recent external enemies; Switzerland and Sweden are but two examples. Also, in a study directed specifically to the topic of loyalty, Harold Guetzkow concludes: "Although an out-group is often useful in serving as a foil in the development of in-group solidarity, it is not a necessary condition for the development of group loyalty."[10] It is at least possible that people can learn to view war, huge military expenditures, waste of resources, pollution, diseases, and natural disasters as "the enemy" of the human race against which they can direct their aggressive tendencies.[11]

In our earlier discussion of nationalism, we noted that the existence of different languages within a country, though not an insurmountable obstacle to building a sense of national identity, nevertheless constitutes a hindrance to that goal. Not being able to communicate directly with other people because of language differences tends to block the process of identification. If people cannot read the same materials or listen to the same radio and television broadcasts, they may develop very different attitudes and beliefs about the world. There is also a basis for suspicion when some people are speaking to one another and others cannot understand what they are saying. It follows that one thing which might help a great deal to develop a sense of community among all the peoples of the world is the use of the same language everywhere.

It is unlikely that people will stop using the language with which they are familiar and start using another. What seems more realistic is that people all over the world could concentrate on learning the same second language. In that way people everywhere could retain their own native languages but at the same time speak directly with people from other countries without the assistance of a translator. In the late nineteenth century, with this very thought in mind, a Polish oculist named L.L. Zamenhof developed an international language called Esperanto. This artificially-constructed language is based on a vocabulary drawn from a mixture of European languages and has an easily-learned, completely regular grammar and phonetic spelling. Interested individuals and groups all over the world have devoted themselves to spreading the use of Esperanto. It is also used in some international broadcasting and international publications. Efforts to have Esperanto adopted as an official language at the League of Nations did not succeed. Similar efforts at the United Nations have so far met with a similar fate, but UNESCO has shown some interest in the work of the Esperantists.[12]

Whether it be Esperanto or some other language, it would be helpful in the long-term development of the world community if the United Nations would take action, declaring some single language to be the one official language of the future. It could be determined that at some definite future date (perhaps 25 or 50 years hence) this language would be the only one to be used at the United Nations and in official international communications. Starting immediately, young people all over the world could be taught this language in addition to their own. Costly translation facilities and multiple printings of all documents could then be avoided. Maximum use of the technological capabilities of worldwide communication and transportation systems would no longer be hindered by the absence of a single language. Just as important would be the role that such a language could play in developing a sense of identity among all the people of the world. Everyone in the whole world could communicate directly with everyone else.

In the absence of such deliberate action by the U.N. it is still possible that some single world language may develop. In fact, English is rapidly becoming such a language not only because it is the official language in many countries but also because of the present influence of American technology and business. The difficulty with English as the world language, in addition to its weird spelling and other irregularities, is that such a development carries with it overtones of cultural imperialism. Not only the English language, but also the cultural traditions and values which are carried in the language, would be thrust on everyone. An artificial language such as Esperanto would avoid this problem. Even though its vocabulary is fundamentally European, Esperanto has from the beginning carried with it a spirit of international cooperation and has been accepted enthusiastically by Japanese, Chinese, and other non-Europeans.

The crucial point, however, is the central role that a single world language, whether Esperanto or some other language, would have in creating a sense of world community. If somehow a single world language could be decided upon, the development of a sense of "we"-ness which includes the whole world would develop much more rapidly. It is a sad commentary on the absence of vision of the political and educational leaders of the nations that so little attention has been directed to this significant problem of a single language for the whole human family.[13]

Before leaving the topic of patriotism and humatriotism, we should take note of how perceptions of international affairs would be different if nationalism were subordinated to globalism. Such a change could be expected to at least partially erode the double standard of morality which now is frequently manifested in the perception of foreign relations. For example, at the time of the Cuban missile crisis in October of 1962, Americans generally believed that it would be very wrong for the Soviets to install missiles in Cuba even though the Cuban government had asked for the missiles and even though the U.S. had its own missiles in Turkey not far from the Russian border. For another example, Americans generally believe there is something wrong about the presence of Cuban troops in Angola and Ethiopia, but at the same time feel that it is quite proper for the U.S. to have military personnel in the Philippines, Okinawa, South Korea, Japan, West Germany, Spain, Panama, and even at the Guantánamo Naval Base in Cuba itself, not to mention military advisers throughout Latin American and the Middle East. On what basis is it concluded that the U.S. has a right to station troops and advisers in many other nations, but that Cuba does not have such a right? If the predominant nationalistic point of view is replaced by a global perspective, this double standard of morality will no longer go unquestioned.

Of course, it is not only American nationalism that leads to the adoption of a double standard of morality in international affairs. Russian nationalism, Israeli nationalism, Palestinian nationalism, Vietnamese nationalism, and so on — all of the nations find it easy to excuse themselves for the very things they find reprehensible if done by other nations. Such a distortion of perceptions provides a fertile ground for wars. An attitude of globalism could serve as a welcome corrective to the double-standard mentality of nationalistic thinking in international affairs.

Even many of those involved in the academic study of international relations could benefit from adopting a global framework which would override the nationalistic perspective which is so automatically assumed in their work. Many scholars in the field of foreign affairs have been unable or unwilling to see world politics from the global point of view, from a perspective where the problem to be addressed is one of governing the whole world for the welfare of the whole human race. They tend to consider global issues strictly from the standpoint of how knowledge of international affairs can be used to help their own national leaders to promote the welfare of their own particular nation. Some scholars do not even ask how a human problem such as the problem of war can be solved. Fortunately there are others who have adopted a global perspective and have come to see that political science need not forever remain the handmaiden of national governments. Humatriotism is needed by everyone, including scholars in the field of international relations.

World Citizenship

It is not sufficient, however, that people begin to identify with all other human beings. People need to take on a readiness to work for the world community and its further development. Such an attitude would lead to more citizen support for globally-minded organizations in their efforts to solve global problems. An acceptance of one's role as a world citizen would lead to personal actions such as learning an international language, conserving resources, eating less meat (which would free more grain for use as human food), and making financial contributions to international agencies such as the International Red Cross and UNICEF and to the international relief organizations of churches and other groups.

The development of a positive attitude toward world citizenship does not preclude taking on responsibilities at the local or national level of community. Just as a good citizen of Illinois can also be a good citizen of the United States, so a good citizen of the United States can also be a good citizen of the world. In fact, citizenship at the various levels of community is important.[14] It would be inappropriate for a citizen of Illinois to seek to promote the interests of that state in a manner detrimental to the larger community of the United States. In the same way, it is inappropriate for a citizen of any nation to seek to promote the interests of that nation in a manner detrimental to the larger world community. A good national citizen will also be a good world citizen, and a good world citizen will also be a good national citizen.[15]

XIV. Reforming the Internal Operation of National Governments

We have considered one approach to promoting peace, modifying the attitudes of individuals. A different strategy is that of reforming the internal operation of national governments. National governments are crucial to the war problem, whether we consider international wars or civil wars. In international wars, the national governments not only carry on the wars; it is also their policies which generate the conditions which may result in war with other nations. In civil wars the national government will be one party in the war, and its policies will have been instrumental in producing the conditions which lead to revolt. Consequently, it is plausible to argue that if national governments operated properly, the problem of war would be solved. There are, of course, various proposals about how national governments should be changed in order to make war less likely.

"The Western approach" assumes that the existence of war is due to nondemocratic national governments. If all national governments were democracies, it is claimed, warfare, both international and intranational would be eliminated or greatly reduced. On the other hand, "the Marxist approach" assumes that the existence of war is due to capitalist-controlled national governments. If all national governments were socialistic, it is claimed, warfare, both international and intranational, would be eliminated or greatly reduced. A third view, the Gandhi-King approach, assumes that any kind of government is likely to perpetrate injustices and that the proper way of countering unjust governmental decisions is to mobilize large-scale nonviolent protests. It claims that if people everywhere could be organized and trained in the techniques of nonviolent resistance, then not only warfare, but also gross injustice, would be eliminated or greatly reduced.

The Western Approach

Defenders of the idea that democracy in every nation is the way to peace generally suppose that international wars are caused by power-hungry dictators who want to expand the area of their domination. As noted in our discussion of the causes of war, the aggressiveness of leaders may be a significant factor in whether the groups they lead will behave aggressively toward other groups. It is claimed by supporters of this Western approach that extremely aggressive persons are more likely to gain control of the government in a dictatorship than in a democracy, because when people elect their leaders they will not vote for persons who advocate war or follow aggressive policies which are likely to lead to war. Furthermore, in a democracy there will be more restraints on what an aggressive leader can do. Authoritarian leaders, on the other hand, are accustomed to using ruthless force to subdue dissenters even in their own countries. Such individuals, it is argued, can be expected to use military means to try to increase the area of land and the number of people over which they have control. Consequently, it can be concluded that democratic nations will tend to have governments which seek peace and compromise, while countries with authoritarian rulers will tend to be militaristic, aggressive, and imperialistic.[1]

In the eyes of most Americans, World War II was a perfect illustration of the correctness of this view. Hitler established his authoritarian rule within Germany before being able to use his militaristic approach to subdue people in other countries. Mussolini began by silencing dissenters in Italy. The Japanese military allowed no public criticism of its policies in Japan. These nations thus were able to launch aggressive attacks on their neighbors without worrying about objections from their own people. If there had been a democratic government, it is argued, at least some of the people in Germany would have protested against Hitler's military expansion in Austria, Czechoslovakia, Poland, Belgium, France, Denmark, and Norway. Some persons would have protested against attacking Britain and Russia and declaring war on the United States. If there had been a democratic government in Japan, surely there would have been some protests against the attack on the U.S. at Pearl Harbor. Also, the Soviet Union headed by the dictator Stalin was able to reach an agreement with Hitler to divide Poland between them. Would the Russian people have approved that move if they had been allowed to express their views?

According to the adherents of this view, it is not only international war which would be ended if all nations were democracies. Such a change would also mean an end to wars within countries. If people can change their rulers at the ballot box, there seems to be no point in engaging in a violent struggle against the government. Dissenters can wait until the next election and try to generate enough support for their views to vote a different government into power. Under such a system, it is claimed, there is no justification for forceful action against the government in power. Even the motivation for trying to organize a violent revolution against the government is removed because it seems to be easier and less dangerous to exert the effort needed to win an election than to launch a successful military revolt.

But historical realities raise some questions about the theory that the institution of democratic governments everywhere would mean the end of war. Democratic governments in Great Britain, France, and the United States seem to have been as imperialistic and to have fought as many wars as the authoritarian governments in Spain, Portugal, and Russia. The involvement of the United States in the Mexican War and then the Spanish-American War can hardly give support to the notion that democratic governments don't engage in expansionistic, aggressive wars. There may have been some protesters, but they did not prevail. More recent American involvement in Asia and Latin America also raises doubts about the inherently pacifist nature of democracies. Furthermore, even if it were the case that democratic governments do not deliberately seek to bring about wars, they might still inadvertently make war more probable because of the policies they follow in international affairs as a result of their voters focusing on domestic affairs and fearing entanglement in the affairs of other nations.[2] Also, regardless of the apparent cogency of the argument about the pointlessness of revolutions in a democracy, the historical reality is that even democratic governments do experience violent revolutions and civil wars. One of the bloodier examples is the American Civil War.

The historical record thus forces us to reexamine the argument that the institution of democratic governments would mean the end of war. A basic assumption of the argument was that ordinary people want peace. The problem is that the people of a nation also want other things. They want a high standard of living and will support policies that give it to them, even though these policies may arouse antagonism in other countries. Furthermore, the identification of people with their nation leads them to support wars which add to the territory and glory of the nation. What the people generally oppose is not war but a losing war or a long drawn-out indecisive war.[3] A war which can be won quickly and which adds to the national territory and prestige will generally have popular support. Even in Germany in World War II, Hitler was quite popular as long as the German forces were winning. In the U.S., the Mexican and the Spanish-American War were both rather popular, despite some protesters.

With regard to war within a country, the "revolution through the ballot box" argument neglects the fact that a minority group may suffer from the tyranny of the majority. In such a situation, an appeal to the ballot box is almost certain to end in defeat for the mistreated minority. The minority may have no wish to rule over the majority, but may simply want to withdraw and form a separate government in order to be free from domination. Having no chance of winning an election, they may feel that resort to violence is the only means of changing the situation, even in a democracy.

A Marxist reading this discussion would object that the whole presentation has been incredibly naive. It is based on the assumption that there are democratic governments where the people really have the power to elect the leaders they want and to follow the policies they approve. In reality, says the Marxist, so-called democratic governments are in fact controlled by capitalists and politicans who are subservient to them. Decisions on whether or not to engage in war are made on the basis of its being advantageous to capitalists. Imperialistic wars against weaker nations will be "sold" to the public through an appeal to nationalism, even though the real motivation is to give capitalists access to raw materials and control over markets. As for a revolution through the ballot box, the capitalists will make sure that the process by which candidates are nominated will be under their control. They will make sure that the mass media and the educational system indoctrinate people to admire capitalism and hate socialism. People who openly advocate socialist ideas will be harassed by the FBI and the local police and ignored by everyone else. Consequently, the Marxist argues, the so-called democratic system can be changed only if working classes use violence to remove the capitalists from their position of behind-the-scenes control.

Even though the argument that democracy in all countries would reduce warfare apparently has some deficiencies, perhaps something can still be said for it. The Marxist critique can actually be used to help undercut the historical cases used previously to show that democracy doesn't stop war. If the Marxist analysis is correct, then the cases cited do not refer to truly democratic nations but only to pseudo-democratic national governments. It could be claimed that it was a small ruling clique that sold the American public on the Mexican War and then on the Spanish-American War, and that the protestors of those wars were not given sufficient opportunity to express their views. What would have happened in a true democracy? It is hard to say. Nevertheless, it is worth noting how so-called democratic governments have had to keep some of their militaristic adventures secret from their own people. One distressing example of such secrecy occurred prior to World War II, when the governments of Britain and France concealed their secret agreements with Mussolini concerning Ethiopia.[4] Another illustration is the U.S. government's concealment from its citizens of events during the Vietnamese War. These cases of government secrecy suggest that government leaders in democracies realize that some of their war-oriented policies would not be generally approved by their own people. Perhaps leaders in truly democratic governments would be less inclined to follow militaristic, aggressive policies than those national leaders who are not obligated to explain or defend their policies before the public.

The Marxist Approach

From the Marxist point of view, it is not authoritarian national governments that cause war, but rather countries where control is in the hands of capitalists. It is assumed that capitalists will subordinate all other interests to that of making money. According to Marxist theory, capitalists make money by exploiting the workers who operate their machines. As more goods are produced and sold, the capitalists make more profit. Consequently, the Marxist sees capitalists as desiring to gain control over more and more of the Earth's resources, the Earth's workers, and the Earth's consumers. The capitalists in the more technologically advanced countries are able to extend their control over less developed countries either directly by turning them into political colonies, or indirectly by supporting native leaders who will be cooperative. Capitalistic or imperialistic wars break out between capitalistic countries as they compete with each other for control of these less developed countries. Wars of national liberation break out when less developed countries struggle to rid themselves of control by foreign capitalists and their native lackeys. There is also the possibility of war between advanced capitalist and advanced Communist countries if the capitalists seek to reestablish capitalism in the Communist country.

According to Lenin, World War I is a good example of a war fought between advanced capitalist countries as they struggled with each other for control of colonies in Africa and Asia. By then the British and French had worked out agreements with each other regarding colonial holdings, but Italy, Japan, and Germany were just getting ready to go colony hunting. In World War I, both Italy and Japan correctly determined that they would better extend their area of control by fighting against Germany and Austria-Hungary and with the French, British, and Russians. Although that war was touched off by conflict in the Balkans, it was Germany's rapidly increasing military power that had led to the opposing alliances which caused the war to spread rapidly once fighting began. World War II is also viewed by Communists as primarily a struggle between the capitalist classes in Germany, Italy, and Japan on the one hand and those in France, the United Kingdom, and the United States on the other. The battle in eastern Europe between Germany and the Soviet Union, however, is taken to be the result of capitalist Germany trying to eliminate socialism in Russia. Examples of wars of national liberation are the Algerian War, when the French were expelled, and the Vietnamese War, in which the Vietnamese Communists drove out first the capitalists of France and then the U.S.-supported Vietnamese capitalist government of South Vietnam.

Marxists also claim that capitalists are to blame for civil wars, because capitalistic governments make laws which justify the exploitation of workers, and workers have no opportunity to gain fair treatment other than through a violent revolution. "Democratic procedures" may be devised to create the illusion that it is possible for the masses to inaugurate changes in policy, but the capitalists ensure that anticapitalist candidates have virtually no chance of getting elected. If such a candidate should somehow manage to get elected, the capitalists will use the military to engineer a coup d'état to remove the elected anticapitalist from power. Events in Chile in 1970–73, when the Marxist Allende was democratically elected and then overthrown by a rightist military group, follow this pattern exactly. These events, say the Marxists, show that the possibility of a lasting peaceful socialist takeover of a capitalist country by a revolution at the ballot box is an illusion. Consequently, according to the Communists, revolutionary war is the only course open to those who desire social justice for the masses. Castro's more enduring revolution in Cuba illustrates the proper Marxist way to get rid of an oppressive capitalist regime and then establish a socialist society.[5]

Once again, however, there are historical realities that raise doubts about the correctness of the Communist doctrines put forth. If simply instituting socialist governments will end war, why is it that the Communist regimes in Russia and China have engaged in battles with each other and are presently preparing for war against each other? Why is it that Vietnamese and Cambodian Communists have fought each other? Why have the Chinese and Vietnamese Communists engaged in warfare against each other. According to Communist doctrine, the institution of socialist regimes should bring the end of war.

Also, civil disorders do not seem to cease when Communist governments take over. Consider the revolts in Hungary in 1956 and in Czechoslovakia in 1968 and the uprisings at various times in East Germany and Poland. If Communism ends the problem of injustice within a society, why must extreme measures be taken to prevent large numbers of people from fleeing these nations? Even very repressive totalitarian governments have not been able to completely silence dissenters or to completely stop defectors from finding asylum in other countries.

The historical record thus suggests that there is something wrong with the Marxist argument. Where does it go awry? A basic assumption of the Marxist view is that capitalists want profits and nothing else, but in fact capitalists are people with other interests, too. They can be, and sometimes are, interested in political freedom and the welfare of the human race as well as their own profits. Marxists also assume that workers always identify with other members of the working class from all over the world, as if nationalism were nonexistent. In fact, the ineffectiveness of the socialist pacifist movement at the beginning of World War I, the conflicts between the Russians on the one hand and the Yugoslavs and Chinese on the other, and the conflict between Vietnam on the one hand and Cambodia and China on the other all indicate that nationalism is a stronger social force than any anticipated class solidarity among the workers of the world.

With regard to civil war, it seems a mistake to assume, as the Marxist does, that a government will be dedicated to justice simply because it is controlled by noncapitalists. Why suppose that socialists will be completely unselfish leaders, dedicated only to the welfare of the society? The Marxist tends to neglect the fact that the desire for political power can make a person indifferent to the concerns of others as surely as the desire for profit can.

The defender of democracy would object that the Marxist analysis concentrates too much on the economic aspects of the social system without paying enough attention to political aspects or to the psychological principles which apply to the behavior of leaders. Some Marxists think that the rise to power of autocratic leaders such as Stalin and Mao was merely an accident, while in fact the system of centralized political control which is practiced in Communist countries may make the concentration of power in the hands of one authoritarian person almost inevitable.

Even though the Marxist view that ending capitalism will end war has been shown to be questionable, we should note that the desire of those with wealth to expand their profits and their area of control has been an important factor in many past wars. It is the capitalistic part of Western ideology, rather than the democratic part of it, which has led the European peoples to exploit others who had less technological knowledge. It is the capitalistic part of Western ideology which has led to wide differences in income, wealth, and power within Western societies. The Marxist criticism that capitalism has not been particularly concerned about social justice seems to some extent correct. But so far, there is little evidence that the socialist systems controlled by Communists abound in justice or freedom, and in the international sphere socialists seem to be as subject to nationalistic enmities as capitalists are.

The Gandhi-King Approach

A third approach to reforming the internal operation of national governments focuses on the problem of justice rather than directly on the problem of war. It assumes that a major cause of war is the resort to violence or threats of violence by those who want to eliminate the injustices perpetrated by those in power. Injustice stems from the fact that, both within nations and on the global level, people with economic, military, and political power use that power to advance their own personal and group interests at the expense of those who lack such power. This unjust behavior on the part of the powerful, for the most part, is not the result of a conscious and deliberate effort to harm other people, for they, like all people, are merely more aware of their own interests than of the interests of others. Injustice is the result of indifference to the interests of those being exploited.

The natural reaction of exploited people is to feel resentment and hatred toward those who exploit them. They become ready to use violence to overthrow and destroy their oppressors. But, argued Gandhi, to react in such a resentful, hateful, and aggressive manner is to become a perpetrator of injustice oneself. Reducing the situation to a mere struggle for power between oppressors and oppressed leaves no room for moral considerations. The side which wins the contest of force will simply impose its will against the other side. Even if the formerly oppressed group wins the struggle for power, it will simply become a new ruling group using threats of violence to control those who lost the fight. There will be no more justice than before.

In order to escape from round after round of conflict in which oppression begets violence which begets counter-violence, an entirely different approach is required. A means must be found which is appropriate to the end of furthering justice. Instead of relying on physical force, Gandhi believes that the champion of justice must appeal to a different kind of power, the power of love and commitment to truth. The person who is thus committed to the power of truth, the *satyagrahi*, will feel no ill will against those whose interests conflict with his own, no matter how oppressive and unjust they may seem to be. Instead of seeking a situation in which he can impose his will on those who have coerced him, he will try to do what will be beneficial for everyone. The *satyagrahi* will dedicate his whole being to the removal of injustice, but he will not hate anyone, even the perpetrator of the most gross injustices. His attitude will be one of trying to help the oppressor to rid himself of his insensitivity to the concerns of others.

What technique can the victims of social oppression use to stop the injustices being committed against them without in turn becoming oppressors? In the development of his own thinking, Gandhi's first answer to this question was to use reason. He thought that if the oppressed party could state its case so clearly and dispassionately to the oppressors that the injustice would be evident to any rational observer, then the oppressors would see their error and change their ways. But Gandhi the lawyer discovered by personal experience that this appeal to reason accomplished virtually nothing toward changing the oppressive policies of the ruling groups. Something else was needed.

The new technique Gandhi developed to give power to truth is known as *nonviolent resistance*. Sometimes his approach is mistakenly called "passive resistance," but the technique he advocated is anything but passive. Gandhi insisted that those who were suffering from injustice must be active in their resistance to it. If they did nothing, the oppression would continue. The oppressed must be committed to the removal of injustice by an appeal to the oppressor's sense of justice. They must act to dramatize their plight and show their willingness to suffer even more, if necessary, to change the situation. Although each individual should do whatever he can to protest injustices, the likelihood of success in changing unjust conditions is much greater when large numbers of people are willing to unite their efforts in nonviolent resistance. Some particular techniques of collective nonviolent resistance are demonstrations, boycotts, strikes, and refusals to comply with orders given by the ruling group. An important part of the Gandhian approach is the openness of the planning for nonviolent resistance. Those whose injustices are being protested are permitted to give their side of the story and are told in advance what types of nonviolent activities will be undertaken, as well as details of when and where they will occur.

It is claimed that nonviolent resistance can end war because it provides a means other than violence by which oppressed people can eliminate injustice. The case of India shows how it can be used by the people of a nation to rid themselves of domination by the government of another nation. The civil rights movement in the U.S., led by Martin Luther King, Jr., shows how it can be used within a nation as a substitute for violent revolution. But the big question for nonviolent resistance is whether it can succeed in eliminating government-supported oppression when there is no threat of violence in the background. The detractors of the nonviolent approach argue that in the cases of India and the U.S., there was a real threat of violent action if the nonviolent approach didn't work. Without that threat in the background, neither Gandhi nor King would have succeeded. Furthermore, it is argued that the British and American governments are not among the more ruthless and oppressive governments the world has ever known. Could the Jews have used nonviolent resistance against Hitler's Nazi government? Could Russian dissidents have used nonviolent resistance against Stalin's ruthless rule? Can massive nonviolent resistance even get started when there is a government which prevents potential dissenters from meeting with each other? Such questions arouse skepticism about how effective nonviolent resistance can be against an extremely determined oppressive government.

The defenders of nonviolent resistance respond that even ruthless governments eventually become reluctant to use violence against nonviolent protesters because the ruthlessness becomes so evident, even to the people who have previously not been protesting against it.[6] Gandhi believed that there is a basic decency about most people that would rebel against obvious oppression. The task is for oppressed people to make their oppressed state obvious to people who are otherwise indifferent. Members of the oppressed group who have been indifferent to trying to change the situation and even some others outside the oppressed group will join the resistance effort once the unjust situation is sufficiently dramatized. To be sure, organizing nonviolent resistance so that it can be effective is not easy. Gandhi liked to compare the need for strategy and for courage required for nonviolent resistance to that required in a military confrontation. The "soldier" of nonviolent resistance needs to be trained and disciplined and should be regarded as just as much a hero as any guerrilla fighter who uses violence to try to eliminate oppression. In fact, participants in nonviolent resistance would be even more worthy of admiration than the guerrilla fighters because they would not be drawn into defiling their own human nature by killing and maiming others in the name of justice.[7]

In the end, however, it seems that the basic assumptions of the Gandhi-King approach can still be called into question. Even if people do have some basic sense of justice, it seems to be a weak motive for action compared with self-preservation. It seems almost self-evident that sufficiently ruthless government leaders can keep most dissenters silent by the use of threats of death and injury, if not to the individual then to those he loves. It is also very questionable whether all or even most wars are the result of the use of violence to eliminate the oppressive policies of some dominant group. In fact, in international affairs it seems that wars are usually fought between one powerful nation or group of nations and another powerful nation or groups of nations. The truly poor nations, economically and militarily, realize that any attempt to use force will bring on defeat. It seems that nonviolent resistance may offer an alternative to violence as a way to remove some injustices in some particular kinds of situations, but it is questionable whether even the widespread use of nonviolent resistance to protest oppression by ruling groups would do much to reduce the frequency of war. In fact, such activity might even lead to more ruthless oppression by those in power.

XV. Reforming the Policies
of National Governments

In the previous chapter, we considered various ideas about how the internal operations of national governments might be changed to lessen the likelihood of war. In this chapter we will examine proposals concerning the policies national governments might adopt to reduce the likelihood of war. Our focus will be mainly on courses of action which might be adopted in relation to other national governments, but in many cases these same approaches might also be applied to relations with antagonistic groups within the nation.

It may be worthwhile to reiterate the point made in the previous chapter, namely, that national governments and the policies they follow are crucial to the war problem. International wars are the result of interactions between various national governments, and wars within nations are usually the result of reactions of various groups to the policies of their own national governments. It seems that war could be eliminated if national governments followed the proper policies. Of course, there may be contextual factors which make it difficult for national governments to follow these ideal policies, but a discussion of that point must be postponed to the next chapter.

As we discuss these various proposals, we need to keep certain points in mind. First, our point of view is to consider policies that might be adopted by any national government. There will be a natural tendency for those who live in the United States to think only in terms of policies that might be adopted by this country, but our aim is to maintain a broader perspective. Some policies that might not seem very attractive to a superpower may make a great deal of sense for other nations. Second, it is not to be supposed that these various policies which we will be considering are mutually exclusive of one another. Some of them are incompatible with others, but there are many others which could readily be followed simultaneously. Third, we need to keep in mind that the problem of war currently confronting humankind has four aspects: the threat of nuclear war between big powers, the threat of conventional war between nations, the threat of war within nations, and the expenditure of huge amounts of money and effort for military purposes. Certain proposals may be directed primarily to one or another of these aspects of the war problem. Even a proposal which promises to deal successfully with one aspect of the problem will probably need to be supplemented by other proposals to deal with other aspects of the problem. Fourth, some of these proposals have received a great deal more attention in the past than others. There may be an unconscious tendency to think that some pro-posals which are unfamiliar are for that reason insignificant. Here the reader is advised to be on guard against the natural tendency to dismiss new ideas as ridiculous just because he has not previously heard of them.

Peace Through Isolationism and Economic Self-Sufficiency

One strategy which national leaders may pursue to keep out of wars is to concentrate on solving the domestic problems of their own nation while seeking to isolate themselves from the conflicts of other nations. The term *isolationism* as used here does not refer to a complete withdrawal from all diplomatic and trade relations with other countries, but rather to a policy of avoiding alliances and refraining from military interventions.[1] At the same time a country pursuing this strategy will usually be com-mitted to using research, technology, and conservation measures to avoid economic dependency on other countries. For example, a country which is dependent on imported oil for energy could be expected to make a massive effort to develop alternative energy sources on the assumption that in the long run this approach will be less expensive than building up military forces in order to try to guarantee the availability of oil.

A good example of a nation which has followed an isolationist policy for some time is Switzerland. The Swiss have steadfastly refrained from entering into any kind of military alliances. They even obtained an ex-plicit exemption from participation in any military sanctions against other nations before joining the League of Nations, and they have been reluctant to join the United Nations because of the collective security provisions of its Charter. They have tried to mind their own business, not developing any close ties with any other particular nations, but not making any enemies either. Under this policy they have managed to stay out of both world wars. They have military forces, but these forces are single-mindedly devoted to defending the homeland against any possible invasion. For the Swiss this policy has worked well, and they presently have one of the world's highest per-capita incomes. Sweden is another example of a country which has done very well by following a neutralist policy while at the same time going beyond a strict self-sufficiency strat-egy as manifested by its willingness to provide substantial amounts of economic assistance to less developed countries.

The success of an isolationist and neutralist policy, however, may depend on factors outside the control of the national leaders. Switzerland and Sweden are countries where much of the land is mountainous. For the most part they do not provide good travel routes for armies of other nations bent on conquest, and the Swiss and Swedish could fairly readily blow up bridges and tunnels which would frustrate would-be invaders. The situation is quite different for countries such as Belgium and Poland. These nations have also tried to stay out of wars, but with little success. Their relatively flat land is very inviting to militant leaders looking for routes for attacking their enemies. Switzerland and Sweden also have been assisted in their isolationist policies by their lack of readily exploitable scarce natural resources. It would seem that a small country with crucial natural resources such as the oil-rich United Arab Emirates would be well advised not to try to defend itself without relying on any allies.

For a good part of its history, the United States tried to follow an isolationist policy, at least with regard to Europe. Nevertheless it found itself dragged into both world wars. Since World War II, the U.S. has followed just the opposite of an isolationist policy, forming alliances and intervening militarily all over the world in an effort to stop the spread of Communism. The Vietnamese War raised some doubts about the desirability of playing "world policeman," and scholar Robert Tucker has argued that the U.S. should now return to a nonmilitaristic, noninterventionist approach.[2] He claims that the less developed countries, Japan, and Western Europe are quite able to protect themselves against Communism on their own and that the U.S. nuclear deterrent is sufficient to keep the Russians or anyone else from attacking the U.S. directly. But Tucker may be wrong. It is quite possible that such a new isolationist policy on the part of the U.S. would be disastrous. It might well encourage Russian expansionism to flourish until the U.S. would once again be pulled into a major war to assist its ideological allies.

A country may also find it difficult to follow a strategy of isolationism and self-development if it is very short of resources. Japan is a good example, for it must import almost all the oil it uses. Development of hydroelectric, solar, and nuclear energy can provide a bit of self-sufficiency, but the need for energy and other natural resources is too great to be met by current technology. Japan's objective situation seems to preclude a policy of national self-sufficiency and noninvolvement in international affairs.

It seems then that the desirability of a policy of isolationism and economic self-sufficiency depends on particular circumstances. A country which is a major power may find it hard to refrain from helping ideological allies when they are in danger of being conquered by a powerful ideological enemy. A country which depends greatly on others for resources must take an interest in the outlook of those nations. A small country with readily exploitable resources is likely to be quickly conquered by aggressive powers if it relies only on its own defensive efforts. A country which provides a good route for conquering armies may not be able to stay out of wars. And when a nation decides not to intervene in the affairs of other nations, it is not thereby assured that other nations will forego the use of force to conquer it or damage its vital interests.

Does isolationism promote peace? It certainly seems that a country which is following an isolationist policy will not be a threat to other nations. Consequently, it is less likely to be attacked. Its lack of alliances means that it is also less likely to be dragged into wars between other nations. On the other hand, if there are other nations committed to the use of military force in expanding their power, an isolationist policy may play right into their hands by allowing them to conquer one country at a time. Even the case of Switzerland needs to be reexamined from this point of view. If Hitler had been successful in maintaining control for some time over all of the rest of continental Europe, would not Switzerland sooner or later have been converted by one means or another into a German-speaking fascist country swearing its allegiance to *der Führer?* If so, Switzerland was saved not by its isolationist policy but by the Allies who put an end to Hitler's rule. Similarly, other countries following an isolationist policy may escape from war for a time, but they face the possibility of being swallowed up by those interested in expanding their power by military means unless they are saved from disaster by others. If there are powers bent on spreading their control without limit by military means, it seems prudent to join with others in resisting such expansionism at its beginning. Isolationism would be a good policy if all other nations would also mind their own business, but there seems always to be some national leaders who feel that they should control more than they already do. The same kind of considerations apply to groups within countries which seek to stay out of political issues. Whether they can preserve their own interests and ideology by noninvolvement in political conflicts will depend on the policies pursued by the other groups in that society. The fate of the Bahais in Iran shows that political noninvolvement does not necessarily save a group from being persecuted.

Peace through Strength

A second strategy which national leaders may pursue in order to prevent wars is to be so strong that no potential enemy will risk attacking them. The Latin phrase *para bellum* (prepare for war) is often used to describe this approach. It applies both to international relations and the situation within a nation. War with other countries breaks out, it is claimed, when stronger nations let weaker ones entertain the hope that they might win in a contest of force. War within a country breaks out when some subservient group comes to believe that they might be able to successfully revolt against the national government. The secret of preserving peace is for those with power to have such an overwhelming amount of it and such an obvious resolve to use it that no other government or group will be tempted to test their strength. Although this policy of *peace through strength* usually focuses on building up the military, we will also consider two other ways of strengthening a national government against potential enemies, namely, developing a civilian-based defense system and forming alliances.

In order to fully appreciate the attractiveness of the peace through strength position, it is important to realize that wars very seldom, if ever, happen by accident. Wars occur when the leaders of at least one government or organized group estimate that they will gain more from fighting a war than they can gain by other means such as diplomatic bargaining.[3]

If a national government is weak, other governments outside and organized groups within are likely to try to take advantage of it. A weak government will regularly be in a position of either peacefully yielding some of its interests to aggressive enemies or being attacked militarily if it does not yield enough to placate its stronger opponents. The only way of avoiding such an unpleasant situation is to be strong—either militarily or by virtue of a civilian-based defense system or good alliances.

In the U.S., many advocates of the peace through military strength approach are very critical of the policies followed by the U.S. government since the end of World War II. At that time the U.S. had a monopoly in nuclear weapons, an overwhelming superiority in arms production, and well-trained armed forces. It was a great mistake, claim the supporters of this view, to disarm so rapidly when it should have been obvious that the Communists would be making moves all over the world to try to expand the territory they control. If U.S. military power had been maintained rather than dismantled, U.S. forces could have saved at least some of Eastern Europe from falling under Communist domination. An all-out effort in China could have kept that country from falling to Mao's Communist forces. In the Korean War, the U.S. should have used its superior military might to attack China itself when the forces from that country began assisting the North Koreans. If the U.S. had given aid to the French in Indo-China when the war first started instead of waiting until 1954, the Communists would not have gained control of that area. According to this view the U.S. has consistently been too restrained and too reluctant to use its military power, leading the Communists to be more daring than they would otherwise have been. It has resulted in U.S. retreat and Communist advances in both Europe and Asia. The only time that Communist expansion has been halted is when the U.S. has indicated its readiness to use all its military force, as in Europe after the formation of the North Atlantic Treaty Organization and as in Cuba in 1962 when the Russians were coerced into removing their missiles.

Supporters of the peace through military strength approach believe that it is still not too late for the U.S. to save itself by a determined effort to regain overwhelming military superiority. Essentially, that means spending more money for military research, development, and production. Why should the U.S. be spending only 5 or 6 percent of its gross national product for the military while the Soviet Union is devoting about 12 to 14 percent of its gross national product for this purpose? If this situation continues over a long period of time, then the Soviets will eventually have newer weapons and a greater military strength than the U.S. They will not be reluctant to use it, as the U.S. has been. Then the U.S. will be forced to knuckle under to Soviet demands or start a war to resist such efforts. That, it is claimed, is precisely how weakness leads to war while military strength and determination would preserve peace.

So far we have been considering this policy of peace through military strength only from the U.S. point of view, but the peace through strength policy could be pursued by any nation, including the Soviet Union. No nation wants to find itself in a position where its interests must be sacrificed because the opponent is stronger. In a world where conflicts of interest are ultimately settled by force and threats of force, being strong is a good way of preventing others from attacking or threatening to attack.

There are some problems, however, with the peace through strength approach when it is focused on building up one's military forces. The nation which is very strong militarily can be fairly confident that it won't be attacked, but can other nations be confident that they won't be attacked by it? Strong military forces may make a nation more secure from attack, but its forces then constitute a threat which makes other nations less secure. The leaders who build up the military might of their countries may be thinking in terms of using those forces to deter an attack on their own country, but once the forces are available it is very tempting to use them to launch an attack on another country. Peace through military strength may thus lead to attempted conquest through war.

A second problem for the peace through military strength approach concerns the actions required of a national government which pursues this policy to its final logical implications. If conflicts are ultimately to be decided by force, then force should be used to eliminate competitors while they are weak. In the international sphere, this approach would require a dominant nation to seek to extend its control over potential enemies by attacking them and conquering them before they become militarily strong enough to offer much resistance. Within a country, peace through military strength would require a national government to seek to silence all criticism and dissent before it has a chance to spread and possibly lead to a revolution. Peace through military strength ultimately means maintaining the status quo by means of the most forceful suppression of any efforts to challenge the power of those who presently are in control. Such an approach seems fitting only for a totalitarian regime bent on eliminating all opposition, whether from some other country or from within.

A third problem for the peace through military strength approach concerns what happens when rival parties both adopt this approach. In the international arena, the result is an unrestrained arms race which consumes more and more of the resources of the countries involved. When the contending nations have nuclear weapons, a balance of terror results which is threatening even to other countries. Rather than solving the war problem, the peace through military strength approach generates one aspect of the problem, the huge cost of preparations for war. The same result occurs within nations when opposing groups commit themselves to the use of military force to resolve their differences. Guns and ammunition are stockpiled by those not in power for the day when they may be able to revolt against the government. The government, on the other hand, builds up its forces and tries to imprison anyone who might participate in a revolt. Ruthlessness begets more ruthlessness in the continuing struggle for power. Even those who would prefer to remain neutral and stay out of the struggle cannot escape the violence. Nations which had been peaceful thus become battlegrounds in which both their human and material resources are consumed. This tragedy has occurred in recent years in countries such as Lebanon, Angola, Afghanistan, Cambodia, and El Salvador.

Thus, the view that peace should be preserved by building up military strength runs into some significant difficulties. It seems to be more a policy for trying to maintain the power of those who now have it than a policy which promotes peace. The peace through military strength advocate, whether Communist or capitalist, must be ready to resort to more and more force to try to silence any effort to modify the present social order, both international and domestic. This attempt to prevent peaceful change may in fact be a major contributory factor to the eventual outbreak of violence. The leaders may begin with some sensitivity to issues of justice and the possible need for change, but the logic of their reliance on force pushes them to assume that their own control must be maintained. Furthermore, when opposing groups both adopt this same approach, an all-out race for military superiority is the result, aggravating rather than solving the war problem. The peace through military strength approach, when carried to its logical conclusion, even encourages violent attacks against potential enemies while they are weak. Thus a proposal which is put forth as a policy to promote peace actually turns out to be a policy which blocks efforts for peaceful change and leads to arms races and the opportunistic use of force.

Can the problems of the peace through military strength policy be avoided by a different approach to building up a nation's strength? Is there some way a national government could increase its fighting ability without thereby threatening its potential enemies, without leading to a coercive effort to resist all change, and without possibly starting an arms race? One proposal for increasing national strength while avoiding such difficulties consists of building up an effective civilian-based defense system.

The basic idea of a civilian-based system of defense is to train all the citizenry of a country in techniques of nonviolent resistance which can be used to frustrate an invader even though he may have an overwhelming superiority of military force. Gene Sharp, the primary spokesman for this idea, notes that the people of a society need to be equipped with a means of fighting so that they can defend themselves rather than relying solely on that small part of the population which constitutes the armed forces of the country.[4] Even if a country has an army of professional soldiers, the people of that country should not be defenseless if their army is defeated. And once a nation dedicates itself to developing a full-fledged system of civilian defense, it may find that building up traditional military forces is superfluous. Such a system of national defense also has the advantages of not being threatening to one's neighbors and of being useful for resistance even to an internal group which attempts to take over the government by force. Consequently, it seems to be an especially appropriate type of defense for a democratic country.

Exactly how could a civilian population defend itself nonviolently against an invading army? It might begin by destroying anything that would be useful to the invaders. Explosives might be used to blow up key bridges, harbor facilities, airports, mines, factories, radio broadcasting towers, and the like. Automobiles could be parked in rows to block highways and streets. Human chains twenty or thirty people deep, unarmed but backed up by reinforcements and determined not to move, could be formed to stand in the way of the advancing enemy. Work which the enemy wanted done simply wouldn't get done. The people would obey no commands but those given by their own leaders, and the leaders would give no commands that would assist the invaders.

The strategy of civilian-based defense depends on the principle that invading military leaders can succeed in accomplishing their goals only if others cooperate by following their orders. If the whole civilian population just refuses to do what they are told, if they refuse to work or provide supplies or give orders to their subordinates in the society, then the invading army will be stymied. They will be in the country but they will have no control over it. They may make threats and even carry some of them out in order to try to get their commands obeyed; but if the whole population stubbornly refuses, then they cannot be subdued regardless of the violence that may be used against them. If their resistance is completely nonviolent, the commanders of the invading army may eventually even have difficulty trying to get their own troops to follow orders to use violence against these nonviolent people.

It may be argued that once the invading force kills a few people the others will be frightened into obeying, but that reaction is precisely what training in civilian defense must overcome. A soldier does not stop fighting just because some of his buddies have been killed. In fact, such an event may make him more determined than ever to fight. Civilian defenders need to be taught to react in the same way except that their fighting will be done nonviolently. They must also realize how important it is that no one turn traitor and cooperate with the invader and that no one begin to use violence, thus undermining the nonviolent resistance. Most important of all, they must be taught to keep firmly before their minds the truth that no matter how many of their friends and family are killed or tortured, the number of casualties would probably have been even greater if they had tried to rely on military resistance and thus invited massive destructive attacks.

The notion of civilian-based defense as an alternative to a traditional military defense system may not seem a very attractive possibility to superpowers such as the U.S. and the Soviet Union, or even to countries such as the United Kingdom, France, and China which have nuclear-tipped missiles to launch at any country which attacks them. But what about countries such as Sweden, Japan, Mexico, and Nigeria, not to mention smaller countries? They do not have a nuclear deterrent. What sort of defense can they hope to develop against a possible attack by a nuclear power? Even if they could develop nuclear weapons and missile launchers, they might not want to do so since the presence of such weapons in their country might invite a nuclear attack. Even a big build-up of conventional weapons might make them a target for attack when they otherwise might not be bothered. Consequently, the civilian-based defense system constitutes an attractive possibility. The governments of Sweden, Norway, and the Netherlands have sponsored official studies of the possibilities of this approach.

Would a system of civilian-based defense work? Advocates point to the partial success of resistance movements in the Ruhr Valley in 1923 when the German population resisted a French-Belgian takeover attempt, in Norway and in Denmark where Hitler's forces were shunned and ignored during World War II, and in the Czechoslovak uprising against the Russians in 1968. In 1920, the German Weimar Republic was saved from an attempted internal takeover by strikes and refusal of the population to cooperate. In these cases there had been no advanced preparation for the resistance effort. It is claimed that a civilian population trained in advance and equipped with hidden resources such as duplicating machines and radio transmitters could be much more successful. If there can be partial successes against military forces without advanced preparation, one could expect even better results with planning and special training in civilian defense.

The skeptics remain unconvinced, however.[5] The crucial issue is human nature. Will people refrain from reacting violently when under violent attack? Will people stand up to threats of violence when they see their own family members being threatened and tortured? As some people yielded to threats and revealed secret hiding places and secret codes, it would become more and more difficult for others to keep up their resistance. Another problem is that the enemy would also be in a position to use nonviolent techniques against them. For example, the invaders could shut off supplies of electricity, food, petroleum, medical care, and so on unless the captured citizenry cooperated. The approach of civilian-based defense, its detractors argue, does not have enough respect for the influence of physical force, especially in an age of mind-altering drugs and brain-washing techniques. The mind is too dependent on the body, too much a part of the body, too dedicated to the continuation of one's own personal existence. Some people may be committed enough to the cause to suffer greatly and possibly die, but it is doubtful that such commitment would be the prevalent response regardless of advance training and preparations. Furthermore, there is always the gruesome possibility that the invading nation would simply kill huge numbers of people and then move some of its own population into the conquered country. Some successful revolutionary movements have massacred substantial proportions of their own people, so the possibility of murdering large numbers of foreigners should not be dismissed too readily.

The advocate of civilian-based defense might still maintain that, especially for smaller countries, this system of defense makes more sense than other alternatives. But is this true? Doesn't alliance with a superpower with a similar ideology offer more security than civilian-based defense? Furthermore, even though a traditional military build-up might not constitute much of a deterrent to a superpower, it might nevertheless be a good policy to follow for opposing other small and middle-sized countries, especially when one considers the influence of military power on international relations even when there is no immediate threat of war. It seems that relying on a civilian-based defense system alone is not a particularly attractive strategy though it may be worth planning in advance to follow such an approach if and when one's military forces have been subdued. If nations were committed to using civilian-based defense rather than building up their military forces, war might be less probable; but it seems that few nations are ready to rely solely on a type of defense whose success seems so questionable.

Peace through strength may involve building up one's military forces or developing a civilian-based defense system, but it may also mean forming alliances with other countries which will provide military assistance if war comes. States with a common interest can enter into a mutual defense pact which declares that an attack on either will be considered an attack on both. By such an alliance both nations have strengthened their power relative to others. Weaker countries will be much less vulnerable to an attack from a potential enemy if they have formed an alliance with a superpower. This situation is not unlike that of a small boy who finds a big, strong friend who will help him resist a bully who has been harassing him. The idea of increasing one's strength by making alliances also applies in the case of conflicting groups within nations. It is not unusual for a revolutionary effort to succeed because of an alliance of dissatisfied groups which nevertheless begin fighting each other once the old regime has been toppled. At the same time, ruling governments may themselves be the result of an alliance of groups working together to preserve the basic structure of the present order.

Though a country which has alliances with other countires may be stronger as a result, the question remains whether it will be less likely to get involved in a war. Some potential enemies that might otherwise consider attacking will probably be deterred, but the stronger nation in the alliance may try to control the policies of the weaker, possibly even resorting to military force to do so. There is also the possibility of a country being dragged into a war if its ally is attacked or of being attacked simply because it has entered into the alliance with the other country. Finally, there is a danger that a country's ally, knowing that it will have assistance, will deliberately act in such a way as to invite an attack. Thus, entering an alliance does not necessarily mean that a nation will be more likely to remain at peace. Upgrading national strength through alliances has some drawbacks not found in the strategies of increasing strength by building up the military and of developing a system of civilian-based defense.

Separate from the issue of whether a country entering an alliance is more or less likely to get into a war is the issue of whether alliances in general make peace more probable or less probable. It can be argued that

World War I was a major war rather than a minor war because of the system of alliances existing before the war began. On the other hand, there is a widely held view that peace is preserved by a *balance of power* between opposing alliances. It is generally believed that if one nation or group of nations acquires an overwhelming military superiority over another nation or group of nations, it will be inclined to start a war to convert its military supremacy into economic and political gain.

There are several different kinds of situations where the balance-of-power concept is relevant. There may be two opposing blocs of nations, neither of which has obvious military superiority over the other. This situation is called a *bipolar balance of power*. Each of the sides is likely to try to gain superiority over the other by various means including recruiting new allies. Peace will be maintained, according to the balance of power view, if neither side gains a great superiority over the other. A second type of situation is the *tripolar system* where there are three opposing nations or groups of nations. In this situation the two weaker states or groups of states will form an alliance against the more powerful state or groups of states. If two of the three states or blocs of states are nearly equal in power, the third state or group of states may act as a "balancer," shifting its support from one group to the other in order to maintain the balance. Many historians and political scientists believe that Britain played just such a role as "balancer" in Europe from 1815 to 1914, thus preventing any major wars during this period.[6] A fourth situation is a *multipolar system* where there are many different nations and groups of nations which keep shifting alliances with each other, thus keeping any nation or group of nations from gaining an overwhelming military superiority. Similar balance of power situations apparently can also be found in the struggles among groups within countries.

The basic premise of the balance of power view of maintaining peace is that wars occur when one side has overwhelming superiority over another. It is assumed that under such circumstances the more powerful side will start a war because it is confident it can win. This basic supposition of the balance of power view is very questionable. When a nation or group of nations has obvious military superiority, other nations and groups of nations tend to be conciliatory and even subservient in order to try to avoid a war they are likely to lose. Of course war might eventually occur if they came to the view that they had to fight to protect what they had not already surrendered. On the other hand, when there is a balance between powers, it might well be that a crucial conflict situation will develop and neither side will back down because neither perceives itself as weaker than the other. War then seems a likely result. It is surprising that the balance of power view is so popular when it is so debatable whether war is more likely when there is an imbalance between powers than when there is a balance. Nations can be expected to seek to form alliances with other nations, especially against nations and groups of nations which seem threatening, but this behavior seems to be more readily explicable on grounds that the nations are protecting their own national interests by getting help against a potential enemy than on grounds that they are trying to preserve peace by maintaining a balance of power.

Seeking peace and security through strength is the prevalent approach among the national governments of the world. The most popular path to strength has been the building up of military forces. Entering into alliances is also widespread, however, while the civilian-based defense system, though not now a significant part of any nation's efforts, could in the future become a common supplementary path for increasing national strength. In a world where conflicts of national interest may ultimately be settled by war, there seems to be no substitute for strength. How else can a country keep from becoming a victim of other nations which have built up their strength? Though the peace through strength approach has some real deficiencies from the point of view of solving the war problem, it seems destined to remain one of the most popular policies for national governments to follow unless there is a substantial modification of the international system.

Peace through Arms Control and Renunciation of War

As noted in the previous section, rival nations both pursuing a policy of peace through military strength are likely to find themselves engaged in an arms race. We earlier noted that arms races are sometimes a contributory factor to the outbreak of war. It would seem that anything which could keep arms races in check would make war less likely. It is the aim of arms control agreements to promote peace by slowing and possibly even reversing arms races.

Our earlier discussion of arms control agreements reviewed the various treaties which have been made during the past 30 years. One of the more interesting treaties from the point of view of preserving peace is the U.S.-Soviet SALT I ABM Treaty of 1972. By restricting each side to only two ABM sites, this treaty maintained a situation of mutual assured destruction. That is, because of the Treaty each side would remain vulnerable to a retaliatory attack by the other, thus minimizing the likelihood that either side would attempt to launch a first strike against the other. Suppose there had been no ABM Treaty. One side conceivably could have developed an extensive ABM capability. As a result it might have considered the possibility of launching a first strike and then using its ABM's to intercept whatever retaliatory strike the other side could manage to launch. The ABM Treaty forestalled such a development, thereby decreasing tension and the likelihood of war.

One of the main problems for those contemplating arms control agreements is being able to know whether the other side is keeping its part of the bargain. Treaties governing the testing of nuclear weapons and limiting the number of strategic weapons have been made possible by technological developments which permit each side to know what the other is doing without needing to rely on "on-site" inspections. Probably the most important advance in this regard has been the development of spy-in-the-sky satellites which carry sophisticated photographic equipment. These satellites can reportedly detect an object as small as a half-dollar. Consequently, it is not difficult to locate the complex of radars and antiballistic missiles which constitute an ABM site or the launching pads for intercontinental ballistic missiles. The problem of inspection can still be a major obstacle, however, with regard to smaller weapons such as cruise missiles. Consequently, agreements limiting these smaller weapons are not to be expected unless some system of "on-site" inspection can be worked out. Such a system is not likely, however, because each side fears the other will use such inspections not merely to make sure that agreements are being kept but also to gain valuable information about military installations which could be used for planning an attack. Even the notion of a neutral "on-site" inspection team is not likely to be acceptable to the superpowers because they do not trust neutral observers to be clever enough not to be duped or neutral enough not to pass valuable information to the other side.

Another problem for arms control agreements is modern science and its capacity to continue developing new kinds of weapons. Arms control agreements often limit only certain kinds of weapons which exist at the time the agreement is made. As new weapons are developed, they are not restricted by earlier agreements. An example of this situation is the ABM Treaty previously mentioned. The stability promoted by that treaty is now in jeopardy because of the development of new kinds of missile-defense systems which do not rely on antiballistic missiles. It has been suggested that treaties should be adopted which restrict not only the production of certain kinds of weapons but also the testing of them. SALT II makes a start in this direction, but for some kinds of weapons the inspection problem exists with regard to testing them as well as monitoring the number produced and deployed.

Another problem with arms control agreements is that the arms race is merely diverted to the development of other weapons and strategies not covered by the agreements. If there is an agreement on the number of missile-launchers each side is permitted, then the race is diverted to the problem of how to put more separately targetable warheads on each missile. If there is an agreement to limit the number of strategic missiles, then there is added emphasis on the building of missiles with less than intercontinental range. If there is an agreement to limit the number of antiballistic missiles, then there is an effort to develop another kind of defense against the other side's missiles. The situation is not unlike that of the mythical Hydra which grew two new heads for each one cut off.

A cynic is likely to note that the arms control agreements that have been adopted by the U.S. and U.S.S.R. tend to cover weapons which both sides have decided are not likely to be very effective anyway (as with the antiballistic-missile missile) or weapons which both sides decide they already have in more than adequate quantity (as with the intercontinental ballistic missiles). To give another example of this principle at work, smaller, not larger, nuclear devices are now needed for military purposes. Thus the U.S. and U.S.S.R. can agree to a ban on testing nuclear devices of over 150 kilotons without greatly inhibiting the further development of those weapons which will be most useful from a military point of view.

The major difficulty with arms control agreements as a road to peace, however, is that even if successful in slowing arms races they do very little to eliminate the danger of war. Suppose, for example, that through arms control agreements all of the nuclear weapons and all the ballistic missiles which now exist could be eliminated. Supposed that even the knowledge of how to build such weapons were eliminated. Would such a development mean the end of war? Obviously not. We would simply regress to the weapons capability of mid-1945. What would be so wonderful about that? Fifty-one million people were killed in World War II, and nuclear weapons accounted for less than 250,000 of the deaths.

In fact, one could even argue that the elimination of nuclear warheads and ballistic missiles would make war *more* likely. Without the threat of such weapons, we might already have had World War III. Those who want to eliminate all nuclear weapons need to ask themselves whether the goal they seek is really desirable.

If agreements limiting certain kinds of weapons do not do much to reduce the likelihood of war, perhaps national governments could go further and renounce any use of force or threats of force to settle their differences. The most obvious example of an effort in this direction was the General Treaty for the Renunciation of War, commonly called the Kellogg-Briand Pact, of 1928. In it the signing parties agreed to renounce war "as an instrument of national policy in their relations with one another."[7] It stated further that "the high contracting parties agree that the settlement or solution of all disputes or conflicts, of whatever nature or of whatever origin they may be, which may arise among them, shall never be sought except by pacific means."[8] Sixty-one nations had signed this pact by the end of 1930, the only important nonsigners being Argentina and Brazil. However, the agreement did not state what should be done if some nation did violate the agreement, which Japan, Paraguay, and Italy had all done by 1936. It is questionable whether the agreement had any influence on the behavior of the nations which had signed it. Still, at the Nuremberg Trials after World War II, this treaty was appealed to as setting forth international law which had been violated by the Nazi leaders.

Another example of an international agreement renouncing the use of force is the Charter of the United Nations. Article 2 says in part:

> 3. All Members shall settle their international disputes by peaceful means in such a manner that international peace and security, and justice, are not endangered.

> 4. All Members shall refrain in their international relations from the threat or use of force against the territorial integrity or political inde-

pendence of any state, or in any other manner inconsistent with the Purposes of the United Nations.[9]

But once again there is no indication of what should be done if this pledge is violated. It is also doubtful whether national governments act much differently because they have joined the U.N. By becoming members of the U.N., however, nations do indicate that they accept these principles as international law.

A more recent example of the use of this approach to peace is the 1973 Agreement Between the U.S. and the U.S.S.R. on the Prevention of Nuclear War. In this agreement

> The Parties agree ... to proceed from the premise that each Party will refrain from the threat or use of force against the other Party, against the allies of the other Party, and against other countries, in circumstances which may endanger international peace and security.[10]

This agreement also indicates that whenever there seems to be a risk of nuclear conflict, the two governments "shall immediately enter into urgent consultations with each other and make every effort to avert this risk."[11]

How much either side feels bound by this agreement is a matter for speculation. Still, it seems pointless to sign such an agreement unless there is at least some expectation by each side that the other will abide by it.

The technique of maintaining peace by renouncing the use of force suffers from a number of deficiencies. The most obvious one is the absence of provisions for enforcement. No punishment is stipulated for those who violate the pledge, no arrangements are made for deciding whether punishment is warranted, and no structure is established to oversee the punishment of violators. Any agreement not to use force to resolve disputes needs to be supplemented by a statement of what means will be used to settle differences. The renunciation of force approach to peace cannot be expected to work until there is also agreement on some alternative trustworthy way of resolving disputes. About all that can be said for pledges by national governments not to use force is that it is probably better for them to make such pledges than to refuse to make them.

The approaches of arms control and the renunciation of force can be joined in a single effort to try to achieve general and complete disarmament. The reader may be surprised to learn that in 1961 the U.S., represented by John McCloy, and the Soviet Union, represented by Valerian Zorin, reached an agreement on principles which should govern negotiations aimed at general and complete disarmament. Among them were the following:

> (1) The aim of negotiations should be general and complete disarmament accompanied by the establishment of reliable procedures for the peaceful settlement of disputes.
>
> (2) When the process is completed, all armed forces will be disbanded, all stockpiles of weapons will be destroyed, all military training will be ended, and all military expenditures will cease.

(3) The disarmament programme should take place in stages with verification of compliance at each stage by an international disarmament organization created within the framework of the U.N.

(4) During the disarmament process institutions for the peaceful settlement of international disputes should be strengthened and a U.N. international peace force should be developed to keep the peace.[12]

These principles were also approved by the U.N. General Assembly.

Unfortunately, there was a significant difference of opinion concealed in the agreement that there would be verification concerning compliance. The Soviets took this to mean that the destroying of weapons would be verified, while the U.S. insisted that the verification must extend also to what arms still remained. This difference received more attention than the areas of agreement. It seemed that the governments involved did not really want to reach a workable agreement. The leaders of national governments have difficulty imagining a world where they will have no military forces to try to protect their national interests, and their distrust of possible enemies is too great to allow them to seriously consider the notion of complete disarmament. Part of the difficulty, of course, is the lack of any clear idea of how international disputes would be resolved in the absence of those military forces which at present give the more powerful nations a superior position in bargaining situations.

Although the prospect of general and complete disarmament seems remote, the value of arms control agreements which have been reached should not be disparaged too much. Almost no existing weapons have been destroyed and the arms race continues full-tilt in areas not covered by the agreements, but some restraints are in place. The problems of inspection and new technological advancements are so great that one can only be surprised that an agreement such as SALT II could be worked out by the adversaries. It is to be hoped that further agreements can be negotiated and ratified. The notion of making all of Europe a nuclear-free zone needs to be explored, as well as the proposal to freeze the testing and production of all nuclear weapons. Nevertheless, arms control agreements do not and cannot end the possibility of war. They merely restrict the area of competition for further arms development and production. It is doubtful whether they even do much to restrain military spending since the restrictions from previously adopted arms control agreements may merely result in larger expenditures for research and development of other kinds of weapons.

Peace through Conciliatory Moves and Gradual Tension Reduction

Arms control agreements and eventually general and complete disarmament seem to be moves in the right direction in the struggle against war, but sometimes tensions and distrust are so great that negotiations between opposing parties cannot even get started. What if anything can be done to move toward peace in those situations where neither side trusts the other enough to contemplate the possibility of arms control agreements?

The best known suggestion for action in this kind of situation is the GRIT proposal of psychologist Charles Osgood.[13] GRIT stands for "Graduated Reciprocation in Tension-Reduction" or "Graduated and Reciprocated Initiatives in Tension-Reduction."[14] The aim of GRIT is to convert a situation of intense tension and distrust into one where it is possible to have negotiated settlements made in good faith. The general idea is for one party to make a series of conciliatory moves announced in advance with a public invitation for the opponent to make reciprocal gestures of his own choosing. At the same time defenses continue to be maintained in case the opponent misinterprets the moves as signs of weakness.

Osgood has worked out his proposal in considerable detail with regard to the confrontation between the U.S. and the U.S.S.R. He suggests, for example, that even while making conciliatory moves the U.S. must maintain its capacity to launch a nuclear retaliatory attack and to meet an attack using conventional weapons with adequate conventional weapons of its own. He notes that the announced conciliatory gestures need to be carried out regardless of whether the other side indicates it will reciprocate, and they need to be continued over a long period of time, not just for a month or two. Conciliatory moves should be planned which will promote cooperative enterprises, which will encourage the transfer of sovereignty from the national to the international level, which will reduce the imbalance between have and have-not nations, and which will strengthen democratic ways of life.

Would such a policy of unilateral conciliatory moves work? Would the U.S. even be willing to try such a policy in its dealings with the Soviet Union? It seems that a policy of this sort was attempted by President Kennedy in 1963 and with some good results, the most obvious one being the adoption of the treaty to stop nuclear testing in the atmosphere signed in August of 1963.[15] The main conciliatory moves consisted of a unilateral stopping of nuclear tests in the atmosphere and the approval of the sale of a large amount of wheat to the Soviet Union.

> For each [conciliatory] move that was made, the Soviets reciprocated. … They participated in a "you move-I move" sequence rather than waiting for simultaneous, negotiated, agree[d]-upon moves. Further, they shifted to multilateral-simultaneous arrangements once the appropriate mood was generated....
>
> … A danger that seems not to have been anticipated by the United States Government did materialize: the Russians responded not just by reciprocating American initiatives but by offering some initiatives of their own … Washington was put on the spot: it had to reciprocate if it were not to weaken the new spirit, but it could lose control of the experiment.[16]

Why was such an apparently successful move for peace which began in June of 1963 not continued past November of 1963?

The reasons were many: the Administration felt that the psychological mood in the West was getting out of hand, with hopes and expectations for more Soviet-American measures running too high; allies, especially West Germany, objected more and more bitterly; and the pre-election year began, in which the Administration seemed ... [to want to make sure that] even if all went sour — if the Soviets resumed testing, orbited bombs, etc. — no credible "appeasement" charge could be made by Republicans.[17]

Another relevant factor may have been President Kennedy's assassination at that time, although some additional conciliatory moves were made by Lyndon Johnson after he was elected in 1964. He continued them for about a year. Increasing U.S. involvement in Vietnam may have made the Russians less ready to respond to conciliatory moves on other fronts. It is also relevant that Khrushchev was removed from his leadership position in the Soviet Union in 1964. Kennedy and Khrushchev had gone through the Cuban missile crisis to the brink of nuclear war in October of 1962 and then led their countries through the détente of 1963, but by the end of 1964 neither man was any longer part of the international decision-making process.

Another example of a unilateral conciliatory move to resolve a conflict was Anwar Sadat's dramatic trip to Jerusalem to address the Israeli Knesset in December 1977. The final consequences of that move are still to be determined, but there is no doubt that it led to negotiations and an agreement between Egypt and Israel that would otherwise have been unthinkable. Sadat's move does not fall within the strategy outlined by Osgood, however, because there was not a series of moves but simply one dramatic gesture. Sadat was not operating from a position of military strength, and he seems to have been motivated partly by the hope of influencing public opinion in the United States, a country which could be expected to act as a mediator in the dispute. Still, Sadat's act was an example of making a conciliatory move to loosen dead-locked confrontation.

It would be a mistake to assume that unilateral conciliatory moves will always be successful. The success of Kennedy's initiatives in 1963 may have resulted from the fact that Kennedy and Khrushchev had come face-to-face with the possibility of nuclear war during the Cuban missile crisis a few months earlier. The success of Sadat's move seems to be due to the fact that he gave the Israelis what they had wanted all along: the recognition by Arab countries that Israel had a right to exist. It is quite conceivable, however, that conciliatory moves could have other results. When the stronger party in a conflict situation makes a conciliatory move, the other party may view this as an opportunity to catch up or surpass the other side in strength. When the weaker party makes a conciliatory move, the stronger may view this as an act of desperation which signals that a complete victory can be won by becoming more aggressive.

Advocates of the gradual tension-reduction approach can reply that there is some risk in any situation. One must also take account of the risk involved when tensions continue to mount and when the production of weapons of mass destruction keeps increasing. Furthermore, the GRIT proposal as worked out by Osgood preserves a retaliatory capability. The gradualist is not suggesting unilateral disarmament, only unilateral conciliatory moves which may induce the other party to reciprocate. The other party may not reciprocate, but how can this be known until the attempt is made? Although our discussion of the peace through tension-reduction approach has been focused on international relations, this same type of strategy could also be applied to group conflicts within nations.

Peace through Good Relations, Moral Restraint, and Cooperative Efforts

Although there are obvious differences between international relations and interpersonal relations, there may nevertheless be some principles operative in the interaction between individuals which can also be applied to the interaction between nations. The GRIT proposal discussed in the previous section is a case in point. It was developed not by an expert in international relations but by a psychologist, Charles Osgood. The presumption made by Osgood is that some principles effective in reducing interpersonal conflict might, with suitable modification, be applicable to reducing international conflict. Undoubtedly one must be careful in making such a move. Nevertheless certain kinds of behavior which tend to keep interpersonal conflict under control should be considered in terms of what they may suggest for more peaceful international relations.

One kind of behavior which seems to promote good interpersonal relations is communicating with those who speak or write to you. In international affairs, the parallel of such politeness would be the maintenance of diplomatic relations with all other countries which indicate a desire to have them. Even if their interests and ideologies are different, nothing is to be gained by refusing to have official dealings with them. Such a response can only create bitterness and almost guarantee unfriendliness in return. Communicating with another person does not mean that one approves of that person's life-style, and in a similar way maintaining diplomatic relations with other countries need not indicate approval of the governments or policies of those countries. In both interpersonal and international relations, the frank and open exchange of views seems more fruitful for preventing violent conflict than the refusal to respond to communications. The courtesies and rituals of diplomatic exchanges can take some of the edge off even the most bitter disputes. One way of promoting peace would be the maintenance of proper diplomatic relations with all other governments that desire them, regardless of their ideologies.

At the same time sometimes in interpersonal relations strong antagonistic feelings develop, and then peace may best be achieved by a separation of the feuding parties. If two persons have found they cannot tolerate each other, perhaps the best course of action is for each to have nothing to do with the other. Similarly, in international relations peace may be furthered if two antagonistic countries simply ignore each other. Unfortunately, such a solution often is not possible in international affairs because of geographical or other factors.

Another important aspect of interpersonal behavior which may provide some ideas about how to solve the problem of violent international conflict is morality. In interpersonal relations morality provides a basis for individual restraint. It is based on notions of reciprocity (don't do things to others that you wouldn't want them to do to you) and the benefit to each person of a peaceful social order (rather than having a situation where each person pursues his own self-interest without regard to the interests of other individuals or the welfare of the group as a whole). Similarly, in international relations morality based on reciprocity and the benefit to all nations of a peaceful international order might serve as a welcome restraint on the actions of national governments.

Many, perhaps most, scholars of international affairs would consider any attempt to apply moral principles to the behavior of nations as completely misguided.[18] They would contend that nations are quite different from individual persons. They would argue that the very purpose of national governments is to promote the interests of the persons in the nation while people do not exist merely to promote their own interests. Individuals are necessarily part of a social order while nations are not necessarily part of a community of nations. Leaders of nations, they contend, must think purely in terms of the preservation of their own nation and the furthering of its interests. To determine policy on the basis of some notion of international morality would be to act contrary to their duty to the nation they lead.

Regardless of how widespread this view is, it must be questioned. The view that the national governments should be concerned only about the people of their own nation neglects the fact that nations are composed of people who have a species-kinship with people of other nations. People in other countries are people too, and our empathy with them does not end at the nation's borders, no matter how much some national governments may try to promote such a limitation of concern. Furthermore, nations more and more do live in a community of nations. Only a few of the larger nations of the world are even close to being self-sufficient communities. The main point to be made in connection with the view that national governments should not be restrained by any kind of moral considerations, however, is that this doctrine of the absence of morality in international relations is itself at least partly responsible for the prevalence of war in the world. If individuals were to be guided in their behavior by a like principle that each person should pursue only personal interests regardless of the effects on others, then the same prevalence of animosity and violence which is found in international relations would be observed in interpersonal relations. A widespread recognition of the need for morality among nations based on the principle of reciprocity and the value to all nations of a peaceful international order would undoubtedly reduce the amount of war in the world. National leaders would be free to promote the interests of their state, but only within the limits permitted by international morality.

Has there ever been anything like moral behavior on the part of nations? A few examples may help to refute the notion that moral behavior is completely unheard-of in international affairs. One of the more outstanding cases occurred in 1956 when U.S. allies Britain, France, and Israel attacked Egypt, then ruled by Nasser and supplied with military equipment by the Russians. Surely expediency dictated that the U.S. would support its allies against a nation generally regarded at that time at least partly in the Communist camp, but the U.S., following principle rather than expediency, worked with the U.S.S.R. in the United Nations to stop the attack made by its own allies on grounds that it violated the U.N. Charter's prohibition against aggression. One could also point to the Marshall Plan undertaken by the U.S. after World War II to assist Western Europe in rebuilding itself economically. This plan was undoubtedly motivated in part by a desire to keep the Communists from gaining control in these countries, but the U.S. might have tried to achieve that aim by continued military occupation and policies similar to those followed by the Soviets in Eastern Europe. Economic assistance to the less developed countries of the world should also be mentioned, especially that which comes through the United Nations with no strings attached, as well as international disaster relief efforts and the acceptance of refugees from other countries. It seems that humanitarian concerns at least sometimes extend beyond national boundaries.

The debate in the U.S. concerning the ratification of the new Panama Canal treaties not long ago reveals the kinds of arguments which can be advanced for and against a foreign policy based on moral restraint. The Carter administration's morally-oriented policy was based on the assumption that the U.S. should be sensitive to the national interests of Panama and to the attitudes of Latin Americans toward the U.S. The heavy-handed manner by which the U.S. had gained control of the Canal Zone in the first place was considered somewhat questionable. The opponents of Carter's moral approach appealed to the national interest of the U.S. They argued that the U.S. was a powerful nation and should not yield anything to a small Latin American country ruled by a dictator. Furthermore, they argued, the decision on the Canal treaties should be evaluated strictly from a military point of view and in the context of the worldwide struggle against the Soviet Union.

These two views on the Canal treaties dramatize how a moral approach which takes account of the interests of other countries and the attitudes of people in those countries differs from a so-called realistic approach which appeals to national self-interest and militaristic considerations. The latter approach is consistent with the peace through military strength strategy previously discussed, but it tends to arouse resentment and hatred. The other nation may not respond militarily at that moment, but a readiness to use violence has been created and may be manifested when the opportunity presents itself. The moral approach, on the other hand, tends to stimulate friendship and increase the long-term prospects for peace. It may, of course, also stimulate the oppressed to be more vocal about their other complaints, but in the long run this reaction seems preferable to ongoing suppressed indignation.

Another principle from interpersonal relations that seems applicable to international relations is that working together on mutually beneficial projects may promote friendship.[19] Of course, it is possible that such joint efforts may also produce tension, so it is important to choose the right kinds of projects. An example of the wrong kind of project was the Apollo-Soyuz Test Project in 1975 in which American and Russian spacecraft were joined in space. The Russians and Americans involved shook hands in space as well as conducting a few joint experiments, and the events were jointly televised to the peoples of both countries and to the rest of the world. Nevertheless, this joint space venture was not a good choice for a cooperative project because of the close connection between space technology and military technology. There were those of both nations who suspected that the other side was using the project to find out more about its technology. The whole project also seemed to be more an artificial propaganda stunt than an effort to accomplish something really useful.

Fortunately, the U.S.-U.S.S.R. cooperation has not been limited to this one venture. During the flourishing of the spirit of détente in 1972–74, the U.S. and the U.S.S.R. signed ten other cooperative agreements which resulted in well over 100 joint projects covering areas such as environmental protection, medical science and public health, agriculture, transportation, ocean research, peaceful uses of atomic energy, other forms of energy, artificial heart research, and housing.[20] The level of cooperation has declined significantly since 1980, however, as the U.S. has reacted to Soviet activities in Afghanistan and Poland.

It is not only with regard to the U.S. and the U.S.S.R. that relations might be improved by carrying out joint projects. In the Middle East the Israelis and Arabs might be able to undertake joint development projects which cross their national boundaries. Perhaps such projects might also be worked out by India and Pakistan. In southern Africa, the white regime of South Africa could work with the black regimes in Angola and Mozambique on projects beneficial to all. On Cyprus, projects could be undertaken which would help both the Greek and Turkish communities.

Closely related to the idea of joint projects is the idea of mutual exchanges. Such exchanges can range from the simple exchange of commodities in trade to the exchange of people between the groups. An extreme example of this approach is the practice of exogamy among primitive peoples. Since young people are required to marry outside their own group, kinship relations are built up between individuals in the different groups. Under such circumstances the likelihood of war among these groups is greatly reduced. Exogamy does not seem very workable in the modern world even though something like it was practiced not too long ago among European royalty. It is still possible, however, to encourage exchanges of entertainers, athletes, artists, teachers, and students. Such exchanges promote an awareness that foreigners are people who have some skills, interests, and attitudes which are not unlike those of the people in one's own country.

Since exogamy seems not to be practical in the modern world, an alternative way of reducing the likelihood of nuclear war between the superpowers might be the mutual exchange of "hostages." Suppose that a substantial number of people from the U.S., especially young people and relatives of government leaders, were living in the various major cities of the Soviet Union while a similar group of Russians were living in the various major cities of the U.S. This arrangement would not only promote cultural interaction but would also reduce the danger of nuclear attack and the suspicion that the other side would launch such an attack.

Another kind of exchange is exchange of information. The Soviets and Americans now each sell some magazines and books about their own country in the other country. Also it is possible with the right kind of radio receiver to listen to broadcasts from the other country. A possible future development would be for each country to permit the other to broadcast a given number of hours each week on many radio and TV stations in a completely uncensored fashion. Such a move would require a great change on the part of both countries, but it would make good sense in terms of increasing understanding. The people of both countries could then learn directly what the government of the other country had to say for itself rather than always having information sifted through the perceptual nets of their own countrymen and politicians.

The mutual exchanges of goods, people, and information could also be expected to be beneficial in other conflict situations. For example, the travel of Egyptians to Israel and of Israelis to Egypt has helped considerably to reduce the feelings of animosity which had been built up during the course of four wars. Travel between the U.S. and Cuba may help to diminish hostility between those countries. Trade and travel between China and capitalist countries can be expected to smooth the development of firmer relations between them.

The great weakness of joint projects and mutual exchanges as a road to peace is that they can be used only when tensions have already been somewhat reduced. Efforts to carry out such projects depend on a willingness on the part of the governments involved to develop friendly relations. Even if it were possible to work out joint projects or exchanges during a period of high tension, they might well be sabotaged in one way or another, leading to more antagonism than if there had been no joint project or exchange efforts in the first place. But once there is a break in a confrontation situation, these joint projects and mutual exchanges can do much to solidify the new spirit of cooperation.

Although this discussion of good relations, morality, and cooperative efforts has focused on the international situation, the same approaches to peace can be applied to the relations between different groups within a nation. Respect for the other side, a sensitivity to the interests of the other side and to the advantages of peace, and the carrying out of cooperative projects can be expected to promote peace while coerciveness, hard-nosed selfishness, and a refusal to undertake joint projects can be expected to increase the probability of violent conflict in the long run.

Peace through Third Party Involvement

When a conflict arises between two parties, there are various devices for trying to resolve it. One, of course, is a contest of force. But in most situations the parties can agree in advance that they do not want to settle the disagreement by force if another way can be found. One of the most common approaches is to bargain. Each side makes offers to the other and responds to offers made by the other. When both parties have a great deal to lose if they cannot come to some kind of agreement, there is a great deal of pressure to be conciliatory. On the other hand, each side tries to get the best bargain it can, and this factor tends to make each party unconciliatory. A bargainer who is "hard-nosed" tends to be rewarded while one who is too conciliatory gives up more to the other side than necessary. Consequently, the bargaining process itself is usually very tense as each side tries to get all it can. Most of the interaction between nations takes place by bargaining.

In some situations, however, bargaining does not resolve the issue and the conflict continues. Is war the necessary outcome? Not necessarily. There are other ways of trying to resolve the dispute. One important alternative is the introduction of a third party to try to help the two sides come to an agreement. This third party may intervene on its own because it wants the dispute settled or it may be invited to participate by the parties in the conflict.

We can distinguish four different roles a third party might play in trying to resolve a conflict: provider of "good offices," mediator, arbitrator, and adjudicator. To *provide "good offices,"* means to assist the parties in a conflict to communicate with each other in a situation where bargaining has not even begun or where it has ceased because of its apparent hopelessness. The "good offices" may consist of conveying messages between parties who have refused to talk to each other or of providing a neutral meeting place for representatives of the two sides so neither one needs to agree to meet at a place favorable to the other.

A *mediator* does more than facilitate communication; he actually makes proposals which he then encourages both sides to accept. In his proposals he is able to bring in an outside perspective about what seems to be a fair agreement. With a mediator neither side needs to worry about appearing to be too conciliatory when it gives in on some point which it earlier held to be nonnegotiable; each side can maintain that it is merely reacting positively to the efforts of the mediator while still being adamantly opposed to the other party. This point is important because the negotiators for both sides need to be able to assure the people they represent that they are getting everything they can for their group. Sometimes a mediator may even exert some pressure on the disputing parties to try to get them to accept his proposed solution. Still, the mediator must get both sides to explicitly accept all aspects of his proposed agreement before the conflict is resolved.

In arbitration, the two parties who can't reach an agreement on the issues which divide them are at least able to agree in advance that they will abide by the decision of an *arbitrator* they both view as neutral. They each present their case to the arbitrator who then renders his judgment about how all aspects of the dispute are to be resolved. The obvious difficulty of this approach is finding an arbitrator whom both sides can really trust.

An *adjudicator* differs from an arbitrator in that he concerns himself only with the legal aspects of the case. He is concerned not with making a decision that will be perceived as fair by the parties involved but only with rendering a judgment about what the law dictates in this particular case. Obviously, some sorts of disputes are best handled by an arbitrator while others, where laws are already prescribed to govern the situation, may best be handled by an adjudicator or judge.

How does all this apply to conflicts between nations and between groups within nations? Sometimes one national government will act as provider of good offices, mediator, or arbitrator in a dispute involving other national governments. On other occasions a particularly respected individual or group of individuals may be called on to act as a third party to help settle a dispute between nations or between groups within a nation. International organizations may also serve as third parties in dispute settlement, especially in the areas of mediation and adjudication, but discussions of their role will be postponed to the next section in which the use of international organizations to promote peace will be the theme.

A good example of third-party intervention on the initiative of the third party itself is U.S. participation in the conflict between Israel and her Arab neighbors. The U.S. is very interested in getting this conflict resolved in order to keep the Russians out of the area. It is also in a good position to act as mediator because it has good reasons to see that both parties involved are happy concerning whatever settlement is made. The U.S. is committed to helping Israel both because of ideological bonds and because of the influence of the Jewish-American community in U.S. politics. At the same time, the U.S. is committed to helping the Arabs, both because of their anti-Communism and because of their oil. It would be a great boon to the U.S. if the Arab-Israeli conflict could be resolved. The U.S. consequently has tried to get the two sides together, especially since 1973 when the Arabs cut off oil shipments. U.S. efforts have played a significant role in the accords between Israel and Egypt. Although the U.S. has indicated repeatedly that it has no desire to impose a settlement, it has motivated both sides to work for a peaceful solution by offering them generous financial assistance as part of the peace package.

Of course, other instances of efforts to settle international disputes by third parties can be given. For example, in 1871 the U.S. and Britain signed the Treaty of Washington which established the Geneva Arbitration Tribunal to settle what was known as the *Alabama* claims. These claims of the U.S. against the British were made on grounds that the British had illegally sold warships, including the *Alabama*, to agents of the Confederacy during the American Civil War. The arbitration panel decided that Britain should pay the U.S. $15,500,000 in damages, the British paid it, and the dispute was ended.[21]

In 1904 Russian warships fired on some British trawlers in the North Sea. The British demanded reparations. A Commission of Inquiry, consisting of naval officers from Britain, Russia, France, the U.S., and Austria-Hungary, was formed to settle the dispute. It decided that the Russians should pay the British 65,000 British pounds. Once again the payment was made and the dispute was over.[22] In 1905 U.S. President Theodore Roosevelt offered to assist in ending the Russo-Japanese War. His offer was accepted, and the U.S. played a major role in mediating the conflict, which ended with the signing of a peace treaty.[23] U.S. President Woodrow Wilson tried to get the opposing sides in World War I to adopt a cease-fire and then negotiate their differences, but without success. At the outset of World War II in Europe, King Léopold of Belgium, President Franklin Roosevelt of the U.S., and Pope Pius XII made appeals to let third parties mediate the conflict but to no avail.[24] In 1949 Egypt and Saudi Arabia successfully mediated a dispute between Syria and Lebanon arising from the killing of some Lebanese civilians by Syrian soldiers and leading to a harmful cessation of trade between the two countries.[25] Turkey and Iran served as mediators in a border dispute between Pakistan and Afghanistan which began in 1947, when Pakistan gained its independence from Britain, and lasted until 1963.[26] In 1967 President Hamani of Niger successfully mediated a dispute between Chad and Sudan which had occurred as a result of Sudanese assistance to Muslim insurgents in Christian-ruled Chad.[27] In 1958, an unhappy conflict flared up between Chile and Argentina concerning the possession of three islands at the southern tip of South America, and the British were called upon to act as arbitrators but without much success.[28] In 1977 Queen Elizabeth II rendered her judgment, based on the opinion of expert legal advisers, that all three of the disputed islands belonged to Chile, but the Argentinians refused to accept this judgment even though they had earlier agreed to abide by whatever decision was made.[29] In 1980 Algeria played a key role in getting U.S. hostages out of Iran. In 1982 the U.S. played a major role in preventing an all-out battle between the Israelis and the Palestine Liberation Organization in Beirut, Lebanon.

The notion of third-party settlement of disputes can also be applied to conflicts within a nation. Sometimes the third party in such disputes may be another nation. For example, a civil war in Yemen in 1962–70 which saw Egyptian and Saudi Arabian intrusion to help the opposing sides was eventually settled with the assistance of Sudan and Saudi

Arabia. At one point, representatives from Iraq and Morocco also helped oversee the withdrawal of foreign troops.[30] For another example, the United Kingdom took an active role in negotiating between blacks and whites in its former colony of Rhodesia (now called Zimbabwe) in order to work out a constitution acceptable to both groups and to supervise the first elections.[31] Of course, the mediators in intranational conflicts are not always, or even usually, persons from another country. Individual arbitrators acceptable to both sides can frequently be found within the society involved.

From a broader point of view, in democratic societies where there is a large middle class, this class in effect functions as an ongoing mediator between the very rich and the poor, between the ultraconservatives and the revolutionaries. In fact, it can be argued that in many less developed countries the situation is explosive because there is no sizable middle class to serve as mediators. Consequently, the rich who want to preserve their positions of privilege and the poor who are pressing hard for a more equal sharing of wealth and power may both feel that only violence and the complete domination of one group by the other can bring the conflict to an end.

It should be evident that third-party mediation has proved to be an effective approach for resolving some difficult conflicts. In order to be successful, the third party must be perceived as impartial and as having a real desire to have the conflict resolved. When the third party also has power and influence which it is willing to use to help enforce an agreement and economic resources which it is willing to use to "sweeten" the agreement, success is even more likely. Of course, there is always the possibility that the third party who seeks to resolve a conflict may end up being viewed as an enemy by both the disputing parties. Nevertheless, it is to be expected that third-party involvement will become more widely used in the future to try to keep conflicts, both international and intranational, from becoming wars. As we will see in the next section, the third party in international disputes may often be an international organization or its representatives.

Peace through Conflict Management Using International Organizations

A relatively new approach to peace which has attracted the attention of many persons interested in international relations is that of controlling or managing conflict through the use of international organizations such as the United Nations and the International Court of Justice.[32] The use of regional international organizations like the Organization of American States, the Council of Europe, the Arab League, and the Organization of African Unity to control conflict among members is also part of this approach,[33] but our discussion will focus on the use of the U.N. and the International Court of Justice.

This peace-through-conflict-management approach to peace began with the development of the League of Nations after World War I and has become much more widespread with the development of the United Nations after World War II. In a very general way one could say that this approach to peace uses an international organization as a third party to deal with conflicts between members of that organization. An organization such as the United Nations can be used in many different ways: to allow for a public airing of differences between disputants, to furnish trained individuals for private mediation, to send special commissions to determine the facts of a conflict situation, to provide armed forces to guard against violations of agreements that have been reached, and so on. The International Court of Justice can render legal judgments about the application of international law to particular conflict situations. In using this approach nations surrender none of their national sovereignty, but yet they make use of the forum and the machinery of international organizations in order to resolve their conflicts.

The way in which the United Nations has operated to promote peace is not exactly what was envisioned at the time that this organization was created in 1945. The plan for preserving peace put forth in the U.N. Charter is called *collective security*. The basic idea of collective security is that any nation which is attacked by an aggressor can expect all the other members of the United Nations to join it in fighting against the aggressor. The closest approximation to this type of response occurred in 1950 when North Korea attacked South Korea. Sixteen nations sent at least some forces to assist South Korea in the battle against North Korea, which had been labeled the aggressor by the U.N. But even this noteworthy case was far from the type of response that should have occurred according to the doctrine of collective security. Most of the fighting in Korea was done by South Korean and American troops. Even the other nations which responded sent relatively small contingents. As might be expected, no Communist countries volunteered to send troops to fight against an ideological ally. More significant is that most non-Communist nations did not send assistance, even though the principle of collective security in the U.N. Charter required it.

On the basis of past experience with the League of Nations as well as the United Nations, collective security does not seem to be a very trustworthy system for stopping aggressive attacks. Nations want the benefit of collective security it they are attacked, but they don't want to take on the costs of making their contribution to collective security if some other nation is attacked. Although the U.N. has now solved the very difficult problem of working out a very precise definition of "aggression,"[34] the even more difficult problem remains of determining in a particular situation whether a given nation is an aggressor or not. Furthermore, even if there is general approval of the notion that a given country is an aggressor, there still may be little response to an appeal for help to fight against that aggressor. The prospects for collective security as a way of preserving peace do not seem good at this time.

Meanwhile, the United Nations has in actual practice developed an approach to controlling conflict not envisioned at the time of its founding, namely, the policing of agreements arrived at by the parties to the conflict after the Security Council (or in some cases the General Assembly) has passed a resolution calling for a cease-fire supervised by U.N. forces. Our earlier chapter on the U.N. included a discussion of this type of effort called *peacekeeping*. In peacekeeping there is no effort to brand one country or another as an aggressor. The attempt rather is to stop the fighting and persuade the countries to resolve their differences in a nonviolent way. It should be evident, however, that this approach can be used only in those circumstances where all the big powers in the Security Council agree or where the General Assembly in view of inaction by the Security Council, passes a resolution calling for a cease-fire under U.N. supervision. Of course, in situations where emotions run high, appeals by the U.N. may simply be ignored.[35] Also, U.N. peacekeeping efforts can be criticized because they merely seek to preserve the status quo rather than allowing for peaceful change.

The formal peacekeeping operations of the U.N. are not the only device which that organization has for promoting peace. Peacekeeping activities come into play only after a situation has become tense and fighting has broken out. Ideally, other kinds of U.N. efforts can keep a potential conflict from reaching the fighting stage. The Secretary-General may confer privately with parties which seem to be heading for a conflict. Fact-finding commissions can be appointed. The General Assembly or the Security Council can pass resolutions which serve as indicators of international public opinion. As a result, national governments may be more restrained than they otherwise would be. The existence of the international organization serves at least to some extent to inhibit its members from pursuing their national interests without regard to consequences for other nations and for the international community as a whole.

It is not possible to evaluate exactly how successful the United Nations has been in defusing conflict situations because some potential conflicts are kept from even coming to public attention by behind-the-scenes meetings of diplomats at the U.N. It is possible, however, to look at the U.N.'s record in handling disputes which have reached the stage of public awareness. In a careful study of the effectiveness of the U.N. in managing conflict in various types of situations R.L. Butterworth concludes that the U.N.

> has been involved in the growth of conditions for world order.... It has done so by acting as a generalized resource for states to try to use in conducting international politics....Shared norms, perceptions, and habits of cooperation have been stimulated and facilitated through the U.N.'s conflict management activities.[36]

Still, he observes, the U.N. has frequently not been successful. He notes that "...the U.N. is usually effective only when substantial collective resources are mobilized"[37] and that "the U.N.'s effectiveness was strongly linked to American leadership."[38] If the U.S. continues to back away from a leadership role at the U.N., that organization may become even less effective in the future than it has been in the past.[39]

It would seem that if nations were really interested in promoting peace, they could make better use of the U.N. and the International Court of Justice than they do now. Instead of thinking simply in terms of how they can use the U.N. to advance their short-term national interests, they could focus their attention on how to make the U.N. more effective as a peacemaking and peacekeeping organization. Some moves to make the U.N. more effective may require changes in the Charter. We will consider these possibilities in the next chapter. For now let us consider some things which could be done without changing the Charter.

In some cases the task is merely to implement some of the provisions in the Charter concerning what the Security Council can do to enforce the peace. If the U.S. and the U.S.S.R. really get serious about using the Security Council to maintain peace, they could make use of Article 43 of the Charter which permits the Security Council to negotiate agreements with member nations by which they commit certain of their armed forces and facilities for use by the United Nations. If such agreements were negotiated in advance, the Security Council and its Military Staff Committee could put together a peacekeeping force much more rapidly than is possible when no forces are committed until after an emergency develops. The preexisting agreements would make quick intervention by the U.N. a much more vivid possibility to would-be aggressors. The Military Staff Committee could draw up plans of action for various kinds of contingencies. They could develop a list of higher ranking officers from middle-sized and small countries who would be qualified to command peacekeeping forces. These officers could be given training specifically for peacekeeping missions. Greater U.N. readiness for action should be a positive factor in promoting peace.

The Security Council could also take a more active role in spotting potential conflicts before fighting actually breaks out. In these situations it could recommend to the parties involved methods by which the dispute might be resolved, including referral of legal disputes to the International Court of Justice. The Security Council could have a roster of skilled mediators and arbitrators to send into conflict situations. A Security Council on the lookout for serious problems would be much different from the present situation where the Security Council frequently does nothing even after fighting has become very intense. Perhaps one way of remedying this situation is to work out an understanding that the veto would not be used to prevent certain kinds of issues from being considered by the Council.

An important change in the funding of peacekeeping operations could be made by building up a reserve to finance future activities. Such a program would eliminate two problems encountered in the Congo peacekeeping effort, namely, the refusal of France and the Soviet Union to pay their share of the cost and the need to stop the operation altogether because of lack of funds. It is also more painless for the contributing nations to pay a little at a time year after year than to receive a big bill all at once for their share of the peacekeeping costs.

If the national governments became serious about arms control and disarmament, they could set up an agency within the U.N. to gather data on the present levels of arms and personnel, to propose agreements to control weapons and size of forces, and to see that agreements are enforced once they are accepted. This international arms control and disarmament agency could use satellites as well as on-site random inspections to verify information provided by national governments. A procedure of gradual disarmament could be adopted, with each nation cutting its weapons and personnel by a certain percentage each year. An inspection agency could issue public statements about the compliance or noncompliance of each nation. If any country failed to cut its weapons and forces by the specified amount, the arms control and disarmament agency could grant a delay to all the other countries in further cut-backs until the offender complied with the terms of the disarmament agreement.[40]

The national governments could also make the U.N. a more effective instrument for peace by giving it more money with which to do its work. In 1979, the total expenditure by the U.N., including peacekeeping operations and all the organizations in the U.N. system, was about $2.5 billion, an amount less than that spent by 32 of the state governments of the United States at that time.[41] The U.N. outlay is less than a half of one percent of what the world spends for military purposes. The voluntary contributions to special U.N. programs (mainly for refugees or economic development) could also be greatly increased. It is unrealistic to expect the U.N. to do much to alleviate the inequities which exist in the world and to work for the solution of global problems in fields such as health, agriculture, pollution, and peacekeeping when it has so little money with which to do the job.

The possibilities of the International Court of Justice should not be overlooked. The Court has been able to play a major role in defusing some tense international situations. In 1951 the Court settled a dispute between Norway and the United Kingdom concerning fishing rights off the Norwegian coast.[42] In 1959 the Court's ruling resolved a boundary dispute between Belgium and the Netherlands,[43] and in 1960 the Court ruled on a boundary dispute between Honduras and Nicaragua, resulting in a settlement.[44] These are but a few of the cases adjudicated by the International Court of Justice. One obvious way in which nations could make better use of the international organizations which are already available would be to submit more cases to the International Court of Justice. There are many international disputes which involve matters not vital to the interests of the disputing parties (such as conflicting claims concerning ownership of small uninhabited islands[45]) that could be submitted to the Court for judgments. Even though the issues may seem minor, the use of the Court would add to its prestige, and the habit of sending matters of dispute to the Court would be strengthened.

National governments could also make U.N. efforts in the field of human rights much more meaningful if the issue were approached in a less political way. Each nation sees the speck in its neighbor's eye but not the beam in its own. Nations which do not have the support of large voting blocs in the General Assembly, such as South Africa and Israel, are condemned for their violations of human rights while other nations such as Argentina, Iran, Cambodia, and Vietnam are not censured although they too are guilty of severe violations. It would help if more national attention and publicity were given to the activities of the Human Rights Commission and less to the politicized voting on resolutions in the General Assembly.

Finally, if national governments wished to do so, they could use the U.N. to promote a global approach to solving the problems facing humanity. At the U.N. Law of the Sea Conference, nations could have put more of the resources in the hands of an international body and less in the hands of national governments. Governments could do more to encourage the celebration of October 24, U.N. Day, as a world holiday. They could decide that at some definite time in the future only one international language, such as Esperanto, would be used for all U.N. meetings, documents, and publications. The speeches and the voting at the U.N. could be focused on the human interest rather than the national interests of the various nations. The lack of more progress toward a peaceful world, it can be argued, is not the fault of the existing international organizations but rather of the national governments which do not make appropriate use of the international organizations to which they belong.[46] Of course, the national governments could claim that the present international system virtually requires them to look out primarily for their own national interests or be at a disadvantage compared to those nations which do adopt a purely nationalistic outlook.

Peace through Promotion of Peace Research and Peace Education

As we have earlier noted, worldwide expenditures for military purposes amount to over $1.5 billion a day. As weapons become ever more sophisticated, the cost of developing and producing them can be expected to increase substantially. Under these circumstances it seems that the national governments should be interested in promoting peace research and peace education so that these huge outlays of resources to the military would become unnecessary.

From the point of view of cutting their own future costs, it is hard to imagine what better investment could be made by national governments than support of peace research, especially when it is recalled that national governments are responsible for maintaining peace among opposing groups in their own society as well as preventing wars with other countries. It seems that nations cannot afford not to invest some of their resources in learning how to promote peace.

Despite the desirability of supporting peace research, few national governments are contributing much to such efforts. In fact, the number of people all over the world actively engaged in peace research has been estimated at 5,000.[47] The financial support for peace research comes from many different sources, such as foundations, trust funds, special grants, membership contributions, university budgets, and direct government contributions.[48] The funding of peace research from all these sources is less than 1 percent of the amount spent for military research in Canada and Sweden, less than 2 percent in the United States, and less than 5 percent in West Germany and India.[49] National governments in countries such as Sweden, Denmark, Finland, France, West Germany, Japan, Norway, and the United Kingdom have given some direct support to peace research.[50] Sweden's Stockholm International Peace Research Institute is probably the outstanding example of a government-assisted institution devoted strictly to the study of peace from an international point of view. The U.S. and the U.S.S.R., the nations that together account for nearly two-thirds of the world's military spending, have done very little in the way of providing support for peace research. Recently the U.S. Congress authorized a Commission to investigate the feasibility of creating a National Academy of Peace and Conflict Resolution, an institution which would not only conduct research related to peace but also train people in the arts of peace-making (mediation, arbitration, and so on) just as the military academies train people in the skills used in war. Hearings have been held, a report issued, and bills introduced in both houses of Congress to establish an Academy, but it is unclear whether the proposed institution will become a reality.[51]

What specific kinds of problems might peace researchers consider? One obvious task would be the evaluation of proposals for solving the war problem, such as those discussed in this book. Research could be done to try to determine how various approaches could be made more effective and to learn how particular approaches could best be applied to particular kinds of situations. Peace researchers could examine periods of peace as well as the beginnings of wars in order to try to learn what factors promote peace and what factors destroy it. The problem of how to educate people to promote peace could be investigated. The various topics discussed in this book provide only a beginning list of the issues which peace researchers need to study.

Peace research can also develop new proposals and techniques for resolving group conflicts and then test their effectiveness. Let us look at but one technique which has been developed to be used when an arbitrator has been enlisted to try to resolve a conflict. It is called the *last-best-offer technique*. After the regular bargaining process has gone as far as it can go, each side is asked to give its "last best offer" to the arbitrator, that is, to indicate the most conciliatory agreement it can bring itself to make. The arbitrator must choose one or the other proposal, whichever one he feels is most fair, to be the final settlement. He can no longer suggest "splitting the difference" between the two offers, a different mediating technique which has the adverse effect of encouraging each side to be more excessive in its demands so that it will be better off after the difference is split evenly. With the last-best-offer technique, each side is led to be as conciliatory as possible in hopes that its proposal will be the one accepted by the arbitrator. Peace researchers could investigate how this and other techniques might be applied both to international disputes and to disputes between groups within countries.

Although peace research involves discovering and evaluating techniques for resolving conflict which are immediately applicable, it must also deal with the more general issue of the relation between justice and peace. It needs to focus on the problem of peace not merely from the point of view of how to preserve the status quo without violence, but also from the point of view of how to remove the injustices and resulting resentments which prompt people to resort to violence. If peace research is not to be simply another instrument in the hands of those with power and privilege, it must focus on the processes by which peaceful change can take place. It needs to address itself to investigating alternatives to violence for those who are presently being treated unfairly by the social system as a whole. On the international level, peace research must be concerned with the plight of the less developed countries and how the international order can be changed in a peaceful way to accommodate the interests of these countries without ignoring those of the more technologically advanced countries. On the domestic level, peace research must deal with the situation of the poor and dispossessed and how the social system can be changed in a peaceful way so that it takes account of their interests as well as those of the rich and powerful.

It seems obvious that supporting peace research would promote justice as well as peace both within nations and among them. In fact, Kenneth Boulding maintains that there is nothing that can be done that would more dramatically increase the probability of the survival of humanity than a massive effort in peace research.[52] Such an effort might make the difference of whether or not we all die in a nuclear holocaust. It could save governments large sums of money now being spent for military forces, weapons, police forces, prisons, and special personnel for suppressing riots. It is distressing to note that national governments are so wedded to resolving conflict by force that they are generally unwilling to fund the efforts to learn about other techniques of conflict resolution.

And what about peace education? Here national governments face a difficult problem. As much as they might like to educate their people to be more informed about and committed to peace, they realize that the present international system may require them to resort to force to protect their national interests. Citizens may be needed to fight a war. Under such circumstances it is not surprising that national governments are less than enthusiastic about promoting peace education. It seems that substantial support for peace education on the part of national governments is not likely until the system of sovereign nations is changed. How that system might be changed to promote peace is the topic of Chapter XVI.

XVI. Reforming the Nation System

So far we have reviewed proposals for promoting peace by reforming the attitudes of individuals, by reforming the internal operations of national governments, and by reforming the policies of national governments. We turn now to another set of proposals based on the view that, as helpful as some of these other proposals may be, there can be no lasting solution to the war problem until the present anarchy among nations is replaced by some kind of system at the international level that puts some limits on national sovereignty.

The present international system consists of over 150 sovereign nations, each devoted to the pursuit of its own national interests. When we say that these nations are *sovereign*, we mean that there is no higher authority to which they are subject. As we have previously noted, even the most significant international organization which presently exists, the United Nations, is based on acceptance of the principle of national sovereignty. Although there are some parts of the U.N. Charter which suggest that the Security Council can require member nations to do certain things, in fact no nation has ever been coerced to obey; and if an effort were made to try to coerce a nation to obey, it could withdraw from the U.N. and escape its jurisdiction.

Those who believe that the system of sovereign nations must be changed before an enduring and dependable peace can be established argue as follows: There are bound to be conflicts of interest between different nations. These conflicts may be resolved by bargaining, mediation, arbitration, and adjudication; but if the conflict is intense and the nations involved have approximately equal military power, it can be expected that situations will arise in which each of these nations will insist on having its own way. So long as there is no higher authority which can settle the dispute, the nations will use threats of force, and ultimately war itself, to try to resolve the conflict in accord with their own interests. The only way to avoid these wars and the military build-ups which are related to them, it is claimed, is to place some restriction on national sovereignty. Those who want disarmament by the nations first and *then* a consideration of alternative nonviolent ways of resolving disputes are hoping for something that can never be. It is only *after* trustworthy nonviolent means of resolving disputes which limit the sovereignty of nations have been developed that one can expect the national governments to seriously consider disarming.

According to those who maintain that the international state system must be changed, part of the difficulty with the present system is the roles that national leaders are required to play. National leaders are expected to do everything possible to promote the national interest. Any conciliatory moves with regard to the concerns of other nations is likely to be taken as a sign of weakness and a betrayal of the nation they lead. A great deal of the power in the world is in the hands of national leaders who must play this role. On the other hand, who has the role of looking out not just for this or that nation but for the whole human race? Who has the job of being concerned more about promoting world peace than about promoting national interests? The present international system lacks anyone with power to play this role. The Secretary-General of the U.N. comes closest to having such a position, but even he serves at the wish of the national governments and dares not say or do anything that might offend the more powerful ones. The representatives of the national governments at the U.N. for the most part view themselves as having a responsibility not to solve world problems but only to protect the interests of the national governments they represent. Under such a system, it is claimed, enduring peace is not likely. It is necessary to change the structure so that the power of those concerned about purely national interests is more limited while the power of those concerned about the welfare of the broader human community is strengthened.

Another difficulty with the present international system, it is claimed, is that the notion of national sovereignty is not consistent with the realities of the modern world. National sovereignty is based ultimately on the two assumptions that nations are self-sufficient social units and that national governments are capable of protecting their citizens from any harm which might be done to them by other groups. But in today's world neither assumption is true. No nation exists which is not at least somewhat dependent on the events that take place in other national societies. Even the largest nations have needs which they themselves cannot meet. National governments also are no longer able to completely protect their citizens from any harm that might be done by other groups. It is obvious that the governments of the smaller and weaker nations could not protect their people from a takeover by a superpower. It follows that the national governments of these smaller and weaker nations are "sovereign" only in theory. Furthermore, even the superpowers cannot protect their own people completely. They cannot stop intercontinental missiles tipped with nuclear warheads from falling on their cities. Even if such an attack were deterred by threat of retaliation, a government cannot save its own citizens from the radioactivity of a nuclear war in which their own nation is not involved. What could the United States do to protect its citizenry from radioactive fallout in the event of a nuclear war between the Soviet Union and China? All the deterrent weaponry in the world would not help. It is no longer true that nations are self-sufficient and that national governments are capable of protecting their citizens from all dangers originating in other societies. As a consequence, it is argued, it is now necessary to move beyond an international system based on the obsolete idea of unlimited national sovereignty.

How might such a change be accomplished? One possibility would be limiting or bypassing national sovereignty with regard to specific international situations. A second possibility is the consolidation of groups of nations into larger political units on the basis of geography, culture, or ideological commitments. A third possibility would be the establishment of a world government over the national governments so that the kinds of political and judicial institutions for resolving conflict now found within nations would be created at the global level.

Those who would like to see the establishment of a world government may differ on which of three possible approaches is most likely to produce such an institution. The *federalist approach* to world government advocates the deliberate decision by national governments to transfer certain powers (such as maintaining armed forces) to a world government while retaining other powers (such as establishing laws concerning the ownership of property) for themselves. The *functionalist approach* to world government advocates the creation of more and more global agencies (such as the World Health Organization, the Food and Agriculture Organization, and the Universal Postal Union) to handle particular global problems until such agencies collectively constitute a world government handling the problems of the global community. The *populist approach* to world government advocates a grass-roots people's movement to establish a democratic world government directly responsible to the people of the world, a global political institution which will control national governments rather than being subservient to them.

Limiting National Sovereignty in Specific Situations

There are many particular ways in which national sovereignty might be limited or bypassed in order to reduce the likelihood of violent conflict.[1] In order to give some organization to our discussion we will consider them under six headings: developing supranational agencies for governing territory not already controlled by nations; modifying voting arrangements in the U.N. in order to diminish the influence of the principle of national sovereignty and increase the importance of the U.N. in conflict resolution; allowing the U.N. to have sources of revenue other than contributions from national governments, thus making the U.N. less dependent on national governments; extending the powers of the International Court of Justice so that it can assist in the resolution of more conflicts; allowing the U.N. and the International Court of Justice to interact directly with private parties to help resolve international conflicts; and using direct action by a nongovernmental group to try to stop the use of armed force by national governments. This discussion aims to call attention to some of the particular ways in which the principle of national sovereignty might be eroded in order to promote the peaceful resolution of conflicts.

One of the more promising approaches to limiting national sovereignty is to prevent it from spreading beyond its present limits. There are still parts of the world, such as the oceans, which so far have not been claimed to be under the jurisdiction of national governments. Traditionally international law has maintained that the oceans cannot be claimed by any nation or made subject to the laws of any country. "The freedom of the seas" has meant that ships could go anywhere on the oceans. It has meant that one could take out of the oceans fish, whales, or whatever else was wanted and dump into the oceans garbage, sewage, radioactive wastes, or whatever else wasn't wanted. In order to protect their coasts, nations were allowed sovereignty over an area out to three miles, called the territorial sea because it was regarded as the territory of the coastal nation. But beyond this three-mile limit, the seas belonged to no one.

Unfortunately, since World War II nations have been expanding their area of control of the oceans. In 1945, the U.S. discovered oil in its continental shelf (the ground which slopes away from land but which is under water) and claimed ownership of all natural resources in the shelf, even beyond the earlier three-mile limit.[2] Chile, Ecuador, and Peru, not having much of a continental shelf but having many fish upon which their economies depended in the waters off their coasts, in 1952 joined together in the Santiago Declaration claiming ownership of the resources in the ocean itself out to a distance of 200 miles.[3] Other nations began claiming resources off their coasts beyond the three-mile limit.

To try to prevent further grabs of ocean resources and to eliminate possible violence from conflicting claims, the U.N. General Assembly in 1969 passed a resolution calling for a moratorium on efforts to exploit the resources of the sea-bed under the oceans until an international regime was established to control such exploitation, and in 1970 it passed another declaring the oceans to be "the common heritage of mankind" and another calling for a Conference on the Law of the Sea.[4] The U.N. Conference on the Law of the Sea (UNCLOS) held its first session in New York in December of 1973 and then had one or two sessions each year until the text of the Law of the Sea Treaty was finalized in 1982. The Treaty provides for a territorial sea twelve miles in width instead of three; for the preservation of the international status of straits even as the width of the territorial sea is otherwise extended; for an economic zone under the control of the coastal state extending out to 200 miles; and for an International Seabed Resources Authority to control the resources of the sea-bed beyond the economic zone of the coastal states. Consequently, when the Treaty goes into effect the area not under the control of national governments will be substantially reduced, but an international agency will be established to govern the exploitation of that portion of the sea-bed which remains beyond national jurisdiction.

From the point of view of the issue of sovereignty, it is this international agency which is especially interesting. For the first time in human history it seems that there will be a region of the earth under the control of an international regime. Once such a supranational government is organized and functioning, it is not hard to imagine a gradual extension of the area for which it is responsible or the creation of similar agencies to govern other areas such as Antarctica[5] and outer space, including the moon and planets.[6] At any rate, the effort to create an international agency to control the resources of the sea-bed represents a first step in ending the expansion of territory controlled by national governments.

A second situation where national sovereignty could be eroded is in the voting arrangements in the Security Council and the General Assembly of the United Nations. In the Security Council each of the five permanent members (the U.S., the U.S.S.R., China, the U.K., and France) has the power to cast a veto, thus blocking action even if all other members of the Security Council favor the action. The extravagant degree of sovereignty granted these five nations could conceivably be trimmed if there were certain situations in which the veto could not be used. For example, the veto power could be eliminated on votes concerning the establishment of fact-finding commissions, the interposition of peacekeeping forces to preserve the status quo, or the admission of nations into the U.N. Perhaps some limitations on the veto would be accepted by the big powers in exchange for modifications on the voting arrangements in the General Assembly.

In the General Assembly at present, each nation, no matter how large or small, powerful or weak, gets one vote. The number of people in a nation and the amount of economic wealth and military power it has make a great deal of difference in the actual conduct of international relations, but these factors are not reflected in the voting of the General Assembly. It is theoretically possible that a resolution could be passed in the General Assembly on the basis of votes of countries which have less than 5 percent of the world's population and less than 1.5 percent of the gross world product.[7] Under such circumstances, who is going to pay much attention to votes in the General Assembly? Resolutions have no binding authority anyway, but the one-vote-per-nation arrangement means that moral influence is minimal too.

A change in the voting rules to take account of factors such as population and economic power could be viewed as putting some constraints on the notion of national sovereignty, especially that part of the doctrine which holds that every nation is equal to every other nation. Richard Hudson has proposed that the voting arrangement in the General Assembly be changed so that the vote on any resolution would be computed three times. On the first computation, each nation gets one vote, and a two-thirds favorable vote is required for the measure to pass this hurdle. On the second computation, each nation's vote is multiplied by its population, and votes of countries representing a majority of the world's population are required for the measure to pass this hurdle. On the third computation, each nation's vote is multiplied by its contribution to the regular U.N. budget, and votes of countries representing two-thirds of the annual contributions to the U.N. are required for the measure to pass this hurdle. A resolution would be adopted by the General Assembly only if it passes all three hurdles.[8] This arrangement would have the effect of giving more moral authority to votes in the General Assembly because they would more accurately reflect the realities of the world situation than a system where each nation gets one vote regardless of its population or wealth. Hudson's proposal is only one of many suggestions put forth on how voting in the General Assembly might be modified.

A third situation where national sovereignty could be eroded concerns the financial arrangements for the U.N. At present the only source of funds for the U.N. is assessments and contributions from national governments.[9] This arrangement means that those governments which make substantial contributions can exert considerable pressure on the U.N. by threatening to refuse to pay certain assessments or to withdraw from the organization entirely if displeased. The U.N. would be much less susceptible to such threats if it had its own source of funds. When the International Seabed Resources Authority discussed above becomes operative, it could tax the resources being taken from the ocean floor and pass some of the revenue along to the U.N. A small tax might also be levied on all resources taken out of the economic zones of the oceans on the principle that all parts of the oceans, even that part which makes up the national economic zones, have been declared to be the common heritage of mankind. It might even be possible to tax arms that cross national boundaries or to assess a proportional tax on any nation's military expenditure that exceeds 3 percent of its GNP. Perhaps the U.N. could collect fines for violation of regulations it might adopt governing air or water pollution which crosses national boundaries. In any case, if the U.N. had its own source of funds, it would be less vulnerable to economic threats from national governments.

The fourth situation where national sovereignty could be eroded concerns the International Court of Justice. At present only national governments can be parties in cases before the Court, and the Court will accept a case only if all parties to the dispute agree in advance to abide by its decision. Only the Security Council, the General Assembly, and other U.N. organs and agencies which first get the approval of the General Assembly can get advisory opinions from the Court. Under these circumstances the Court has not been very busy. Why not expand the powers of the Court? One possible change would be to allow the Security Council to get binding decisions from the Court rather than merely advisory ones. A second possible change would be to allow the Secretary-General and regional international organizations such as the Organization of American States to ask for advisory opinions. A third possible change, a much more radical one which would have a much greater impact on national sovereignty, would be to allow a national government to get an advisory opinion from the Court in a conflict situation even though the other governments involved have refused to accept the jurisdiction of the Court. Other changes of the same sort are also possible. The point is that the International Court of Justice could take a much more active role in resolving international conflicts if such changes were made.

A fifth way of making national sovereignty less of an obstacle in international conflict resolution would be to permit greater interaction between individuals on the one hand and the U.N. and the International Court of Justice on the other. As the U.N. was originally conceived, the only place in which there was to be any interaction between the U.N. and individuals was the Secretariat, where persons are hired as employees of the U.N. The Economic and Social Council was permitted to consult with nongovernmental organizations concerned with matters related to its activities. Otherwise, the U.N. and the International Court of Justice could do business only with national governments and their representatives. But some changes toward more direct interaction between the U.N. and private parties are already taking place. In the area of human rights, the International Covenant of Civil and Political Rights contains an optional Protocol by which a national government can give its citizens the right to appeal directly as individuals to the U.N. Human Rights Committee when they feel that their rights granted by the Covenant have been violated. Another significant development occurred at the U.N. Special Session on Disarmament in 1978 when representatives of nongovernmental organizations interested in disarmament were allowed to address the session.

What further changes might be made in permitting the U.N. and the International Court of Justice to interact directly with individuals and nongovernmental organizations? One idea is to let the U.N. directly recruit individuals to serve in the U.N. peacekeeping forces rather than relying on contingents of armed forces from national governments. Another idea is to have a time set aside at each session of the General Assembly for addresses by representatives of nongovernmental organizations and individuals interested in global problems. With regard to judicial issues, there already exist international conventions which prohibit certain activities such as hijacking airplanes on international flights or using violence against diplomats, activities carried on by individuals rather than national governments. Why not have the International Court of Justice create a separate International Criminal Court to deal with those individuals who are accused of violating these international laws? Why not also establish international courts to handle civil cases between private parties from different countries or between a private party and a foreign government? Among other things, such courts would provide a setting for resolving legal disputes between governments and transnational corporations.

A sixth approach to limiting national sovereignty involves the use at the international level of the Gandhian idea of nonviolent resistance. This approach involves the creation of a nongovernmental organization composed of individuals from all over the world who are willing to participate in unarmed and nonviolent activities at points of conflict anywhere in the world. These people would be dedicated to direct nonviolent action to oppose the use of force by national governments. Such a World Peace Brigade was organized in 1962 but lost its momentum by 1964 because of financial difficulties and differences of opinion on whether to emphasize reconciliation of the opposing sides from an impartial point of view or confrontation to advance the interests of oppressed people. Another difficulty was that action seemed always to be related to issues of justice within a country rather than being addressed to international conflicts. Nevertheless, Robert Johansen has recently proposed the creation of a nongovernmental, international nonviolent police force which would engage in mediation as well as nonviolent direct action, and efforts are underway to try to rehabilitate the World Peace Brigade under the new title Peace Brigades International.[10] Such an international group could serve as a moral force which might act as a check on national armed forces when they are used for purposes such as suppressing people in other countries.

There are, then, many changes that could be made to limit or bypass the sovereignty of national governments that would facilitate the peaceful resolution of conflicts. Still other ideas could be suggested. There are many ways of eroding national sovereignty which are more modest than the grander schemes to which we now turn.

Consolidating Nations into Larger Units

When nations decide to associate with each other to carry on joint activities, they can work out different structural arrangements for their collective enterprise. They may decide on a looser organization called a "confederation" or "league," or they may prefer a tighter organization called a "federation" or "federal union." In a *confederation* or *league* each nation retains complete sovereignty. The central body composed of representatives from the member nations may make recommendations for collective action, but each country retains for itself the right to act or not act in accord with the recommendations of the central body. Each member nation is free to leave the association at any time and for any reason. Furthermore, the central body has no right to deal with the individual citizens of the member nations but rather must confine itself to dealing with the governments of the nations which belong to it. International organizations such as the United Nations and the Organization of American States exemplify this confederate type of organization.

In the tighter kind of organization called a *federation* the structure is different. In this system certain areas of decision-making are given to a new central "federal" government and the member nations surrender their power to make decisions regarding these matters. However, the power to make decisions in all other areas is retained by the members. In a federal system there is, then, a divided sovereignty. The central government has the authority to make laws concerning certain types of issues, while the member nations have the authority to make laws concerning all other issues. On those issues where the central government has authority, laws will be made on the basis of some agreed-upon procedure usually involving voting by representatives. Each member nation will be obligated to abide by the decisions made by these procedures on these delegated issues regardless of its own interest. Furthermore, in a federal arrangement members usually are not free to dissociate themselves from the central government once they have joined. If they were free to leave, the central organization would be reluctant to make any decision which any member nation didn't like and the result in practice would be similar to the loose association found in a confederation. Finally, in a federal structure the central "federal" government will have the authority to arrest, judge, and imprison individual persons who violate those laws made by the central government. The member nations, of course, will have their own particular laws and will have the authority to arrest, judge, and imprison individual persons who violate these laws. The governments of the U.S. and the U.S.S.R. as well as those of many other nations are examples of this federal type of organization.

The history of the United States furnishes an excellent opportunity for appreciating the differences between a confederation and a federation. Even though 1776, the date of the Declaration of Independence, is usually taken to mark the beginning of the United States of America, the fact is that there was no federal government until 1789 when George Washington became the first President. The Revolutionary War (1775–81) was fought by 13 sovereign states joined in a collective war effort against British rule. The participants thought of themselves as New Yorkers or Pennsylvanians or Virginians rather than Americans. During the period 1781 to 1788, they cooperated together under the Articles of Confederation with an organization structurally very similar to the present United Nations. Each state had one vote in the Continental Congress, and the Congress could pass resolutions making recommendations to the states but could not make binding laws. In 1787 at a meeting in Philadelphia whose announced purpose was to formulate amendments to the Articles of Confederation, a Federal Constitution was drawn up to replace the Articles. The Federalists, under the leadership of Hamilton, Madison, and Jay, led the state-by-state battle for ratification of the Constitution which would convert the confederate structure then existing into the federal structure of the United States of America. The main argument for federation was that many problems facing the states (maintenance of good currency, payment of war debts, restrictions on trade and travel between states, foreign relations with European countries, growing tension between some states) could not be solved without a federal government.

After the creation of the federal government in 1789, the precise limits of the powers of the federal government had to be worked out in practice. Eventually the American Civil War (1861–65) was fought to determine whether states could secede from the federal union when they felt that the federal government was exceeding its authority. Those who favored secession claimed that states were totally sovereign and had the right to determine their own policies free from interference by the federal government. On the other hand, the defenders of the Union claimed that if some states were allowed to secede it would be the end of the federal government and the states of North America would revert to a confederacy. The outcome of the war was the preservation of the federal nature of the central government and the firm establishment of the principle that no state could secede from that government.

Returning to the present international situation, some thinkers claim that it would be desirable for various groups of nations of the world to join together in a common effort to advance the welfare of their people and to protect themselves from exploitation and conquest by outside nations. For example, how many countries in Africa or Latin America are in a position to defend themselves against exploitation and domination by more developed countries? For another example, how can the countries of Western Europe hope to defend themselves separately against possible attack from the Soviet Union? And how can they expect to compete economically with the U.S. if each acts separately in terms of its own national interest? It seems that the best hope for many nations of the world is to unite with other countries in a larger, more powerful organization. Such organizations may be based on geographical proximity, similarity of culture, ideological agreement, or some combination of these.

We have previously mentioned the existence of various regional political organizations such as the Organization of American States, the Organization of African Unity, and the Arab League. They are all examples of loose confederations formed basically to keep outside nations from intervening in their part of the world. Even the European Community, which may someday become a federal United States of Europe, is still largely a confederate organization. These confederate structures do not basically alter the present system of sovereign nations because they do not limit the sovereignty of their members. In the present discussion the notion of consolidating nations into larger units as a road to peace will be limited to the forming of federations.

The argument for such federations is that they alone in the long run will be strong enough to protect the nations involved from being dominated by others. The federal structure promotes peace by decreasing vulnerability from outside attack and by providing political and judicial institutions for the nonviolent resolution of conflicts among their own members, and it promotes justice by decreasing vulnerability to exploitation. A United States of Western Europe, for example, should be able to protect itself militarily from an attack by the Soviet Union even without U.S. assistance and could be more effective at preventing domination of its economy by the U.S. or Japan. It could also help control conflicts among its own members.

The development of regional federations in Africa and Latin America would also be significant. A united Africa could be more effective in keeping non-Africans out of Africa, thus preventing both military and economic exploitation. It could help to keep peace among the various nations in the region. A united Latin America would be more effective in resolving conflicts among its members and in protecting itself against economic exploitation by American, Japanese, and European businesses. In both instances, however, the nationalistic attitudes, the unevenness in size and wealth of the countries involved, and the competition among the nations of the region with each other make the creation of such federations very unlikely. For example, in Latin America Brazil conceives of itself as a future superpower. It would be reluctant to join any Latin American federation unless it was given a commanding role in the organization, but the other nations of that region probably would not join any federation in which Brazil was given a commanding role.

Although federations are usually based on geographical proximity, they can also be based on other factors such as ideology. Some champions of capitalistic democracy have suggested that all "free nations" should join together in a federation in order to preserve their way of life from both fascists and Communists. In 1938 when Hitler was threatening Europe, Clarence Streit advanced the idea of an Atlantic Union, a federation of the mature democracies on both sides of the North Atlantic plus the nations which at that time made up the British Empire.[11] Other nations could be admitted to the Union of the Free as they demonstrated their capability for conducting their affairs in a democratic way. Streit and his followers see this Union of the Free as a step toward eventual world government, since it could grow to include more and more nations. The Union of the Free can't *start* as a world government, however, since there are too many nations in the world who are not committed to or experienced enough in the system of democratic government. If a world government were to be established at present, the people who understand how democracy works would be outvoted by national governments with autocratic systems. But a Union of all the mature democracies would create an extremely powerful supernation which could dominate the world scene and the United Nations in the same way that the United States dominates the Western Hemisphere and the Organization of American States. This Union would be a much more effective way to stop the spread of totalitarianism, whether of the left or right, than the present international system in which the sovereign national democracies often are competing with each other rather than working together. On the other hand, a federation limited to the European democracies would be a mistake, since it would tend to accentuate differences between the U.S. and Europe rather than bringing them together as the Union of the Free would do.

In response to the charge that such a Union would probably provoke a retaliatory response from those left out of the federation, resulting in the formation of a union of many nondemocracies or the total incorporation of the countries of Eastern Europe into the Soviet Union, defenders of the Federal Union of the Free nations note that even a union of totalitarian states would have little power compared with the union of the democracies.

In fact, the countries of Eastern Europe are mere puppets of the Soviet Union anyway. It is only prudent, say the advocates of Federal Union, for the democracies to unite in order to be more effective in the battle against Communism. Under present conditions the Communists may be able to extend their control over the other nations of Europe one by one — first Italy, then France, then Spain, then Portugal. A Union of democracies, it is claimed, would be able to stop this gradual spread of a united Communism over the separate national governments of Europe.

What can be said about this proposal? First, the attempt to create a Union of the Free might in fact cause dissension among the democracies because it would force the nations involved to focus on their differences as they tried to work out rules for the union. Who would get how many votes in the central parliament? Would the leader be selected by parliament or elected directly by the people? What language or languages would be used? Thus there is a problem of whether or not the attempt to bring the democracies together might have the opposite effect of arousing quarrels.

Secondly, with regard to the issue of peace, it seems that the establishment of a Union of the Free would accentuate the ideological antagonisms already present in the world. As noted above, the Communists would probably counter by forming their own union. An international system of many nations with various ideological commitments would be replaced by a system of a few supernations each dedicated to the preservation of a particular ideology. Wouldn't this situation make war more likely than the present situation, where there are nationalistic deviations in both camps? It is true that a Union of the Free might make it very difficult for the Communists to gain control in Italy, but at the same time, if Streit's proposal had been enacted and the Communists had responded with the creation of their own union, then Yugoslavia and China would still be under the control of Moscow. The competition between West and East to control the nations of the Third World would become even more intense since once a nation became part of one supernation the other supernation would no longer have any opportunity to influence it. Nationalism in the sense of loyalty to a relatively small nation would be virtually eliminated, but there would be a new system in which ideological commitments would coincide with regional political boundaries, producing a new supernationalism. It is doubtful that the likelihood of war would be diminished by such a development.

Defenders of the Union of the Free would respond that as long as the Union of the democracies continues to be more powerful than the Communist Union, there would be no war. The proposal for a Union of democracies is based on the supposition that political democracy necessarily produces peace and restraint in foreign policy. It claims that if the democracies will unite their efforts, they will be able to prevail over everyone else by superior force, but at the same time it assumes that these democracies will not perpetrate any injustices themselves. The colonial and neocolonial exploitation of Asia, Africa, and Latin America by the

Western capitalist nations does not justify such an assumption. Streit's inclusion of the Union of South Africa in the Union of the Free is especially likely to arouse skepticism.[12] For anyone who is convinced that current Western democratic capitalism represents the last word in social justice, the creation of an Atlantic Union of the Free may seem to be the ideal way to promote global peace and justice. Others who are less confident about the ultimate wisdom and justice of contemporary Western democratic capitalism will be more skeptical about whether this proposal provides the best way to a peaceful and just world.

World Government through Federation by National Governments

In the previous section the difference between a confederation and a federation was discussed. It was also noted that the United States of America began as a confederation but was then converted to a federation by the states because the confederate structure was unable to adequately handle many of the problems facing the emerging American community. World federalists argue that the national governments of the world should follow a similar course of action[13] and convert the United Nations into a federal-type central government because its present confederate structure does not adequately handle many of the problems facing the world community—problems such as pollution control, planning for a global language, and management of the international financial system as well as nonviolent resolution of international disputes. Essentially, this approach to world peace proposes that national governments delegate certain powers (such as the authority to own and control the production of weapons of war) to a central federal government while retaining for themselves other powers (such as the making of laws governing property ownership, education, and family relationships). Some world federalists would like to see many powers shifted to the central government so that it could deal with all the various global problems facing the world community; they are called *maximalist* world federalists. Others would want to shift only those few powers directly related to the problem of war and disarmament; they are called *minimalist* world federalists. In either case there would be a drastic change in the international state system. National governments would transfer authority to deal with certain kinds of issues to a new world government, a government which would be quite different from present national governments not only because of its extensive scope and the heterogeneity of the people it governed, but also because there would be no external enemy against whom defense would be needed.[14]

In this respect a federal world government would be quite different from the federal union of democratic nations previously discussed. The advocate of a federal world government argues that a union of any part of humanity against some other part of humanity is going to leave unchanged the fundamental situation of sovereign entities aligned against each other. Force and threats of force would then still be the determining factors in conflict situations. The basic argument of the advocate of the Union of the Free is that democratic capitalism will prevail if the free nations will only unify their efforts and take advantage of their superior power. Peace will come as a consequence of that strategy. The advocate of world federalism, on the other hand, focuses on the need to change the method by which ideological conflicts are resolved. The federalist wants conflict to be settled within a political and judicial structure which makes resort to violence unnecessary and unacceptable.

The world federalist claims that the institution of government which has been somewhat successful at providing for the peaceful resolution of conflict within villages, within city-states, within provinces, and within nations should now be extended not merely to geographical regions or groups of nations with a common ideology but to the whole world. He claims that modern technology has created a global community which needs global political and judicial structures. Fast postal service, air transportation, and radio and other communications services have linked people more closely with those of other nations than with many of their own countrymen. More and more the national boundaries marked on maps make less and less difference to the everyday lives of people and the associations they form. These national boundaries are already less significant for the world community than the boundaries between the states were at the time the federal government of the United States was created. The world is ready, the world federalist says, for world government.[15]

One obvious question to be raised is whether there is any hope whatever that such a federal world government could possibly be brought into existence in the very near, or even the distant, future. We will turn to that issue shortly. For the moment, let us suppose that such a federal world government could be created. Would it put an end to war? It should be recalled that there are two kinds of war, those between governments and those within a governed territory, that is, civil wars. If all the peoples and territory of the Earth were under one government, there would be an end to "external" wars unless a violent conflict arose with visitors from another planet. But the possibility of civil war would remain. In fact, civil wars might become more common just because there would be no external enemy which might otherwise inhibit any movement toward disunity. Even the United States, which the world federalist likes to point to as an ideal example of a federation which evolved from a confederation, had a brutal civil war. If federation did not prevent war among the states of the United States, what likelihood is there that it would prevent war among the nations of the world?

In response to this challenge, an advocate of a federal world government would argue that one war in 200 years is a much better record than probably would have developed had there been no federal government in the area of the world that now makes up the U.S. The establishment of a federal government for the United States promoted a peaceful expansion to the West and led the various state governments to converge in their structure and ideology. Completely sovereign states probably would have competed with each other for control of the West and may well have diverged more and more from each other in their structure and ideology. Wars probably would have been as common as they have been in Europe. The American experience thus suggests that federal world government would probably greatly reduce the probability of war even if it would not necessarily eliminate it entirely.

But, the opponent of federal world government will argue, one cannot put much confidence in a generalization drawn from a single instance. Furthermore, it is claimed, there are some instances which suggest that sometimes nations live more peacefully together under separate national governments than they would if an effort were made to bring them under a single central government. For example, Norway and Sweden seem to have had more peaceful relations with each other after they decided to establish separate governments than when efforts were being made to bring them under a single government.[16] Canada and the U.S., Sweden and Finland, Spain and Portugal, and many other neighboring but sovereign nations live in peace with each other with no expectation of war between them even though there is no government uniting them. It seems that where nations are peacefully inclined toward each other a government over them is unneeded while if they are not peacefully inclined toward each other it would be impossible to form such a government.

One response which the defender of world federalism would make to this point is that nations which are peacefully inclined toward one another at one time may not always be so inclined and that a common government over them would help to cement a community of interest between them and make it more likely that any conflicts which do arise are fought out in the political and judicial arena rather than with arms. Other federations such as Switzerland, India, Yugoslavia, and the Soviet Union show that the experience of the American federation in maintaining peace is not unique. Another response would be that most individual persons get along peacefully with others most of the time but no one would conclude from this situation that government over individual persons is unneeded or undesirable. Government is needed not so much for the many who would live together in peace anyway, but for the few who will go on a rampage if they are not stopped by force mobilized by the community as a whole. Also, the existence of the government as an agency for conflict resolution through its political and judicial processes tends to keep adversaries from thinking in terms of using violence to resolve their differences.[17] Furthermore, a federal world government would make it feasible to enforce arms control measures since enforcement would involve action against those individual persons who possess and make weapons of war rather than seeking to regulate whole national governments as must be done in a confederation. That is why world government is the best hope, not only for ending actual war but also for ending the military build-ups that are an important part of the war problem.

One of the main concerns voiced by opponents of a world government is the worry that such a government might become a vehicle for a world dictatorship from which there would be no escape. This same kind of concern was voiced by those who opposed the Constitution of the United States of America as a replacement for the Articles of Confederation. The advocate of federal world government would use the same response which was used in connection with the creation of the American federation, namely, that tyranny can be prevented by creating a government with checks and balances both within the central government and between the central government and the member states as well as by incorporating into the constitution of the central government a Bill of Rights limiting its power over individuals. Perhaps the constitution of a world government could also contain a Bill of Rights for member nations limiting what the central government could do with regard to them. Another factor which could be expected to help keep a dictatorship from developing at the world level is the absence of any external enemies. If we look at national governments, we see that the restriction of the rights of citizens is often justified on grounds that it is necessary to protect the nation from its external enemies. Such an appeal would not be available to the leaders of a world government. With regard to this issue of protecting the rights of individuals, the advocate of world federalism can even advance an additional argument for his position, namely, that the presence of a federal world government would tend to undermine national totalitarian and militaristic governments because they would no longer be able to victimize their own populations on grounds that such suppression is necessary for national security.

The opponent of world federalism might also raise the question whether countries with such different ideologies as those of the U.S. and the U.S.S.R. could be accommodated within a central government. The world federalist's response to this question has several parts. First, it could be noted that both these countries would be interested in keeping the powers of the central government quite limited, while retaining as many powers as possible in the governments of the nations.[18] Thus each country could continue to run its domestic affairs in accord with its own ideology. Second, though the U.S. and the U.S.S.R. have different ideologies, they are both themselves federations and consequently would be familiar with the idea of different levels of government having responsibility for different kinds of issues. Third, it should be noted that people do not need to have complete ideological agreement in order to live together in peace; they need only agree on what procedures will be used to resolve their conflicts. At one time it was generally thought that Catholics and Protestants could not possibly live together peacefully within the same nation, but subsequent developments have shown that it can be done once certain rules for resolving and regulating conflicts are put into force. There is no reason that democratic capitalists and Communists cannot devise some system of mechanisms and understandings which would govern the resolution of conflicts between them. Fourth, the ideologies of democratic capitalism and Communism seem to be agreed on the basic goal of social institutions, namely, to promote the welfare of the human race as a whole. They differ only on the best means of reaching that goal. There is no reason that conflicts between these views cannot be resolved on some basis other than military confrontation. The key to such peaceful resolution, say world federalists, is to focus on the techniques and mechanisms that are required for resolving the conflicts peacefully rather than thinking only in terms of the contents of the ideologies.

Assuming that the development of a federal world government would be desirable, is there any chance that such a government could be established? From a theoretical point of view, the transition would involve a change from resolving disputes on the basis of military power, where what counts is the size of armed forces and the destructive efficiency of weapons, to one of resolving disputes on the basis of political power, where what counts is the number of votes and the skills of legislators. The crucial task would be to work out a voting system which would be fair to all and which would protect the interests of every national government at least as much as that interest is protected now. Since the smaller nations of the world are presently generally at the mercy of the larger countries, they would have much to gain by joining a world government which provides legal protection from exploitation by other nations. The middle-sized countries would also gain more control over their own destinies than they have under the present system, where questions of life and death are decided in Moscow and Washington.

What about the superpowers? Now they can usually stop any developments which they oppose except those dependent on the activities of the other superpower. Their military capability, as compared to that of the rest of the world, continues to be substantial, though as more nations acquire nuclear warheads and sophisticated weaponry it becomes more risky for them to try to dominate the middle-sized countries. Also, events in Vietnam, Iran, Afghanistan, and Central America show that there are limits to what military power can accomplish. Another problem facing both superpowers is the high cost of the arms race which consumes more and more of their resources while other nations such as Japan make rapid economic progress. Under the circumstances it would be advantageous for the superpowers to enter into an agreement which would put restraints on their arms race and at the same time institutionalize to some extent their present predominant position in international affairs. The challenge is to work out a specific system or mechanism which both superpowers could accept and which would also be acceptable to the other nations of the world.

A continuing effort is underway within the United Nations to try to increase its influence in world affairs. In 1974 the U.N. General Assembly created an ad hoc Committee on the Charter and on Strengthening the Role of the Organization, and in 1975 the General Assembly voted to make this a Special Committee of the General Assembly. As might be expected, the U.S., the U.S.S.R., France, and Britain have not been enthusiastic supporters of this committee because they fear that any proposed changes will diminish their positions of privilege within the U.N. while giving the U.N. itself more power. Meanwhile, the General Assembly has succeeded in keeping the Committee functioning despite the opposition of the big powers.[19] A committee to deliberate about how the U.N. might be strengthened is obviously a long way from a federal world government, but advocates of world federalism like to note that the convention which drew up the U.S. Constitution was originally called merely to revise the Articles of Confederation. The hope of world federalists is also strengthened by the fact that many national legislators in countries such as Denmark, Canada, the Netherlands, the United Kingdom, and Japan support the idea of world government while in the United States in 1980 almost one-third of the Congress belonged to Members of Congress for Peace through Law.[20]

Even the most optimistic advocates of world federalism do not see such a government coming into existence in the next 25 years. Yet many see such a development as inevitable. A crucial question is how best to structure such a government so that it will maintain peace and still allow for the peaceful change which is necessary if injustice is to be reduced. The various national governments need to be studied to learn which of the various existing political structures and procedures best promote justice and the resolution of group conflicts. The strong emphasis on political justice embodied in the ideology of the West and the strong emphasis on economic justice embodied in the ideology of the East both need to be incorporated into the coming world government. The advocates of federal world government believe that the ever-increasing cost of the arms race and the absence of real security in a world where national conflicts are resolved by force and threats of force will cause leaders to see that it is in their nation's interests to develop a federal world government to adjudicate their disagreements and to police their agreements.

World Government through Functionalism

Many of those who recognize the need to change the international system agree with the world federalists that problems need to be considered on a global basis but do not agree that a structured federal world government brought into existence by the deliberate action of the national governments is the best or most feasible way to make the shift away from international anarchy. These thinkers emphasize the interdependence of the nations of the world and the desirability of building structures to solve various global problems on a problem-by-problem basis. They believe that many decisions about global problems can be made on a consensus basis without emphasizing voting if discussions can be focused on solving specific global problems rather than on abstract principles.[21]

Earlier, when dealing with presently existing international institutions, we discussed the various functional agencies associated with the

United Nations such as the World Health Organization, the International Labor Organization, and the Universal Postal Union. Functionalists believe that the best way to change the international system is to continue to create more and more such agencies to work on the various particular problems facing humanity. In the long run, they claim, this approach is much more likely to lead to a gradual limiting of national sovereignty than an effort to try to get the various national governments to explicitly agree to limit their sovereignty. If functional agencies are created, they will gradually develop the competence and authority to deal with the particular problems to which they are devoted. The national governments will find these functional agencies and the bureaucracies they have developed extremely helpful in carrying on the actual business of international problem solving. Gradually, the functionalist notes, the agencies will make more and more of the decisions which need to be made concerning international issues while the national governments will find it less and less important to concern themselves with these matters. There will be no need for an explicit transfer of sovereignty because real power and authority will gradually have shifted to the global functional agencies.

To better understand this functionalist approach, let us consider what happens within national governments. Many important decisions are now made by individual bureaucrats. In the U.S., for example, the President and Congress cannot keep track of every decision concerning government action. The President delegates authority to Cabinet officers, who in turn delegate it to others, who in turn delegate it to others. Guidelines for action may be given by the President or a Cabinet member, but there are many decisions not governed by guidelines and others where there is considerable room for judgment about how the guidelines should be applied to a particular case. People not at the top of the bureaucracy know more about some situations than those of higher rank and consequently must advise the higher-ups concerning what should be done in specific cases. As long as things are running smoothly, those higher up in the bureaucracy don't want to be bothered with such decisions. In the same way, international functional agencies can build bureaucracies of experts to handle the practical problems of the international community. As long as these agencies adequately perform the tasks for which they were established, the national governments are not likely to intrude. The functional agencies will serve as the "departments" of a gradually developing world "government" which handle many of the real day-to-day problems of the global community.

Critics of the functionalist approach object that this proposed way of proceeding overlooks the areas of intense conflict between nations. They claim that national governments will use their power to keep functional agencies from carrying out any policies which they find contrary to their own interests and allow the agencies to do only what doesn't offend any national government. Otherwise, the offended national government will withdraw its support of the functional agency or try to obstruct its activities. But, functionalists will reply, in most cases the national governments will find the functional agency too useful to themselves to take such negative actions. For example, it would be difficult even for a large and powerful nation to withdraw from the Universal Postal Union and work out separate agreements for transfer of international mail with all the other countries in the world. Furthermore, even if some nations don't want to belong to a particular international functional agency (for example, the Communist countries do not belong to the International Monetary Fund), the agency can still serve others who do want to participate. International interdependence is such that nations which stay out or withdraw from an international functional agency will probably hurt themselves more than they will hurt the agency.

But will the development of global functional agencies help solve the problem of war? Even if these agencies successfully handle their particular assignments, won't the arms race continue? Won't the issues vital to the interests of national governments still be resolved on the basis of force and threats of force? To this point functionalists will make two responses. First, it may not be possible to do everything at once, but over a period of time the success of functional agencies will make it clear to all nations that they have more to gain by working together than by engaging in confrontation tactics. The number of issues viewed as worth fighting about will gradually diminish to zero. Second, the functionalists will note that the problem of arms control and disarmament should be handled by a functional agency deliberately designed to take care of this problem. Such an agency might develop its own system of surveillance satellites to keep track of the military activities of all nations.[22] It might also develop proposals for arms limitation. The representatives of the various nations on the International Arms Control and Disarmament Agency could work to develop disarmament policies on which they could all agree. Once policies were adopted the functional agency could see that they were implemented. If any nation failed to carry out its part of the disarmament plan, the International Agency could announce this fact to all other countries and delay any further disarmament until the offending nation complied. Obviously, if some powerful nation refused to continue to cooperate, the disarmament could not go on. But what alternative could there be? Would the other nations of the world or a world government try to use military force to try to force the reluctant country to disarm? Disarmament is possible only when all the nations, and especially the more powerful ones, are ready to take this action together.

We can readily imagine a debate between a world federalist and a functionalist concerning the functionalist approach to disarmament. The federalist would make two main points. First, he would go back to his basic thesis that disarmament cannot be expected until an effective judicial system is in place to resolve intense conflicts of interest. To this point the functionalist could reply that some kind of arms control might be possible even if the situation did not yet permit complete disarmament. Furthermore, he would argue, it is the existence of various kinds of

functional agencies, including one for arms control, that would best prepare the way for a situation where formal political and judicial systems
for resolving conflict could be developed and accepted.

The second argument of the federalist would be the claim that a
functional arms control and disarmament agency could not be as effective
as a disarmament plan carried out by a world government because only
under the federalist approach could individual violators of the disarmament agreement be arrested and penalized. A functional agency could
deal only with the national governments. The functionalist would reply
that it is not individuals but national governments which purchase
modern weapons and hire people to use them. As long as these governments want weapons and armies, they will not permit the arrest of their
citizens who make them and practice using them. It may be true that
national governments would not need arms to protect their interests if
there were an effective world government which protected them, but, the
functionalist claims, it is also the case that the national governments
would not need arms to protect their interests if the various functional
agencies were successfully solving the various global problems to which
they were addressing themselves. The functionalist argues that either the
national governments would find cooperation more satisfying than military confrontation (in which case a formal world government is merely
icing on the cake) or they would not (in which case even a federal world
government could not prevent a civil war). The federalist would respond
that there are possibilities between these extremes. Nevertheless, the functionalist would reply, the gradual transfer of power to global agencies is
much less threatening to national governments than the federalist plan for
a sudden and explicit transfer of particular powers from national governments to a new central world government.

This hypothetical debate concerning the desirability and feasibility
of trying to establish a functional International Arms Control and Disarmament Agency points up the basic differences between the federalist
and functionalist approaches. Both have as their ultimate goal a governing structure for the world community, but they advocate different means
for achieving that goal. The federalist wants to make a frontal attack on
unrestricted national sovereignty because he believes that national
leaders, the persons who have primary responsibility for dealing with
international problems, should be able to see the desirability, and even
the necessity, of transferring some of the powers of national governments
to a central limited world government. That government could then use
its powers to enforce a disarmament agreement by dealing with actual
individuals who might try to violate it. This federalist approach seeks to
create a world community from the "top down." The functionalist, on the
other hand, maintains that the world community must become more
accustomed to working together through the development of many different functional agencies before a full-fledged world government can be
created. This functionalist approach maintains that one must work from
the "bottom up," from a sense of world community to the development

of a formal political structure to govern it. Of course, there is no reason that both of these approaches could not be tried simultaneously.

World Government through Direct Citizen Action

There are still other thinkers who agree with the world federalists and the functionalists that the present system of nations with unlimited sovereignty must be replaced by the development of some global institutions, but they differ about how this can best be accomplished. They believe that the federalists are naive to believe that national governments are going to voluntarily and explicitly transfer even a few of their powers to a central world government. They also think the functionalists are naive to pay so little attention to power politics and the drive of national governments to promote their own interests at the expense of other nations. The more powerful nations will cooperate with the global functional agencies only so long as they can use them to preserve the advantages which they have over other nations. National leaders are too clever to allow their positions of superior power to be gradually eroded in those areas which are important for the struggle for goods, power, and status. It is true that there cannot be a transformed peaceful world until the national governments are made at least somewhat subordinate to a world government, but the national governments themselves will never initiate efforts which require them to give up any power. Consequently, the only hope for a peaceful world is for citizen action to create a globally-oriented social and political system directly, that is, by somehow by-passing the national governments. There are several different ideas about how to do this.

One approach focuses on changing the attitudes and patterns of behavior of individuals without making any particular effort at present to develop a global political structure. Each person can be encouraged to think and act as a world citizen. Any laws or commands of national governments which are inconsistent with this outlook are to be ignored. A notable example of someone who advocates such an approach is Garry Davis. In 1948, he pitched a tent on the grounds of the Palais de Chaillot in Paris where the U.N. General Assembly was meeting and declared himself to be a world citizen and consequently not subject to the jurisdiction of national laws.[23] He has also encouraged others to adopt the view that their primary loyalty is to the whole of humanity rather than to a nation and to openly declare themselves to be world citizens. Many persons have signed statements indicating that they consider themselves to be world citizens, though few of them totally reject the jurisdiction of national governments as Davis did. A list of such world citizens is being kept in Paris and San Francisco by the International Registry of World Citizens.[24] These world citizens are invited to get together at World Citizens Assemblies held about every third year. The last one was in Japan in 1980.

Another version of the "world citizen" approach focuses on cities and organizations rather than individual persons. An effort is made to get city councils or boards of aldermen to adopt resolutions declaring all people in their community to be world citizens.[25] A city which has adopted such a resolution is said to be "mundialized" (from the Latin word "mundus" meaning "world"). The adoption of a resolution of mundialization may include related provisions such as flying or displaying the United Nations flag, forming a sister-city relationship with a city in another country, making a regular contribution to the U.N. Special Account in lieu of world taxes, and urging educational institutions in the community to promote a global outlook among their students. The idea of adopting statements of mundialization has also been extended from city councils to other organizations such as universities, schools, churches, and lodges as well as to other political units such as state governments. For example, in the U.S. proclamations of world citizenship have been issued by political leaders in Minnesota, Illinois, and Iowa. The basic idea of the mundialization effort is to develop and give concrete expression to a global outlook without working through national governments.

A third version of the "world citizen" approach is represented by W. Warren Wagar's call for the development of a world civilization.[26] Wagar is addressing himself mainly to young social activists whose concern for justice leads them to protest against wars, military spending, draft registration, and the various activities of "the establishment." His message is that the activists' concern for justice is admirable but that their understanding of the obstacle and how to remove it is faulty. The obstacle to justice, he says, is not some particular "establishment" in some particular national society, not capitalism or Communism, but the archaic system of sovereign nations. The way to overcome it is to form a worldwide political party which will work behind the scenes until the moment is ripe to take power and establish a world government. What is required, he says, is the building of a new global civilization based on common concerns for justice on a worldwide scale, for personal freedom for all people, for preservation of the earth, and for truth and meaning. It is to the building of such a world civilization that everyone should be devoted.

A second kind of populist approach to world government focuses on the idea of creating some kind of council or committee of outstanding individuals from all over the world which will serve as a concrete embodiment of the conscience of the world community. This approach is based on the same kind of commitment to a global orientation as the first approach just discussed, but it recognizes a need for a focal point for generating pronouncements and possibly concerted action. According to one plan proposed by Joseph H.C. Creyghton of the Netherlands,[27] a citizens' group asks over 100 outstanding persons from all over the world to form an "Emergency World Council." This Council then asks nine highly respected persons from various countries to form a provisional world government. At the appropriate time, this group would announce that they are assuming worldwide political authority. Within three years they would announce the procedures for direct election of the members of a world parliament by all citizens of the world *without any prior approval from national governments*. Once the world parliament is convened, it would draft a constitution for a permanent world government. The only power possessed by the provisional world government or by the permanent one to follow it would be the support given by the citizenry who voluntarily follow its directives. The hope is that at the critical moment a large proportion of the people of the world would follow the directives of the world government even if the national governments tried to stop them. For example, some national governments might forbid their citizens to participate in the elections of representatives to the world government. The key test would then be whether people in those nations would try to vote anyway. The difficulty with this approach, of course, is the improbability that many people would follow the world government directives when national governments ordered them to do otherwise and backed up those orders with police power.

A second version of this approach would emphasize the ethical dimension rather than the legislative one. French philosopher Jacques Maritain suggested that a small council of persons deemed to be especially wise, disinterested, and trustworthy be selected to speak out as the conscience of humanity on social issues.[28] Such persons might be nominated by religious organizations, universities, and governments and then elected by the people of all nations. Those elected would lose their national citizenships and would have no power of any kind with which to enforce their judgments. Unlike a court, no individual or nation could bring questions before the group. The council would give moral judgments concerning what is just only on issues of its own choosing. Such a council could influence the formation of public opinion in those situations. Maritain is especially concerned that individual citizens be given guidance concerning whether a war in which their own country is involved is a just war. The world council he proposes could give a disinterested answer, as compared to the biased answer a citizen would get from his own government. Once again, the problem is how many people would pay attention to the world council.

British philosopher Bertrand Russell went beyond proposing a council of this kind. He established the Bertrand Russell Peace Foundation to cast the public spotlight on institutionalized violence, and this Foundation in turn organized public tribunals to examine cases of gross violation of human rights by national governments.[29] Tribunals have been held to hear evidence and render verdicts concerning matters such as war crimes committed by the U.S. in Vietnam, repression in Chile after the overthrow of the Allende government, and the exclusion of persons from public employment in West Germany on grounds of their political views. The Russell Foundation also held public hearings on the invasion of Czechoslovakia by Russian and East German military forces. The members of the tribunals are selected by the Russell Foundation from among leading thinkers of various nations. The evidence uncovered and the verdicts rendered are published in the hope of influencing world public opinion.

Another proposal along these same lines is Gerald Gottleib's call for the establishment of a "Court of Man."[30] Noting that history reveals several instances where courts operated without any governmental power to enforce their decisions, Gottleib claims that the same thing could be done for the global community. This approach can work, he claims, because people have a tendency to obey law which they regard as fair even if there is no coercive enforcement of it. The jurisdiction of the Court of Man would be "crimes against humanity and against the peace,"[31] but it would approach these matters as civil rather than criminal cases; that is, aggrieved individuals, groups, and states could appeal to the court for judgments concerning what restitution is due them because of violations of international law. The justices on the Court would be drawn from various cultural, racial, geographical, and religious backgrounds, and regional subcourts might be established if the number of cases warranted. At first the only device for enforcement would be the publication of the judgment of the Court, but eventually national governments and the U.N. might lend support to enforcing the judgments. Such a Court would directly promote the development of world law but would not be a world government. Still, its existence might be instrumental in changing the international system because an aggrieved state could appeal to the Court rather than threatening to use force to protect its interests. Unlike the International Court of Justice, in the Court of Man the state accused of wrongdoing would not need to consent to participate before the case would be heard. Once again the big question is how many people would pay any attention to the decisions of this Court. It would seem that the national governments would do whatever they could to prevent it from coming into existence or from being noticed if it did get organized.

A third general approach for direct citizen action consists of getting a worldwide assembly of "world citizens" to draft a "World Constitution" which is then presented to the people of the world for their acceptance.[32] This effort derives from a World Constituent Assembly held in Interlaken, Switzerland and Wolfach, Germany in 1968 which began drafting a "Constitution for the Federation of the Earth." A subsequent Assembly held in Innsbruck, Austria in 1977 adopted the Constitution and approved long-range plans for generating support for its ratification by votes of the people in national referendums. An effort is being made to get universities, town councils, and other organizations to indicate their acceptance of this Constitution. Also, regional conferences of persons in favor of the Constitution are to be held. Ultimately the success of this effort depends on national governments authorizing referendums to ratify the proposed Constitution, but this plan differs from the traditional approach of world federalists because it contains a grass-roots program for pushing the national governments into action. The big question, as always, is whether there will be enough citizen involvement to create much of a stir.

Although the federalist, functionalist, and populist approaches to world government may seem to be in competition with each other, they can also be viewed as complementing each other.[33] Those who wish to avoid emphasizing one or another particular approach may even drop the term "world government" in favor of the term *world order*. This expression indicates that the desired global political order must promote the values of social justice, economic well-being, and ecological balance as well as peace.[34] Advocates of world order have become reluctant to use the term "world government" because they feel that such an expression suggests a political institution designed to protect only the interests of those who already have power. Nevertheless, they believe that the present system of sovereign nations must give way to a new global political order.

The federalist, functionalist, and populist approaches all seem to be necessary if a new global political order is ever to become a reality. Since the national governments now have the highest level of political power, it seems that the federalists are right in saying that a global system of governance cannot be established without the acquiescence, sooner or later, of these national governments. It seems that the functionalists are right in saying that, at least for the near future, it is easier to erode sovereignty by building up global functional agencies than by launching a direct attack on unlimited national sovereignty. Finally, it seems that the direct-citizen-action advocates are right in saying that most national governments are not going to move toward a new world political order until they are pushed very hard in that direction by a substantial grass-roots movement.[35]

A Note to the Reader

I hope that you are saying to yourself, "I see that the war problem is the most important problem confronting humanity. I wonder what I might do to be part of the solution." There are obviously many things you can do, some of which have been explicitly mentioned in the text. You can look through the various proposals for solving the war problem and see several possibilities, especially with regard to reforming the attitudes of individuals — including your own.

But if you are really serious about helping to solve the problem, you need to associate yourself in a formal way with some of the many organizations working against war. Most of these organizations publish a newsletter or other literature, and if you join you will continuously receive materials which will keep you informed and motivated. You will be alerted about when to write letters to have maximum impact on public decision-making. You will be able to mesh your own particular talents with those of others in an integrated effort. You will be helping to promote peace by financially supporting the efforts of specialists. Your membership will also help the organization you support to be noticed by political and media leaders. There would be a great deal more concern about the war-peace issue if the membership of peace organizations grew to four or five times its present level.

One of the most informative organizational newsletters is *The Interdependent*, a monthly newspaper which one receives as a member of the United Nations Association of the United States of America (300 E. 42nd St., New York, NY 10017). The UNA-USA is a nonpolitical organization which seeks to build public support for the United Nations and an internationalistic outlook. If your interest is in political action to try to improve the U.N., you may want to get the "Global Statesmanship" ratings of members of Congress and other publications of the Campaign for U.N. Reform (600 Valley Rd., Wayne, NJ 07470). If you feel that the best hope for world peace is the development of global political and judicial institutions, you may wish to join the World Federalists Association (1011 Arlington Blvd., Arlington, VA 22209), which seeks to generate public support for the world federalist idea in the U.S., or the World Constitution and Parliament Association (1480 Hoyt St., Suite 31, Lakewood, CO 80215), which emphasizes direct citizen action for world government. Commentary on current events from a world federalist point of view can be found in the monthly publication *World Peace News* (777 U.N. Plaza, New York, NY 10017). An emphasis on global thinking and a global approach to the problems confronting humanity is promoted by Planetary Citizens (P.O. Box 1715, New Rochelle, NY 10802). Both the UNA-USA and the World Federalists have local organizations, generally but not exclusively in the larger metropolitan areas, and both are parts of a worldwide network of similar organizations in other countries.

Some peace organizations focus on the wastefulness and inappropriateness of high levels of military spending. A valuable source for up-to-date facts on the thinking and planning of the U.S. military establishment from a critical point of view, one on which even Congressmen rely, is *The Defense Monitor* published monthly by the Center for Defense Information (600 Maryland Ave. SW, Washington, DC 20024). Another organization, SANE (711 G Street SE, Washington, DC 20003), focuses its efforts on countering the military-industrial complex, seeking to do this in part through the development of plans by which present arms suppliers could convert from military to civilian production. Mobilization for Survival (3601 Locust Walk, Philadelphia, PA 19104) seeks to coordinate public demonstrations against nuclear weapons and military spending and in support of the allocation of more public funds for meeting human needs.

Many peace organizations emphasize the need for social justice as well as for peace. One such worldwide organization is the Women's International League for Peace and Freedom (1213 Race St., Philadelphia, PA 19107). Amnesty International (304 W. 58th St., New York, NY 10019) has received much acclaim for its work in writing letters and staging demonstrations in support of political prisoners who have not advocated the use of violence but who nevertheless have been imprisoned and tortured for opposing some of the oppressive policies of their governments. Another organization working in the area of the advancement of human rights is the International League for Human Rights (236 E. 46 St., New York, NY 10017).

Nonviolence is a central theme in the work of peace organizations such as the War Resister's League (339 Lafayette St., New York, NY 10012), Clergy and Laity Concerned (198 Broadway, New York, NY 10038), and the Fellowship of Reconciliation (Box 271, Nyack, NY 10960). One group which deserves special mention because of its fine newsletter concerning the legislative scene in Washington is the Friends Committee on National Legislation (245 Second St. NE, Washington, DC 20002).

Three current national campaigns should also be mentioned. Probably the most widely known is the Nuclear Weapons Freeze Campaign (4144 Lindell, St. Louis, MO 63108). Another is the National Peace Academy Campaign (110 Maryland Ave. NE, Washington, DC 20002) which is seeking support for legislation which would make a U.S. Peace Academy a reality. A less well known political effort is the aim to extend the principle of conscientious objection so that taxpayers can refuse to have their tax dollars used for military purposes. The organization behind this effort is the National Council for a World Peace Tax Fund (2111 Florida Ave. NW, Washington, DC 20008).

Some organizations focus their efforts on the development and distribution of peace-oriented literature. World Priorities (3013 Dunbarton

Ave. NW, Washington, DC 20007) publishes the very valuable annual report on *World Military and Social Expenditures* as well as other materials. The World Policy Institute (formerly the Institute for World Order, 777 U.N. Plaza, New York, NY 10017) publishes ideas of scholars on how world order can become a reality and promotes the development of global education at the college level. The World Without War Council (175 Fifth Avenue, New York, NY 10010) seeks to mobilize public concern about the war problem and does this partly by operating a bookstore (421 South Wabash, Chicago, IL 60605) from which a great variety of peace-oriented literature can be purchased.

The trouble with mentioning specific organizations either here or in the footnotes is that many other worthwhile organizations are not mentioned. Information about 2,000 peace organizations can be found in *The American Peace Directory* (available for $5 from Westview Press, 5500 Central Ave., Boulder, CO 80915). It should be evident that there is no shortage of organizations. What is needed is more people to support them. For most organizations the annual membership fee is $15–25, and many offer a reduced rate for students, retired persons, and others on limited income.

The mention of contributing money, even a small amount, may dampen the enthusiasm of some people. Many people want peace, but not *that* much. Yet we must recognize that what we really value is indicated not primarily by what we say but by how we spend our time and money. In general people have not put much of their time or their money into the struggle to eliminate war. Their efforts have been directed instead to getting more for themselves, regardless of what that might mean for others, and to imposing their will and ideology on others rather than to developing mutual respect. Perhaps someday people will change their ways; but then, again, probably they won't. When dealing with the war problem the disturbing thought which comes to mind again and again is that people are likely to get just what they deserve.

Chapter Notes

Chapter I. The Nature of the War Problem

1. Lester Brown, *World Without Borders* (New York: Random House, 1972), p. 156.
2. Barry Commoner, "Ecosystems are Circular: Part II," *American Forests*, Vol. 80, No.5 (May 1974), p. 60.
3. Ruth Leger Sivard, *World Military and Social Expenditures, 1982* (World Priorities, 3013 Dumbarton Ave. NW, Washington, DC 20007, 1982), p. 6. Hereafter this publication will be referred to as "*WSME, 1982.*" The 1981 edition will be referred to as "*WSME, 1981.*"
4. Sivard, *WMSE, 1982*, chart on p. 19.
5. Stockhold International Peace Research Institute (SIPRI), *World Armaments and Disarmament: SIPRI Yearbook 1981* (London: Taylor & Francis Ltd., 1981), p. xvii.
6. Frank Barnaby, "World Armament and Disarmament," *The Bulletin of the Atomic Scientists*, Vol. 32, No. 6 (June 1976), p. 26.
7. Sivard, *WMSE, 1982*, p. 30. The table indicates that 59 percent are literate, which means that 41 percent are illiterate.
8. Sivard, *WMSE, 1982*, p. 27. The military expenditure for the developing countries is $112.386 billion while the expenditure for education for these countries is $89.154 billion, so the ratio is 1.26 to 1.
9. A significant book-length treatment of this aspect of the war problem is Jonathan Schell's *The Fate of the Earth* (New York: Alfred A. Knopf, 1982).
10. *The Defense Monitor* (published by the Center for Defense Information, 600 Maryland Ave. SW, Washington, DC 20024), Vol. 4, No. 2 (February 1975), pp. 1–3, reported that at that time the U.S. had 30,000 nuclear warheads, 8,000 of them on strategic (very long range) weapons and 22,000 on tactical weapons. A more recent issue of *The Defense Monitor*, Vol. 8, No. 2 (February 1979), p. 4, estimated that the Soviets have 20,000 nuclear warheads and that the United Kingdom, France, and China together have several thousand. At least one-fourth of these warheads are on strategic weapons and thus available for use in a long-range attack on the homeland of an enemy country.
11. For an inside view of the Cuban missile crisis, see Robert F. Kennedy, *Thirteen Days* (New York: W.W. Norton, 1969).
12. It has been estimated that 25,000,000 lives have been lost in these conventional wars since the end of World War II (World War I took 20,000,000). See István Kende, "116 Wars in 30 Years" in David Carlton and Carlo Schaerf (eds.), *Arms Control and Technological Innovation* (New York: Wiley, 1976), p. 304.
13. Norwegian peace researcher Johan Galtung has noted that of the 120 wars between 1946 and 1976, 114 took place in the less developed countries of the world. See *World Press Review*, Vol. 26, No. 7 (July 1979), p. 8.
14. Stockholm International Peace Research Institute (SIPRI), *World Armaments and Disarmament: SIPRI Yearbook 1974* (Cambridge, MA: MIT Press, 1974), p. 5.
15. *World Armaments and Disarmament: SIPRI Yearbook 1974*, p. 151.

Chapter II. The Conceptual Framework

1. Lewis Richardson in *Statistics of Deadly Quarrels* (Pittsburgh: Boxwood, 1960) used 317 (that is, $10^{2.5}$) deaths as the minimum. Quincy Wright in *A Study of War* (Chicago: University of Chicago, 1942) relied on the number of troops involved rather than the number of casualties and decided that a conflict would be counted as a war if at least 50,000 troops were committed to the fighting or if the war was recognized as a war in the legal sense (p. 626). J. David Singer and Melvin Small in *The Wages of War, 1816–1965: A Statistical Handbook*

(New York: Wiley, 1972) worked out very precise criteria for deciding whether to count an armed conflict as a war. An inter-state war is taken into account only if there were at least 1,000 battle fatalities (p. 35) while imperial and colonial wars are taken into account only if the imperialistic or colonial power suffered at least 1,000 battle fatalities per year (pp. 36–37). Singer and Small did not consider civil wars in their study.

2. See for example Johan Galtung, "Violence, Peace, and Peace Research" in the *Journal of Peace Research*, VI (1961), pp. 167–91.

3. In this book the term "just war" is used to mean a war which is justified on moral grounds. This term has been used in other ways. For example, the term is sometimes used to refer to a defensive war as opposed to a violent effort to change the existing state of affairs. In the Middle Ages a "just war" was simply a war which was authorized by the authorities rather than a "wildcat" war, and in Roman times a "just war" was one fought in accord with the rules of war as laid down by the state and religious authorities. See "War, Laws of" in *Encyclopaedia Britannica*, 15th ed. (1974), Vol. 19, p. 539. A well-known discussion of modern just war theory is Paul Ramsey's *The Just War: Force and Political Responsibility* (New York: Scribner's 1968). For a significant more recent discussion of this topic see Michael Walzer, *Just and Unjust Wars: A Moral Argument with Historical Illustrations* (New York: Basic Books, 1977).

4. See Thomas Hobbes, *Leviathan*, Chapter XIII in *The English Works of Thomas Hobbes* edited by Sir William Molesworth (London: John Bohn, 1839, reprinted 1966), Vol. 3, p. 113.

5. Plato, *Republic*, Book I, pp. 331e, and 332c.

6. Harrop A. Freeman, "Pacifism and Law" in Robert Ginsberg (ed.), *The Critique of War: Contemporary Philosophical Explorations* (Chicago: Henry Regnery, 1969), pp. 284–96, presents the interesting thesis that once government machinery is in place, the less powerful will gradually become able to make use of that machinery to protect themselves from oppression by the powerful. See pp. 291–93.

7. For example, see Riseri Frondizi, "The Ideological Origins of the Third World War" in Ginsberg, *The Critique of War*, pp. 77–95, especially p. 89 and pp. 93–95.

8. Kenneth E. Boulding, *Stable Peace* (Austin, Texas: University of Texas, 1978), p. 67.

Chapter III. The Historical Framework

1. Quincy Wright, *A Study of War* (1942), Vol. I, p. 61. Wright devotes a whole chapter to primitive warfare (Vol. I, pp. 53–100) as well as an appendix on the "Relation between Warlikeness and Other Characteristics of Primitive Peoples" (Vol. I, pp. 560–61). Margaret Mead notes that the Eskimos and the Lepchas of Sikkim do not understand the notion of war, "not even defensive war." Her article "Warfare Is Only an Invention — Not a Biological Necessity" was originally published in *Asia*, Vol. 40, No. 8 (August 1940), pp. 402–05 and has been reprinted in various collections including Leon Bramson and George W. Goethals (eds.), *War: Studies from Psychology, Sociology, Anthropology*, Rev. ed. (New York: Basic Books, 1968), pp. 269–74 and Charles R. Beitz and Theodore Herman (eds.) *Peace and War* (San Francisco: W.H. Freeman, 1973), pp. 112–18. The quoted phrase is from the third paragraph of this article. Something bordering on warfare has been observed among chimpanzees. See Jane Goodall, "Life and Death at Gombe," *National Geographic*, Vol. 155, No. 5 (May 1979), pp. 592–621.

2. See Robert Ardrey, *African Genesis* (New York: Dell, 1967), pp. 102–03.

3. Frederick L. Schuman, *International Politics*, 7th ed. (New York: McGraw-Hill, 1969), p. 34. This text contains a relatively brief history of international politics and war from 5000 B.C. to 1945 A.D. on pp. 33–99. The subsequent account of post-World War II history is much more detailed.

4. Schuman, *International Politics*, pp. 38–39.

5. H.R. Haldeman, *The Ends of Power* (New York: Times Books, 1978), p. 92. See also pp. 88–94. Even if Haldeman's version of this incident is not exactly correct, it seems probable that something like this happened for which the Chinese leaders were very grateful to Nixon. Why else would they invite him back to China even after he had resigned from the Presidency because of the Watergate scandal?

6. Robert Ardrey in *African Genesis* suggests that man should be defined as the weapon-

making animal. See pp. 185–207, especially 207. For a somewhat humorous satirical treatment of the history of warfare and the development of new weapons see Richard Armour, *It All Started with Stones and Clubs* (New York: McGraw-Hill, 1967).

7. An excellent critical review of these attempts can be found in Singer and Small, *The Wages of War, 1816–1965*, pp. 7–11. See also Francis A. Beer, *How Much War in History: Definitions, Estimates, Extrapolations, and Trends* (Beverly Hills, CA: Sage Publications, 1974) and Francis A. Beer, *Peace Against War: The Ecology of International Violence* (San Francisco: W.H. Freeman, 1981), pp. 20–49. For reports on another recent effort to list all major conflicts from 1740 to 1978 see the following articles by Gernot Köhler: "Gaston Bouthoul and René Carrère: A List of the 366 Major Armed Conflicts of the Period 1740–1974," *Peace Research*, X (1978), 83–108 and "Gaston Bouthoul and René Carrère: Major Armed Conflicts, 1965 to 1 July 1978," *Peace Research*, XI (1979), 183–86. For data on wars since 1960 see Sivard, *WMSE, 1982*, p. 15.

8. The investigators themselves tell us that in many cases the evidence for their estimates is very weak. See Singer and Small, *The Wages of War, 1816–1965*, p. 4; Beer, *How Much War in History*, pp. 7 and 30; Wright, *A Study of War*, Vol. I, pp. 101–03; and Sivard, *WMSE, 1982*, p. 36.

9. *The Wages of War, 1816–1965*.

10. Wright and his fellow researchers focused on wars from 1480 to 1940, but he did not limit himself to that more recent period when making judgments about long-term trends.

11. Wright, *A Study of War*, Vol. I, pp. 234–35. Wright considers the points of agreement and disagreement between his own generalizations and those drawn by Lewis F. Richardson in *Statistics of Deadly Quarrels* in his introduction to Richardson's work. See pp. vii–xiii of the 1960 edition edited by Wright and C.C. Lineau (Pittsburgh: Boxwood Press and Chicago: Quadrangle Books).

12. Wright, *A Study of War*, Vol. I, p. 236.

13. Wright, *A Study of War*, Vol. I, p. 237.

14. Wright, *A Study of War*, Vol. I, p. 242.

15. Singer and Small, *The Wages of War, 1816–1965*, p. 201.

16. Singer and Small, *The Wages of War, 1816–1965*, pp. 200–201.

17. Singer and Small, *The Wages of War, 1816–1965*, pp. 66–68.

18. Singer and Small, *The Wages of War, 1816–1965*, pp. 189–90 and 197.

19. Singer and Small, *The Wages of War, 1816–1965*, p. 201.

20. Beer, *How Much War*, p. 20; also Beer, *Peace Against War*, pp. 38–39, 41, and 46.

21. Beer, *How Much War in History*, p. 31.

22. See note 5 for Chapter 1. At the same time it should be noted that in the 20-year period 1960–79 the Gross World Product (GWP) has increased faster than military spending. In 1960 world military expenditures constituted 6.8 percent of the GWP while in 1979 world military expenditures constituted 4.5 percent of the GWP. In 1980 world military expenditures went up to 4.6 percent of the GWP, and recent increases in military spending by the U.S. will probably cause this percentage to keep going up. These figures are the result of appropriate mathematical calculations on the data provided on page 26 of Sivard, *WMSE, 1982*.

23. See Gernot Köhler, "Exponential Military Growth," *Peace Research*, Vol. 9, No. 4 (October 1977), pp. 165–75, especially p. 171. This generalization seems to hold even with regard to such peaceful nations as Sweden and Switzerland. According to *World Military Expenditures and Arms Transfers 1969–1978* (Washington: U.S. Arms Control and Disarmament Agency, 1980) Sweden's military expenditures ranged between 3.3 and 3.7 percent of GNP while Switzerland's ranged between 1.9 and 2.3 percent (p. 68). There are some notable exceptions, however. The military expenditures of Japan ranged between .8 and .9 percent of GNP (p. 54), those of Austria ranged between 1.0 and 1.3 percent (p. 39), and Iceland had no military expenditures at all for the whole ten-year period (p. 52). At the other extreme the military expenditures of the Soviet Union ranged between 12.2 and 13.6 percent of GNP (p. 66) while those of embattled Israel ranged between 19.1 and 38.0 percent of GNP (p. 53). The calculation of military spending for the Soviet Union presents some difficulties (p. 26). On this issue see also pp. 38–39 of Sivard, *WMSE, 1982* and W.T. Lee, "Soviet Defense Expenditures" in William Schneider, Jr. and Francis P. Hoeber (eds.) *Arms, Men, and Military Budgets: Issues for Fiscal Year 1977* (New York: Crane, Russak & Co., 1976), pp. 254–84.

24. Sivard, *WMSE, 1981*, p. 15.

25. John Somerville, "Scientific-Technological Progress and the New Problem of Preventing the Annihilation of the Human World," *Peace Research*, Vol. 11 (1979), pp. 11–18. The quotation is from page 17.

26. *An alternative to War or Surrender* (Urbana: University of Illinois, 1962), pp. 47–48.
27. Sivard, *WMSE, 1981*, p. 15.
28. See Bill Wickersham, "Murphy's Law and Nuclear Disarmament," *Prioritas*, Vol. 1, No. 1 (October 1976), pp. 9–14.
29. Singer and Small, *The Wages of War, 1816–1965*, p. 399.
30. From September 1, 1939 to August 14, 1945 is 2,175 days. If there were 15,000,000 battle deaths altogether (Singer and Small, p. 67), then the average for World War II would be 6,896.55 deaths per day.
31. From June 24, 1950 to July 27, 1953 is 1,130 days. If there were 2,000,000 battle deaths altogether (Singer and Small, p. 68), then the average for the Korean War would be 1,769.9 deaths per day.
32. The U.S. military budget for the fiscal year October 1, 1981 to September 30, 1982 is $199.7 billion (*Time*, Vol. 118, No. 27, December 28, 1981, p. 34). The population of the U.S. is approximately 235,000,000. The figure of $71 per month in the text is the result of dividing $199.7 billion by 235,000,000 to get $849.79 per person for the year and then dividing by 12 to get $70.82 per person each month.

Chapter IV. The Cause of War: General Considerations

1. Theodore Lentz, "Introduction," in Theodore Lentz (ed.) *Humatriotism* (St. Louis: The Futures Press, 1976), p. 28. (Publisher's address: 6251 San Bonita, St. Louis, MO 63105.)
2. See for example Matthew Melko's *Fifty-Two Peaceful Societies* (Oakville, Ontario: Canadian Peace Research Institute Press, 1973). Melko has made some modifications of his original data as the result of comments received from others. See his "Note on the Dating of the Phoenician Peace" in *Peace Research*, Vol. 7 (1975), p. 108. For a more recent refinement of this effort see Matthew Melko and Richard D. Weigel, *Peace in the Ancient World* (Jefferson, NC: McFarland, 1981).
3. For an example of such an inference see Norman Alcock, *The War Disease* (Oakville, Ontario: Canadian Peace Research Institute Press, 1972), pp. 152–53. It is remarkable that Alcock nevertheless takes note of Lewis Richardson's care in concluding that arms races are only sometimes the cause of war. See pp. 70–71.
4. See for example John Stoessinger, *Why Nations Go To War*, 3rd ed. (New York: St. Martin's Press, 1981). After analyzing the beginnings of seven recent wars, Stoessinger indicates in the final chapter that he believes he can extract certain generalizations or common themes from his case studies. The kind of detailed case studies he conducts seem to be necessary in order to proceed to the classification of wars on the basis of their causes.
5. Mention should be made of the "Correlates of War" project being carried out by J. David Singer and his associates. They attempt to check various theories about the cause of war by trying to calculate the correlations between the presence of the purported causes of war and the actual occurrence of wars. See J. David Singer, *Explaining War: Causes and Correlates of War* (Beverly Hills: Sage, 1979) and J. David Singer, *Correlates of War–II* (New York: Free Press, 1980). For a brief discussion of the limitations of this approach see David W. Ziegler, *War, Peace, and International Politics*, 2nd ed. (Boston: Little, Brown, 1981), pp. 120–23 and 421.
6. Leonard Berkowitz, "The Concept of Aggressive Drive: Some Additional Considerations" in L. Berkowitz (ed.), *Advances in Experimental Social Psychology*, Vol. 2 (New York: Academic Press, 1965), p. 302.
7. For a forceful statement of the view that the causes of individual aggression are different from the causes of war see Ralph L. Holloway, "Human Aggression: The Need for a Species-Specific Framework" in Morton Fried, Marvin Harris, and Robert Murphy (eds.), *War: The Anthropology of Armed Conflict and Aggression* (Garden City, NY: Natural History Press, 1967), pp. 29–48, especially pp. 29–30. For an earlier statement of this view, see Bronislaw Malinowski, "An Anthropological Analysis of War," *American Journal of Sociology*, Vol. 46, No. 2 (January 1941), pp. 521–50, especially pp. 523–33.
8. A good collection of excerpts from selections relating individual aggression to warfare can be found in William A. Nesbitt (ed.), *Human Nature and War*. This booklet for students was published by the State Education Department of New York, 99 Washington Ave., Albany, NY 12210 in 1973.
9. For a good collection of three selections, one dealing with each type of theory about

human aggression, see Richard A. Falk and Samuel S. Kim (eds.), *The War System: An Interdisciplinary Approach* (Boulder, CO: Westview Press, 1980), pp. 77–156.

10. *On Aggression* (New York: Harcourt, Brace, Janovich, 1966), p. 52. The relevant passage is reprinted in Nesbitt, *Human Nature and War*, p. 9.

11. *Civilization and Its Discontents* (New York: Norton, 1930), p. 67. The relevant passage is reprinted in Nesbitt, *Human Nature and War*, p. 14.

12. *The Territorial Imperative* (New York: Atheneum, 1961).

13. *African Genesis*, p. 325.

14. *The Naked Ape* (New York: McGraw-Hill, 1967).

15. "Human Violence: Some Causes and Implications" in Beitz and Herman, *Peace and War*, pp. 119–43. This article contains a rather extensive bibliography on the physiological basis of aggression. Corning would probably object to being grouped with Lorenz, Ardrey, and Morris because his views are considerably different from theirs. Still, his emphasis on the physiological basis for aggressive behavior seems to require classifying his view as one that emphasizes the biological rather than the cultural or psychological aspects of aggression. At the same time it should be noted that for Corning, as well as for others such as Freud who emphasize the biological or instinctual basis of aggression, the solution to the war problem is to be found in politics rather than biology.

16. Peggy Durdin, "From the Space Age to the Tasaday Age," *New York Times Magazine*, October 8, 1972, pp. 14ff., partially reprinted in Nesbitt, *Human Nature and War*, pp. 45–47.

17. Geoffrey Gorer, "Man Has No 'Killer Instinct'," *New York Times Magazine*, November 27, 1966, pp. 47ff., partially reprinted in Nesbitt, *Human Nature and War*, pp. 49–52.

18. Mead, "Warfare Is Only an Invention – Not a Biological Necessity." See Note 1 for Chapter III.

19. Ardrey, *African Genesis*, pp. 359–60. Also see Freud's response to Einstein in *Why War?* (Paris: International Institute of Intellectual Cooperation, 1933), reprinted in Peter Mayer (ed.), *The Pacifist Conscience* (Chicago: Henry Regnery, 1967), pp. 235–48; see especially pp. 247–48.

20. Corning, "Human Violence" in Beitz and Herman, *Peace and War*, pp. 131–43.

21. "The Fashionable View of Man as a Naked Ape Is: 1. An Insult to Apes, 2. Simplistic, 3. Male-oriented, 4. Rubbish," *New York Times Magazine*, September 3, 1972, pp. 10ff., partially reprinted in Nesbitt, *Human Nature and War*, pp. 29–33. See also Sally Carrighar, "War Is Not in Our Genes," *New York Times Magazine*, September 10, 1967, pp. 74ff., reprinted in *UNESCO Courier*, Vol. 23, No. 8 (August–September, 1970), pp. 40–45 and partially reprinted in Nesbitt, *Human Nature and War*, pp. 23–28. But in defense of group territoriality in primates see Ardrey, *African Genesis*, pp. 46, 77, 82–85, and 107–10 and Goodall, "Life and Death at Gombe," *National Geographic*, Vol. 155, No. 5 (May 1979), p. 599.

22. J. Dollard, L.W. Doob, N.E. Miller, O.H. Mowrer, and R.R. Sears, *Frustration and Aggression* (New Haven: Yale University, 1939). See especially p. 1.

23. Leonard Berkowitz, "The Frustration-Aggression Hypothesis Revisited" in L. Berkowitz (ed.), *Roots of Aggression* (New York: Atherton, 1969), pp. 1–28.

24. Stanley Milgrim, *Obedience to Authority: An Experimental View* (New York: Harper and Row, 1974). See especially pp. 165–68.

25. Arnold H. Buss, *The Psychology of Aggression* (New York: Wiley, 1961), pp. 20–23.

26. Richard J. Borden, "Social Situational Influences on Aggression: A Review of Experimental Findings and Implications," *Peace Research*, Vol. 7 (1975), pp. 97–107.

27. William Eckhardt, "A Conformity Theory of Aggression," *Journal of Peace Research*, Vol. 11 (1974), pp. 31–39.

28. For a good general statement of this approach see John Dewey, "Does Human Nature Change?", *The Rotarian*, February 1938, reprinted in Mary Mothersill (ed.) *Ethics* (New York: Macmillan, 1965), pp. 83–91. Another good general statement of this view is Mark A. May's "War, Peace, and Social Learning" in Bramson and Goethals, *War: Studies from Psychology, Sociology, Anthropology*, pp. 151–58.

29. Mead, "Warfare Is Only an Invention – Not a Biological Necessity." See Note 1 for Chapter III.

30. *African Genesis*, pp. 107–10.

31. Stoessinger, *Why Nations Go To War*, pp. 208–09, makes this same point as a result of his case studies of seven wars in the twentieth century. Corning, "Human Violence" in Beitz and Herman, *Peace and War*, pp. 129–30, also discusses the issue of the significance of

the aggressiveness of leaders for the problem of war, especially in terms of the issue of male vs. female leaders.

32. See E.F.M. Durbin and John Bowlby, "Personal Aggressiveness and War" in Bramson and Goethals, *War: Studies from Psychology, Sociology, Anthropology*, pp. 94–95. See also Edward C. Tolman, "Drives Toward War" in this same book of readings, pp. 165–68.

33. Ross Stagner, *Psychological Aspects of International Conflict* (Belmont, CA: Wadsworth, 1967), pp. 109–10.

34. Stagner, *Psychological Aspects of International Conflict*, pp. 148–49 and Kenneth Grundy, "The Causes of Political Violence" in Beitz and Herman, *Peace and War*, pp. 50–68.

Chapter V. Group Competition and Group Identification

1. Anatol Rapoport in *Fights, Games, and Debates* (Ann Arbor, MI: University of Michigan, 1960), pp. 9–12, makes some excellent points about the differences between the three different activities mentioned in his title. He notes that even in debates it is assumed that the aim is to get the other person to come over to one's own opinion. The search for objective truth must take a different form. It must be what Rapoport calls an argument (p. 273). It consists of a dialectic of escaping error rather than of defending a particular theory no matter what objections are raised.

2. Frondizi, "The Ideological Origins of the Third World War" in Ginsberg, *The Critique of War*, pp. 77–95, especially p. 81 and pp. 87–88.

3. Freeman, "Pacifism and Law" in Ginsberg, *The Critique of War*, pp. 284–96, especially pp. 293–94.

4. Joseph A. Schumpeter, *Imperialism and Social Classes* (Cleveland: World Publishing Co., 1955), argues for the thesis that "objectless" expansionism (that is, expansionism with no reasonable objective in terms of the welfare of the nation involved) occurs regularly and in fact may be the cause of a majority of the international wars that have occurred. See especially p. 6 and pp. 24–25.

5. See Ziegler, *War, Peace, and International Politics*, pp. 97–98.

6. For a list of separatist efforts of the recent past see Steven J. Rosen and Walter S. Jones, *The Logic of International Relations*, 3rd ed. (Cambridge, MA: Winthrop, 1980), p. 312.

7. The situation of the Somalis is somewhat duplicated by that of the Bakongos in Zaire, Congo, Cabinda, and Angola and by that of the Kurds in Iraq, Iran, Turkey, and the Soviet Union except that in these two cases there is no existing political entity to serve as a core for the unification effort.

8. For a more extended discussion of this aspect of nationalism by a psychologist see Stagner, *Psychological Aspects of International Conflict*, pp. 17–83.

Chapter VI. Other Views about Causes of War

1. This "Arms Race Game" is an adaptation of the "Prisoner's Dilemma" game. See Rapoport, *Fights, Games, and Debates*, pp. 173–74.

2. Alcock, *The War Disease*, pp. 169–70.

3. See Alan G. Newcombe, "A Foreign Policy for Peace," *Gandhi Marg*, Vol. 16 (1972), pp. 254–65. A slightly revised version of this article is reprinted in Israel W. Charny (ed.), *Strategies Against Violence: Design for Nonviolent Change* (Boulder, CO: Westview, 1978), pp. 3–18. See also Alcock, *The War Disease*, pp. 164–73.

4. Lewis F. Richardson, *Arms and Insecurity* (Pittsburgh: Boxwood Press, 1960), pp. 12–36. See also Alcock, *The War Disease*, pp. 70–83 and 200–212.

5. Lewis F. Richardson, "Could An Arms Race End Without Fighting?",*Nature*, Vol. 168 (1951), pp. 567–68 and Richardson, *Arms and Insecurity*, pp. 35–36 and p. 76.

6. Richardson, *Arms and Insecurity*, p. 70.

7. Ziegler, *War, Peace, and International Politics*, p. 117, argues that the view that individual aggressive leaders are a cause of war cannot be correct because there are many wars in which there seem to be no villains. Ziegler's argument is cogent only against the view that individual aggressive leaders are a necessary condition of war. It does not apply to the thesis that individual aggressive leaders are a contributory factor to war. The view that national

leaders play a key role in determining whether or not their countries will engage in war is convincingly defended by Bruce Bueno de Mesquita in *The War Trap* (New Haven: Yale University, 1981), pp. 19–29.

8. See Kenneth Waltz, *Man, the State, and War* (New York: Columbia University, 1959), pp. 8–9.

9. The term "military-industrial complex" seems to have been coined by Malcolm Moos and popularized by President Eisenhower when he used it in 1961 in his farewell address. See Alvin R. Sunseri, "The Military-Industrial Complex in Iowa" in Benjamin F. Cooling (ed.), *War, Business, and American Society: Historical Perspectives on the Military-Industrial Complex* (Port Washington, NY: Kennikat, 1977), p. 158.

10. Anne Trotter, "Development of the Merchants-of-Death Theory" in Cooling, *War, Business, and American Society*, p. 96.

11. Trotter, "Development of the Merchants-of-Death Theory" in Cooling, *War, Business, and American Society*, pp. 97–98.

12. Trotter, "Development of the Merchants-of-Death Theory" in Cooling, *War, Business, and American Society*, p. 94.

13. Trotter, "Development of the Merchants-of-Death Theory" in Cooling, *War, Business and American Society*, pp. 101–03.

14. Benjamin F. Cooling, "Introduction" in Cooling, *War, Business, and American Society*, p. 3.

15. See for example Seymour Melman (ed.), *The War Economy of the United States* (New York: St. Martin's, 1971).

16. See C. Wright Mills, *The Causes of World War Three* (New York: Simon and Schuster, 1958), pp. 17–19, 47–50, and 86–89.

17. Stagner, *Psychological Aspects of International Conflict*, p. 137.

18. For a good discussion of the thesis that war is caused by a few individuals seeking personal gain see Bernard Brodie, *War and Politics* (New York: Macmillan, 1973), pp. 283–302.

19. The best source for these basic ideas is *The Communist Manifesto* by Marx and Engels. The *Manifesto* along with other relevant selections can be found in *The Marx-Engels Reader* edited by Robert C. Tucker (New York: Norton, 1972) and in *Karl Marx: Selected Readings* (Oxford: Oxford University, 1977) edited by David McLellan. See also Frederick Engels, *Herr Eugen Düring's Revolution in Science*, tr. by Emile Burns (New York: International Publishers, 1939), especially pp. 292–310.

20. V.I. Lenin, *Imperialism: The Highest Stage of Capitalism* (New York: International Publishers, 1939), especially pp. 9–14 and 76–98.

21. *Philosophy of Right*, tr. by T.M. Knox (Oxford: The Clarendon Press, 1942), p. 295.

22. For a brief account of Bismarck's efforts and views see Ziegler, *War, Peace, and International Politics*, pp. 7–20.

23. For an attempt to show that there is a correlation between external war and domestic conflict in "polyarchic" (democratic) states see Jonathan Wilkenfeld, "Domestic and Foreign Conflict Behavior of Nations," *Journal of Peace Research*, Vol. 5 (1968), pp. 56–69. Wilkenfeld cites various earlier studies that had concluded that there was no correlation between foreign conflict and domestic conflict such as Rudolph J. Rummel, "Dimensions of Conflict Behavior Within and Between Nations," *General Systems*, Vol. 8 (1963), pp. 1–50.

24. This letter is reprinted in John Somerville and Ronald E. Santoni (eds.) *Social and Political Philosophy* (Garden City, NY: Doubleday, 1963), pp. 259–60.

25. Quincy Wright, *A Study of War*, abridged by Louise Leonard Wright (Chicago: University of Chicago, 1964), p. 428.

Chapter VII. The Value of War

1. It is surprising how widespread the tendency is to assume that since wars have some supposed good consequence they are therefore begun in order to achieve that end. For example, in the list of twelve theories about the cause of war discussed by Rosen and Jones in *The Logic of International Relations*, pp. 307–36, two of them (the eighth and the eleventh) involve this mistake.

2. Frank B. Livingstone, "The Effects of Warfare on the Biology of the Human Species" in Fried, Harris, and Murphy, *War: The Anthropology of Armed Conflict and Aggression*, p. 5.

3. Some nations suffered more than others with the Soviet Union losing 9 percent of its population during that war while Germany lost 5 percent of its population, England and France about 1 percent, and the U.S. only .2 percent. See Livingstone, "The Effects of Warfare" in Fried, Harris, and Murphy, *War: The Anthropology of Armed Conflict and Aggression*, p. 5.

4. Livingstone, "The Effects of Warfare" in Fried, Harris, and Murphy, *War: The Anthropology of Armed Conflict and Aggression*, p. 5.

5. Livingstone, "The Effects of Warfare" in Fried, Harris, and Murphy, *War: The Anthropology of Armed Conflict and Aggression*, p. 5. Frederick P. Thieme, discussant of Livingstone's paper at the 1967 symposium of the American Anthropological Association on the effects of war on the human species, agreed with Livingstone's judgment on this matter. See p. 16 of the Fried, Harris, and Murphy book.

6. Livingstone, "The Effects of Warfare" in Fried, Harris, and Murphy, *War: The Anthropology of Armed Conflict and Aggression*, pp. 6–8. Interestingly Livingstone is making the point that the genetic consequences are so slight that one need not be concerned that modern war has an *adverse* effect on the gene pool, an effect which might be expected when it is supposed that there is a tendency for the *better fit* persons to be called to serve in combat situations during war. Our concern in the text is the opposite view that war is *good* because then the *less fit* are less likely to survive and reproduce.

7. "The Biological Consequences of War" in Fried, Harris, and Murphy, *War: The Anthropology of Armed Conflict and Aggression*, p. 18.

8. The situation in earlier times among more primitive people may have been somewhat different. In fact, primitive warfare may have been an important factor in both population control and genetic selection. See Livingstone, "The Effects of Warfare" in Fried, Harris, and Murphy, *War: The Anthropology of Armed Conflict and Aggression*, pp. 8–11; Corning, "Human Violence" in Beitz and Herman, *Peace and War*, p. 126; and Stanislav Andreski, "Evolution and War," *Science Journal*, Vol. 7 (January, 1971), p. 91.

9. John Nef, "Political, Technological, and Cultural Aspects of War" in Ginsberg, *The Critique of War*, pp. 120–37, especially pp. 130–31.

10. *Philosophy of Right*, p. 295.

11. From *The Political and Social Doctrine of Fascism* (tr. by Jane Soames) as reprinted in Somerville and Santoni, *Social and Political Philosophy*, p. 431.

12. Reprinted in Bramson and Goethals, *War: Studies from Psychology, Sociology, Anthropology*, pp. 21–31.

13. William James, "The Moral Equivalent of War" in Bramson and Goethals, *War: Studies from Psychology, Sociology, Anthropology*, p. 29. James seems naively optimistic in supposing that a government with so many people at its command would have them disinterestedly pursue justice rather than its own national interest. American Peace Corps volunteers are frequently disillusioned to find that they have become agents of American foreign policy rather than disinterested workers for justice. It is difficult to believe that things would be different under the program James proposes.

14. See Andrew Vayda, "Hypotheses about Functions of War" in Fried, Harris, and Murphy, *War: The Anthropology of Armed Conflict and Aggression*, p. 88.

15. *Newsweek*, Vol. 74, No. 4 (July 28, 1969), p. 54 and *Time*, Vol. 94, No. 4 (July 25, 1969), pp. 29–30.

Chapter VIII. Ideological Aspects of the Contemporary Situation

1. Adam Smith (1723–1790) in *An Inquiry into the Nature and Causes of the Wealth of the Nations* (ed. by J.R. McCulloch, Edinburgh: Adam and Charles Black, 1863), Book IV, Chapter II, p. 199, poetically describes this operation of the market system as the working of an "invisible hand." The basic ideas of capitalism and the implications of its natural international dimensions are put forward by Smith in this work.

2. It is sometimes claimed that capitalism is racist and imperialistic. It may in fact be the case that capitalists have been racists, but that characteristic is not essential to the capitalist system. In fact, racism is foreign to it since the only things which matter in capitalism are competence as a worker or investor and the possession of money in order to buy as a consumer

or to invest as a saver. The race, religion, sex, or age of the individual is irrelevant. It may also be the case that some capitalists have been imperialistic, but nationalistic imperialism is contrary to the theory of capitalism. The capitalist is interested in making profit on his investment regardless of where that might be. He favors a worldwide market economy rather than a system of national tariffs and regulations. There is only one type of discrimination which is necessarily part of capitalism and that is discrimination against the poor. The poor are discriminated against because they do not have enough money to serve as potential customers or to invest and earn profits.

3. Although this view of history is fundamental in Marx's thought, the most sustained discussions of historical materialism occur in Frederick Engels, *Herr Eugen Dühring's Revolution in Science*, pp. 292–310 and Frederick Engels, *Ludwig Feuerbach and the End of Classical German Philosophy* (tr. anonymous, Peking: Foreign Languages Press, 1976), pp. 38–59.

4. Marx and Engels seem to assume without argument that the dominant class in a mass-production society will be the factory workers (the proletariat). They fail to consider an alternative possibility, that the new dominant class will be the managers. The important role now played by managers in both capitalist and socialist countries gives some plausibility to this alternative view. Such a view would also make the shift from individualistic capitalism to the collectivist type of production analogous to what Marx and Engels claim happened during earlier transitions. In no earlier shift did the oppressed class of the previous stage become the new ruling class. The new dominant class was always a new class brought into existence by the new mode of production. In the shift from small-scale manufacturing to mass production the new class which arises with decision-making power upon which both stockholders and factory workers depend is the managerial class.

5. This phrase from *Critique of the Gotha Program* can be found in McLellan, *Karl Marx: Selected Writings*, p. 569 and Tucker, *The Marx-Engels Reader*, p. 388.

6. David Lane, *Politics and Society in the U.S.S.R.* (New York: Random House, 1971), pp. 11–14.

7. Lane, *Politics and Society in the U.S.S.R.*, p. 129.

8. It is ironic that while Marxism is based on the premise that economic power automatically generates political power, it nevertheless focuses its efforts to bring about social change on using force to gain control of the *political* system. This imperative of Marxist *practical* philosophy suggests that, contrary to Marxist *theoretical* philosophy, the political system is the controller of the economic system. Otherwise, the proper approach for Marxists would be to get more wealth into the hands of the proletariat so they would as a result acquire more political power. Could increased wages secured by militant labor unions be a better route to the classless society than armed revolutions? If not, then political power must have some basis other than economic power and the materialistic interpretation of history needs to be discarded.

9. John Somerville, "Marxism and War" in Ginsberg, *The Critique of War*, p. 149.

Chapter IX. Economic Aspects of the Contemporary Situation

1. See for example Sivard *WMSE, 1982*, pp. 26–35.

2. The ready availability of data for many countries leads us to use the "per capita GNP" even though it is not a wholly satisfactory measure of the material conditions of life. It will tend to exaggerate the differences between the developed and less developed countries because the Gross National Product (GNP) does not include goods made or services provided where no payment was made. The "per capita GNP" also gives no indication of how evenly or unevenly the income is distributed with a country. In order to have a better measure of the quality of life in less developed countries the Overseas Development Council, a nongovernmental organization in Washington, D.C., has developed a new measure of welfare called the "Physical Quality of Life Index." The PQLI is a composite figure based on indexes for three widely used social indicators: the infant mortality rate, the life expectancy of a one-year-old child, and the literacy rate in that country. For more information about the "Physical Quality of Life Index" see Martin M. McLaughlin et al., *The United States and World Development: Agenda 1979* (New York: Praeger, 1979), pp. 129–44 and Morris D. Morris, *Measuring the*

Condition of the World's Poor: The Physical Quality of Life Index (New York: Pergamon, 1979).

3. These figures are taken from Sivard, *WMSE, 1982*, pp. 30–35.

4. Sivard, *WMSE, 1982*, p. 30. Even though a division is made between developed and less developed countries, it should be realized that in actuality there is a continuum of different levels of development and wealth.

5. For an extended account of the rationale for a New International Economic Order from the point of view of the less developed countries, see Jan Tinbergen (Coordinator), *RIO: Reshaping the International Order* [A Report to the Club of Rome] (New York: E.P. Dutton, 1976) and James B. McGinnis, *Bread and Justice: Toward a New International Economic Order* (New York: Paulist Press, 1979).

6. William A. Rugh, "Saudi Arabia," *The Wilson Quarterly*, Vol. III, No. 1 (Winter 1979), pp. 60–61.

7. In 1979 the per capita GNP was $5,228 for Spain, $4,382 for Ireland, $566 for Honduras, and $462 for Egypt. Sivard, *WMSE, 1982*, pp. 30–35.

8. McLaughlin, *U.S. and World Development: Agenda 1979*, p. 176 and Lester Brown, *World Without Borders* (New York: Random House, 1972), pp. 42–44.

9. See Harland Cleveland, *The Third Try at World Order* (New York: Aspen Institute for Humanistic Studies, 1977), p. 104 for projections for 1985 by the World Bank.

10. Lester Brown, *The Twenty-Ninth Day* (New York: Norton, 1978), especially pp. 242–71.

11. One of the most optimistic forecasts for the future of the less developed countries is that given by Herman Kahn and his associates at the Hudson Institute in their book *The Next 200 Years* (New York: William Morrow & Co., 1976). In that book it is argued that the less developed countries will develop much more rapidly than the present developed countries did because of the following factors: they will have capital as the result of being able to sell oil and other raw materials to the richer countries; their people will be able to gain skills and money by working temporarily in rich countries and then taking their money home with them; they will be able to attract capital because they will have lower wages than the developed countries; they will be able to get money from tourists from the richer countries; they will be able to borrow developed technology from the more advanced nations; they will be able to copy successful institutions and devices developed by others; they will be able to gain income by engaging in activities which are too polluting or menial for more developed countries; they will be able to develop their own industry through the use of protective tariffs; they will not need to spend much on military defense; and they will get foreign aid from richer countries (pp. 34–49). Kahn's optimistic forecast is "that the current 100–1 ratio of per capita product between the wealthiest 10 percent and the poorest 20 percent of the world population could shrink to about 5–1 after 200 years, give or take a factor of two or three" (pp. 55–57). Mention of a factor of three suggests that it might take 600 years to get this ratio! And if we look at the absolute figures projected by Kahn rather than merely the ratios, we get a very different perspective. In 1975 the average income for the wealthiest 10 percent of the world's population was about $7,000 while for the poorest 20 percent it was about $70 per person, a difference of $6,930. According to the very optimistic projections of Kahn and his associates, in 200 years the figures would be $45,000 per person for the richest 10 percent and $9,000 per person for the poorest 20 percent, a difference of $36,000. The ratio would be less but the *gap* between the rich and poor would be much greater *in absolute terms* than it was in 1975. Incidentally, these figures are in constant dollars, so the projected upward shift is due entirely to increased productivity and not inflation. It should also be noted that this forecast assumes that there will be no damaging shortages of raw materials and that the rate of increase in the rich countries will fall off as more attention is directed to services and less to the production of goods. It should also be noted that the authors of this forecast admit (p. 57) that population growth in the less developed countries might not fall off as rapidly as projected so that the 100 to 1 ratio between richest and poorest might persist for 200 years! Even Kahn's optimistic forecast does not portray a very bright future for the poorer countries.

12. McLaughlin, *U.S. and World Development: Agenda 1979*, p. 182.

13. McLaughlin, *U.S. and World Development: Agenda 1979*, p. 182.

14. McLaughlin, *U.S. and World Development: Agenda 1979*, p. 182.

15. For more explanation and examples see Paul A. Samuelson, *Economics*, 9th ed. (New York: McGraw-Hill, 1973), pp. 84–89.

16. Samuelson, *Economics*, pp. 87–88.

17. Samuelson, *Economics*, p. 87 and p. 768.
18. McLaughlin, *U.S. and World Development: Agenda 1979*, p. 182. Note that the ratio of the top fifth to the bottom fifth for France is 28.26 to 1 (53.7/1.9) while for Sri Lanka, a less developed country, it is only 7.67 to 1 (46/6). See also Brown, *World Without Borders*, pp. 47–48.
19. Sivard, *WMSE, 1982*, p. 19.
20. Samuelson, *Economics*, p. 768.
21. Samuelson, *Economics*, p. 768.
22. These and the other figures in this paragraph are from U.S. Arms Control and Disarmament Agency, *World Military Expenditures and Arms Transfers 1969-78*, pp. 38–74. One developed country, Iceland, also spends less than .5 percent of its GNP for military purposes.
23. Sivard, *WMSE, 1982*, p. 27. The figure of 4.61 percent was calculated by dividing $112.4 billion by $2,439.1 billion, the total of the GNP's of the less developed countries.
24. Sivard, *WMSE, 1982*, p. 27. The figure of 4.52 percent was calculated by dividing $365.6 billion by $8,083.1 billion, the total of the GNP's of the developed countries.
25. Sivard, *WMSE, 1982*, p. 27. The figure of .3 percent was calculated by dividing $24.3 billion by $8083.1 billion, the total of the GNP's of the developed countries.
26. In 1979 the Soviet Union gave $1.432 billion in foreign assistance representing only .13 percent of its GNP while all the nations of the Warsaw Pact including the U.S.S.R. gave $1.852 billion or .12 percent of the combined GNP's of these nations. On the other hand, the nations of NATO including the U.S. and Canada gave $17.720 billion or .34 percent of the combined GNP's of these nations. The basic data is from Sivard, *WMSE, 1982*, p. 27.
27. For a recent statement on the problem of the distribution of wealth at the global level see *North-South: A Program of Survival*, the report of the Independent Commission on International Development Issues under the chairmanship of Willy Brandt (Cambridge: MA: MIT Press, 1980). On page 4 of this report it is noted that "the military expenditure of only half a day would suffice to finance the whole malaria eradication programme of the World Health Organization...."
28. A good succinct statement on the relation between poverty and guerrilla warfare is Vladimir Dedijer's "Guerrilla Warfare: The Poor Man's Power" in Beitz and Herman, *Peace and War*, pp. 41–49.

Chapter X. Military Aspects of the Contemporary Situation

1. Sheldon Novick, "The Secret of the Atom Bomb," *Environment*, Vol. 18, No. 6 (July/August 1976), p. 10. The first bomb had been used in the test at Alamagordo, New Mexico. Novick notes that two other bombs were made and then immediately exploded in 1946 (pp. 11–12). The U.S. had only a very few atomic bombs on hand in 1947 and didn't have a model suitable for mass production until 1948 (p. 16). This same information is presented by Novick in his book *The Electric War: The Fight Over Nuclear Power* (San Francisco: Sierra Club, 1976), pp. 15–17 and 24–30. The information that the U.S. had no atomic bombs in reserve after dropping two on Japan is also given by Bernard Brodie in *War and Politics*, pp. 51–52.
2. For a discussion of this point see *World Armaments and Disarmament: SIPRI Yearbook 1981*, pp. 38–45.
3. Nuclear weapons are measured in terms of the equivalent explosive power of a given number of tons of TNT. The Hiroshima bomb was equivalent to 12,000–14,000 tons (12–14 kilotons) of TNT. Some hydrogen bombs now available have an explosive force equivalent to 25,000,000 tons (25 megatons) of TNT.
4. Novick, "The Secret of the Atom Bomb" in *Environment*, p. 16.
5. *The Defense Monitor*, Vol. 4, No. 2 (February 1975), p. 1.
6. Philip Morrison and Paul F. Walker, "A New Strategy for Military Spending," *Scientific American*, Vol. 239, No. 4 (October 1978), p. 55. It should be noted that some nuclear weapons are being retired on a rather regular basis, so the total is not always increasing. The U.S. total of nuclear warheads peaked at 32,000 in 1967. See William Arkin, Thomas Cochran, and Milton Hoenig, "The U.S. Nuclear Stockpile" in *Arms Control Today*, Vol. 12, No. 4 (April 1982), p. 2.

7. *The Defense Monitor*, Vol. 8, No. 2 (February 1979), p. 4.

8. *The Defense Monitor*, Vol. 8, No. 2 (February 1979), p. 4.

9. "Science and the Citizen," *Scientific American*, Vol. 229, No. 4 (October 1973), p. 47.

10. *World Armaments and Disarmament: SIPRI Yearbook 1981*, pp. 22–23.

11. Kosta Tsipis, "Cruise Missiles," *Scientific American*, Vol. 236, No. 2 (February 1977), pp. 20–29.

12. Richard L. Garwin, "Charged Particle Beam Weapons?", *The Bulletin of the Atomic Scientists*, Vol. 34, No. 8 (October 1978), pp. 24–27; Frank Barnaby, "World Arsenals in 1981," *The Bulletin of the Atomic Scientists*, Vol. 37, No. 7 (August/September 1981), pp. 20–21; and *World Armaments and Disarmament: SIPRI Yearbook 1981*, pp. 264–71. A good source of information about space-based missile defense systems is the Institute for Space and Security Studies, 7720 Mary Cassatt Dr., Potomac, MD 20854.

13. See Clarence A. Robinson, Jr., "Decisions Reached on Nuclear Weapons," *Aviation Week and Space Technology*, Vol. 115, No. 15 (October 12, 1981), pp. 18–23.

14. For a detailed discussion of the agreement and how it has been maintained despite occasional violations, see James Eayrs, "Arms Control on the Great Lakes," *Disarmament and Arms Control*, Vol. 2, No. 4 (Autumn 1964), pp. 372–404.

15. Hans Wehberg, *The Limitation of Armaments*, tr. by Edwin Zeydel (Washington: Carnegie Endowment for International Peace, 1921), pp. 23–25.

16. Wehberg, *The Limitation of Armaments*, pp. 26–28.

17. *Encyclopaedia Britannica*, 15th ed. (1974), "Naval Ships and Craft," Vol. 12, p. 894.

18. Information about this Treaty and the other multilateral treaties discussed in the text can be found in *World Armaments and Disarmament: SIPRI Yearbook 1981*, pp. 413–38. The number of nations given in the text includes the Byelorussian Soviet Socialist Republic and the Ukranian Soviet Socialist Republic as separate countries because of their separate representation in the United Nations. For the texts of these arms control agreements see *1982 Edition, Arms Control and Disarmament Agreements: Texts and History of Negotiations*, U.S. Arms Control and Disarmament Agency (US ACDA, Washington, DC 20451).

19. The U.S.-U.S.S.R. bilateral agreements are summarized in *World Armaments and Disarmament: SIPRI Yearbook 1981*, pp. 439–44. The texts can be found in US ACDA, *1982 Edition, Arms Control and Disarmament Agreements*.

20. See *World Armaments and Disarmament: SIPRI Yearbook 1981*, pp. 264–71 and Robert Darroch, "The War in Space," *World Press Review*, Vol. 29, No. 1 (January 1981), pp. 32–33.

21. "The Grand Forks Pyramid," *Nation*, Vol. 221, No. 20 (Dec. 13, 1975), p. 613.

22. US ACDA, *1982 Edition, Arms Control and Disarmament Agreements*, p. 154.

23. This number can go up to 1,618 if the Soviets decide to keep 210 of their old SS–7 and SS–8 ICBM's, but in that case their maximum number of submarine-launched ballistic missiles would be reduced by 210. See US ACDA, *1982 Edition, Arms Control and Disarmament Agreements*, pp. 148–49.

24. This number can go up to 1,054 if the Americans decide to keep 54 of their old Titan ICBM's, but in that case their maximum number of submarine-launched ballistic missiles would be reduced by 54. See US ACDA, *1982 Edition, Arms Control and Disarmament Agreements*, pp. 148–49.

25. US ACDA, *1982 Edition, Arms Control and Disarmament Agreements*, p. 148–49.

26. *The Defense Monitor*, Vol. I, No. 3 (July 1972), p. 1.

27. *The Defense Monitor*, Vol. I, No. 3 (July 1972), p. 1.

28. US ACDA, *1982 Edition, Arms Control and Disarmament Agreements*, pp. 164–70.

29. US ACDA, *1982 Edition, Arms Control and Disarmament Agreements*, pp. 171–89.

30. *Time*, Vol. 110, No. 20 (November 14, 1977), pp. 34–35.

31. The text of the SALT II Treaty can be found in US ACDA, *1982 Edition, Arms Control and Disarmament Agreements*, pp. 242–77.

32. One statement of the charges is Melvin Laird's "Arms Control: The Russians Are Cheating," *Reader's Digest*, Vol. 111, No. 668 (December 1977), pp. 97–101. These charges are addressed in detail in a special report on "Compliance with SALT I Agreements" from the State Department to the Senate Committee on Foreign Relations (Special Report No. 55 from the Bureau of Public Affairs, U.S. Department of State, Washington, DC 20520). The report is also printed in *The Congressional Record* for February 28, 1978, pp. S2553–S2556.

33. For more details, see John Cox, *Overkill: Weapons of the Nuclear Age* (New York: Thomas Y. Crowell, 1977), pp. 62–66.

34. Morrison and Walker, "A New Strategy for Military Spending" in *Scientific American*, pp. 56–57.

35. Morrison and Walker, "A New Strategy for Military Spending" in *Scientific American*, pp. 55–60. See also "Battlefield of the 1990's," *U.S. News and World Report*, Vol. 83, No. 1 (July 4, 1977), pp. 48–50.

Chapter XI. Institutional Aspects of the Contemporary Situation

1. Schuman, *International Politics*, pp. 219–24.

2. Poland was unable to send a representative to the San Francisco conference but was permitted to sign as the fifty-first charter member. The other charter members were Argentina, Australia, Belgium, Bolivia, Brazil, Byelorussian Soviet Socialist Republic, Canada, Chile, China, Colombia, Costa Rica, Cuba, Czechoslovakia, Denmark, Dominican Republic, Ecuador, Egypt, El Salvador, Ethiopia, France, Greece, Guatemala, Haiti, Honduras, India, Iran, Iraq, Lebanon, Liberia, Luxembourg, Mexico, Netherlands, New Zealand, Nicaragua, Norway, Panama, Paraguay, Peru, Philippines, Saudi Arabia, South Africa, Syria, Turkey, Ukranian Soviet Socialist Republic, Union of Soviet Socialist Republics, United Kingdom, United States of America, Uruguay, Venezuela, and Yugoslavia. Byelorussian S.S.R. and Ukranian S.S.R. are not really separate countries but they were allowed separate votes as one of the compromises which made the U.N. possible.

3. One recent book about the U.N. which contains much detailed information in a readily usable form is Moshe Y. Sachs (ed.), *The United Nations: A Handbook on the United Nations: Its Structure, History, Purposes, Activities, and Agencies* (New York: Wiley, 1977).

4. Even then problems may arise. For example, the U.S. has agreed to commit itself in advance to the jurisdiction of the Court, but the Connally Amendment to the Senate's acceptance of the Statutes of the International Court of Justice indicates that the U.S. will not accept this jurisdiction in cases which the U.S. (rather than the Court) decides fall within its domestic jurisdiction. Since the U.S. can decide which matters fall within its domestic jurisdiction, the Connally Amendment in effect nullifies the U.S.'s advance commitment to accept the jurisdiction of the Court. Many other nations have also adopted "Connally-type" reservations to their acceptance of the Statutes of the International Court of Justice.

5. Sachs, *The United Nations*, p. 36.

6. For a review of major U.N. peacekeeping operations see Sachs, *The United Nations*, pp. 45–52.

7. For a succinct but thorough history of developments in the Middle East since 1946 see *The Middle East*, 5th ed. (Congressional Quarterly, 1414 22nd St. NW, Washington, DC 20037, 1981), pp. 9–29.

8. Charter of the U.N., Article 47. See Schuman, *International Politics*, pp. 696–97.

9. See Sachs, *The United Nations*, pp. 51–52 for details on the financial problems on the U.N.'s peacekeeping efforts.

10. Inis L. Claude, Jr., *Swords into Plowshares: The Problems and Progress of International Organization*, 3rd ed. rev. (New York: Random House, 1964), p. 334.

11. See "U.S. Contributions to the U.N. in 1979," a one-page fact sheet available from the U.N. Association of the U.S.A., 300 East 42nd St., New York, NY 10017.

12. See *U.S. News and World Report*, Vol. 87, No. 12 (September 17, 1979), p. 63.

13. The texts of these documents plus a great deal of other related information on human rights can be found in Robert Woito (ed.), *International Human Rights Kit* (World Without War Publications, 421 So. Wabash, Chicago, IL 60605, 1977).

14. UNIDO became a specialized agency in the U.N. system in 1979. See *The Interdependent*, Vol. 6, No. 5 (May 1979), p. 5. *The Interdependent* is a publication of the U.N. Association of the U.S.A. whose address is in note 11 above.

15. Donald A. Henderson, "Smallpox — Epitaph for a Killer?", *National Geographic*, Vol. 154, No. 6 (December 1978), pp. 796–805.

16. *Keesing's Contemporary Archives*, Vol. XXV (1979), pp. 29893–29900. It has been determined that Greece will have 24 representatives, bringing the new total to 434.

17. Article 71 of the U.N. Charter reads as follows: "The Economic and Social Council may make suitable arrangements for consultation with nongovernmental organizations which

are concerned with matters within its competence. Such arrangements may be made with international organizations and, where appropriate, with national organizations after consultation with the Member of the United Nations concerned." (From Schuman, *International Politics*, p. 700)

18. For a list of these nongovernmental organizations officially affiliated with the United Nations see Sachs, *The United Nations*, pp. 229–34.

19. *United Nations Monthly Chronicle*, Vol. 15, No. 6 (June 1978), p. 27 and Vol. 15, No. 7 (July 1978), p. 4.

20. *Washington Newsletter*, No. 397 (November 1977) of the Friends Committee on National Legislation, 245 Second St. NE, Washington, DC 20002, p. 6. Eisenhower made this comment in London on August 31, 1959.

Chapter XII. Legal Aspects of the Contemporary Situation

1. The discussion of international law in this chapter is confined to that part which deals with the relations between nations and which is called *public international law*. Not discussed here is that other part of international law, *private international law*, which deals with private persons and property in international situations where there are problems about which national government has jurisdiction and which national laws are applicable.

2. For a short discussion of the early development of international law, see Schuman, *International Politics*, pp. 67–71. For a discussion of the principles of international law, see pp. 115–48 of the same work.

3. Article 10 of the League Covenant says: "The Members of the League undertake to respect and preserve as against external aggression the territorial integrity and existing political independence of all Members of the League. In case of any such aggression or in case of any threat or danger of such aggression, the Council shall advise upon the means by which this obligation shall be fulfilled." (From Schuman, *International Politics*, p. 711)

4. The U.N. Charter reads as follows:

Article 41. The Security Council may decide what measures not involving the use of armed force are to be employed to give effect to its decisions, and it may call upon the Members of the United Nations to apply such measures. These may include complete or partial interruption of economic relations and of rail, sea, air, postal, telegraphic, radio, and other means of communication, and the severance of diplomatic relations.

Article 42. Should the Security Council consider that measures provided for in Article 41 would be inadequate or have proved to be inadequate, it may take such action by air, sea, or land forces as may be necessary to maintain or restore international peace and security. Such action may include demonstrations, blockade, and other operations by air, sea, or land forces of Members of the United Nations.

Article 43. 1. All Members of the United Nations, in order to contribute to the maintenance of international peace and security, undertake to make available to the Security Council, on its call and in accordance with a special agreement or agreements, armed forces, assistance, and facilities, including rights of passage, necessary for the purpose of maintaining international peace and security.

2. Such agreement or agreements shall govern the numbers and types of forces, their degree of readiness and general location, and the nature of the facilities and assistance to be provided.

3. The agreement or agreements shall be negotiated as soon as possible on the initiative of the Security Council. They shall be concluded between the Security Council and Members or between the Security Council and groups of Members and shall be subject to ratification by the signatory states in accordance with their respective constitutional processes. (From Schuman, *International Politics*, p. 696).

5. Woito, *International Human Rights Kit*, pp. 90–91.

6. The U.N. General Assembly directed its Law Commission to "formulate the principles of international law recognized in the Charter of the Nürnberg Tribunal and in the judgment of the Tribunal." The seven principles formulated can be found in Woito, *International Human Rights Kit*, p. 76.

7. Schuman, *International Politics*, p. 147n.

8. Rules for warfare were first advanced by Hugo Grotius in his *On the Law of War and Peace* (1625). They have been developed by various conventions, the most important of which are the Geneva Conventions (developed at meetings in 1864, 1929, and 1949) and the two Hague Conventions (1899 and 1907). Other conventions such as the Convention on Genocide (1948) and the one protecting cultural property (1954) also apply to wartime situations. The laws of war also include rules about the treatment and obligations of neutrals. For a more detailed account, see "War, Laws of" in *Encyclopaedia Britannica*, 15th ed. (1974), Vol. 19, pp. 538–42 and Schuman, *International Politics*, pp. 134–39.

9. See the Preamble and Article 2 of the U.N. Charter. Schuman, *International Politics*, pp. 689–90.

10. *Charter of the United Nations and Statute of the International Court of Justice* (Office of Public Information, United Nations, NY, 1968), pp. 75–76.

11. Schuman, *International Politics*, pp. 220–21.

Chapter XIII. Reforming the Attitudes of Individuals

1. A moving plea for greater effort on the part of the U.S. in educating its people about other cultures and about world affairs can be found in Edwin O. Reischauer, *Toward the 21st Century: Education for a Changing World* (New York: Knopf, 1973).

2. The War Resisters League, 339 Lafayette Street, New York, NY 10012, publishes an annual calendar which contains information about the ideas and past use of nonviolent resistance. A good introduction to various philosophies of nonviolence is Mayer, *The Pacifist Conscience*.

3. A good brief introduction to the life and teachings of Gandhi is Louis Fischer, *Gandhi: His Life and Message for the World* (New York: New American Library, 1954). For an overview of Gandhi's thought see Joan V. Bondurant, *Conquest of Violence: The Gandhian Philosophy of Conflict* (Princeton, N.J.: Princeton University, 1958) and the selections from Gandhi's writings in *All Men Are Brothers* (New York: Seabury, 1980). For an introduction to the life and teachings of Martin Luther King, Jr. one might well begin with his own *Stride Toward Freedom: The Montgomery Story* (New York: Harper and Row, 1958). On pp. 102–07, King gives his own presentation of the basic principles of the philosophy of nonviolent resistance.

4. One such pledge, composed by Lillian Genser of Wayne State University in Detroit, goes as follows:

> I pledge allegiance to the world, To cherish every living thing,
>
> To care for earth and seas and air, With peace and justice everywhere.

5. For more information, contact Dorothy Schneider, 4452 Caminito Fuente, San Diego, CA 92116.

6. For more information about the UNICEF collection, contact U.S. Committee for UNICEF, 331 E. 38th Street, New York, NY 10016.

7. The term "humatriotism" was formulated by Theodore Lentz of St. Louis. See Note 1 for Chapter IV.

8. *African Genesis*, p. 256.

9. *Civilization and Its Discontents*, p. 61.

10. *Multiple Loyalties: Theoretical Approach to a Problem in International Organization* (Princeton, NJ: Princeton University's Center for Research on World Political Institutions, 1955), pp. 49–50.

11. An approach along these lines is suggested by William James in his essay "The Moral Equivalent of War" which is reprinted in Bramson and Goethals, *War: Studies from Psychology, Sociology, Anthropology*, pp. 21–31.

12. For more information about Esperanto, contact the Esperanto League of North America, Box 1129, El Cerrito, CA 94530.

13. For example, consider the contents of the book *Many Voices, One World* (London: Kogan Page, New York: Unipub, and Paris: Unesco, 1980), which is a report of the International Commission for the Study of Communication Problems appointed in 1977 by Amadou-Mahtar M'Bow, Director-General of UNESCO and headed by Sean McBride. This Commission analyzed language and communication problems only from the point of view of national governments and did not mention Esperanto or even the idea of a single international language for everyone. It is unbelievable that an international commission set up by

a U.N. agency to study communication problems can manage to not even address itself to this crucial issue.

14. It is noteworthy that both the Boy Scouts and the Girl Scouts offer a merit badge for citizenship in the world to those scouts who fulfill the appropriate requirements as well as badges for citizenship in the community and citizenship in the nation.

15. A book which should be helpful to teachers interested in the issue of developing a global perspective in their pupils is James M. Becker (ed.), *Schooling for a Global Age* (New York: McGraw-Hill, 1979). There are many organizations promoting education for peace, several of which have developed helpful materials or newsletters. Some of them are:

Jane Addams Peace Association, 1213 Race St., Philadelphia, PA 19107.

American Friends Service Committee, Peace Studies Program, 980 N. Fair Oaks, Pasadena, CA 91103.

Association for World Education, 3 Harbor Dr., Huntington, NY 11743.

Center for Teaching Peace & Conflict Studies, Wayne State University, 5229 Cass Avenue, Detroit, MI 48202.

Children's Creative Response to Conflict Program, Avery Pub. Group, Wayne, NJ 07470.

Conference on Peace Research in History, Department of History, New York University, 19 University Pl., New York, NY 10003.

Consortium on Peace Research, Education, and Development (COPRED), Center for Peaceful Change, Stopher Hall, Kent State University, Kent, OH 44242.

Council on Learning, 271 North Ave., New Rochell, NY 10801.

Friends Peace Committee of the Philadelphia Yearly Meeting of Friends — Children and Nonviolence Program, 1515 Cherry St., Philadelphia, PA 19102.

Global Education Associates, 522 Park Ave., East Orange, NJ 07017.

Global Perspectives in Education, Suite 235, Hotel Claremont, Oakland, CA 94705.

Global Perspectives in Education, 218 E. 18th St., New York, NY 10003.

Intercommunity Center for Justice & Peace, 20 Washington Sq. No., New York, NY 10011.

Institute for Peace & Justice, 4144 Lindell, St. Louis, MO 63108.

International Peace Studies Newsletter, Center for Peace Studies, The University of Akron, Akron, OH 44325.

Charles F. Kettering Foundation, Suite 300, 5335 Far Hills Ave., Dayton, OH 45429.

Mid-America Program, Social Studies Development Center, 513 No. Park, Bloomington, IN 47401

Peacemaking, Militarism, & Education Program, c/o Betty Reardon, Box 171, Teachers College, Columbia University, New York, NY 10027.

Planetary Citizens, P.O. Box 1715, New Rochelle, NY 10802.

Project for Global Education, 777 United Nations Plaza, New York, NY 10017.

UNA-USA School Program, 345 E. 46th St., New York, NY 10017.

University of the State of New York — Learning Resources in International Studies, Suite 1026, 60 E. 42nd St., New York, NY 10017.

WORLD EAGLE, 64 Washburn Ave., Wellesley, MA 02181.

World Education, 1414 Sixth Ave., New York, NY 10019.

World Federalist Association, P.O. Box 15250, Washington, DC 20003

World Policy Institute, 777 U.N. Plaza, New York, NY 10017.

World Without War Publications, 421 South Wabash, Chicago, IL 60605: *The War Peace Film Guide* by John Dowling is useful.

Chapter XIV. Reforming the Internal Operations of National Governments

1. Such views about the desirability of democracy as a way of reducing the likelihood of war go back at least to the eighteenth-century philosophers Rousseau, Montesquieu, and Kant. See Michael E. Howard, *War and the Liberal Conscience* (New Brunswick, NJ: Rutgers University, 1978), pp. 23–28.

2. Wright, *A Study of War*, Vol. II, pp. 843–48.

3. For support of this statement on the basis of public reactions in the U.S. during the Vietnamese War, see Robert W. Tucker, *A New Isolationism: Threat or Promise* (New York: Universe Books, 1972), pp. 99–101.

4. Schuman, *International Politics*, pp. 220–21.

5. For a recent collection of articles on the current Communist view on the war problem see *Problems of War and Peace* prepared by the Institute of Philosophy, the Academy of Sciences of the USSR and translated into English by Bryan Bean (Moscow: Progress Publishers, 1972).

6. Gene Sharp, *Exploring Nonviolent Alternatives* (Boston: Porter Sargent, 1970), lists 85 cases of nonviolent action (pp. 115–23) and indicates that slightly more than 60 percent occurred under dictatorships. With regard to success, Sharp says only that "in some of these cases the nonviolent actionists partly or fully succeeded in achieving the desired objectives." (p.122)

7. For a recent collection of articles on nonviolent resistance, see Severyn T. Bruyn and Paula M. Rayman (eds.), *Nonviolent Action and Social Change* (New York: Irvington Publishers, 1979). A classic on all phases of nonviolent resistance is Gene Sharp, *The Politics of Nonviolent Action* (3 vols.) (Boston: Porter Sargent, 1973).

Chapter XV. Reforming the Policies of National Governments

1. This is the definition of isolationism offered by Tucker in *A New Isolationism*, p. 12.

2. See *A New Isolationism: Threat or Promise*.

3. For a recent carefully worked out and well-documented defense of this proposition see Bueno de Mesquita, *The War Trap*.

4. Gene Sharp, "Making the Abolition of War a Realistic Goal." This essay was originally published in the December 1980 Newsletter of the World Without War Issues Center – Midwest. It was reprinted as a separate booklet by the Institute for World Order as a result of winning the Wallach Awards Competition for 1979–80 and is also reprinted in Carolyn M. Stephenson (ed.), *Alternative Methods for International Security* (Washington: University Press of America, 1982), pp. 127–40. See also Gene Sharp, "Civilian-Based Defense as a Peace Strategy," *Peace and Change*, Vol. 7, No. 4 (Fall 1981), pp. 53–58 and his "National Defense without Armaments," *War/Peace Report*, Vol. 10, No. 4 (April 1970), pp. 3–10 (reprinted in Beitz and Herman, *Peace and War*, pp. 349–67).

5. For a restrained but cogent response to Sharp's proposal, see Michael Walzer, *Just and Unjust Wars: A Moral Argument with Historical Illustrations*, pp. 329–35. See also Thomas C. Schelling, "Some Questions on Civilian Defense" originally printed in Adam Roberts (ed.), *Civilian Resistance as a National Defense* (Harrisburg: Stackpole, 1968), pp. 302–08 and reprinted in Beitz and Herman, *Peace and War*, pp. 368–74.

6. For a discussion of this point see Rosen and Jones, *The Logic of International Relations*, pp. 240–44.

7. Schuman, *International Politics*, p. 248.

8. Schuman, *International Politics*, p. 248.

9. Schuman, *International Politics*, p. 690.

10. US ACDA, *1980 Edition, Arms Control and Disarmament Agreements*, p. 159.

11. US ACDA, *1980 Edition, Arms Control and Disarmament Agreements*, p. 160.

12. *New York Times*, September 21, 1961, p. 10. These same principles are incorporated in House Concurrent Resolution 392 introduced in the U.S. House of Representatives on August 5, 1982, by Congressman George Brown of California.

13. See his *An Alternative to War or Surrender* (Urbana, IL: University of Illinois, 1962).

14. The latter formulation is used by Osgood in his preface to the 1970 edition of *An Alternative to War or Surrender*.

15. Amatai Etzioni, "The Kennedy Experiment," *The Western Political Quarterly*, Vol. XX (1967), pp. 361–80 (reprinted in Amatai Etzioni and Martin Wenglinsky (eds.), *War and Its Prevention* (New York: Harper and Row, 1970), pp. 215–42). Etzioni has also developed his own general presentation of the gradual-tension-reduction approach in his book *The Hard Way to Peace: A New Strategy* (New York: Collier Books, 1962).

16. Etzioni, "The Kennedy Experiment," *West. Pol. Quart.*, pp. 368–69.

17. Etzioni, "The Kennedy Experiment," *West. Pol. Quart.*, pp. 367–68.

18. For a recent succinct review of the issues and various views related to this question, see Stanley Hoffmann, *Duties Beyond Borders: On the Limits and Possibilities of Ethical*

International Politics (Syracuse: Syracuse University, 1981), pp. 10–27. Hoffman himself rejects the prevalent view. See pp. 190–91 for a summary of his position.

19. The work describing the classical experiments with boys on the value of cooperative projects in overcoming group antagonism is Muzafer Sherif's *In Common Predicament* (Boston: Houghton Mifflin, 1966).

20. "Review of U.S.-U.S.S.R. Cooperative Agreements on Science and Technology: Special Oversight Report No. 6," Subcommittee on Domestic and International Scientific Planning and Analysis of the Committee on Science and Technology, U.S. House of Representatives, 94th Congress, Second Session. Serial VV, November 1976, p. 9.

21. Ziegler, *War, Peace, and International Politics*, pp. 293–94 and Schuman, *International Politics*, p. 141.

22. Schuman, *International Politics*, p. 156.

23. Schuman, *International Politics*, p. 154.

24. Schuman, *International Politics*, p. 155.

25. Robert L. Butterworth, *Managing Interstate Conflict, 1945–74: Data with Synopses* (Pittsburgh: University Center for International Studies, 1976), pp. 131–32.

26. Butterworth, *Managing Interstate Conflict*, pp. 94–96.

27. Butterworth, *Managing Interstate Conflict*, pp. 392–93.

28. Butterworth, *Managing Interstate Conflict*, pp. 235–37.

29. *New York Times*, Dec. 6, 1977, p. 8 and Jan. 26, 1978, p. 6.

30. Butterworth, *Managing Interstate Conflict*, pp. 341–44.

31. See *Time*, Vol. 114, No. 22 (November 26, 1979), pp. 62–64.

32. For a succinct statement of the philosophy behind this conflict-management-using-international-organizations approach to peace, see Robert L. Butterworth, *Moderation from Management: International Organization and Peace* (Pittsburgh: University Center for International Studies, 1978), pp. 1–14 and 120–26.

33. For a summary of efforts by regional organizations to manage international conflicts see Ziegler, *War, Peace, and International Politics*, pp. 196–203.

34. Sachs, *The United Nations*, p. 123.

35. See John P. Lovell, *The Search for Peace: An Appraisal of Alternative Approaches* (Pittsburgh: International Studies Association, Occasional Paper No. 4, 1974), pp. 17–18.

36. Butterworth, *Moderation from Management*, pp. 62–63. See pp. 33–71 for a detailed account of the record of the U.N. in managing various types of conflict situations.

37. Butterworth, *Moderation from Management*, p. 66.

38. Butterworth, *Moderation from Management*, p. 66.

39. Butterworth, *Moderation from Management*, p. 67.

40. For further details of such a proposal see Grenville Clark and Louis Sohn, *World Peace through World Law*, 3rd ed. enlarged (Cambridge, MA: Harvard University, 1966), pp. xxv, 379–92, and 415–47.

41. See *U.S. News and World Report*, Vol. 87, No. 12 (September 17, 1979), p. 63 and *The World Almanac and Book of Facts, 1982*, p. 102.

42. Butterworth, *Managing Interstate Conflict*, p. 132.

43. Butterworth, *Managing Interstate Conflict*, p. 224.

44. Butterworth, *Managing Interstate Conflict*, p. 225.

45. In May 1974 the U.S. Senate adopted a group of five resolutions (S. 74, 75, 76, 77, 78), known as the Taft-Cranston Resolutions, indicating that it was the sense of the Senate that the President of the U.S. should take various actions to promote greater use of the International Court of Justice. Resolution 74 called on the President to "direct the Secretary of State to consider submitting to the International Court of Justice as many as possible of the approximately 28 territorial disputes involving our country and a number of close allies over desolate and largely uninhabited islands in the Caribbean Sea and the Pacific Ocean." See *The Congressional Record* of the 93rd Congress, 2nd Session, Vol. 120, Part 12 (May 20, 1974), pp. 15264–15266.

46. For a nation-by-nation evaluation of the voting of member states in the U.N. General Assembly on selected issues of concern to the advancement of the total human community, see the annual reports on the General Assembly prepared by Donald Keys, 777 U.N. Plaza, Room 10-D, New York, NY 10017. Starting in 1981 these reports on voting records are being published in Keys's *UN and Planet Report*.

47. United Nations Educational, Scientific, and Cultural Organization, *Peace Research: Trend Report and World Directory* (Paris: UNESCO, 1978–79), p. 26.

48. UNESCO, *Peace Research*, pp. 35–222.

49. UNESCO, *Peace Research*, pp. 21–24.

50. UNESCO, *Peace Research*, pp. 54–55, 79–80, 85–86, 87–93, 98–100, 126–27, 147–48, 166–67.

51. For more information contact National Peace Academy Campaign, 110 Maryland Avenue NE, Washington, DC 20002.

52. Kenneth Boulding, *The Meaning of the Twentieth Century* (New York: Harper, 1964), p. 103.

Chapter XVI. Reforming the Nation System

1. I am indebted to the Campaign for U.N. Reform, 600 Valley Road, Wayne, NJ 07470 for several of the ideas in this section. A good summary of proposals for reforming the U.N. is a report prepared by the Foreign Affairs and National Defense Division of the Congressional Research Service, Library of Congress, for the Committee on Foreign Relations of the U.S. Senate (96th Congress, 1st Session) entitled "Reform of the United Nations: An Analysis of the President's Proposals and Their Comparison with Proposals of Other Countries." This report was published in October 1979 by the U.S. Government Printing Office in Washington, D.C.

2. D. Evan T. Luard, *The Control of the Sea-Bed: A New International Issue* (London: Heineman, 1974), p. 35.

3. Luard, *The Control of the Sea-Bed*, p. 30 and pp. 144–46.

4. Luard, *The Control of the Sea-Bed*, pp. 139–42 and 146–49. The recent Conference, which began in 1973, is actually the third international conference on the law of the sea, the first having been held in 1958 and the second in 1960. The first conference, held in Geneva, generated four conventions covering matters such as definitions of terms, rights and responsibilities in the various "zones" of the ocean, conservation of the living resources of the high seas, and ownership of the continental shelf by the coastal state, but none of these conventions has been accepted by a majority of the nations of the world. For a history of the three law of the sea conferences, see Luard, *The Control of the Sea-Bed*, pp. 29–48, 83–96, and 127–68.

5. "The Struggle for Antarctica's Riches," *World Press Review*, Vol. 24, No. 12 (December 1977), pp. 21–23.

6. In December 1979 the U.N. General Assembly accepted the draft of an Agreement covering the Activities of States on the Moon and Other Celestial Bodies and asked the Secretary-General to open the Agreement for signature and ratification. Article 11 of the Agreement declares that "the moon and its natural resources are the common heritage of mankind" and calls for the establishment of "an international regime ... to govern the exploitation of the natural resources of the moon as such exploitation is about to become feasible." The Agreement will come into force after five nations accede to it. For more details see *Keesing's Contemporary Archives*, May 2, 1980, pp. 30226–28.

7. Richard Hudson, "Time for Mutations in the United Nations," *The Bulletin of the Atomic Scientists*, Vol. 32, No. 9 (November 1976), p. 40.

8. Hudson, "Time for Mutations," *Bull. of Atom. Sci.*, pp. 39–43. It might be fairer to require only a simple majority with regard to contributions since there seems to be no rationale for making financial contributions more important than population. Alternatively, one might require a two-thirds vote on the second computation as well as on the first and third. Hudson himself has modified his proposal in this latter way as he has applied it to the problem of voting in the Assembly of the Seabed Authority. See *Global Report* for July–August 1980, p. 4 distributed by the Center for War-Peace Studies, 218 E. 18th St., New York, NY 10003. Hudson's most recent modifications of his "Binding Triad" proposal can be found in Special Study No. 6 published in October 1982 by the Center for War-Peace Studies. The precise details are not as important, however, as the general approach. There are other international organizations, such as the International Monetary Fund and the European Parliament, where voting is weighted rather than being one vote per nation, so establishing such a system in the General Assembly would not be without precedent.

9. There are a couple of exceptions to the principle that the U.N. and its various programs must be funded by contributions from national governments. For example, individual persons can contribute to UNICEF and to the U.N. Special Account, a fund used at the discretion of the Secretary-General, usually to help refugees.

10. The information in this paragraph is from Beverly Woodward, "Nonviolent Struggle, Nonviolent Defense, and Nonviolent Peacemaking," *Peace and Change*, Vol. 7, No. 4 (Fall 1981), pp. 62–63 and Carolyn Stephenson, "Alternative Methods for International Security: A Review of the Literature" in the same volume. Those interested in learning more about present efforts to establish a nonviolent peacemaking force can contact Peace Brigades International, Box 1222, Walla Walla, WA 99362.

11. Clarence Streit, *Union Now* (printed privately in 1938; then published by Harper Brothers in New York in 1939 with an enlarged postwar edition by the same publisher in 1948). Streit's view is being promoted by Federal Union, Inc., Post Office Box 75920, Washington, DC 20013 and the International Association for a Union of Democracies, 414 W. 20th St., New York, NY 10011. A study which is somewhat related to Streit's proposal is *Political Community and the North Atlantic Area* by Karl W. Deutsch and others (Princeton, NJ: Princeton University, 1957 and New York: Greenwood, 1969).

12. Streit apparently had no qualms about the racial policies of the Union of South Africa since he includes that country in his list of places where federal democracy has been tried and worked (*Union Now*, p. 6) and includes it as one of the 15 founder democracies of the Union of the Free (p. 9).

13. For a view of American history in the 1780's as a model for the formation of a federal world government, see Carl Van Doren, *The Great Rehearsal* (New York: The Viking Press, 1948).

14. It is worth noting that at present state governments in the U.S. likewise do not need to concern themselves with defense against external enemies and that after a world government had been established national governments would no longer need to maintain military forces for defense.

15. The idea of a world government brought about through the agreement of the leaders of all nations rather than by conquest seems to have been first advanced in 1623 by Parisian monk Eméric Crucé in a book entitled *The New Cineas* (tr. by C. Frederick Farrell, Jr. and Edith R. Farrell, New York and London: Garland, 1972). The idea of a world government brought about by consent has also been espoused by philosophers such as Rousseau, Kant, Bentham, and Russell and noted scientists such as Einstein. For a brief history of early advocates of world government, see Schuman, *International Politics*, pp. 203–06. For a more complete review which also covers more recent thinkers, see Finn Laursen, *Federalism and World Order: Compendium I* (Copenhagen: World Federalist Youth, 1970). Two of the more influential works about world federalism published during World War II were Mortimer J. Adler, *How to Think about War and Peace* (New York: Simon and Schuster, 1944) and Emery Reves, *The Anatomy of Peace* (New York and London: Harper and Brothers, 1945; recently republished by Peter Smith, Publisher, Magnolia, MA 01930). A significant proposal addressed to creating a minimal federal world government through modification or expansion of the U.N. is given in Clark and Sohn, *World Peace through World Law*. The world federalist idea is promoted in the U.S. by the World Federalist Association, P.O. Box 15250, Washington, DC 20003; the American Movement for World Government, 20 West 40th St., New York, NY 10018; the Campaign for World Government, 331 Park Ave., Room 304, Glencoe, IL 60022; and The Federalist Caucus, Box 19482, Portland, OR 97219.

16. Inis L. Claude, Jr., *Power and International Relations* (New York: Random House, 1962), pp. 214–15.

17. Lewis Richardson, in his historical study of wars from 1820 to 1945, concludes that once a single government is established over previously sovereign groups, the longer these groups are under a common government the less likely they are to go to war with each other. See *Statistics of Deadly Quarrels*, pp. xi, 189–90, 295–96, 311–13.

18. The plan advanced by Clark and Sohn in *World Peace through World Law* is an example of a minimalist approach which might be acceptable to both the U.S. and the U.S.S.R.

19. For information about this committee and its work, see the reports on the U.N. General Assembly compiled by Donald Keys. See Note 46 for Chapter XV.

20. Sandford Z. Persons, "The Only Bicameral and Bipartisan Organization in the Congress" *Center Report*, Vol. 8, No. 5 (December 1975) (Center for the Study of Democratic Institutions, 256 Eucalyptus Hill Dr., Santa Barbara, CA 93103), pp. 27–28. The Parliamentarians for World Order (Uganda House, 7th Floor, 336 E. 45 St., New York, NY 10017) now have 600 members from the parliaments of 25 countries.

21. See Harland Cleveland, *The Third Try at World Order* (New York: Aspen Institute for Humanistic Studies, 1977), pp. 77–78. Cleveland's book constitutes a recent statement of

the functionalist approach. An earlier and very influential statement of the functionalist view is David Mitrany's *A Working Peace System* (London: Royal Institute of International Affairs, 1943). A more recent significant discussion of functionalism is Ernst B. Haas's *Beyond the Nation-State: Functionalism and International Organization* (Stanford: Stanford University, 1964).

22. The creation of such an agency was proposed by Sri Lanka at the 1978 U.N. Special Session on Disarmament, and France proposed an international satellite agency to help monitor arms control agreements. See *Keesing's Contemporary Archives*, October 20, 1978, p. 29263.

23. *New York Times*, September 12, 1948, p. 30 and September 13, 1948, p. 5.

24. The Paris address is 66 Bd. Vincent Auriol, 75013 Paris, France. The U.S. address is Douglas Mattern, 312 Sutter St., Room 608, San Francisco, CA 94108. A similar registration effort is carried on by Planetary Citizens, P.O. Box 1715, New Rochelle, NY 10802. Garry Davis has more recently organized the World Service Authority, 1012 14th St. NW, Washington, DC 20005 to register world citizens and to issue passports, birth and marriage certificates, and so on for refugees and stateless persons.

25. Alan Newcombe and Hanna Newcombe, "Mundialization: World Community at the Doorstep" in Israel W. Charny (ed.), *Strategies against Violence: Design for Nonviolent Change* (Boulder, CO: Westview Press, 1978), pp. 314–30.

26. W. Warren Wagar, *Building the City of Man* (San Francisco: W.H. Freeman, 1972). For other expressions of a somewhat similar approach, see Gerald Mische and Patricia Mische, *Toward a Human World Order* (New York: Paulist Press, 1977) and Donald Keys, *Earth at Omega: The Passage to Planetization* (available from Planetary Citizens, P.O. Box 1715, New Rochelle, NY 10802).

27. Joseph H.C. Creyghton, *Internationale Anarchie* (Amsterdam: De Brug-Djambatan, 1962). See also Johan M.L.F. Keijser (ed.), *Political World Union 1962–1981: A Documentary Appraisal* (The Hague: Working Group World Union, 1982) (available from Johan Keijser in care of Hesbjerg Peace Research Institute, Hesbjergvej 50, DK-5491 BLOMMENSLYST (Fyn), Denmark).

28. Jacques Maritain, *Man and the State* (Chicago: University of Chicago, 1951), pp. 212–16.

29. The Bertrand Russell Peace Foundation is located in Bertrand Russell House, Gamble St., Nottingham NG7 4ET, England.

30. Gerald H. Gottlieb, "The Court of Man," *Center Magazine*, Vol. 2, No. 1 (January 1969) (Center for the Study of Democratic Institutions, 256 Eucalyptus Hill Dr., Santa Barbara, CA 93103), pp. 20–31.

31. Gottleib, "The Court of Man," *Center Magazine*, p. 25.

32. This endeavor is being coordinated by the World Constitution and Parliament Association, 1480 Hoyt St., Suite 31, Lakewood, CO 80215.

33. See Hanna Newcombe, "Alternative Approaches to World Government — II" in *Peace Research Reviews*, Vol. 5, No. 2 (February 1974). For a compilation of abstracts which deal with many books and articles addressed to the development of a just and peaceful world society, see Hanna Newcombe (compiler), *World Unification Plans and Analyses* (Peace Research Institute — Dundas, 25 Dundana Ave., Dundas, Ontario L9H 4E5, Canada, 1980).

34. The "world order" approach is promoted by the World Policy Institute (formerly the Institute for World Order), 777 U.N. Plaza, New York, NY 10017. Individuals associated with this approach include Richard A. Falk, Samuel S. Kim, and Saul H. Mendlovitz.

35. Part IV of this book is an attempt to give an overview of proposals for solving the war problem. For another overview see Carolyn M. Stephenson, "Alternative Methods for International Security: A Review of the Literature," *Peace and Change*, Vol. 7, No. 4 (Fall 1981), pp. 85–110. This article, along with other related articles, is also available in Stephenson (ed.), *Alternative Methods for International Security*.

Selected Bibliography

Adler, Mortimer J. *How to Think about War and Peace*. New York: Simon & Schuster, 1944.

Beer, Francis A. *How Much War in History: Definitions, Estimates, Extrapolations, and Trends*. Beverly Hills, CA: Sage Publications, 1974.

———. *Peace Against War: The Ecology of International Violence*. San Francisco: W.H. Freeman, 1981.

Beitz, Charles R., and Theodore Herman (eds.). *Peace and War*. San Francisco: W.H. Freeman, 1973.

Boulding, Kenneth E. *Stable Peace*. Austin: University of Texas Press, 1978.

Bramson, Leon, and George W. Goethals (eds.). *War: Studies from Psychology, Sociology, Anthropology*, rev. ed. New York: Basic Books, 1968.

Brodie, Bernard, *War and Politics*. New York: Macmillan, 1973.

Bueno de Mesquita, Bruce. *The War Trap*. New Haven: Yale University Press, 1981.

Butterworth, Robert L. *Managing Interstate Conflict, 1945–74: Data with Synopses*. Pittsburgh: University Center for International Studies, 1976.

———. *Moderation from Management: International Organization and Peace*. Pittsburgh: University Center for International Studies, 1978.

Charny, Israel W. (ed.). *Strategies Against Violence: Design for Nonviolent Change*. Boulder, CO: Westview, 1978.

Clark, Grenville, and Louis Sohn. *World Peace through World Law*, 3rd ed. enlarged. Cambridge, MA: Harvard University Press, 1966.

Claude, Inis L., Jr. *Swords into Plowshares: The Problems and Progress of International Organization*, 3rd ed. rev. New York: Random House, 1964.

Cleveland, Harland. *The Third Try at World Order*. New York: Aspen Institute for Humanistic Studies, 1977.

Cooling, Benjamin F. (ed.). *War, Business, and American Society: Historical Perspectives on the Military-Industrial Complex*. Port Washington, NY: Kennikat, 1977.

Etzioni, Amatai. *The Hard Way to Peace: A New Strategy*. (New York: Collier Books, 1962.

Falk, Richard, and Samuel S. Kim (eds.). *The War System: An Interdisciplinary Approach*. Boulder, CO: Westview, 1980.

———, ———, and Saul H. Mendlovitz (eds.). *Toward a Just World Order*. Boulder, CO: Westview, 1982.

Fried, Morton, Marvin Harris, and Robert Murphy (eds.). *War: The Anthropology of Armed Conflict and Aggression*. Garden City, NY: Natural History Press, 1967.

Ginsberg, Robert (ed.). *The Critique of War: Contemporary Philosophical Explorations*. Chicago: Henry Regnery, 1969.

Haas, Ernst B. *Beyond the Nation-State: Functionalism and International Organization*. Stanford, CA: Stanford University Press, 1964.

Hoffman, Stanley. *Studies Beyond Borders: On the Limits and Possibilities of Ethical International Politics*. Syracuse, NY: Syracuse University Press, 1981.

Independent Commission on International Development Issues, Willy Brandt, Chair. *North-South: A Program of Survival*. Cambridge, MA: MIT Press, 1980.

Institute of Philosophy, Academy of Sciences of the U.S.S.R. *Problems of War and Peace*, tr. by Bryan Bean. Moscow: Progress Publishers, 1972.

Lovell, John P. *The Search for Peace: An Appraisal of Alternative Approaches*. Pittsburgh: International Studies Association, Occasional Paper No. 4, 1974.

McGinnis, James B. *Bread and Justice: Toward a New International Economic Order*. New York: Paulist Press, 1979.

Mayer, Peter (ed.). *The Pacifist Conscience*. Chicago: Henry Regnery, 1967.

Mische, Gerald, and Patricia Mische. *Toward a Human World Order*. New York: Paulist Press, 1977.

Mitrany, David. *A Working Peace System*. London: Royal Institute of International Affairs, 1943.

Nesbitt, William A. (ed.). *Human Nature and War*. Albany: State Education Department of New York, 1973.

Osgood, Charles E. *An Alternative to War or Surrender*. Urbana: University of Illinois Press, 1962.

Rapoport, Anatol. *Fights, Games, and Debates*. Ann Arbor: University of Michigan Press, 1960.

Reves, Emery. *The Anatomy of Peace*. New York: Harper & Brothers, 1945.

Richardson, Lewis F. *Arms and Insecurity*. Pittsburgh: Boxwood Press, 1960.

_____. *Statistics of Deadly Quarrels*. Pittsburgh: Boxwood, 1960.

Rosen, Steven J. and Walter S. Jones. *The Logic of International Relations*, 3rd ed. Cambridge, MA: Winthrop, 1980.

Schell, Jonathan. *The Fate of the Earth*. New York: Alfred A. Knopf, 1982.

Schuman, Frederick L. *International Politics*, 7th ed. New York: McGraw-Hill, 1969.

Sharp, Gene. *Exploring Nonviolent Alternatives*. Boston: Porter Sargent, 1970.

_____. *The Politics of Nonviolent Action* (3 vols.). Boston: Porter Sargent, 1973.

Singer, J. David, and Melvin Small. *The Wages of War, 1816–1965: A Statistical Handbook*. New York: Wiley, 1972.

Sivard, Ruth Leger. *World Military and Social Expenditures, 1982*. Washington, DC: World Priorities, 1982.

Stephenson, Carolyn M. (ed.). *Alternative Methods for International Security*. Washington, DC: University Press of America, 1982.

Stockholm International Peace Research Institute. *World Armaments and Disarmament: SIPRI Yearbook 1981*. London: Taylor & Francis, 1981.

Stoessinger, John. *Why Nations Go to War*, 3rd ed. New York: St. Martin's, 1981.

Streit, Clarence. *Union Now*, enlarged ed. New York: Harper & Brothers, 1948.

Tinbergen, Jan (coordinator). *RIO: Reshaping the International Order*. New York: E.P. Dutton, 1976.

Wagar, W. Warren. *Building the City of Man*. San Francisco: W.H. Freeman, 1972.

Waltz, Kenneth. *Man, the State, and War*. New York: Columbia University Press, 1959.

Walzer, Michael. *Just and Unjust Wars: A Moral Argument with Historical Illustrations*. New York: Basic Books, 1977.

Woito, Robert S. *To End War: A New Approach to International Conflict*. New York: Pilgrim Press, 1982.

Wright, Quincy. *A Study of War*. Chicago: University of Chicago Press, 1942; abridged ed. by Louise Wright, 1964.

Ziegler, David W. *War, Peace, and International Politics*, 2nd ed. Boston: Little, Brown, 1981.

Index

ABM Treaty (Anti-Ballistic Missile Treaty) 120, 127, 130, 204, 205
accidental nuclear war 33, 124
adjudication 217, 227, 244
Afghanistan 4, 67, 98, 131, 199, 214, 218, 243
Africa 4, 20, 21, 23, 34, 48, 58, 81, 101, 102, 142, 154, 160, 187, 214, 236, 238
aggression, nation against nation 161, 162, 163, 168, 213, 220, 222
aggression of individuals & war 37, 39–46, 178, 179, 183–86, 189
air-to-surface ballistic missile (ASBM) 129
Alabama claims 218
Albania & Albanians 140
Alexander the Great 20, 45
Algeria & Algerians 24, 58, 60, 116, 187, 219
Allende, Salvador 115, 187, 250
alliances, motivation for 158–59, 195, 201–204
America 21, 102, 154, 160
American Civil War *see* U.S. Civil War
American Indians 65, 73, 160
Amnesty International 154
Andean Development Corporation 152
Angola 24, 60, 116, 180, 199, 214
Antarctic Treaty 125, 130
Antarctica 231
anti-ballistic-missile missile (ABM) 118, 119, 120, 123, 127, 204, 205
ANZUS 152
Apollo-Soyuz Test Project 214
Arab-Israeli Wars 4, 5, 25, 33, 34, 67, 73, 112, 132, 138–40
Arab League 154, 219, 236
Arabs 4, 25, 73, 138, 139, 140, 143, 210, 214, 217
Arapesh 41
arbitration 74, 217, 222, 225–26, 227, 244
Ardrey, Robert 40, 44, 178
Argentina 4, 46, 72, 124, 147, 155, 206, 218, 224
arms control agreements 124–30, 144, 204–208, 223, 241, 246–47
arms race 62–64, 66, 198, 199, 204, 206, 243, 246
arms race game 62–64
Articles of Confederation 235, 242, 244
Asia 4, 21, 101, 102, 160, 185, 187, 197, 238
Assyrian Empire 20
Atlantic Charter 135

Atlantic Union *see* Union of the Free
atomic (fission) bomb 4, 24, 32, 74–75, 78, 117, 118, 122
Australia 101, 102, 152
Austria & Austrians 21, 22, 58, 137, 147, 149, 184, 187, 218, 251
automated battlefield 132–33
Avenol, Joseph 135

Babylonian Empire 20
Bahais 155, 196
balance of power 134, 203–204
Balkans 187
ballistic missile defense system 120, 124, 130, 205
Bangladesh 5, 57, 102
Barbados 112
bargaining 74, 196, 216, 227
Beer, Francis 31
Begin, Menachim 25
Belgium 22, 23, 152, 153, 184, 194, 201, 223
Benelux 152
Berkowitz, Leonard 42
Berlin 117
Berlinguer, Enrico 98
Bertrand Russell Peace Foundation 250
Biafra 5, 57
biological-instinctual theories of aggression 40–42, 42–43
Biological Weapons Convention 127, 130
bipolar balance of power 203
Bismarck, Otto von 72
Botswana 112
Boulding, Kenneth 226
Brazil 5, 126, 130, 206, 237
Brezhnev, Leonid 128, 129
Britain & British 4, 5, 21, 22, 23, 24, 25, 28, 64, 65, 66, 67, 72, 73, 98, 102, 111, 122, 124, 125, 126, 127, 128, 130, 134, 135, 136, 137, 138, 139, 152, 153, 168, 184, 186, 187, 191, 200, 203, 213, 218, 219, 223, 225, 231, 235, 243, 244, 250
British Commonwealth (British Empire) 25, 142, 152–53, 237
Brown, Lester 3
Buddhism 155
Bulgaria & Bulgarians 22, 140
Burma 137
Butterworth, R.L. 221
Byelorussian Soviet Socialist Republic 142